PAPER FORTUNES

PAPER

FORTUNE$

Modern Wall Street:

Where It's Been and

Where It's Going

ROY C. SMITH

ST. MARTIN'S PRESS ♨ NEW YORK

www.stmartins.com

Library of Congress Cataloging-in-Publication Data

Smith, Roy C., 1938–
    Paper fortunes : modern Wall Street : where it's been and where it's
going / Roy C. Smith.
        p. cm.
    ISBN 978-0-312-38217-9
    1. New York Stock Exchange—History.   2. Finance—United States—History.
3. Investments—United States—History.   4. Investment banking—United States—
History.   5. Investment advisors—United States—History.   I. Title.
    HG4572.S658 2010
    332.64'273—dc22

                                                                2009033522

First Edition: January 2010

10 9 8 7 6 5 4 3 2 1

CONTENTS

PAPER FORTUNES

INTRODUCTION

IN THE SUMMER OF 1965, between years at Harvard Business School, I worked in the International Finance Department at Corning Glass Works, in the sleepy little town of Corning, New York. My direct boss was a Frenchman, Pierre Roederer, who was married to a Frenchwoman, Madeleine. Near the end of the summer, the Roederers gave a family swimming party at their home in honor of two friends or relatives of Madeleine's who were visiting from Paris. My wife, two-year-old daughter, and I arrived at the event to discover two good-looking French girls sunning themselves by the pool, topless. This was not normal procedure in Corning, New York, at the time, but in this little bit of France in the Finger Lakes it seemed all right. The girls were accompanied by two young American guys they had collected in New York City. These men didn't know anyone at the party, so they decided to talk to me.

"What's a summer job like here?" one said.

"Okay, sort of quiet."

"Man, you ought to be in Wall Street, that's where the action is." They were both junior employees at investment banks that I (who knew nothing about investment banks) had never heard of.

"Guy like you is going to go nuts in a place like this. They don't do any real deals, do they?"

"I've been working on financing a three-million-dollar glass plant in Brazil."

"That's no deal. Just a plant. And how many plants get financed, anyway? One or two a year at the most, right? We're used to working on five, six deals at once, maybe twenty or more in a year. Stock deals, bond deals, mergers. All sorts of different things. It's never dull.

"Man, you ought to look into becoming an investment banker, not settle for being just another dull corporate guy living out here in the sticks, going nowhere."

This went on for a while, and I was interested. Twenty or more deals a year sounded great. Variety, different problems and issues, different colleagues and clients. An opportunity to show what I could do. Not being dull and living in the sticks. All this sounded great to me. It was up my alley, and after my first year at Harvard, I had found that I had a knack for finance, a subject that had been totally new to me.

Later, I told my wife that I had met two investment bankers who sounded interesting.

"I thought you didn't want to get involved with Wall Street," she said. "Didn't you say it was too greedy and pushy when I asked you about it while you were looking for a summer job? You didn't even want to interview at investment banks."

"True, but maybe I was being too quick to form a view. It sounds a lot more interesting than I thought."

"Are you sure it wasn't the naked French girls?"

The next day, I asked around among my bosses. "Does Corning have an investment bank? Could you arrange for me to meet someone there when I go back to school?"

"Corning has used Goldman Sachs for years. We haven't done much with them for the last few, but Corning International has a board of directors, and Sidney Weinberg, one of their top guys, is a member of it. I guess we could set something up for you."

They did. They described me over the phone and said I would be calling for an informational interview. I talked to a secretary, and a date was set. At the end of the summer I appeared at Goldman Sachs, then located at 20 Broad Street, next door to the Stock Exchange, for a meeting with Sidney Weinberg. A pleasant, dapper man in his forties appeared and took me into his office for a chat, then introduced me around to some of his partners. I enjoyed myself and looked forward to having another interview, though none was promised at the time.

A month or two later, I was in class at business school when a young woman entered and handed a note to the instructor. The instructor looked up at me and signaled for me to come down to talk to him.

"The dean wants to see you at his house, right away."

Such things didn't happen at the Harvard Business School; something really important must have come up. I was sure that our apartment building had been blown up and everyone in it killed, or something like that, so I hurried off to the dean's house, a prominent Georgian building on campus that I had never been in before. I knocked on the door and introduced myself to a butler, who showed me to an austere sitting room. A few minutes later, in walked a very short older man in a trim three-piece suit with an old-fashioned gold watch chain and brightly polished shoes. I stood up to shake his hand, and at six foot six, I towered over him.

"I'm Sidney Weinberg," he said, pronouncing it "Wein-boig."

That couldn't be, I thought; this isn't the guy I met in New York.

"Would you like to work [woik] at Goldman Sachs?"

I said something about how impressed with the firm I had been but that it was early days yet and I hadn't started interviewing.

He asked if I was a Baker Scholar (the top 2.5 percent of the first-year class), and I admitted that I was not.

"Well, we might have a place for you if you're willing to work hard. Somebody will call you." Then he stood up, shook my hand again, and left the room to return to the meeting he had left to talk to me. I left and rushed to the library to look up Sidney J. Weinberg in *Who's Who*. The guy I had been talking to turned out to be the real Sidney Weinberg after all. I learned that he had been the senior partner of Goldman Sachs since 1930, and was clearly a very important man. Though he had only an eighth-grade education, he had been close to Presidents Roosevelt, Truman, Eisenhower, Kennedy, and Johnson, and was one of America's leading corporate directors, at one time serving on the boards of thirty-five companies, and in addition, was an overseer of Harvard Business School (which explained why he had been at the dean's house that day). Also, I learned he had two sons: Sidney James Weinberg, Jr., and John Livingston Weinberg. Both worked at Goldman Sachs, which explained the other mysterious Sidney Weinberg, the son commonly known as Jim, who was the one on the Corning International board. The Corning people, I supposed, had called Sidney's office, which had directed them to Jim, who saw me and reported to his father that he had done so.

Harvard Business School is a big place. My class had about eight hundred students in it, divided during the first year into eight sections of about ninety that took all of their classes together in a large amphitheater-like room. After our summer jobs, we all talked over our experiences and what we thought we wanted to do for real jobs when we graduated. In my section was a suave, formally dressed New Yorker, Steve Fenster, who was a brilliant Harvard summa cum laude who seemed to know everything about finance and Wall Street. Steve had worked at Morgan Stanley during the summer but was headed to the Pentagon, where he was to serve a few years as a "whiz kid" defense analyst for Robert McNamara, a former HBS star who was then secretary of defense. In our section there were three other students whom Steve thought ought to work in investment banking: Michael Bloomberg, whom he steered to Salomon Brothers, a rough-and-ready trading firm with no interest in pedigree; Jud Reis, whom he praised to his bosses at Morgan Stanley; and me. Once he heard about my interview with the wrong Sidney Weinberg, Steve encouraged me to push ahead at Goldman Sachs. Shortly afterward I was invited back to New York for more interviews, and a job offer appeared by Christmas. I felt comfortable with the people at Goldman Sachs, and though I had been interviewing at other firms, I decided that this was the offer I wanted, and I accepted it. This decision began a career that lasted thirty-three years as associate, vice-president, partner, and limited partner, and ended when Goldman Sachs incorporated and went public in 1999 and had no further need of limited partners. In fact, all of us who were Steve's advisees ended up where he placed us; Steve himself joined Lehman Brothers after the Pentagon, where, like the rest of us, he became a partner specializing in complex corporate restructuring and where, because he was so smart, he was respectfully known as "the Professor." Several others from our class went to Wall Street then, including Tom James (Raymond James), Wick Simmons (Prudential Securities), and Tom Weisel (Montgomery Securities, Thomas Weisel Partners), who became CEOs of their firms, but the total number of us was probably well under 5 percent of the class as a whole. Steve Fenster later developed cancer and left Wall Street to join the faculty of Harvard Business School, where he served for a couple of years. Steve also encouraged Jud Reis and me to teach (Jud at the University of Virginia), and remained a close counselor to Mike Bloomberg and a director of his sensational company, Bloomberg L.P., until he died in 1995.

In 1988, after consulting extensively with Steve, I resigned as a general partner of Goldman Sachs to accept a full-time position on the faculty of

New York University's Stern School of Business as a professor of finance, where I have remained until now, teaching investment banking in its various and ever-changing forms.

Thus I have had an interesting vantage point from which to view the development of an industry—the capital markets industry—that has changed beyond all expectations since I joined it. This is an industry that has grown to become one of the most vital, dynamic, and controversial in the world. Starting from a nexus of twenty or so small partnerships capitalized (in aggregate) with less than $100 million, located in New York and largely confined by the borders of the United States, the industry has been transformed perhaps more than any other during the last four decades to one that now consists of ten or so fiercely competitive giant global players, all publicly owned, with market capitalizations totaling, at one point, more than $1 trillion. Their businesses stretch from New York to London, Frankfurt, Bombay, Tokyo, and Shanghai. Three-fourths of the approximately $12 trillion in capital raised annually by corporations, banks, and governments is now sourced from capital markets that contain outstanding debt and equity securities valued, at the end of 2007, in excess of $140 trillion. This capital is owned and traded by investors of all types, from all over the world—institutional investors such as pension and mutual funds, banks and insurance companies, private wealth managers, sovereign investment funds, foundations, endowments, hedge funds, and other speculators of many types.

Despite this dynamic and continuous growth, very few Wall Street firms have survived the change and the prosperity it induced. Almost all of the firms that were among the top twenty in 1966 are no longer in business under the same name; the partnerships are all gone and several once-mighty houses have fallen or been swept up in forced or transformational mergers. Other well-known firms have been acquired, chewed up, and spat out later by large businesses outside of Wall Street that couldn't make them work. Only one firm, after the tumultuous events of the autumn of 2008, remained more or less the same as it was (notwithstanding converting from a partnership to a publicly owned company, and then to a bank holding company): Goldman Sachs.

The journey from 1966 until now has been one of great adventure, filled with danger and opportunity, which continues even now as the industry contemplates an uncertain future. The journey, however, has been challenged by deregulation, new technologies, globalization, and continually increasing scrutiny by regulators, prosecutors, and litigants. The industry has adopted entirely new attitudes toward exposure to risk, and eagerly pursued opportunities in market making, proprietary trading, wholesale lending, and "private equity." Over the past forty years traditional corporate underwriting and advisory services came to account for only a relatively small part of the industry's revenue stream. And the larger firms today generate half or more of their revenue from activities outside the United States, where half or more of their employees (many of whom don't speak English) reside. New products and services are introduced every year, as older ones rapidly grow obsolete or become commoditized.

The firms in the business now all live by their stock prices, which rise and fall with market cycles, triumphs, and mistakes. Booms and bubbles, followed by panic and plunges in the markets that exaggerate highs and lows, have become commonplace. Those who are successful in these activities have found their compensation to be stupendous, at least while their firms are performing well. However, success can be fickle, and market shifts that derail an entire product line occur frequently. Management turnover is high, and layoffs periodic. Increasingly, employees and managing directors alike realize that they are worth only what they can produce—"You eat what you kill," as some say—and even successful careers, which used to last well into one's sixties, are often over in one's forties. It's a different industry in a great many ways; it is still changing and evolving and it is still very risky, as the last few years have witnessed.

The story of the transition of this industry from there to here is an extraordinary one, filled with the exertions of a great many interesting and colorful characters, especially the leaders struggling with the task of guiding and preserving their firms as they passed through challenging and difficult times. They had to find intelligent strategies to do so, strategies the people at the firms were willing and able to implement. Bright, talented, and loyal people had to be recruited and retained through the markets' many up and downs. Controls and guidelines had to be installed that kept them out of trouble without destroying incentives. Many of these leaders made contributions that shaped the future of their firms for many years to come. Their stories make up much of the fabric of this book, which on the whole is aimed at providing a wide-angle historical look at the capital markets industry as it has traveled from where it was back in the 1960s to where it is today.

In assembling these chapters I have had a lot of help from former colleagues, competitors, and friends involved in the industry. Several have read sections of the book to address its errors and omissions: Arthur Zeikel (Merrill Lynch), Charles Murphy (First Boston and CSFB), Gerry Rosenfeld (Salomon Brothers), Jud Reis (Morgan Stanley), and Jim Weinberg, Bob Friedman, and Peter Sachs (Goldman Sachs). Dick Scribner and Joe McLaughlan offered their recollections and assistance interpreting some of the legal and regulatory changes that occurred, and Steve Brown at New York University's Leonard Stern School of Business helped on hedge funds. I also benefited from advice given by Larry Zicklin, Lloyd Blankfein, Michael Coles, and from the memoirs and other published works of many industry participants and observers. To all of them I owe my appreciation and the disclaimer that I, not they, am responsible for all the opinions and analysis expressed.

1

ARMAGEDDON

ON SEPTEMBER 15, 2008, a harried and exhausted Richard Fuld reluctantly authorized the filing for bankruptcy of Lehman Brothers, the 158-year-old firm he (and only he) had headed since it was spun off from American Express in 1994. At the time, Lehman was the fourth-largest independent investment bank in the United States. Its bankruptcy filing reported liabilities of $613 billion, which made it nearly three times larger than America's previous largest bankruptcy, that of WorldCom in 2002.

Fuld, sixty-two, had not enjoyed the balmy weather that summer at all. An intense man under any circumstances, he had been locked in a life-or-death struggle to save his firm that began soon after Bear Stearns's merger into JPMorgan Chase in March—when Lehman's stock fell nearly 50 percent following rumors that Lehman would be the market's next victim, before recovering to close out the day with a drop of only 19 percent. A former trader known within the firm as "the Gorilla" for his domineering ways, Fuld was an autocratic leader accustomed to giving orders and ignoring dissent. He was angered by the idea that the market might doubt Lehman's ability to weather the storm. So he roused his associates and ordered everyone to hit the phones to get the word out to clients, counterparties, and the press that Lehman was no Bear Stearns and would survive. This was what he had done to turn the stock around in 1998, when markets were rattled by the sudden failure of Long-Term Capital

Management, a large hedge fund, and again in 2002, when the market turned viciously on Wall Street firms after the collapse of WorldCom. The approach had worked before, and Fuld was confident that it would again.

Lehman Brothers, after all, had made itself a reputation for being a scrappy, street-smart overachiever who moved quickly to take risks and was nimble enough to get out in time. The firm had been especially active in the mortgage origination and securitization businesses, which had been very profitable. Fuld was given much of the credit for Lehman's success, and in 2006 the board granted him a ten-year stock award bonus valued at $186 million. In October of 2007, despite generally negative views about the economy, and after the mortgage-backed securities market had already begun to fall sharply, Lehman joined Tishman Speyer, a property developer, in a $15 billion acquisition of Archstone-Smith Trust, an owner of a large portfolio of residential apartments. Archstone had a $30 billion investment in commercial real estate that, together with another $46 billion or so of Lehman's mortgage-backed securities (MBS), would serve as a millstone around the neck of the firm as the markets soured.[1]

Fuld sensed in early 2008 that although Lehman had raised some new capital earlier in the year, he would need more if he was going to get through the current difficult market unscathed. So, soon after Bear Stearns fell, Lehman approached Warren Buffett, the seventy-eight-year-old chairman of Berkshire Hathaway, to propose an investment. Buffett was interested and proposed his usual recipe of high-coupon preferred stock with expensive warrants, which Fuld rejected as being too costly. A few days later Lehman issued $4 billion in convertible debentures to the public at a better price.[2]

In May, David Einhorn, manager of the hedge fund Greenlight Capital and one of Lehman's biggest critics and short sellers, gave a speech to a group of influential investors criticizing the firm's performance and the valuation of its mortgage-backed assets. Einhorn, who would make a fortune on his negative bet on Lehman, was constantly telling anyone who would listen of Lehman's problems, and soon other short sellers took up positions.

In June, a group of Lehman executives flew to Seoul to attempt to negotiate a substantial investment from the Korea Development Bank, headed then by a former Lehman executive. They returned a few days later without a deal, but with discussions still in process. On June 9 the firm preannounced its second-quarter results, which showed a loss of $2.9 million, down from a profit of $489 million in the first quarter, and an increase in its holdings of Alt-A mortgages (those with a risk rating between prime and subprime), which some observers felt were not marked down enough to reflect their true trading values. After the results were announced, Fuld polled his top executives to ask them what else they thought Lehman should do. They thought there needed to be management changes, and some apparently suggested that Joe Gregory, Fuld's close friend and the firm's longtime president and chief operating officer, should resign. Reluctantly, Gregory stepped forward and volunteered to take the heat and resign along with Erin Callan, a former investment banker who had served for a year as Lehman's CFO and thus had become a principal lightning rod. The changes seemed to make little difference to Lehman's stock price, however, which dropped from $40 per share at the beginning of May to $17 by the beginning of July.

In August the Koreans came back with an offer to buy 25 percent of the firm at the then market price, but Fuld thought the price was too low and was reluctant to give up any control. The Koreans also wanted a better fix on the valuation of Lehman's asset-backed securities, but in any case, the Korea Development Bank would have to obtain government approval to make the investment, which Korean sources seemed to doubt would occur.

The situation was made even more acute when Treasury Secretary Henry Paulson told Fuld that he had better look for a merger partner right away, suggesting that there was likely to be no other way out for Lehman. This was painful news for a man who was fiercely committed to the idea of Lehman's remaining an independent firm, something he had especially learned to value after experiencing Lehman being owned by American Express for nearly ten years. According to a colleague, Fuld had exclaimed in December 2007, "As long as I am alive this firm will never be sold. And if it is sold after I die, I will reach back from the grave and prevent it."[3]

Nevertheless, Fuld canvassed the market broadly for a strategic investor. Over the summer he contacted Bank of America, HSBC, Met Life, GE Capital, and the ruler of Dubai. In July, Fuld suggested to Timothy Geithner, then president of the New York Federal Reserve Bank, that the Fed allow Lehman to become a bank holding company, and thus be regulated (and protected) by the federal banking system. This was an unprecedented request, one that would force the Fed to assume responsibility for all or some of the assets of Lehman. Geithner brushed off the proposal without much discussion, saying it wouldn't be enough to solve Lehman's current problems. He may not have been ready to allow such a radical change in banking regulation or he might not have liked Lehman's collateral, but no reasons were given for why the idea, later successfully put forward by Goldman Sachs and Morgan Stanley, was dismissed.

Lehman also came up with a plan to create a new company that would be capitalized by the firm and to which Lehman's troubled assets would be off-loaded. This company would then be spun off to shareholders, leaving Lehman with a clean balance sheet. The plan was approved by the Securities and Exchange Commission, but would take about three months to be put into effect. By then, however, time was running short.[4]

In the meantime, Lehman borrowed heavily from a facility set up by the European Central Bank; it eschewed borrowing from a post–Bear Stearns Federal Reserve credit facility for investment banks in order not to appear to be desperate to its U.S. creditors. The word got out, though, that Lehman was scrambling for capital, and this caused a number of its hedge fund and other brokerage customers to withdraw funds from the firm, compounding its problems. By early September the Korean talks were pronounced dead and Lehman's stock fell another 45 percent, erasing a decade of market gains.[5]

On September 9, after the Korean investment was abandoned, Fuld had to turn to Bank of America and Barclays Bank, the only potential merger partners still showing any signs of interest. On the same day, JPMorgan Chase, Lehman's clearing bank, had asked for $5 billion more in collateral to support its trading lines to the firm. This was the bank's second request for additional collateral, over and above $5 billion requested five days earlier.

The next day, September 10, Lehman convened a conference call for investors and attempted to reassure them by announcing a major restructuring plan, together with the announcement that it expected to lose an additional $3.9 billion in the third quarter. The restructuring plan would involve selling all or part of its blue-chip investment management division, Neuberger Berman (estimated then to be worth about $7 billion), and cutting its dividend. Fuld said the plan would "create a very clean, liquid balance sheet," and that the firm was on the "right track to put these last two quarters behind us." The call did not mention raising new capital, and when asked whether the firm would need to add another $4 billion, Ian Lowitt, the firm's new CFO, seeking to avoid panicking the market further, replied that "we don't feel we need to raise that extra amount." The following day, September 11, the market price of Lehman credit default swaps (CDS)—the cost to insure against losses on $10 million of its debt for five years—soared to $800,000 a year, up from $219,000 at the end of May. More institutional investors withdrew funds, and Fuld went back to Geithner to tell him that Lehman was running out of cash and would have to borrow a sizeable amount from the Fed's broker-dealer facility in order to stay in business on Monday. Paulson, meanwhile, was putting out the word that the taxpayer should not be expected to rescue every failing bank, while at the same time urging Bank of America's chairman, Ken Lewis, to consider acquiring Lehman.

On Friday, September 12, the credit rating agencies warned that they would downgrade Lehman's debt (forcing it to provide more collateral to back up its trading positions) if it didn't raise fresh equity capital by Monday morning, and JPMorgan froze $17 billion in cash and securities that it was holding for Lehman, denying the firm access to its own funds.[6] The freeze created chaos at Lehman as customers seeking to withdraw their funds could not and as money transfers between offices, or to meet maturing overnight loans, were blocked. Paulson and Geithner convened a meeting at the New York Fed of Wall Street leaders and challenged them to find a private solution to Lehman's troubles, saying it was in their best interest to do so.

Much of Saturday was spent trying to unlock Lehman's cash positions, and to advance merger discussions with Bank of America and Barclays, both of which needed to become more comfortable with Lehman's financial position to take on its business without some sort of guaranty from the Fed. The Fed, on the other hand, was scrambling to identify acceptable collateral that might be put up for an additional loan, but it was unable to come up with enough to meet its strict requirements. Questions were raised about the relatively high valuation of Lehman's large portfolio of commercial real estate holdings, which analysts would later suggest was overvalued by as much as 35 percent.[7]

Meanwhile, a key meeting convened at the New York Fed. John Thain, CEO of Merrill Lynch, was there, along with Lloyd Blankfein, CEO of Goldman Sachs, and John Mack, CEO of Morgan Stanley. The group spent hours trying to put together a deal to purchase $30 billion or so of Lehman's troubled assets, but was too unsure of their value to proceed without a government guarantee of the sort that had been extended to facilitate the Bear Stearns deal. The government was unwilling to extend such a deal, so the meeting broke up inconclusively.

Back at Lehman, meetings were simultaneously being held with representatives of the New York Fed, Bank of America, Barclays, the rating agencies, and with Lehman's lawyers, who, should all else fail, were exploring filing for bankruptcy. Fuld and his senior colleagues were required at all of these meetings and hopped from one to another all day.

By this time, Thain was convinced that Lehman was likely to be left to fall into bankruptcy, and if so, the market would come after Merrill next. Though he was confident that Merrill had more cash and a better story, he knew that the bank was vulnerable. "This could be me sitting here next Friday," Thain was reported to have said. After the Saturday meeting at the New York Fed, he stepped out onto the sidewalk behind the bank, called Ken Lewis at home in Charlotte, North Carolina, and suggested that Bank of America acquire Merrill instead of Lehman. "I can be there in a few hours," Lewis told him.[8] The idea appealed to Lewis, whose interest in Lehman's sophisticated, fast-moving, but dangerous bond trading business was probably limited to being able to get it at a very low price with a government guaranty (which Paulson kept saying wasn't going to happen). Indeed, Lewis had told the *Financial Times* some months earlier, after some disappointing trading losses of his own, that "I have had all the fun I can stand from investment banking." He was much more interested in the prospect of owning Merrill's huge retail brokerage and mutual fund management businesses, knowing he could either suppress or close down the investment banking parts that had gotten Merrill in trouble.

When Thain returned to the New York Fed after calling Lewis, he was told by his colleagues that some top Goldman Sachs representatives had suggested buying a 9.9 percent interest in Merrill Lynch and extending it a $10 billion line of credit. Then John Mack of Morgan Stanley said that Merrill should merge with it. There were follow-up meetings, but Thain was concerned that the firms did not "share our sense of urgency."[9]

But Lewis did, and moved rapidly to settle a deal with Thain.

Merrill's move left Lehman dealing only with Barclays, who also wanted a guaranty, though a more modest one than Bank of America had required. But it didn't want Lehman's troubled assets, which Fuld had figured he could spin off to shareholders. Paulson and Geithner, according to some on the scene, had talked a group of banks into backstopping the spin-off deal with a $55 billion facility, which seemed to be the last step needed to prevent Lehman's bankruptcy.[10] But the Barclays deal could work only if the Fed guaranteed all of Lehman's trading positions when the markets opened on Monday. No other Wall Street firm was willing to do this, so Barclays considered doing it itself, but it was prevented by London Stock Exchange rules from making such a large pledge without first getting shareholder approval. The Fed tried to get the British government to waive the rules, but it refused on the grounds that if rules had to be waived to save a floundering American firm, they should be American rules.

By Sunday afternoon, September 14, Lehman was out of options. Barclays couldn't move without a guaranty, the Fed did not believe it could make such a guaranty without adequate collateral, and the Treasury was not ready or willing to bail out Lehman with its funds. Paulson, who had just nationalized the two federally chartered national mortgage finance companies, and was just beginning to deal with a teetering AIG, had made it clear that he wasn't about to underwrite the moral hazard in the system by rescuing yet another stricken firm that had been sunk by its own actions, though he might have found a way to fudge things for a few weeks so Lehman could complete a deal with Barclays. Paulson believed that the market had had enough time to grasp the situation at Lehman and to protect itself accordingly. He was going to draw the line at bailing out Lehman.

A senior Fed official asked Harvey Miller, Lehman's bankruptcy lawyer from Weil, Gotshal, and Manges, if Lehman was ready to file. "No," he said, "you need more of a plan to prepare to do this." Lehman had tens of billions of dollars in derivative positions with thousands of counterparties. Unless these trades were unwound in an orderly way, or taken over by someone else, bankruptcy "would cause financial Armageddon," Miller said.[11] No one seemed to consider keeping Lehman alive on life support long enough to find a merger partner or properly prepare for bankruptcy.

ALL HELL BREAKS LOOSE

After the Fed's intervention in March 2008 to assist JPMorgan in acquiring Bear Stearns, the markets had seemed to relax a bit. The government, after all, had set the too-big-to-fail bar at Bear Stearns, signaling that those investment banks larger than Bear Stearns would be given similar treatment if need be. Their lenders, in other words, could expect to be guaranteed by either a merger partner or the Fed itself. By early June 2008, the S&P 500 index had risen about 5 percent, and Washington Mutual, the country's largest (but weakened) savings bank, had been able to reject a merger proposal from JPMorgan and raise $7 billion in new capital from a group of private equity firms led by Texas Pacific Group (TPG).

Later in June, Bank of America announced that it had completed its acquisition of troubled mortgage broker Countrywide Financial at a renegotiated, knockdown price and was optimistic about its long-term prospects. Its crosstown rival in Charlotte, Wachovia Bank, however, announced that the board had requested the resignation of Ken Thompson, its long-standing and dynamic CEO, after reporting $8.9 billion in mortgage write-downs for its second quarter.

In July, the Federal Deposit Insurance Corporation (FDIC) took over IndyMac Bank, a $34 billion California thrift institution, the largest bank takeover since the banking crisis of the 1980s. Also in July, Merrill Lynch would report a second-quarter loss of $4.7 billion and a sale of approximately $30 billion in securitized commercial loans to the private equity group Lone Star Funds for only twenty-two cents on the dollar. The price, most commentators thought, was well below the debt's intrinsic value, but Merrill, headed by John Thain since December 2007, wanted to get rid of the debt to put its exposure to weakening debt prices behind it. Merrill's stock price rose in subsequent weeks.

Late in July, Secretary Paulson sought congressional approval to advance funds to the Federal National Mortgage Association (Fannie Mae) and the Federal Home Mortgage Corporation (Freddie Mac), the two home-mortgage finance giants, if they should need them. Both of these companies were struggling with a long history of being chronically undercapitalized, and current market conditions were devaluing the assets they held, but both were also considered to carry implicit guarantees of the U.S. government and appeared to be able to roll over their maturing obligations without difficulty. The mortgage companies had strong supporters in Congress who claimed that they were solid, healthy institutions. No one but the Treasury seemed to think they were on their way out, but the requested funds were to be for just in case. With total assets of $890 billion, it was pretty clear that Fannie Mae would have to be considered too big to fail no matter what it cost to bail it out. The same would be true for the somewhat smaller Freddie Mac. The news of Paulson's request did not stir much up—for some time the markets had realized that the government might have to do something to help out these companies— and August went on to be the quiet month in the markets that it is supposed to be. Credit markets were operating normally, the economy was still thought to be expanding,* if slowly, oil prices were dropping, and

___

* The U.S. economy had actually entered a recession in December 2007, according to a

Ben Bernanke was feeling more relaxed about the markets; as he said in August, "A lot can still go wrong, but at least I can see a path that will bring us out of this entire episode relatively intact."[12]

The lull ended abruptly on September 7 with the government's sudden nationalizing of Fannie Mae and Freddie Mac by taking them into "conservatorship" in much the same way it might have seized two failing S&Ls. Paulson's explanation for why he took them over was a little vague:

> Based on what we have learned about these institutions over the last four weeks—including what we learned about their capital requirements—and given the condition of financial markets today, I concluded that it would not have been in the best interests of the taxpayer for Treasury to simply to make an equity investment in these enterprises in their present form.[13]

The government jumped in with both feet. It provided a net worth support agreement to the two agencies, bought $1 billion in 10 percent senior preferred stock, with warrants representing a 79.9 percent ownership in each firm, and arranged for them to pay the Treasury a quarterly consulting fee starting in 2010. It also dismissed the boards of the two companies, appointed new CEOs, and guaranteed all the debt (but not the preferred stock in which many U.S. banks had invested portions of their reserves). The most alarming part of the seizing of the shareholder-owned companies was that it revealed just how aggressive their managements had been in pursuing growth and profit opportunities—by buying large amounts of mortgage-backed securities from the market (something that was not part of their missions)—despite their weak capital structure and the highly uncertain mortgage-backed securities market. Both firms were out of money and would need to raise more, now with an explicit government guaranty, in order to return actively to the mortgage finance market, where their presence was badly needed to support falling home sales.

Fannie and Freddie were taken over just a few days before Lehman's last week began. This was a week that would end with Lehman's equity worth nothing and its considerable amount of long- and short-term debt worth less than ten cents on the dollar. It would also end with Merrill Lynch being snatched up in a last-minute rescue, leaving only two of the

---

November 2008 announcement by the National Bureau of Economic Research, which keeps the official records of when recessions begin and end.

five largest independent U.S. investment banks still standing to face a hurricane of market anxiety, uncertainty, and fear.

THE HAMMER

Hank Paulson was a reluctant secretary of the treasury when he took office in the summer of 2006, having declined the position when sounded out about it once or twice before. Paulson is a comparatively simple man, by Wall Street standards: he is a Christian Scientist who doesn't drink alcohol and prefers bird-watching and hanging out on weekends at the family farm in Illinois to the New York social scene. He was in his eighth year as CEO of Goldman Sachs, where he was respected and doing his best to live up to the high standards of competence and dedication set by a series of predecessors. He was also a loyal Republican, having served as a White House Fellow in the Nixon administration. When John Snow was replaced as treasury secretary, President George Bush wanted someone who would be seen as more authoritative and on top of things and he was attracted to the former Dartmouth football player, whose nickname was the Hammer. In the end, Bush was able to persuade Paulson to give it all up to join him for the last two years on his sinking ship in Washington. Paulson was able, however, to extract a commitment that if he accepted the job, he would be the undisputed chief economic officer of the administration and have the support of the president for whatever actions he believed were appropriate. No doubt many rookie secretaries of the treasury have had such promises made to them only to find out otherwise once they arrived, but the president supported Paulson through all his untiring efforts and ordeals, and his seizing of leadership of the economic realm was never contested within the administration.

Paulson, however, was ignorant of Washington's wily political ways and roundabout tactics, which frustrated him as they do everyone who comes into office unprepared for them. He had never had any kind of political or economic experience or training to prepare him for what began to unfold within a few months of his taking up the job. No one filling the Treasury position had ever had any more or better training in markets and finance, but the events that occurred on his watch were simply entirely new to the financial system and would come to test it beyond anything since the 1930s. As he put it in an article in *The New York Times*:

There is no playbook for responding to turmoil we have never faced. We adjusted our strategy to reflect the facts of a severe market crisis, always keeping focused on our goal: to stabilize a financial system that is integral to the everyday lives of all Americans. . . . If we have learned anything throughout this year, we have learned that this financial crisis is unpredictable and difficult to counteract.

Paulson is smart, courageous, self-confident, and forceful, and he brought with him more than thirty years of experience in financial markets during the tumultuous and eventful periods later described in this book, experiences that, above all, required accepting reality and finding ways to adapt to superior forces in the marketplace. He is blunt, direct, and arbitrary; he pursues his objectives with great focus and intensity, prefers working with a small coterie of trusted subordinates (some of whom were brought from Goldman Sachs), and can be indifferent to people he doesn't think are important to his current mission. He doesn't care much for the media or the glitzy business of being a Washington celebrity, and he is not naturally a good communicator, but on the whole, at the time of his appointment, he was about as good a package as you could find to lead the country through the next two years of economic and financial trouble. And he seemed to team up very well with scholarly Ben Bernanke, an expert on the economic issues of the Great Depression, and his cohort of savvy financial professionals at the Federal Reserve and the New York Fed.

AN AVALANCHE OF SELLING

Unfortunately, however, the Lehman bankruptcy on September 15 sent the wrong signal to the market. According to one analyst: "Prior to Lehman, there was an almost unshakable faith that the senior creditors and counterparties of large systematically important financial institutions would not face the risk of outright default. This confidence was built up ever since the failure of Continental Illinois in 1984 (at the time the seventh largest bank in the United States), a failure in which bondholders were [fully paid out.]"[14]

The essential problem that Paulson and Bernanke were dealing with was the bursting of an extremely overleveraged speculative bubble. This was unlike the technology bubble of the 1990s, which was surely speculative but not nearly so leveraged. The bubble was based on rising prices in housing, a phenomenon that was fully global, and it had been turbo-charged by banks' use of sophisticated financial techniques. The banks bundled mortgages together to create securities that would be rated AAA because they were secured by the mortgaged assets (whose prices were rising). Because the collateral was so highly rated, investors and interme-diaries could (and did) borrow almost the entire purchase price. Interna-tional bank minimum capital adequacy rules (to which the Fed subscribed and helped create) permitted this, because secured assets were not consid-ered risky, and thus required less capital to support them than unsecured assets. The turbocharging, however, found ways to inject large amounts of lesser-quality subprime mortgages into the securities packages and to finance great inventories of them by borrowing in the short-term com-mercial paper market at low cost. While all this was going on, banks were also increasing their activities in corporate and consumer loans, and lev-eraging up the riskier end of those markets in order to report earnings increases that would appeal to their stockholders.

When the bubble burst and the overvaluation of the housing stock became evident, everything seemed to run downhill at once, at an acce-lerating rate of speed. Defaults on subprime mortgages rose, causing all the collateral for collateralized mortgage obligations (CMOs) to be questioned—it was never clear how much subprime any particular CMO contained—which caused all CMO prices to fall, causing margin calls to be made, which required additional capital, which forced additional sales at distressed prices and brought down CMO prices further, a process that repeated itself continually.

As this happened, banks, investment banks, and hedge funds were forced to write down the securities they held, with the losses reflected im-mediately in write-offs of capital, which required more to be raised to re-place it. Counterparties, clearing agents, and rating agencies all cried for more capital, the issuance of which in a falling market was not easy. Capi-tal raised at low prices diluted the share prices of the banks, dropping them further and making it even harder to raise yet more capital when the losses continued into the next quarter. This condition also reduced the funds that banks had to lend elsewhere and caused their access to com-mercial paper and other money markets to dry up, putting pressure on their abilities to raise funding from other institutional sources and raising flags everywhere.

A plunging stock price became a new form of a run on the banks, causing all those with a stake in particular banks to question their confidence in them. This nasty downward spiral would continue until the market for CMOs and other forms of risky debt bottomed out, or the bank ran out of capital and had to be dealt with by regulators. As banks' funding abilities became impaired, they hunkered down and became unwilling to lend to either commercial or consumer clients, and all types of credit markets dried up, leading the economy into a steep recession.

What made all this worse was the concentration of the collateralized mortgage and debt obligations (CMOs and CDOs, non-mortgage asset-backed securities) within about thirty huge global financial companies, each with assets of around $1 trillion or more, and a few hundred hedge funds and other investors, which were sitting on great piles of depreciating securities they had originated or bought from banks. These largest financial companies were opaque and hard to understand, and nearly all of them, directly or indirectly, were involved with troubled housing and mortgage assets. This concentration of exposures brought major concerns to the public markets for stocks and bonds around the world, the market capitalization of which as of December 31, 2007, was a vast $140 trillion, and triggered a rush for safety as large institutional investors began to sell out positions. No one wanted to be caught holding financial industry paper once the scale and interconnectedness of these exposures became apparent.

An avalanche of selling began at the end of the summer of 2008, and hit its maximum velocity during September and October, after the Lehman bankruptcy. The selling would appear in violent waves, hiking stock market volatility fourfold, to an all-time record. At best all of the resources applied by the U.S. government from various quarters to intervene in the markets never exceeded a few trillion dollars, with another $2 or $3 trillion coming from European countries, and this was simply not enough to stop the avalanche once it began. The only way to stop it was for the market to regain sufficient confidence in the world's principal financial institutions for money to start flowing back into them.

A CATASTROPHIC BANKRUPTCY

The great sigh of relief heard among creditors after Bear Stearns's merger into JPMorgan in March was really one of gratitude for the Fed's having extended its too-big-to-fail doctrine to investment banks for the first time, an act that confirmed that the government would do what it had to do to protect the financial system, even if that meant bending the rules in place at the time. Lehman creditors must have assumed that they, too, would be safe, given that Lehman was significantly larger, and therefore more of a threat to the system than Bear Stearns. This was evident by the fact that Lehman's short-term debt was still held on the eve of bankruptcy by many money market funds, which in the United States accounted for $3.5 trillion in liquid investments.

One of these, the $62 billion Reserve Primary Fund, the country's oldest money market fund, held $785 million in Lehman notes, which, after bankruptcy, were valued at zero, causing the fund to drop the value of its assets to less than $1 per share ("breaking the buck"), a disastrous event in the money market fund industry, and one that had happened only once before, to a small fund fourteen years earlier, without the sponsoring fund managers investing additional capital of their own to stabilize the share prices. Money market investors do not take chances that they might incur principal losses; the value of a money market fund is expected to remain above $1 per share for every dollar deposited, no matter what. If it doesn't, investors will withdraw their funds, not just from the offending fund but from all others that might seem to look like it. By the end of the week following the Lehman bankruptcy, approximately $400 billion in funds had been withdrawn from the money market industry, and the Treasury was forced to guarantee money market funds "temporarily" against any further such losses. After Lehman, these investors, fearing what they didn't know out there in the markets, wanted nothing to do with corporate risk, and sent their funds into Treasuries and federally guaranteed mortgage paper. Money market funds primarily invest in corporate commercial paper and bank certificates of deposit. So the withdrawals dried up low-cost, short-term corporate and bank credit further and forced commercial paper issuers to fall back on their standby bank lines of credit, which banks had to scramble to fulfill.

The next effect was on Lehman's holders of $130 billion of its bonds. In early September these were trading at about ninety-five cents on the dollar, indicating that the bond investors were not expecting Lehman to be anywhere near a bankruptcy situation. The bond price dropped to about forty cents on the dollar just after the bankruptcy, but after an auction of Lehman credit default swaps in October, the price fell to ten cents.[15] In addition to Lehman's direct credit exposures, there were approximately $400 billion of these credit default swaps written on Lehman's credit by others, through which insurance protection was available to those willing to pay for it. But after some considerable netting of long and short positions by investors, only about $6 billion in such swaps (1.5 percent of the notional amount) remained outstanding to be settled after bankruptcy, according to the International Swap Dealers Association. This was a much smaller after-netting loss than had been feared would result from the more than 350 protection contracts written. These derivative exposures, apparently much feared by regulators, had proved not to contain the risks that they were thought to.

There were other problems, though. Hedge funds using Lehman as a prime broker in London found their collateral frozen by the bankruptcy, and some of this collateral had been hypothecated (borrowed against legally) by Lehman, ensuring that it would take a long time to unravel who was entitled to what, during which time the hedge fund assets, and thus many of the funds themselves, would remain frozen. Furthermore, the claims of the hedge funds were expected to be thrown in with the rest of the unsecured creditors to fight over what was left in bankruptcy proceedings.

Thus, the lucrative "prime brokerage" business (with hedge funds) of several large investment banks came under pressure, with hedge funds shying away from any exposure to weaker banks and transferring their business to more substantial custodians. JPMorgan, which acquired a very successful prime brokerage business with Bear Stearns, announced a 25 percent increase in this business during the third quarter of 2008.

The Lehman bankruptcy, as Harvey Miller had forecast, was chaotic, and as a result destroyed as much as $75 billion in value that should have been available to creditors if the process had been more orderly, according to a study prepared by Alvarez and Marsal, bankruptcy agents retained by Lehman. A more orderly (and normal) process would have allowed many assets to be sold at higher values and would have prevented the loss of about $50 billion resulting from the sudden closeout of nearly a million separate derivates contracts, including many in which Lehman was owed money. The Fed, however, got back all of its money invested in Lehman from asset sales after the bankruptcy.[16]

Dick Fuld, however, recovered very little of what was tied up in the shares that he owned in the firm, shares that were once worth nearly $1 billion. Perhaps an equally painful cost to him was the humiliation of the failure, and the sadness of being responsible for the collapse of a firm that had been the home and livelihood of thousands of colleagues and friends who had once looked up to him, but who now seemed to take great satisfaction in his embarrassment and disgrace. Many were very angry, including the former partners of Neuberger Berman, who had sold their firm to Lehman in 2003 for $2.6 billion: half the purchase price and half of their annual bonuses for the next five years were paid in restricted Lehman stock, which was now worthless. For employees and former executives who would lose their jobs and stakes in the firm, Dick Fuld had become the dark villain who had caused it all to happen.

The first Sunday morning following Lehman's bankruptcy, Fuld was working out in the Lehman Brothers gymnasium. A competitive squash player and fitness freak, he believed that exercise was necessary to keep the mind sharp and improve the body's ability to tolerate stress, something he certainly felt he needed just then, when (according to an unusual report from a CNBC and *Vanity Fair* contributor who claims to be quoting "two very senior sources"), he "was on a treadmill with a heart monitor on. Someone was in the corner, pumping iron and he walked over and he knocked him out cold."[17]

If this event truly happened, then it was only a part of the unhappy chain of events involving Fuld that followed the bankruptcy filing. First, he had to preside over the dismantling of the firm he had served since he was a college student in 1967: Barclays Bank would acquire Lehman's North American assets for a trivial price, and its European and Asian assets would be bought by Nomura Securities for not much more. Neuberger Berman would be sold back to the managers of the firm, after a bargain basement sale to two private equity firms came undone.

Also, Fuld was summoned to Washington by the House Committee on Oversight and Government Reform, chaired by Congressman Henry Waxman, to be held up in front of the committee members for public rebuke and to be photographed in front of unknown protestors displaying signs that read "Shame" and "Cap Greed." In his testimony, Fuld was asked what had caused Lehman's failure: "Ultimately what happened to Lehman Brothers was caused by a lack of confidence. This was not a lack of confidence in just Lehman Brothers, but what has been called a storm of fear enveloping the entire investment banking field and our financial institutions generally."[18]

He went on to attribute the failure to a "litany of destabilizing factors," including increased costs of borrowing, accounting rules that forced the bank to write down positions to fire-sale prices, imminent threats of downgrades by credit rating agencies, and short-selling of the stock, but he said, "I take full responsibility for the decisions I made." Not long after these hearings, the Justice Department opened a criminal investigation to determine whether Fuld or others at Lehman had committed fraud in their statements as to the health and viability of the firm, and whether Lehman needed more capital when it said it didn't, during its last months of duress.

Many Wall Street leaders would be unable to deny a certain amount of sympathy for Fuld, thinking how easily they, too, could have ended up in his shoes, had circumstances and timing been a little different.

ALL FALL DOWN

The day after Lehman's bankruptcy filing, the Fed and the Treasury, in a sudden turnaround in their positions on bailouts, announced an $85 billion two-year loan from the New York Fed to AIG, the largest American insurance company, which had strayed deep into the dangerous territory of structured financial products, in order to save it from bankruptcy. According to a statement by the Fed:

> In current circumstances a disorderly failure of AIG could add to already significant levels of financial market fragility and lead to substantially higher borrowing costs, reduced household wealth and materially weaker economic performance. . . . This loan will facilitate a process under which AIG will sell certain of its businesses in an orderly manner, with the least possible disruption to the overall economy.[19]

It was, in essence, a self-liquidation plan. Paulson and Bernanke had been very reluctant to intervene in AIG, invoking for the second time in six months the "unusual and exigent circumstances" clause of the Federal Reserve Act, which gives the Fed the authority to lend outside the banking industry. They were persuaded, however, by the great extent of "interconnectedness" of AIG with the already spooked credit markets. What they had in mind was to provide bridge financing for a couple of years to enable the company to sell off its lucrative insurance and other businesses to repay the loan, with the taxpayers taking 80 percent of whatever was left over for the stockholders. The market capitalization of AIG had been $178 billion a year before, so the assumption was that the loan, which would be secured by the insurance businesses, would be safe. In return for such a bailout of the creditors and stockholders of AIG, Paulson would insist on bringing the company, once one of America's most admired corporations, to its knees. It would have to pay a punitive interest rate of 8.5 percent over LIBOR* and the government would be issued warrants for 79.9 percent of AIG's common stock. Paulson would also insist that the board replace AIG's relatively new CEO, Robert Willumstad, with Edward Liddy, a respected former head of insurer Allstate Corp. and a one-time director of Goldman Sachs, who agreed to work for one dollar per year.

Paulson, who agreed to the AIG loan only the day before it was made, obviously concluded that AIG was too big to fail, whereas Lehman was not. Even though a nonbank insurance company, AIG had fallen into the same trap as some of the large banks. Its relatively small AIG Financial Products division plunged $140 billion into European CMOs, $78 billion into U.S. CDOs, and sold approximately $450 billion in protection to buyers of corporate credit default swaps (CDSs), which survived the crisis relatively intact, and $75 billion of subprime CDSs, which did not. It had been the market's biggest buyer of subprime swaps, which meant it would become its biggest loser from them.[20] This London-based structured financial products unit, which had been enormously profitable for many years through 2007, was now hemorrhaging, reporting $25 billion in losses in the second quarter alone.

As prices declined, the rating agencies demanded that AIG increase the collateral available to support this business by about $60 billion in order to retain its AA corporate credit rating. Failure to post the collateral would sharply devalue the credit default swaps guaranteed by AIG, and plunge the company's creditworthiness into desperate straits, causing collateral losses to counterparts, according to one analyst, of as much as $180 billion.[21] Its valuable insurance companies, which were separately regulated, were separate subsidiaries of the holding company, and thus their funds and resources were unavailable to holding company creditors.

AIG had raised $20 billion in new capital earlier in the year, and had hired Goldman Sachs and Morgan Stanley to help it raise an additional $40 billion to avoid the ratings downgrade. Several offers came from private equity firms: JC Flowers submitted a plan that would give it the right to buy AIG for 25 percent of its current market value, and proposals from Kohlberg Kravis and Roberts (KKR) and Texas Pacific Group (TPG)

---

* London interbank offered rate, the wholesale borrowing rate between banks, set in London daily.

required a bridge loan from the Fed. CEO Robert Willumstad contacted Geithner at the New York Fed to ask for the bridge loan. Reports of the company's worsening circumstances plunged AIG's stock price into free-fall; by Friday, September 12, it had dropped to $4 per share from just under $50 in March. On September 15, Standard & Poor's cut its bond rating to A-, Moody's followed suit, and the company concluded that it might have to declare bankruptcy if it couldn't raise new capital by September 17 to meet its collateral obligations. Perhaps because of this dire outlook, or the sudden drop in the stock price, or other pleas from those who feared the effects of the downgrade on the counterparty credit markets, which were already in sad shape, Bernanke and Paulson changed their minds and came up with the loan scheme that was quickly cobbled together just as Lehman sank into bankruptcy.

Cut off from any further opportunity to raise capital or credit, the AIG board accepted the loan deal under duress, having been told it had no choice. The deal virtually nationalized AIG, but it left the shareholders' remaining residual interest intact, though it had been virtually extinguished. Paulson wanted very much to signal that, as in the case of Fannie Mae and Freddie Mac, if the government was going to step in, the conditions it imposed would be very tough, so there would be no rewards for those who had steered the company into trouble, and taxpayers would have as little risk as possible of being out of pocket. But of course there were many direct beneficiaries of the bailout: AIG's trading counterparties (several major banks and broker-dealers) and creditors.

In less than a month, AIG was in trouble again. The Fed had to extend an additional $38 billion to the company to keep its securities lending business from collapsing. Before its initial rescue, AIG had loaned out securities it held, and invested the cash proceeds foolishly (or desperately) in longer-dated mortgage assets that it believed to be undervalued, only to find that the prices of these assets had declined substantially by the time the borrowed securities were returned and the cash had to be repaid. Thus much of the original $85 billion loan had to be used to shore up this business rather than fund its core credit exposures. This embarrassment was increased when a congressional committee investigating AIG's executive compensation and perks discovered that the company had spent $370,000 on a lush executive retreat a week after the original rescue loan was made. AIG would continue to be a thorn in the side of the Fed and the Treasury, which were compelled to renegotiate the terms of their bailout two or three more times in order to keep the holding company with all its CDS positions from sinking. Its insurance assets could not be sold for decent prices in the depressed markets that immediately followed the bailout, and the cash and other assets in the insurance subsidiaries remained out of reach. The government could only grin and bear it; sooner or later the CDS portfolio would mature and the capital used as collateral would be returned. But it was certainly an uncomfortable wait.

After AIG's rescue, the LIBOR shot up to 6.5 percent from just over 2 percent, as lending between banks suddenly dried up.

On September 17, Goldman Sachs and Morgan Stanley announced third-quarter results (Goldman was down 70 percent from 2007; Morgan was down only modestly; both were profitable). Both firms announced Basel tier-one capital ratios* of 11.6 and 12.3, respectively, as compared to 8.5 for an average of a large bank peer group. But the market buzz had it then that neither firm could survive, despite its fine reputation and success in staving off difficulties so far, because neither was a bank and thus would not be able to rely on a stable deposit base in times of crisis. And, after Lehman, there was no reason to believe the government would assist them if their access to funds dried up as confidence in them drained away. On September 18, the stock prices of the two investment banks declined by 25 and 43 percent, respectively. Morgan Stanley, perhaps as a maneuver to throw off the dogs, announced that it had opened merger talks with Wachovia Bank, the new CEO of which was Robert Steel, until recently deputy secretary of the Treasury, and a longtime Goldman Sachs partner and Paulson associate.

The stock market was signaling a complete loss of confidence in all financial stocks, and the sinking prices in the banking sector alarmed the government regulators watching from the sidelines. As stock prices fell, the credit markets picked up the concern—the banks would be unable to raise new capital, which most of them would need sooner or later as their write-offs continued—and began to withdraw funds. The government onlookers believed that financial stocks were being shorted by hedge funds and other speculators, making the credit market problems worse.

So, on September 18, the SEC stepped in with another unprecedented move: it banned short-selling in shares of 799 companies with financial and banking activities.

Earlier in the year the SEC had banned "naked short-selling" (selling

---

* Minimum risk-adjusted capital adequacy ratios imposed by banking regulators in accordance with a global agreement negotiated in Basel, Switzerland, in 1987.

shares before they had been borrowed in order to sell them short), and prevented short-selling in any of nineteen financial stocks. A year earlier, the SEC, after an extensive study, had rescinded the "uptick" rule, which prevented short-selling unless the prior trade in the stock had been at a higher price. The SEC stated that its study showed that there was no evidence that the time-honored rule was effective, and some claimed that it was a form of interference in free pricing by the market. The removal of the uptick rule, however, was seen by some as making it easier to sell short, while the restriction on naked short-selling made it harder. But the idea that the SEC should prevent short-selling at all, and do so for a designated group of stocks, was thought by many economists and professionals to be well beyond the government's role in the market. The short-selling ban, however, seemed to make very little difference—financial stocks continued to be hammered—though the ban may have contributed to the increase in volatility.

On September 19, now frightened that the whole credit structure might be falling apart, Paulson and Bernanke requested that Congress authorize a $700 billion market stabilization fund (the Troubled Assets Relief Program, or TARP, which was quickly and irrevocably dubbed by the press as the "bailout fund"), which the Congress voted down on September 29, driving the Dow Jones down 778 points that day. Paulson and Bernanke pulled out all the stops to get the bill reintroduced and passed—turning the effort into a high-stakes, do-or-die moment that required vivid pictures of the economic disaster that would occur if the measure was not approved, which rattled the markets further. The Dow Jones average began and ended the month of September at about the same level, but daily swings of four hundred to five hundred points became normal, and several times exceeded this range. The volatility of the stock market (measured by the VIX index) began the month at 20 percent (about average for the past year) and then promptly doubled.

THE END OF WALL STREET

Also on September 19, both Goldman Sachs and Morgan Stanley announced that they had applied to the Fed to become bank holding companies. The move was a great surprise, as both firms had long prized their independence from the federal banking system with its stricter regulatory disciplines. In reality, however, the moves were not so dramatic.

Both firms, since the early part of the year, had had bank inspectors from the Fed embedded inside them, reporting their changing financial positions to the federal authorities daily. The firms were told that they would be considered too big to fail and would have to conform at least to tier-one minimum capital reporting standards for their core capital, for the foreseeable future. Both firms also had for several years owned banks through subsidiaries (domestic and European), which took customer deposits and could access interbank markets. They were already regarded as nonbank holding companies by the Fed, so it was not such a big deal to shift to becoming bank holding companies, especially if the Fed was already telling them that they would be regulated as if they were anyway. The advantage in doing so would be to gain access to the Fed's lending window if needed. The Fed wanted the two firms to act together so one would not be left behind to be ganged up on by a confused and frightened marketplace that might feel the need to withdraw funds from the lone survivor, thus threatening its safety.

The news resulted in a sharp turnaround in the stock prices of both firms, reversing the run and suggesting that the move had been well timed. But the action clearly had important lasting significance beyond its timing. Though the firms would continue in the same businesses they had been in before, and not necessarily rush out to establish themselves as branch banks, the change was seen by many as representing the end of an era. *The Wall Street Journal* ran an editorial entitled "The End of Wall Street," noting that all of the top five stand-alone investment banks were now "gone," and with them the independent, lightly regulated, freewheeling form of market capitalism that had thrived or failed according to the skill and fortune of their principal investors since the beginning of the American republic.

> In a single week, the era of the independent investment bank has ended. Wall Street as we have known it for decades has ceased to exist. Six months ago there were five major investment banks. Two, Lehman and Bear Stearns, have failed, Merrill Lynch is selling itself to Bank of America, and now the last two are becoming commercial banks. Adam Smith, that great market disciplinarian, is punishing excesses and remaking American finance long before Congress can get into the act.[22]

On September 22, Morgan Stanley announced that it would sell approximately $9 billion in stock (representing a 21 percent interest) to

Mitsubishi UFJ Bank. The deal left the merger talks with Wachovia Bank, announced five days earlier, up in the air, but apparently Wachovia was never intended to be a serious alternative.

On September 24, Goldman Sachs announced a deal with America's best-known investor, Warren Buffett, in which his Berkshire Hathaway Corporation would acquire $5 billion in new 10 percent preferred stock, with warrants to purchase $5 billion in common stock at $115 per share (making the cost of the capital to Goldman above 20 percent), and followed this deal with an immediate sale of another $5 billion in stock in the market at $123 per share. The Buffett stamp of approval and the addition of $10 billion in new capital "should quickly end the credit-market debate about the capitalization and liquidity position of Goldman Sachs," said Brad Hintz, a well-regarded analyst at Alliance Bernstein, who follows the securities industry.

MORE BANKS ARE SWEPT AWAY

While the market was still digesting the story of Warren Buffett's return to Wall Street, and Washington's struggle with TARP, another Washington, Washington Mutual (WaMu), a large savings and loan institution in Seattle, announced that it was urgently seeking a merger partner to avoid seizure by the government. WaMu had been very aggressive in generating adjustable-rate and subprime mortgages and had been reporting losses for several quarters. Starting on September 15, WaMu's depositors had been heading for the exits, yanking $17 billion in just ten days. That was enough to jolt the Office of Thrift Supervision into action, and it closed the bank on September 25 and asked the FDIC to arrange an auction of its assets the next day. This was the biggest bank failure in U.S. history, in a year in which twenty-four other banks would be seized by their regulators, the largest number in fifteen years.

Several banks took a look at WaMu, but were discouraged by the quantity of assets that would have to be written down. JPMorgan Chase, however, which just a few months earlier had made an offer to acquire the thrift for $4 per share but had been rebuffed by WaMu in favor of a private equity investment from TPG, was willing to step forward. It made a deal with the FDIC on September 26 to acquire $310 billion in banking assets and $182 billion in deposits for a bargain price of $1.9 billion. WaMu's equity investors would receive nothing—TPG and its co-investors would lose $7 billion on a five-month investment—and unlike all of the 2008 rescue situations that preceded it, its holders of unsecured debt and other creditors would have to take their chances in bankruptcy. The quick flip would cost the FDIC nothing. Morgan would mark down WaMu's assets by an additional $31 billion, but the transaction would still add to its earnings per share, the bank said. The acquisition would create the country's second-largest branch network—5,400 branches in 23 states—and bring Morgan's balance sheet up to $2 trillion in assets.[23]

While WaMu's fate was being decided, Wachovia Bank (which had just made an offer for Morgan Stanley) was struggling hard to save itself. Wachovia was the country's fourth-largest bank holding company, a product of more than one hundred mergers over the preceding two decades. Like Bank of America, it was headquartered in Charlotte, where it had its origins. In 2006, Wachovia acquired Golden West Financial Corporation of Oakland, California, a savings and loan organization, for $25 billion. Golden West added about $120 billion in residential mortgages to its balance sheet, including many of the risky adjustable-rate type. When the housing market began to sink, Wachovia was faced with a near-continuous need for write-downs on its mortgage portfolio. Wachovia also announced that business customers had withdrawn 25 percent of their deposits, and "low-cost core" deposits declined 8 percent.

By early September, the bank realized it would need to raise substantial additional capital, arrange a "strategic partner," or merge with another company, and hired advisors to help them develop alternatives. During the week in which Wachovia was in merger discussions with Morgan Stanley, it also engaged in discussions with other prospective partners, including Citigroup, after several telephone calls from Vikram Pandit, its CEO. Wachovia's stock price, which had dropped more than 80 percent during the past year, closed at ten dollars per share, and the market began to reflect concerns that it might not be able to complete a deal without government support. On September 29, a few days after JPMorgan acquired the assets of WaMu, Wachovia announced a complex deal with Citigroup and the FDIC in which Citigroup would acquire $700 billion of Wachovia's banking assets and liabilities (but none of its nonbanking and securities activities) for $2.16 billion in stock, and the FDIC would provide loss protection on up to $312 billion in mortgage-related and other assets, for which Citigroup would issue approximately $12 billion in additional preferred stock and warrants to the FDIC. Citigroup also promised to raise an additional $10 billion in common stock to support the deal. Citi's stock traded off 12 percent on the news. Its stockholders must have thought that even at such a low price, the true cost of an acquisition of Wachovia, with all its troubled assets, and all the new Citigroup stock to be issued at prices half what they were a few months ago, would still be very high.

The following day, the FDIC announced it would seek an increase from Congress in the $100,000 bank deposit guaranty to $250,000 to reassure nervous depositors, and the SEC and the Financial Accounting Standards Board announced a further review of recently applied Fair Value Accounting rules, which many had complained were forcing banks to take unnecessary write-offs and thus be forced to raise unneeded capital in difficult markets. The SEC had already approved some loosening of Fair Value Accounting for banks, to ease the pressure on them, much to the disgust of accounting purists who believed that the changes would make the financial statements of banks even more opaque and unreliable.

On Friday, October 3, after a week of pleading, arm-twisting, and predictions of catastrophe, a revised TARP bill was passed by Congress. The long-awaited procedures for intervention in the mortgage-backed securities market, however, would still have to be devised, and it would take a couple of months more before intervention could occur, a Treasury spokesman said. This seemed a long time to wait for implementation of a program that had been described as so essential and urgent.

By the same Friday, the Citigroup–Wachovia deal was off. A new bidder had appeared: Wells Fargo (which had considered Wachovia in the preceding weeks but dropped out) made an offer of $7 per share, or $15.4 billion, for all of Wachovia, with no FDIC support, leaving the Citigroup deal in the dust. Even at the higher price, Wells Fargo was acquiring Wachovia at only about 30 percent of book value; but the real incentive came from a little-noticed overnight change in the tax rules by the Treasury on September 30, the day after the Citigroup deal was announced. The rule change would allow profitable banks to use the tax losses from loan write-offs of banks they acquired much more generously than before. This was a huge benefit to Wells Fargo; one tax expert estimated that it would generate additional tax savings from the Wachovia deal of $19.4 billion, more than the entire cost of the deal. (The Treasury ruling would not benefit Citigroup, which was fettered by substantial tax losses of its own, to nearly the same extent.)[24]

What was the Treasury up to? It had pushed Wachovia into selling itself and, after a week of refusing to assist buyers, had then changed its mind and agreed to the FDIC credit protection deal in order to allow Citigroup to move ahead; then, on the same day that it did, it quietly arranged a tax rule change that would cost the taxpayers tens of billions so Wells Fargo could top the deal with Citigroup it had just agreed to. Perhaps it wanted to keep a wobbly Citigroup from going in over its head with an acquisition that might weaken it further, a sensible point. Or perhaps it only wanted to replace the government-supported Citigroup deal with one that had no government support. It is impossible to know, but the market can be forgiven for thinking that the government seemed to be lurching from one thing to another without any sort of underlying plan.

MARKET TURMOIL

By early October the stock market had become seriously nervous and afraid; the S&P 500 dropped 27 percent in the next four weeks of October, and then recovered, only to fall backward again by late November to its low point for the year. The extraordinary levels of volatility in stock markets soured the stomachs of investors of all types, sophisticated and not—and the volatility was absolutely screeching—the VIX index jumped from 40 (about twice the average level for the past few years) to 80, an all-time high. On October 10, the Dow Jones index fell sharply, and then rose equally fast, traversing more than 1,000 points in a single day. Stocks of banks and other financial service companies, after reporting more writedowns and dividend cuts during the third quarter, plunged even more than the market, creating a crisis for them as investors appeared to be withdrawing all support.

During October the Fed intervened heavily in commercial paper and the interbank markets, supported money market funds (to prevent a flood of withdrawals), and negotiated extended currency swap lines with foreign central banks. The governments of the European Union countries, equally concerned about their sinking markets, announced plans to commit "whatever it would take" (about $2 trillion) to support their banking systems, including major interventions in the UK, Germany, France, Italy, Holland, and Belgium. In Switzerland, the government purchased $60 billion in troubled mortgage-backed assets from UBS, to keep it from staggering beneath their weight, and forced several changes in top management.

DE-LEVERAGING

It had now become clear that rapidly falling real estate prices had set off a downward pricing spiral in the MBS market that had spread to other asset-backed securities, resulting in more markdowns, margin calls, and an all-hands-on-deck effort to reduce leverage as rapidly as possible. The market-panicking consequences of the Lehman bankruptcy only made the situation worse, accelerating price declines and the depletion of bank capital and choking off liquidity in both bank credit and capital markets, which in no time came to a halt. Within just a few weeks, the mortgage crisis had spread to become a broad financial crisis, and this was about to descend on the real economy, driving a mild recession into a steep and nasty one.

One hedge fund manager, Jud Reis of Sire Partners, explained the months of September and October 2008 to his investors as follows:

> As the credit markets seized up there was massive pressure on all sorts of securities as banks and investors demanded liquidity. Increased demand for liquidity combined with reduced supply created havoc in the markets. As banks could not finance as easily or as cheaply as they had been accustomed to, they forced their customers and themselves to sell assets. As the wave of selling forced prices lower, others rushed to sell lest they be left standing with no chair when the music stopped. Leveraged investors had no choice but to sell assets. Some prime brokers faced uneconomic funding costs forcing them to reduce credit to their customers. The cost of credit to others increased substantially which had the same effect. For some, credit became unavailable. The push for liquidity forced hedge funds to cover shorts as well as sell longs. Mutual funds had to sell to fund redemptions from panicked investors. Variable annuities were put back to insurance companies, forcing further sales. Institutions who had sold structured products with guaranteed values rushed to sell the securities supporting those values before it was too late and they were underwater. The proprietary trading desks of banks and securities firms were ordered to drastically reduce positions as these institutions no longer had access to the leverage which had financed those positions.

Hedge fund investors withdrew $43 billion in September. Mutual fund investors withdrew about $100 billion in October, forcing fund managers to sell stocks they were perfectly prepared to hold on to. In the fourth quarter of 2008, Morgan Stanley and Goldman Sachs between them reduced assets by a stunning $527 billion. Other large financial institutions had similarly rushed to unload assets.

MORE EFFORTS TO PROTECT THE BANKS

Paulson was increasingly concerned about the severity of the coming recession, and he was also afraid that the continuously worsening position of the large banks would cause them to lose the confidence of their depositors and creditors, and not just one or two, but several large banks might have to be taken over by the FDIC, there being almost no other banks left to rescue them through unassisted mergers. He wondered if there wasn't a way to prop up the banks while also stimulating the economy. The British prime minister, Gordon Brown, had launched a program of government investments in bank capital, which, he figured, could be leveraged nine or ten times with deposits to stimulate lending. Maybe, he thought, such a program would be more helpful right then than using TARP money to try to stabilize the mortgage-backed securities market, its previously advertised purpose.

Paulson decided it would be, and on October 13 he promptly launched a voluntary "Capital Purchase Plan." Through it the Treasury would invest $125 billion of the $350 billion in TARP funds that Congress had authorized the secretary to invest without further approval in preferred stock in nine large U.S. bank holding companies, including the new ones, Goldman Sachs and Morgan Stanley.

He chose to invest initially in the nine largest banks because he did not want to single out weak banks, which might then experience runs. So he insisted (even though the program was supposed to be voluntary) that all of the top nine banks take infusions of capital: as much as $25 billion for Citigroup, JPMorgan Chase, and Bank of America, and $10 billion for Goldman Sachs and Morgan Stanley, and lesser amounts for the others. To induce the banks to agree, Paulson told them, "If a capital infusion is not appealing, you should be aware that your regulator will require it in any circumstances."[25]

The investments were in preferred stock with modest 5 percent dividend rates (for the first five years), and 15 percent stock participation warrants,* but otherwise the preferred stock had no restrictions on the use of proceeds from the financing or on the payment of dividends, though the banks had to agree to get approval for dividend increases and common stock repurchases, and to accept certain (originally modest) limits on executive compensation. The Treasury said it hoped the banks would lend the money to consumers, businesses, and others that would help revive economic activity, though this never happened. The MBS market intervention plan, for which TARP was fought over so hard and intensely, was abandoned. Paulson's plans for TARP had changed, he said, "because the facts had changed." The ABX indices of asset-backed securities prices dropped sharply, to their lowest levels for the year.

The following day, the FDIC announced that it would guarantee all bank securities issued in the interbank market through 2009, and would also insure the commercial paper issued by GE Capital and some other nonbank entities. The Fed and other government agencies had by now committed $1.7 trillion in loan guarantees and support obligations, yet still the stock market, and especially financial stocks, continued to sink. Third-quarter results announced by the banks, many reporting continuing losses, did nothing to improve things.

Within a month of the Treasury's plan to invest in banks, forty-two regional banks had indicated they were interested in signing up for the government's capital purchase program. On November 11, American Express announced that it, too, had been approved to become a bank holding company, the Fed having waived its customary thirty-day waiting period because of exigent market conditions. The company's credit card default rate had doubled over the past year, and October had been the first month since 1993 that card companies were unable to sell bonds backed by card receivables.

After announcing its fourth consecutive quarterly loss (totaling about $20 billion) on November 16, Vikram Pandit of Citigroup said that the bank would eliminate fifty-two thousand jobs over the next year, twice the number targeted a month before. He confirmed that the bank would continue to sell off nonessential business units and other assets, but he remained committed to Citigroup's universal banking strategy. Some analysts

---

* The terms were far more generous to the banks than the terms of the 10 percent preferred stock of Goldman Sachs (with 100 percent stock participation warrants) purchased by Warren Buffett.

then thought that the worst was behind the bank; a consensus of them expected fourth-quarter results to reflect a further loss, but one of less than $1 billion. Still, Citi's stock price hit a twelve-year low of $8.89. Four days later, the stock dropped to $4.71, even as Saudi prince Alwaleed bin Talal said he would invest about $350 million to increase his holdings in the bank from 4 percent to 5. The sinking stock price sparked concern that depositors might withdraw funds from the bank, destabilizing it further. Or possibly instead, it reflected concerns that the government might seize the bank, as it had Fannie Mae and AIG, or prop it up with another highly dilutive equity injection, neither of which would be good for stockholders. On November 21, Citigroup's stock reached a low of $3.05 per share, for a market capitalization of less than $20 billion. Two years earlier the market capitalization of Citigroup had been in excess of $240 billion, the largest in the world for a financial services business.

On November 24, the Treasury, the Fed, and the FDIC made a joint announcement that the three agencies would make an additional cash infusion of $20 billion of TARP funds into Citigroup, and the FDIC would guarantee $306 billion in specified real estate–backed loans and securities for a period of up to ten years, with the first $29 billion of such losses (and 10 percent of the rest) being absorbed by Citigroup, in exchange for $27 billion in new 8 percent preferred stock, with warrants to acquire common stock (to the extent of 15 percent of the value of the preferred) at $10.61 per share (the average of the closing prices over the last twenty trading days). Citigroup would also agree to limit quarterly dividends to $0.01 per share. The stock recovered to the $6.5-to-$7.5-per-share range.

The Treasury appeared to have gotten what it wanted. It believed it had sent a clear signal that the bank would not be allowed to fail or be taken over, and therefore the market could relax and go about its business. It had also avoided nationalizing the bank in the usual sense the term implied. It neither took it into conservatorship (like Fannie Mae) nor did it take up a majority of the voting stock or force a management change as it had done at AIG. But it did invest, in a little more than a month, a total of $52 billion in cash and $270 billion in guarantees in a company with a market capitalization of $40 billion to $45 billion (at the time of the first investment, and half that at the time of the second investment) for nonvoting equity securities with a combined dividend return of 6.5 percent, and warrants exercisable at a premium of nearly 200 percent above the closing price on the date of the investment, for a total of less than 10 percent of the outstanding shares. Anyone else doing such a deal would have insisted on more Buffett-like terms, which would have provided at least a 60 percent voting interest, suggesting that the taxpayer didn't do so well on this one. Not to mention the fact that the taxpayer had invested in a distressed bank without insisting on any changes in management or the board of directors that had striven, unwaveringly and unsuccessfully, to pursue an extremely aggressive multi-platform universal banking business model. This was the model that had led the bank headfirst into every one of the dangerous lending areas that had developed through bubbles and otherwise over the past ten years. This was the same business model that had been fully discredited by Citigroup's stock price performance over the preceding eight years, and had cost it two CEOs and forced at least a dozen senior management changes. It was not at all clear why Citigroup had been treated so much more favorably than AIG.

Meanwhile, another important decision awaited the Washington team before it could turn everything over to the incoming Obama administration (which would include Timothy Geithner as secretary of the treasury): the future of General Motors and the rest of the automobile industry. Congress had declined to assist the industry without a plan for it to recover viability by undertaking major reforms. Many members of Congress (as well as many economists and other professional observers) believed that the best way to work out what was to be reformed, and who was to give up what to do so, was in court through the bankruptcy process. The companies, however, were terrified that bankruptcy would frighten away customers, dealers, and suppliers and create havoc from which the big American companies might never recover. But in the absence of congressional approval of an industry bailout bill, General Motors and Chrysler were headed for the rocks. (Ford was not in such immediate distress.) Unless, that is, they were given a last-minute reprieve by TARP, which they were. On December 19, the Treasury announced that it would provide $13.4 billion in loans to GM and Chrysler: these would be three-year-term loans to bridge the period until the new administration came up with a plan that Congress would approve. There would be no new financing, however, unless the companies met certain restructuring criteria by March 31, 2009.

This effort, however, would not be enough; car buyers couldn't get financing for new cars in the credit-constrained market, so GMAC, General

Motors's sales financing subsidiary (which was 51 percent owned by Cerberus, the private equity group that also owned Chrysler), was to be recapitalized and turned into yet another improbable bank holding company. This however, would require $30 billion in new capital being added to GMAC to satisfy the Fed, its new regulator.*

This capital was to come from asking GMAC's holders of $39 billion in debt to exchange it for new equity shares, something most were reluctant to do. If GMAC, which lost more than $5 billion in 2008, were to fail, the bondholders would be far better off in bankruptcy proceedings as debtors than they would be as stockholders. The deal was sweetened, arms were twisted, and the deadline for the deal was extended several times, until GMAC could report that $21.2 billion of debt had been exchanged (54 percent of the total; the target had been 75 percent). On December 29, Treasury announced that TARP would commit the last of its approved funds to purchasing $5 billion in 8 percent GMAC preferred stock (with warrants to acquire 5 million shares of common stock) and it would make another $1 billion loan to General Motors so that it (together with Cerberus) could acquire $2 billion more of GMAC's stock through a shareholders' rights issue. When you added it all up, the sum of the new capital finding its way into GMAC was close enough to $30 billion to satisfy the Fed.

The deal was particularly complex for Cerberus, a private equity fund, which paid $7.6 billion for its stake in GMAC in 2006 because under the bank holding company rules, industrial companies cannot own more than 15 percent of the voting stock of a bank holding company, so it decided to distribute most of its GMAC holdings directly to its investors, leaving it with 14.9 percent. It also had to discontinue the annual "consulting" fees it charged GMAC.

General Motors could now get back into the car-selling business, it hoped, using a recharged GMAC to fund the purchases. It immediately set out to clear up the unsold inventory by offering 0 percent car loans and lowering the credit standards of acceptable customers considerably. But it was difficult to see how this was going to help get Cerberus its money back (or to prevent GMAC from running up more bad debts, which might threaten its solvency again).

---

* In December GMAC Financial Services chairman J. Ezra Merkin, who was also chairman of the hedge fund Ascott Partners, resigned after reporting losses of $1.8 billion in funds managed by Bernard Madoff.

ASSESSING THE DAMAGE

After the $306 billion in guarantees to Citigroup, the Bloomberg news service estimated that various agencies of the U.S. government had committed a cumulative total of $7.7 trillion to support financial markets and institutions during the crisis: $4.74 trillion for the nine or ten different initiatives put in place by the Fed, $1.54 trillion in guarantees provided by the FDIC, $900 billion provided by the Treasury, and $500 billion from the Federal Housing Authority (FHA) and Fannie Mae and Freddie Mac, the government-sponsored enterprises (GSEs), to support home mortgage purchases and refinancing.[26] All of this unprecedented effort was to check the wave after wave of selling of mortgage assets, credit instruments, and shares by investors of all types, from all over the world, which had been occurring for more than a year. The onslaught had displaced market liquidity in all forms of financial paper to virtually nil, and it had remained like this for months at a time, paralyzing economies everywhere.

The first responder to the crisis was the Fed, which reacted vigorously. As Paul Krugman, the 2008 Nobel Prize winner in economics, said of his former Princeton colleague Ben Bernanke, "I don't think any other central banker in the world would have done as much by way of expanding credit, putting the Fed into unconventional assets, and so on. Now, you might say that it all hasn't been enough. But I guess I think that's more a reflection of the limits to the Fed's power than of Bernanke getting it wrong. And things could have been much worse."[27]

Paulson's reviews have been more mixed. The Lehman bankruptcy catapulted the markets into panic and made everything worse. Offended by the moral hazard of bailouts,* he wanted to draw a line at Lehman, and did. He and Bernanke claim they had no authority to guarantee Lehman's assets, even briefly—but who was checking?

Paulson's flip-flopping on TARP also came in for criticism. First he asked for $700 billion to stabilize the collapsing asset-backed securities markets (the falling prices of which forced banks and others to write down their holdings, repeatedly, as the market continued to fail to find

---

* He may also have been offended by the $1.7 billion fortune that PIMCO, the bond investor, made on its large investments in the debt of Fannie Mae and Freddie Mac before Paulson ordered them into conservatorship.

buyers). Then he switched the strategy in favor of partially nationalizing the largest banks in the country, then suggested that having used about half of the fund, he was finished and would let the incoming administration decide what to do next. According to *The Economist*:

> Distressed markets tend not to react well to offers of salvation being abruptly withdrawn. Holders of toxic mortgage-backed securities had pinned their hopes on the American government's plan to buy large piles of the stuff through auctions as part of the TARP. The decision to abandon that approach has left them shattered. The ABX index, which is linked to residential mortgages, plumbed new depths.[28]

Finally, choosing to support the so-called healthy banks by large injections of government-owned capital may not have been the best way to aid them. An announcement that the government would guaranty all deposits and other liabilities of major banks "while it worked with them" to return their balance sheets to normal might have been enough to keep the wolves away. Instead the program of semi-nationalization left all banks appearing to be in trouble and some in a position of being force-fed more capital than they might have needed, without a clear exit strategy for how they could pay it back. Maybe it would have been better after all to have helped the distressed banks get rid of the troubled assets by forcing their sale to TARP. Even so, by the end of 2008, the Capital Purchase Program had been extended to $250 billion in investments in about fifty institutions, most of which had requested the funds voluntarily. For many of them the capital was cheap at a time when it was otherwise hard to come by.

The Bush government triumvirate (Paulson, Bernanke, and Geithner) acted boldly, often without clear authorization, quickly, and imaginatively, and the size and speed of their responses prevented things from worsening. It was without doubt a difficult struggle, one in which walls collapsed and bastions fell, but the system held, and though there were many casualties, the great majority of the world's largest and most complex financial intermediation institutions would return to duty and the high ground of relative normality would be regained within several months. Many European bankers and economists were quite praiseworthy of Paulson and Bernanke for their quick and resolute reaction to worsening events, in contrast to what they regarded as a too-slow and conventional response by their European counterparts.

Still, there were wounds and wreckage to be dealt with, and the financial markets and the economy as a whole were a long way from reaching the bottom when the government was turned over to the incoming administration in January of 2009. Indeed, the damage to some of the main institutions of finance was enough for many to wonder whether a distinctive fifty-year era of aggressive, freely competitive capital markets had come to an end. Wall Street had not started out in any way resembling what it had become. Much had changed over those fifty years, but the industry that had been deposited on the doorstep of the Obama administration in desperate need of care and feeding, for all its past growth, wealth, and power, was clearly in for another round of changes that would reshape and define its future.

Looking back over those fifty years, one can see both harbingers of the coming disaster and lessons to be drawn for the future reshaping of Wall Street.

2

THE "NEW MEN" OF FINANCE

AFTER ALL THE DIFFICULTIES and disruptions in Wall Street that followed the 1929 crash—the Depression, new securities laws, and World War II—the industry was trying to get back to normal in 1947. Just then, after nearly two decades of chaos, slump, and struggle, the Justice Department decided to bring a major antitrust action against the seventeen largest Wall Street underwriters of new issues of securities for restraint of trade and monopolistic behavior. The case seemed strange, because the government had already moved to regulate the industry: in 1934 the Securities and Exchange Act was signed into law, fully empowering the Securities and Exchange Commission (SEC) to regulate all aspects of the securities business. So why was the Justice Department getting into the act so long after this had happened? Especially since the industry had been small and relatively inactive for the past fifteen years: only 2,600 new underwritten issues had been brought since 1935 (about 170 a year for the whole industry), and 13 percent of these were done through openly competitive bidding. Yet the government was alleging that the industry's leading firms, since about 1915, had turned the market for new issues of securities into a monopoly by their use of underwriting "syndicates." The syndicates were groups of firms formed, on a case-by-case basis, to guarantee the price and distribution of each issue of stocks or bonds. They were necessary for the simple reason that the issues being brought were larger than the comparatively small private firms that were to underwrite them, so the firms needed to band together to form the capital and to share the risk. The case was tried before Judge Harold Medina, who issued a ruling in October 1953 that decided the matter in favor of the defendants and ended the issue. But Judge Medina's lengthy opinion revealed a great deal about the capital markets industry that had emerged since the enactment in 1933 of the Glass-Steagall Act (which forced commercial banks and investment banks to separate their businesses) and the unprecedented, extensive new securities laws. These and other new federal regulations would shape and constrain financial services businesses for generations to come.

The defendants included ten firms that were incorporated and seven general partnerships. Morgan Stanley had fourteen general partners, all of whom were sued individually, as was the case for all the other partnerships, each of which had about the same number of partners. The total capitalization of the seventeen defendants was $107 million (an average of $6.3 million per firm) at a time when the entire securities industry had capital of $484 million. Judge Medina prepared a league table to rank the underwriters by their relative market shares over the preceding fifteen years, using a method he devised to prorate co-managerships among them. At the top of this list was Blyth and Co., the only West Coast–based firm and a leader of most issues from that region. Next was Morgan Stanley, the heir to all the blue-chip clients of JPMorgan, then First Boston Corporation (not a member of the NYSE because it was a publicly held company owned by seven thousand shareholders), Smith Barney, Dillon Read, Lehman Brothers, Kuhn Loeb, Harriman Ripley, and in tenth place, Goldman Sachs. The next seven firms included such unforgettable names as Stone and Webster, Glore Forgan, Harris Hall and Co., and Union Securities, but they did not include names more familiar today such as Merrill Lynch, Salomon Brothers, or Paine Webber. By general consensus the most prestigious firms—those that declared themselves entitled to participate in a "special bracket" of underwriters ranking above all others—were Morgan Stanley, Kuhn Loeb, First Boston, and Dillon Read. The special bracket owed its entitlement to past glories dating back to the railroad days. Two of the firms, Kuhn Loeb and Dillon Read, were already beginning to fade, but certainly the other two were not.

The special (or "bulge") bracket and a few other firms were essentially wholesalers who put together the syndicates that both underwrote the risk of the issues and sold them to investors. These firms originated more than their share of the underwriting business. They had the contact with the issuers, and skillfully and jealously maintained their relationships with them; client relationships almost never changed once they were established. The SEC discouraged competition among underwriters of new issues by requiring a period of approximately thirty days for regulatory procedures from the time an issuer had to name an underwriter (upon filing a registration statement) and when the issue could be sold. No firm could guarantee the price for a stock or a bond thirty days in advance, so there was no competition based on offering the highest stock price or lowest interest rate. In addition to underwriting, investment bankers also arranged unregistered "private placements" (non-underwritten direct sales of a stock or bond issue to a small group of insurance companies or other institutional investors) for which there had been 1,900 issues in the 1935–1949 period. There were hardly any mergers or acquisitions in the 1930s or 1940s. Relationships with clients entailed giving advice on different corporate matters; assisting with introductions to important investors, government officials, and chief executives of other companies; and occasionally being represented on the board. Judge Medina calculated that for the fifteen years he reviewed, investment bankers' board memberships correlated with underwriting managerships on average for about 12 percent of the deals. This percentage was much less for Morgan Stanley (2 percent), where the relationships were mainly inherited, and much greater for Goldman Sachs (55 percent), where Sidney Weinberg was the firm's principal rainmaker.[1]

Wall Street, of course, let out a great sigh of relief when the Medina ruling was announced, but it was clear that the case was about the past, while the industry was facing a new and different future. After World War II, American industry began to expand to supply the long-suppressed consumer demand for products and services related to a "good life": housing, transportation, entertainment, and leisure activities. But progress was uneven: economic expansion periods were closely followed by downturns. Businesses were optimistic, but with vivid memories of difficult times still fresh, many were cautious. The 1950s saw this cautious optimism carried forward, but the 1950s were also the years of the Korean War, and the early days of the cold war and of civil rights activism. Nevertheless, the 1950s saw the initial public offering of Ford Motor Company, worth nearly $700 million, a revival of corporate bond markets, and the first sign of mergers and acquisitions since the 1920s.

In 1952, Harry Markowitz published his seminal, Nobel-winning article on portfolio allocation under uncertainty beginning the development of modern portfolio theory, an extensive and continuing academic investigation into the subject of optimal asset allocation that demonstrated the importance to pension funds of holding large concentrations of equity securities in their portfolios. This work appeared just as financial institutions were emerging as the principal American investors. They were just in time to make use of the theory, and they did. These institutions, which owned $9.5 billion in assets listed on the New York Stock Exchange in 1949, owned $70 billion of such assets, or 20 percent of all listed securities, in 1960.[2] They would expand further over the next four decades, to own two thirds of all American equity securities and to be responsible for trading approximately 90 percent of them.

The 1950s ended in recession, but the fundamental postwar shift of economic plates was still occurring when seventy-year-old Dwight Eisenhower "passed the torch" as president to forty-three-year-old John Kennedy in 1960. This was a very symbolic event as all over the country the older generation that had endured a lifetime of wars and Depression were being replaced by younger people with much more buoyant outlooks. The Kennedy-Johnson years included many stressful and challenging events, but they also contained the longest continuous run of economic growth in America's history (106 months, a record that was later broken in the Clinton years) and a seven-year stretch (1962–1968) in which average annual real GDP growth was over 5 percent. The stock market reflected the excitement in strong bull market rallies in 1960–1961, 1962–1965, and 1967–1968, during which the Dow Jones average doubled. The underwriting business reflected all this activity as corporations took advantage of friendly markets to make investments that would increase their growth rates and appeal to investors.

THE NEW MEN

America has long been indebted to Britain for what it taught about the industrial revolution, which began in the late eighteenth century and ran through much of the nineteenth. The industrial revolution enabled Britain to develop the world's most prosperous economy and, because of the resources this provided, to rule much of the world. English capital markets had made it all possible, according to Walter Bagehot, at the time the editor of *The Economist*, who published a small book in 1873 called

Lombard Street, which described these markets and what made them tick. England's economic glory, he suggested, was based on the supply and accessibility of capital. After all, he pointed out, what would have been the good of inventing a railroad back in Elizabethan times if there was no way to raise the capital to build it? Bagehot pointed out that in England, in the City of London, "there was a place called Lombard Street where in all but the rarest of times, money can always be obtained upon good security, or upon decent prospects of probable gain. Such a market was a luxury which no other country has ever enjoyed with even comparable equality before."[3]

The real power of the market, he went on to suggest, is its ability to offer the benefits of leverage to those working their way up in the system, whose goals are to displace the people at the top. Everywhere, Bagehot noted, "small traders have arisen who discount their bills, and with the capital so borrowed, harass and press upon, if they do not eradicate, the old capitalist." The new trader, he explained, has a natural advantage in the system:

> If a merchant has £50,000, to gain 10 percent on it he must make £5,000 a year, and he must charge for his goods accordingly; but if another has only £10,000 and borrows £40,000 by discounts (no extreme instance in our modern trade), he has the same capital of £50,000 to use, but can sell much cheaper. If the rate at which he borrows is 5 percent, he will have to pay £2,000 a year [in interest]; and if like the old trader he makes £5,000 a year, he will still, after paying his interest, obtain £3,000 a year, or 30 percent on his own £10,000. As most merchants are content with much less than 30 percent, he will be able, if he wishes, to forego some of that profit, lower the price of the commodity, and drive the old-fashioned trader—the man who trades only on his own money—out of the market.

Thus the ambitious "New Man" (Bagehot's 1873 term; of course it meant man or woman), with little to lose and ample access to credit through the market, can earn a greater return on his money than a risk-averse capitalist who borrows little or nothing. The higher return enables the New Man to undercut the other man's prices and take business from him. True, the New Man may lose on the venture and be taken out of the game, but there is always another New Man on his way up who is willing to replace him. As the richer man has a lot to lose, he risks it less, and thus is always in the game continually defending himself against one newcomer or another or until he finally packs it in and retires to the country.

"This increasingly democratic structure of English commerce," Bagehot continued, "is very unpopular. It prevents the long duration of great families of merchant princes . . . who are pushed out by the dirty crowd of little new men." This, on the whole, is good for the system, he concludes, as "the rough and vulgar structure of English commerce is the secret of its life."[4]

And the secret of America's as well. Indeed, in America we are all New Men, or we were not too long ago: the Astors, Vanderbilts, Goulds, Rockefellers, Baruchs, Fords, and Weinbergs. The timeless parade goes on to include the New Men since their day: the Buffetts, Icahns, Gateses, Weills, Kravises, and Schwartzmans. The New Men come—they leverage their capital and their skills—and displace the market leaders who preceded them, until they are overtaken themselves. This is the way of all markets, especially of financial markets, and most especially of all, of Wall Street, no longer just a street in the city of New York, but also the symbol for the entire capital markets industry. Throughout this book, I refer to Wall Street and capital markets, and investment banks and wholesale banks, somewhat interchangeably; reflecting the current reality of the competitive marketplace in global capital market services, the old Wall Street investment banks have been combined and/or compete with a few large, former commercial banks that are now referred to as "universal banks."

MR. WALL STREET

Sidney Weinberg's long and eventful career was ending just as mine was beginning. He had just officially passed day-to-day command of Goldman Sachs to a successor, Gustave L. (Gus) Levy, and moved from the firm's offices at 20 Broad Street into a small office rented for him in the Seagram's Building on Park Avenue, but he wasn't gone. He remained in control of the firm's partnership—deciding who was admitted and what percentage interest each partner received when the partnership was reconstituted every other year—and thus he was an important force in the firm until he died at age seventy-seven in 1969. Though the firm had a very successful institutional brokerage and trading business, Weinberg was mainly interested in the investment banking business the firm performed for corporate clients. Almost all of that business was brought into the firm by Weinberg and his sons (who helped their father manage some of his many clients) to such an extent that the firm might easily have been renamed Sidney Weinberg and Co., and no one would have noticed the difference. Beyond these businesses—corporate finance and institutional sales and trading—the firm did little else. No fixed income, no commodities or foreign exchange, no real estate, no asset management (except for a few rich families looked after by individual partners), and only a modest amount of arbitrage trading. Nor did the firm make much money. When Sidney Weinberg died he is reported to have left an estate of only a few million dollars, despite having owned by far the largest share interest in the partnership for nearly forty years. This was an almost trivial amount compared to the fortunes complied by his contemporaries on Wall Street—Robert ("Bobbie") Lehman, André Meyer, and Ferdinand Eberstadt—all of whom, while heading significant firms of their own, were very active traders and venture investors. Weinberg insisted that he was not a trader, that he never traded, and that all of his effort went into being the best investment banker he could be. That distinction was more important to him than money.

What the distinction meant in practice was the acceptance he invariably received in the corridors of government and in the boardrooms of America's greatest corporations, whose leaders were the men who really made things happen, those who mattered the most. At one point between 1950 and 1965, Sidney Weinberg was on the board of directors of Ford Motor Company, General Electric, Sears Roebuck, BF Goodrich, Kraft Foods, and Owens Corning Fiberglass, among many others. Many of these companies at this time were led by men who were the quintessence of old-line, stuffy, WASP establishment America, men from old families and good schools with little time or interest in uneducated Brooklyn Jews with heavy accents.

So a question came to my mind right away as soon as I had looked him up in the library following our brief interview: How had this Sidney Weinberg ended up where he had, considering where'd he started? That must have been a particularly difficult, virtually impossible journey to make.

Sidney Weinberg was born in 1891, the third of eleven children of an immigrant wholesale liquor dealer of limited means. He went to work early, dropped out of school in 1906, and joined Goldman Sachs in 1907 as an assistant to the porter, cleaning partners' hats and shoes and emptying the cuspidors. Goldman Sachs was founded in 1869 by Henry Goldman and his son-in-law, Samuel Sachs, to conduct a business brokering commercial paper (short-term IOUs issued by corporations for working capital) to the banks in Wall Street. The firm prospered as a commercial paper dealer, and in 1906 it branched out into underwriting public offerings of stock for growing corporations such as Sears Roebuck and General Cigar. This was a pioneering endeavor in a market that then only recognized stocks of railroads and large industrial enterprises. As a young flunky, Weinberg did whatever he was asked, and rose within the firm to become office boy. In this position he attracted the attention and interest of Paul J. Sachs, a partner, who "took him in hand." (Paul was one of four sons or nephews of Samuel Sachs who were partners in the firm; he left the firm in 1915 to become director of the Fogg Gallery and a professor of fine art at Harvard University.) Weinberg joined the navy in World War I as a cook, and returned to Goldman Sachs afterward as a commercial paper salesman. While Weinberg was away, Henry Goldman, who had been the firm's organizing genius most responsible for its success, retired in an angry split with his Sachs in-laws over his strong allegiances to the Imperial German cause, and the Sachses decided to reach out for a dynamic outsider to restart the firm's business after the war. They chose Waddill Catchings, a Southerner with impeccable WASP credentials, a degree from Harvard Law School, and experience at the prestigious New York law firm of Sullivan and Cromwell, to become senior partner in 1918. When Weinberg retuned from the navy, he filled in whatever gaps he noticed in the management structure of the firm, which Catchings and the Sachses happily let him do as their confidence in him grew. In 1927, twenty years after joining the firm, the indispensable Weinberg was rewarded by being made a junior partner, an enormous leap for a former porter's assistant.

The 1920s provided a roaring bull market and a corporate merger boom, which Goldman Sachs was able to participate in, thanks to Catchings and his white-shoe contacts. Catchings also pushed for an increase in the firm's trading activities, which in the rising market made a lot of money. By 1928, Catchings had become the firm's principal rainmaker, and he insisted on having the largest partnership share, which the Sachses, more than a little intimidated by him, agreed to readily. He also insisted on launching a leveraged investment trust called Goldman Sachs Trading Corporation (GSTC), which would buy stock in the market much like a closed-end mutual fund. The firm put up $10 million (half its capital) and hoped to raise $40 million or more, but the feeding frenzy going on in the market enabled them to bring in $100 million. By February 1929, the GSTC stock had doubled, and by June (when two of the Sachs brothers were away in Europe), Goldman Sachs Trading Corporation had suddenly spawned the Shenandoah Corporation, another leveraged investment trust, of which GSTC would own 40 percent. In August, Shenandoah gave birth to yet another, even larger fund, the Blue Ridge Corporation, of which Shenandoah owned 86 percent. This structure is what came to be called a "pyramid scheme." With this arrangement, Goldman Sachs, with a $10 million investment, controlled a fund that controlled investments in three trusts worth $500 million.[5]

It was all fun while it lasted, especially for Waddill Catchings, who joined thirty corporate boards, including Chrysler Corp. and Warner Brothers, and was set to make a killing. The markets in GSTC, Shenandoah, and Blue Ridge all soared in the last months of the bull market in 1929, and Goldman Sachs made more money than it had in its entire history. But it was soon over. The market crashed in October, and shares of GSTC, which had reached a high of $326, fell to as low as $1.75. The other funds also collapsed and the firm lost almost everything. As "one of the greatest investment debacles of the twentieth century," the outcome of the GSTC brought the Goldman Sachs name into disrepute.[6]

When asked many years later why Goldman Sachs had plunged into the investment trust business, Walter Sachs explained, "To conquer the world. Not only [because of] greed for money, but [greed for] power sparked it and that was the great mistake. I confess that we were all influenced by greed."[7]

The Sachses were devastated by the loss of the money, certainly, but they were especially upset by the loss of the firm's good name, which had sustained them all their lives and with which they had been entrusted since Henry Goldman's departure. If Henry had still been there, they felt, the disaster surely would never have happened.

The Sachses, Arthur, Walter, and Howard, pulled themselves together and did what they had to do after the collapse of GSTC—they fired Catchings, whom they thought had been blinded and addled by the runaway market, and set about trying to restore their name and fortune, which they thought would take a decade or more to do. They all resigned themselves to the task, but knew that none of them was up to leading the firm to recovery. So they turned to the indispensable Sidney, despite the fact that he had been closely associated with Catchings and the investment trusts, and offered him the place of senior partner with a one-third interest, together with their willingness to forgive any losses that that interest might require Sidney to shoulder. This was an extraordinarily generous offer to make, especially the loss guaranty, which had to be applied many times over the following years. In the aftermath of the sell-off of GSTC assets, the settling of lawsuits, and operating losses in the interim, Goldman Sachs's capital was reduced to $5 million in 1936. It had been nearly that amount thirty years before, and it would not be until the mid-1950s before the firm's capital would again exceed $10 million. It would not be until 1934 before the firm led an underwriting issue, and until 1935 before it became profitable again, though in those years of the Great Depression the firm had lots of company in its distress.[8]

The massive failure of risk management on the part of the owners of the firm (who did not step in to limit exposures) was not lost on the Sachses or on Weinberg, and inevitably this failure colored their future attitudes about greed, capital, and speculation. No wonder Weinberg didn't trade. Waddill Catchings, however, continued to do so. He was involved with a variety of corporate deals, and ran a small mutual fund before retiring to Florida, where he died a very rich man in 1968.

For Weinberg, the GSTC affair turned out to be a stroke of enormous good fortune. Had it not happened, or had it ended less violently, Catchings would have remained where he was and Sidney would have served out his time, like most of the rest of his partners, in comfort and obscurity. Instead he was presented with an opportunity no unschooled, accent-laden Brooklyn nobody could ever have dreamt of: to lead at the age of thirty-nine, without a capital investment, a group of Harvard-educated, art-collecting grandees who made up one of New York's oldest, blue-blooded German Jewish investment banking partnerships. Of course, the state of the firm's business was so bad that neither the Sachses nor Weinberg had any alternatives. Neither could do much else. And there was still a very good chance in 1930 that the firm would not survive the economic depression that was on its way.

I have often asked friends of mine in the business what they would have done had they been in Sidney Weinberg's shoes then. The question has a particular resonance now. "How would you, in the midst of the Depression, save the firm, restore its reputation, and make yourself the best-known investment banker in America within thirty years? What's your basic plan?" Few have ever come up with much of anything in the way of an answer to the question, and Weinberg never revealed one.

But I think he did have a plan, and some principles that he set out to employ in his effort to regain the lost ground. First, he had to stop the bleeding. He sent the Sachses back to work in the commercial paper business, which had always produced a decent cash flow. Next, he retained John Foster Dulles, then a senior partner at Sullivan and Cromwell*, to represent the firm in the various GSTC matters that had to be dealt with. This would take a few years, but he would need to cap the firm's losses and try to liquidate the investment trusts as quickly and painlessly as possible. Then he would need to find a way to exploit his modest connection to Franklin D. Roosevelt, the governor of New York, who was going to run for the presidency in 1932. Roosevelt would need some help raising funds and gaining whatever support he could on Wall Street, where most of the important people regarded him as a traitor to his class. So the indispensable Sidney made himself available to the Roosevelt machine, no doubt to their mutual benefit. By the time Roosevelt was elected and sworn in, the Depression had deepened and been accompanied by widespread failure of the banking system. Roosevelt's first action as president was to declare a bank holiday to try to prevent a national bank run. Roosevelt complained that he didn't know anybody on Wall Street and didn't know whom to talk to there to sort out the financial mess. Weinberg heard the complaint and offered to help. His offer was accepted and he set out to see all the people who might have been able to do something. He would say something like, "The president of the United States sent me to ask you if you would like to meet with him and his advisors to discuss the banking crisis, and economic policy for the next few years. Maybe you don't like the guy, but the country is in trouble and he's asking for your help. You owe it to yourself and all of us to meet with him." The pitch usually worked, and the meetings that followed were useful for everyone, so the next meetings were easier to arrange. Those who declined to meet, or who were difficult, would be dropped from future invitations. It soon became clear that having access to the country's top economic policymakers was worth something, and Weinberg's phone began to ring.

In 1933 the indispensable Sidney organized the President's Business Council, at which business leaders from all over the country—not just from Wall Street—would be invited to meet with the president and his economic people to discuss views on how to break the Depression. The business leaders welcomed the opportunity to explain their views to an administration that they feared might become excessively socialist. Weinberg was the gatekeeper for these events, and became the go-to man for

---

* Dulles was secretary of state in the presidential cabinet of Dwight Eisenhower.

access to the administration on all business and financial issues. But he didn't stop there. Important government positions had to be filled by experienced executives in the myriad new government agencies created to increase employment and economic activity. Weinberg became the indispensable headhunter for these positions, and before long was also helping corporations find board members or executives who knew how to navigate the many channels of influence and access. Weinberg did not use these occasions to hustle anyone for business—there wasn't much going on in the markets and Goldman Sachs was still recovering then—so the business leaders did not consider him to be a hustler. Instead he was very useful.

Weinberg knew that if he was going to make it with these guys, he would have to be able to deliver very high-quality advice when asked about something, so he made sure that Goldman Sachs was populated with bright, articulate, presentable young men with the best academic credentials who could help him study corporations (or anything else) and write up highly professional analyses or reports. He began looking for these people at business schools, especially Harvard, and by 1967, when he was celebrating the sixtieth anniversary of his career on Wall Street and was being called Mr. Wall Street by *The New York Times*, he was credited with having "trained more than a hundred graduates of the Harvard Business School," probably averaging about three a year since 1935 or so.[9]

When the country drew close to World War II, Weinberg was called upon to help the government recruit industrialists and financiers for top positions in the administration. He was an assistant director of the War Production Board during the war and came to be known as "the body snatcher" for his ability to find top people for the civilian side of the war effort. He filled the same role during the Korean War. By 1950, Weinberg was more than indispensable to the Truman administration, he was also the link between business and government, and knowing everyone, he was the man to talk to if you needed to meet anyone, or attract someone to a board of directors, or fill a senior executive position. Sidney realized that this was his comparative advantage, so he kept close track of everyone, used his own people to study who might be useful where, and always took seriously requests for help, as if pursuing a corporate assignment. His reputation soon led to his being asked onto boards where no one with his background could ever have expected to sit. When on a board, he would use his bright Harvard Business School associates to study every proposal and alternative and to prepare him for every meeting. He was always likable, humorous, lighthearted, and fun, but he also knew when to be blunt and direct. He was intensely loyal to the companies he served, even insisting on consuming only their products in his daily life. He would almost always turn out to be everyone's idea of a perfect, well-prepared, valuable, and supportive director. For more than twenty years Weinberg would attend two hundred or more board or corporate meetings a year. For important politicians he could go one step further and help arrange financing for their campaigns.

All of this he did without developing an ego that was too big for him to be threatening or difficult for those he was associating with. He was one of the boys, not one of those who had to stand out among them. He was a workaholic with few distractions or interests other than doing what he did: hanging out with the corporate and government "boys" who ran things in the country and who considered him to be an extremely valuable colleague.

Sidney's role as investment banker grew with all this activity, and over the years he arranged hundreds of financings for his many clients. The most important of all these transactions was the $650 million initial public offering of Ford Motor Company common stock in January 1956. This was not only the largest stock offering ever done, one in which every underwriter in the country participated except Morgan Stanley, which participated only in underwritings it led, it was also one of the more complicated deals ever done.

Henry Ford II replaced his grandfather as CEO of the company in 1947 and inherited a mess. The elder Ford had been senile and erratic for years and had allowed the company to become very run down. It was losing money, had terrible labor problems, and needed to be turned around, which Henry II was attempting to do. But also his grandfather had transferred 90 percent of the company's stock to the Ford Foundation to avoid estate taxes and had given the foundation a nonvoting class of shares that received no dividends. With no dividends, the foundation had no money to disperse, and without disbursements it couldn't remain a tax-exempt foundation. The family, however, which owned only 10 percent of the stock, wanted more economic participation and also didn't want to risk losing control of the company. It took two years to work this out, but the foundation was recapitalized and the issue finally came to market and was a big success, with Weinberg receiving full credit in the press for masterminding the operation. It was the highlight of his career.

Back at Goldman Sachs, Weinberg's mark on the firm was clear. He was the boss, autocratic and prickly in his own way, and the Sachses were consigned to the backseat. The firm's main job was to support Weinberg's various activities, and this was not to be questioned. Only Walter and Howard Sachs from the family were left in the partnership in 1950. Nine of the thirteen partners (and most of the Harvard men who were not yet partners) were gentiles; most of them had been brought in by Weinberg. The firm made very little money in the difficult years before 1945, and not a great deal afterward, despite Sidney's rising personal acclaim. According to Jim Weinberg, "During the twenty years from 1929 to 1949, the good news about Goldman Sachs was that it had made $8 million; the bad news was that it had lost $14 million." The extraordinary thing, he added, "was that the Sachs family hung in there through all that time without pulling the plug on the firm. They deserve a lot of credit for having the faith in my dad and his partners to see the firm through those terrible years."

After his experience with GSTC, Weinberg feared trading and speculating and losing his and the firm's reputation through some sort of reckless mistake or another. He always aimed to be part of the center of the establishment and make his living by giving good advice in important situations. Gus Levy, a talented trader who was made a partner in 1945, had become the firm's moneymaker. Sidney and Gus had a lot in common—they were both hardworking, ambitious, undereducated Jews from very limited means with no background at all on Wall Street, but with a special gift for dealing with markets and people. They were both dedicated and grateful to Goldman Sachs for the opportunity it gave them and for the sense of belonging to an old, respected firm.

But the two had some fundamental differences, too. Gus was a natural risk-taker who aimed to make a fortune, not just a living, and to do it by trading and helping others invest. That meant he would have to be where the action in this world took him, which was not often toward the center of the establishment, which in any event wouldn't be available to him with Weinberg still around. In the end, Weinberg recognized Levy's claim to be his successor; he brought in a lot of income, much more than anyone else, and surely would leave if Weinberg picked one of the other partners. Levy was chosen and appropriately given much of the authority that Weinberg had wielded for more than thirty years. Weinberg had had his day, and it was time. Gus Levy was the best there was, and Weinberg wished him well, but he also worried that the firm might not be able to hold on to his blue-chip clients and play the important roles in business and government that it had under him.

Goldman Sachs, despite Weinberg's long client list, was nowhere near the top of the underwriting league tables in 1967, when the leadership transition occurred, nor was Sidney Weinberg one of Wall Street's wealthier proprietors. As someone who eschewed "trading," he wasn't even close to that distinction. But here he was, on his sixtieth anniversary, vividly dubbed Mr. Wall Street—the best-known and -respected figure in the industry—by the nation's most respected newspaper. That must have meant a lot to him. From where he'd started it was an incredible achievement. Sidney Weinberg had become the quintessential New Man of his time.

Even so, the bulge bracket still ruled on Wall Street, though it was under pressure.

Morgan Stanley was founded in 1935 to handle the blue-chip securities business of J.P. Morgan & Co. by former Morgan partners Henry S. Morgan and Harold Stanley and by Perry Hall and others from Drexel and Co. It had 24 percent of the underwriting market as soon as it opened its doors. It was by far the leading investment banking firm in the 1960s. Its clients included the biggest and most prestigious industrial companies in America, and it attended to those clients closely with good service and a lot of support. Morgan had a reputation for hiring only blue bloods with money and brains, but it was much more competitive than that. It actively recruited bright Harvard Business School students with no claim to blood or money, and most of them did very well at the firm. It was very jealous of its top ranking and proudly defended it. Unlike all other firms, it haughtily refused to allow co-managers in its deals, or to be co-managers in deals led by others. In the middle sixties the firm was small—many of the partners sat in one large Dickensian room behind matching large mahogany rolltop desks so they could easily communicate with one another when they needed to.

First Boston was another powerful firm with a large client base centered in Pittsburgh and many connections in Washington and in foreign capitals. First Boston was incorporated in 1932 as the investment banking subsidiary of the First National Bank of Boston, which spun it off after the passage of Glass-Steagall to a group cobbled together from different investment banking subsidiaries of other commercial banks. It merged with the former investment banking arm of Mellon Bank in 1946, attracting capital and clients from the hugely wealthy Mellon family and its related businesses.

Dillon Read was organized in 1920 by Clarence Dillon, an active financial entrepreneur in the bull market of the 1920s, where he made a very large fortune. In the 1960s he was in his eighties and not active in the firm. Dillon's chosen successor was James Forrestal, who was secretary of the navy during World War II but died just afterward. Clarence Dillon's son, Douglas Dillon, was John F. Kennedy's secretary of the treasury, and did not return to the firm after his government service. Dillon Read was fading as a major investment bank by the mid-1960s.

So was Kuhn Loeb, the only Jewish firm among the bulge bracket that owed its prominence to the leadership of its former senior partner, Jacob Schiff, in placing railroad securities with investors in Europe before World War I.

Indeed, the postwar period required investment banks to become much more competitive than they had been for decades. Not only were new industries developing, a new investor base was forming as well. Financial institutions such as bank trust departments (which managed a great deal of private wealth), insurance companies, state and corporate pension funds, and investment companies of various types were replacing their retiring managers from the 1940s and 1950s with a generation of younger, more optimistic and performance-oriented financial professionals. These new investment managers, eager to participate in all the new opportunities before them, began to change the market for corporate securities in significant ways. And they were accompanied by a mass of young, middle-class salaried professionals who were coming out of the woodwork again to participate in the excitement of the 1960s through purchases of individual stocks or mutual funds just as they had followed the latest nightclub dancing craze called "go-go."

3

THE GO-GO YEARS

IN THE LATE 1960S, the mutual fund industry greatly expanded its sales efforts after nearly thirty years of hiding from the industry's hapless record of the 1930s. The economy was booming, markets were rising, and investors all over the country wanted to participate in the stock market—they had few other opportunities to make the kinds of returns that the stock market was showing, and this time they could do so with the assurance of strict government regulations protecting them against the unprincipled predators who had fleeced their parents' generation in the 1920s. Equity mutual fund assets increased in the 1960s, from $16 billion to $45 billion. Especially attractive to these mutual funds were the rapidly growing companies that exploited new technologies or management methods, such as IBM, Litton Industries, Texas Instruments, and Polaroid. Mutual funds began to compete on the basis of their investment performance, and the appeal of smart, young, aggressive fund managers who seemed to be able to push up returns by finding the latest trends and acting on them quickly. These managers were a far cry from the plodding, careful, and risk-averse investment managers from the 1930s and 1940s whom they had displaced. They came to be known as gunslingers, for their reported willingness to shoot first (to establish positions early) and ask questions later.

THE GUNSLINGERS

The gunslingers were quick; they caught the market's moves, which were mainly up. They traded almost everything they owned. They could turn over an entire portfolio during a year, some even more often. Other managers sponsored special funds, called "hedge funds," which were free to be traded on margin and to short stocks and to trade in other kinds of securities and commodities. All the gunslingers were intensely competitive with one another, and on the surface anyway, they were unbelievably self-confident. "Adam Smith" wrote about them in his 1967 bestseller, *The Money Game*, giving made-up names to real characters right out of *Guys and Dolls*, such as "Odd Lot Robert," "The Great Winfield," "Poor Grenville," and "Scarsdale Fats."[1]

They were bold, and quick to act, but they were professional, too. They read the long research reports published by the new firm of Donaldson, Lufkin and Jenrette, founded by three young men right out of Harvard Business School in 1960 to produce solid, thorough research that their business school professors would have been proud of: full of facts and figures, and explanations of investment "concepts." DLJ was the first new firm to be set up on Wall Street since 1932, and its whole approach was different. Its output was aimed entirely at professional investment managers in large financial institutions. The gunslingers read the reports, but they seemed to rely more on what they heard on the telephone and spent most of their working days glued to the receiver. Many had special angles that they used in investing, but all of them were looking for "growth stocks"—stocks of companies whose earnings per share increased at 15 percent or more per year—and there were quite a few of these around in the 1962–1966 bull market.

One of the star gunslingers of the go-go years was Gerald Tsai, a Chinese-born portfolio manager of Fidelity Capital Fund, which had started up in 1957. He had a great sense of market timing and always seemed to be riding the right stocks. The fund became the flagship for Fidelity and attracted lots of money. In 1965, his fund was up 50 percent on turnover of 120 percent. Tsai specialized in a few selected growth stocks, traded in big blocks, and drove tough bargains with his brokers. His performance was terrific, but his name wasn't Johnson, and Fidelity's principal owner, Edward Johnson (a legend in the mutual fund business who was always called "Mr. Johnson"), had a son named Ned who would take over the firm from his father. Tsai, therefore, quit at the end of 1965 and announced that he would open and manage a new fund, the Manhattan Fund, and hoped to raise something like $25 million for it. But the deal was much too hot for that modest sum, and by the time the subscription period was over, the fund would open for business with $247 million under management. Unfortunately, the appearance of the Manhattan Fund coincided with the end of the bull market that had done so much to make Tsai famous. The Manhattan Fund never achieved the success its investors were looking for, and therefore they withdrew, causing a skeptical John Kenneth Galbraith to comment, "Genius is a rising market."[2]

THE FIRST HIGH-TECH BILLIONAIRE

On September 12, 1968, an initial public offering of 650,000 shares of Electronic Data Systems Corp. (EDS) was launched by R. W. Pressprich, a third- or fourth-tier investment bank, at $16.50 per share, valuing the small data processing company founded by H. Ross Perot at about $200 million. EDS was a very hot company—it processed Medicare, Medicaid, and related payments in various states—and was growing rapidly. The gunslingers loved the technology sector and couldn't get enough of it. EDS was fairly visible, and fifteen or more investment banks made their ways to Dallas to pitch an IPO to the company's shrewd but crusty, countrified bumpkin–like founder. The market was good, they said, so they could do the offering at, say, thirty times earnings. Or fifty times, or even seventy times. Most entrepreneurs would be wildly enthusiastic about any multiple over thirty, but Perot wanted to have a philosophical discussion. Was it moral to go public? Though never close to rich during his lifetime to date, he seemed to disdain money. He certainly didn't want any interference from investors in running his company. One of the last of the bankers to show up was Kenneth Langone of R. W. Pressprich, a fast-talking, street-smart salesman who reported

> Perot said he would give me thirty minutes to make my pitch but then he used up the whole time talking himself. So when the time was up, I stood up and said I had to go. He said why and I said, well, you said you could only give me thirty minutes and the time is up.

Then he said, you can't go yet, I haven't finished. So I stayed and he went on, then I got to make my pitch and we talked all through dinner and well into the night.[3]

Langone had come to make an aggressive pitch. He knew he would have to have something convincing to say, as most of the country's top investment banks had already made theirs. He thought the market would justify selling the stock for one hundred times earnings, and he told Perot this. But it took more time with the man to win his confidence and to persuade him that a public offering was something he could live with. Perot was unaware of the pedigree of the other firms, and not much interested. He liked Langone, and once they had spent the requisite amount of time "visiting together," the deal was his. It was quite a deal when it finally came a few months later. Only 650,000 shares would be sold out of 11.5 million—a float of less than 6 percent, a tiny amount for a trading market—of which half would be sold by the company and half by Perot. At $16.50, the stock was priced at 118 times earnings, and subsequently it went to a premium. Perot was thrilled. He spoke with Langone every day and visited him in New York when he was in town. Langone talked the bigger institutions into the stock, which rose and rose until early 1969, when it was selling at $160. With his 9 million shares, Perot was then worth on paper nearly $1.5 billion. He saw himself as an example of success for hardworking young people starting out with very little.* He was indeed the first such person to make himself a billionaire through the opportunities available to him through Wall Street.

Perot has been a rich man ever since, and still presents himself as an irascible, down-home country boy, but just as he was made instantly rich by Wall Street, a few months later he became the first man to lose $450 million in a single day, also thanks to the good offices of Wall Street. The year 1969 was rough for the stock market. Vietnam and the economy were not mixing well; social protests were rising all over, from the Black Panthers to student demonstrators against the war. But despite all this bad news, the market in EDS had not declined—it was still trading around $160. On April 22, EDS announced good but not spectacular results, and the market hesitated, acting momentarily like the cartoon figure that runs off a cliff and remains suspended in air pedaling franti-

---

* Perot was a third-party presidential candidate in 1992, winning 19 percent of the popular vote.

cally until gravity catches up with the joke and takes over. The stock dropped 50 or 60 points almost instantly, after its moment of suspended belief. "The roof fell in," said Langone, and neither he nor anyone else exactly knew why.[4] The answer lay in the ruins of the over-the-counter market, an awkward, ineffective system for making good trading markets in smaller-company stocks vulnerable to changing news and results. There had to be a better way to make such markets.

THE BIRTH OF NASDAQ

During the 1960s, stocks traded on the New York Stock Exchange, which had fairly strict standards for admission, or on the American Stock Exchange, where the standards were less strict, or in the informal "over-the-counter" (OTC) market, where standards were not strict at all. Many smaller companies, including some, such as EDS, that had just gone public, had to rely on the OTC market at least for a time until they could be eligible for one of the principal exchanges. The OTC market relied upon the daily issuance by the National Quotation Bureau of bid and asked quotes for all the OTC stocks provided by market makers the day before and printed up on pink sheets of paper. According to Gordon Macklin, the first president of the NASDAQ stock market, "The way quotes in over-the-counter stocks were disseminated in those days was each brokerage firm would write down the quotes of the companies they were trading, and somebody would come by, pick up the sheets of quotes, and run it through a mimeograph machine, and then distribute it back out overnight to the brokers. . . . Every morning when you came to work there would be what we called the 'pink sheets.' The problem was the pink sheets were gathered at different times, and printed at different times, so the quotes were old by the time you got them."[5]

In 1963, the SEC published a paper on conditions in the markets for stocks and opened up the possibility of trading over the counter through an electronic, computer-based system to provide better transparency and price discovery. The National Association of Securities Dealers was created by Congress in 1938 to provide a regulatory overview for the OTC market. (The stock exchanges had their own embedded regulatory arms.) The NASD was based in Washington and staffed by employees of Wall Street firms seconded to it. This was not a very tight regulatory system in itself, but the SEC had regulatory power over all markets, and the NASD was allowed to function alongside it as a "self-regulatory organization," or SRO. In this case the NASD took up the initiative to attempt to create an electronic trading system and retained a computer company called Bunker-Ramo to build it. Some Wall Street firms volunteered to participate in a pilot system, where bugs were worked out. The system would connect desktop boxes to a central data station located in Connecticut through thousands of miles of telephone lines, and the result would show more or less real-time quotes from numerous market makers in hundreds of stocks. Some thought it was a miracle; others, a waste of time and money. But the National Association of Securities Dealers Automated Quotation Market (NASDAQ) opened for business in April of 1971 and began to trade. By the end of the following year, it accounted for about 25 percent of all shares traded on the major exchanges (NYSE, American Stock Exchange, and NASDAQ combined), about twice the share of the American Stock Exchange. NASDAQ was then the second-largest exchange in America, and lots of companies wanted to get on it. Companies completing IPOs in particular wanted a good place for their after-market trading to occur.* Later, technology companies such as Intel, Cisco, and Microsoft would be drawn to the NASDAQ market because they couldn't understand why a market like the NYSE's, with people standing around a trading post yelling at one another, could be more efficient than a seamless computer-supported system that worked 24/7. To ease the way for technology companies to trade on NASDAQ, Gordon Macklin made listing standards "user friendly" by eliminating the need for companies to be profitable. Thirty years later the volume of shares traded on NASDAQ would approximate those traded on the NYSE, though the dollar value of the shares would be somewhat less.

MERGERS, RAIDERS, AND CHINESE MONEY

The gunslingers, and those who serviced them on the sales and trading side, were where the action and the glamour were. Investment bankers were where the tedious, plodding part was, but this business, too, was affected by all the market activity ginned up by the gunslingers and their cohorts. The business I joined in 1966 directly from business school was

---

* Bernard L. Madoff served on the board of directors of NASD (1984–1987) and NAS-DAQ (1989–1991) and was chairman in 1991.

small, intimate, and eager to find opportunities for success. Goldman Sachs, like most of the rest of the firms (except Merrill Lynch and the other national brokerage firms), employed about five hundred people, all of whom knew one another. Investment banking didn't pay well in the early years—I was offered $9,500 with no mention of a bonus, much less than three other offers outside Wall Street that I also received—but if you kept your nose clean and did what you were told, you could expect to become a partner someday, and partners were thought to be very well paid. The work was a combination of time-consuming statistical and analytical work, with some legal and regulatory review, but it was accompanied by frequent interaction with clients, which was what most of us enjoyed the most. The clients were senior corporate officers, usually much older though not very knowledgeable about financial markets, but they listened to us and appeared to appreciate our advice. All of us worked on several different projects at once, assigned somewhat randomly, so the variety of the subject matter and people we worked with was great and constantly changing. I was assigned to one of Goldman Sachs's two revenue-generating departments, the Buying Department, which dealt with underwriting and corporate finance (there was also the market-leading commercial paper business that dated back to the founding of the firm in 1869).* The Selling Department was for equity trading and commission brokerage with institutional investors; there was no retail brokerage activity, except for a few rich families, and no Fixed Income Department.

Goldman Sachs was then a middle-ranked underwriter. Most of our clients were brought in to the firm by Sidney Weinberg, but increasingly there were new clients—usually smaller or midsize companies—that had been solicited by Goldman Sachs's highly focused New Business Department, established by one of Sidney's Harvard men, John C. Whitehead, during the 1950s and still run by him. However, despite our investment banking efforts, by far the greatest share of the firm's profits then came from institutional trading and sales, an area of the firm developed and ferociously pursued by Gus Levy, who had replaced Sidney Weinberg as the firm's chief executive just before I arrived.

Levy joined the firm in the 1930s, looked after the OTC business, managed a proprietary trading account that arbitraged various corporate reorganizations or mergers, and cast his eye on the growing institutional

---

* Commercial paper is a short-term promissory note issued by a corporation for working capital purposes.

business. He was relentless in his pursuit of business for the firm and soon discovered that he could be to institutional investors what Sidney Weinberg had been to corporations—a leader who stood out from all the rest—if he was prepared to help them trade large blocks of securities that might appear to be too big for the market. Levy pioneered this business by using the firm's capital to position all or parts of trades that the gunslingers at major insurance companies or mutual funds wanted to make without moving the markets. By 1966, Goldman Sachs was the leader among a handful of firms engaged in block trading (none of the others being important investment banks). This was a very profitable business because of the minimum commission rates required by the New York Stock Exchange regardless of the size of the trade. In a large-block trade there was often a fat commission on both sides, from the buyer and the seller. Gus Levy also attracted a sizeable stable of investment banking clients of his own, many of whom were from among the New Men of the times—traders, deal makers, and heads of fast-growth companies—who were also frequent buyers or sellers of blocks of shares. These rough-edged clients were not at all like the well-connected establishment types favored by Sidney Weinberg, so some tension developed between the two of them. But between the firm's old clients and the new ones, and because of the boiling activity in the corporate securities markets, there was plenty for us plodders to do, and the firm was good about handing out increased responsibilities to those it thought could manage them.

THE CONGLOMERATES

In those years, the appetite for growth companies to invest in was so strong that Wall Street had to go out and create some. The developing technology sector involving computers, electronics, photo processing, and copying were exciting and promising, but there were not enough of them to satisfy the demand, so a new type of growth company emerged: the "conglomerate." This was a holding company that acquired a large number of businesses of all types from different industries. Like gunslingers, the conglomerates (a somewhat pejorative term none of them liked) bought and sold many companies, acting quickly and maintaining a frenetic pace, often with several deals pending at once. At some point a decade or so later, most of them became unmanageable and were dissolved, but in the mid-1960s they were hot, and indeed, they made sense.

The earliest of the conglomerates was born under the banner of necessity. Royal Little, a feisty New Englander, wanted to shelter wartime profits of his small textile business, Textron, from heavy income taxes by consolidating with money-losing companies that he might be able to turn around. There were not many money losers in the textile industry (which ran at full capacity during the war), so he had to step outside the industry to find what he was looking for. He found and acquired several such companies, then several more. These companies then did pretty well in the postwar markets, but the textile industry didn't. In the 1950s, Little decided to forego textiles and concentrate on his diversified investments that had done so well. Then he devised a "strategy" that explained the decision he had already made. By 1966, several years after Royal Little's retirement, Textron had acquired and sold hundreds of companies and had achieved combined sales of over $1 billion. By then Textron had established itself as a growth company and its price-earnings ratio was north of 20.

Conglomerates marketed themselves as growth stocks during a time when gunslingers valued growth over everything else. As growth stocks, the conglomerates benefited from high price-earnings ratios, which meant that when they acquired another company with a lower price-earnings ratio under the permissive "pooling of interests" accounting rules of the times, the combined earnings per share went up. In poolings of interest you just added the financials of the two companies together without creating any "goodwill" that might have to be amortized or written off. Usually, the pro forma earnings per share of a conglomerate after an acquisition would be higher than before the deal, thus creating growth (or at least the appearance of growth). The more deals to flow through the process, the greater would be the growth, especially when leverage was utilized, regardless of what the deals were or how fast they were growing, making the whole idea of conglomerates somewhat gimmicky. But for many years the gimmick was overlooked and the growth was rewarded by increasing stock prices. It was not long before Textron had its emulators.

One of those was ITT (once International Telegraph and Telephone), which had been an overseas phone line business that suffered a painful expropriation when Fidel Castro took control of Cuba. Harold Geneen took over as president of ITT in 1959 and soon persuaded the board to adopt a strategy of redeploying the company's assets into businesses inside the United States. The program was to be accelerated by acquisitions, but these might be constrained by the government's then very tough antitrust policy, which tried to block any large company acquisition in the same industry. So Geneen ended up with a conglomerate strategy of his own, one that within a few years involved the acquisition of a hundred or so very diversified companies: Avis Rent-a-Car, the Nancy Taylor Finishing School, a car parking company, Cleveland Motels, a pump manufacturer, a speedwriting company, Bobbs-Merrill publishers, Pennsylvania Glass Sand, Levitt Homes, Rayioner (a maker of chemical cellulose and a major timberland owner), Continental Baking, Sheraton Hotels, and Hartford Insurance, among many others. Many other such conglomerates were assembled in the 1960s, such that by the end of 1969, *Moody's Industrial Manual* listed dozens of them as "diversified industry" companies. Among them, these companies had acquired thousands of companies and helped to establish America's first postwar merger wave (the third in the century), one that resulted in the disappearance of more than twenty-five thousand companies during the 1960s.[6] The conglomerate spirit and its DNA would reappear in the 1980s in the form of the "leveraged buyout" firms, and in the 1990s as "private equity" investments.

THE MERGER WAVE

The first American merger wave occurred at the beginning of the twentieth century, when companies combined into entities that could conduct business nationally, funded through access to capital markets. The $1.4 billion U.S. Steel merger of 1902—valued at about $20 billion in 1988 dollars, when the RJR Nabisco deal was done, which until then was the largest deal ever done—was an example of the transactions that occurred then. A second merger wave occurred in the 1920s, during a time of new technologies, rising stock prices, and an enthusiasm for pyramided utility holding companies that resulted in 80 percent of the electric power companies in the country being acquired by holding companies. The third wave began in the mid-1960s and involved many industrial company mergers as well as conglomerate ones. Much of American industry was beginning to feel its oats again and was seeking growth solutions of its own, and mergers were certainly a way to create growth, as long as the Justice Department allowed them to do so. But as a result of the combined activity of old industrial companies (Sidney Weinberg's group) and the new conglomerate entrepreneurs (Gus Levy's guys), there was again in

America an active "market for corporate control," that is, a place where you could go to acquire control of another company, and many companies took advantage of it.

Sidney Weinberg's type of client started the merger wave in the mid-1950s, when they went looking for opportunities to combine strategically with others in order to diversify against business cycles or to strengthen themselves against the threat of competition. A landmark deal in 1955 was the merger of Warner-Hudnut Inc. and The Lambert Company into a $100 million pharmaceutical giant, Warner-Lambert. Wall Street financiers André Meyer and Ferdinand Eberstadt had heard that an inside block of Warner-Hudnut was coming on the market and quickly organized a private syndicate to buy 44 percent of the company, then pushed the company to set off on an acquisition binge in order to increase its stock price. In 1955, Warner-Hudnut focused on The Lambert Company, makers of Listerine, which was represented by Sidney Weinberg. Weinberg took a very dim view of the Meyer-Eberstadt group, which he regarded as speculators, and dug his heels in, which resulted in a deal at a very attractive price for the shareholders of Lambert.[7] Weinberg knew that his client had benefited greatly from his efforts and reportedly charged Lambert a fee of $1 million, the largest fee ever charged by Goldman Sachs until then, and one of the few then ever charged for merger advice. There were many other large companies seeking mergers in the late 1950s, an activity that kept the Justice Department busy deciding which to allow and which to prevent. Other of Sidney's clients used the market to take advantage of favorable pricing opportunities to sell their businesses, to shed ones that no longer fit, or to find new managers for family-owned businesses with no heir on the scene.

Gus Levy's clients, on the other hand, were inclined to use the market as the means to acquire growth. Gus was close to James Ling of Ling Temco Vought, and to several other conglomerators, and he knew many more focused smaller companies seeking to expand their market positions through acquisitions. The gunslingers, of course, loved the acquisition business, because shareholders of target companies were offered premiums over the market value of the stock as an inducement to tender their shares to the buyer. The risk arbitrageurs also loved the acquisition business. They bought shares in the market on the news of an offer, at a discount from the offered price, betting that the deal would go through and the full offered price—or a higher one yet—would be realized.

ARBITRAGEURS

Gus Levy had long been an arbitrageur himself, focusing before mergers came along on such opportunities as the breakup of Electric Bond and Share and other utility holding companies that the Justice Department wanted broken up in the 1940s. By the early 1960s, he had turned this business over to his partner L. Jay Tenenbaum. "L. Jay" is a legendary figure at Goldman Sachs, a master of the game of arbitrage who trained Robert Rubin, a future senior partner of the firm, who, like me, joined Goldman Sachs in 1966. The main investment banks were not in the arbitrage business—it required a high tolerance for trading risks and a willingness to get involved with messy, unpopular deals that serious investment bankers then did not want to be seen with. The other major arbitrage players then were Salim Lewis of Bear Stearns, Harry Cohn of L.F. Rothschild, and Bernard ("Bunny") Lasker of Lasker, Stone and Stern.

The arbitrage business could be pretty exciting. An aggressive buyer might suddenly announce on a Saturday evening, when management was off its guard, that on Monday it was making a cash offer direct to shareholders to purchase up to 51 percent of the company at, say, $24 per share, a price 20 percent above Friday's closing price of $20, on a first-come, first-served basis, with the offer expiring in a few days. Such an offer, called a "Saturday night special" after the cheap handgun used in street muggings, gave the target company almost no time to respond to the offer or to communicate to shareholders. The first-come, first-served aspect meant that the gunslingers and their ilk would tender all of their shares as fast as they could, knowing that shares not taken up in the cash offer would be forced to take some sort of junk securities for the remaining 49 percent. An arbitrageur would buy all the stock he could at the market price, usually a little less than the offer price, say $22.50, hoping to get it all accepted by the buyer, to whom he would tender it immediately. If he did, he made $1.50 per share on a $22.50 investment, or 6.7 percent, but he made it in only five days, so the annualized return was 489 percent. If money was borrowed to buy the shares, then the investment return could be a good deal higher yet, but if some of the stock was returned (the buyer having already received the 51 percent), then the return would be reduced by the sale of the securities received in exchange for the rest of the stock at any value less than $24. The arbitrageur had to find the stock, buy it, and tender it very quickly to make this work, and had to hope that nothing interfered with the buyer's intention or capability to purchase the stock. If the deal came undone, the stock would certainly drop to $20 or less, potentially leaving the arbitrageur with a big loss. By 1968, Congress realized that the ordinary investor was getting screwed by the first-come, first-served feature and passed the Williams Act, which outlawed this feature in favor of prorated offers, and extended the time available to investors to tender their shares. The Williams Act did slow the pace somewhat, and protected unwary investors from being blindsided, but the deals continued to flow as conglomerates and financial entrepreneurs (called raiders in the 1960s) continued to be in the market to buy what they thought to be underperforming companies.

ENTREPRENEURIAL BANKERS

All through the merger wave of the 1960s, hostile deals were strictly the preserve of the financial entrepreneurs and their bankers. The blue-chips didn't do such things; such deals were considered sordid, encouraged bad behavior in corporate America generally, and were beneath them. Most of the old-line investment banks (including Goldman Sachs, despite Gus Levy's connections with many of the perpetrators) did not represent raiders. Therefore, the population of takeover players narrowed down to raiders, targets, and "white knights," usually large blue-chip corporations who were prepared to rush in to rescue a target under fire but not to fire the first shot.

There were two established firms, however, whose entrepreneurial instincts were strong and whose sympathies were with the raiders (though they didn't call them that). One was Lehman Brothers, run since 1925 by the elegant, soft-spoken, polo-playing heir to the family fortune, Robert ("Bobbie") Lehman. Bobbie Lehman was the last of the "Own Crowd" of German Jewish banking families who emigrated in the nineteenth century to run a major firm. He was probably best known in New York for the outstanding art collection he inherited from his father and added to over many years. He was chairman of the Board of Trustees of the Metropolitan Museum of Art and, at his death, one of America's richest men. Bobbie had replaced his father as senior partner when he was thirty-four, rode the last few years of the 1920s bull market, and then confronted the Depression and war years. He expanded the firm's investment banking business before, during, and after World War II by associating with important industrialists and military figures, and by financing technology companies they were interested in. He actively and very successfully invested the firm's capital in venture and other investment schemes introduced by friends and associates, something the rest of Wall Street was, for the most part, unwilling to do. He was an early backer of Juan Trippe, founder of Pan American Airways, and David Sarnoff of RCA and an early investor in the retailing industry and the Hollywood film business. To do all this he needed more capital and contacts, so he invited several non-family members into the Lehman partnership for the first time. Bobbie claimed that he "bet on people," and he appears to have been a good judge of them. He was never very involved with the details of the investment banking business, but he alone decided who would become partner, and what their shares would be, and what investments the firm would make. He was the Sun King of Lehman Brothers, far above all the other partners, untouchable, and virtually worshipped by them. Bobbie, one of his partners would say, "didn't know preferred stock from livestock, but was a hell of a psychologist." He skillfully played the partners off one another to increase the competition among them, thinking this would maximize their production, and apparently enjoyed from a distance the vicious fights they got into. Bobbie was the lion tamer in the cage, and when he died at seventy-eight in 1967, the lions became nasty and uncontrollable. There was no consensus for a successor, so politics roiled, and some senior partners withdrew from the firm, taking their substantial capital with them. Finally Fred Ehrman, a cousin of Bobbie's who had joined the firm in 1941, succeeded as senior partner. But Ehrman was greatly disliked by many of the other, mostly younger partners, and a coup was staged in 1973 in which Peter G. Peterson, the former CEO of Bell and Howell, who had just joined the firm from the Nixon administration where he had been secretary of commerce, was installed as chief executive.[8] Peterson did not have an easy time of it, but he did calm things down enough for his warring partners to get back to work and earn some money for the firm. Several of them were involved in merger deals, where Lehman's collection of well-placed industrialists, entrepreneurs, and dealmakers came in handy. Some of the deals were hostile, and some threatened to be, but Lehman Brothers did not worry about it. Bobbie Lehman had been a backer of Litton Industries, an early conglomerate, and was an active supporter of some of the others.

Another firm that benefited a great deal in the 1960s from the merger business was Lazard Frères, which was then run by an autocratic, acerbic

Frenchman named André Meyer, who joined Lazard's French parent firm in 1925, emigrated to the United States in 1940 to escape the Nazis, and in 1943, when he was forty-five, elbowed out Lazard's long-serving, highly respected New York partner, Frank Altschul. According to his biographer Cary Reich:

> Meyer was greedy, vindictive, domineering, and often quite sadistic. His constant browbeating and temper-tantrums made life unbearable for his business associates and his family. No matter how wealthy he became, and he became *very* wealthy, he could not stop plotting and scheming to build an even bigger fortune.[9]

Meyer's role model was Bobbie Lehman, whom he admired as someone who made a lot of money, ruthlessly controlled his partners and clients, and possessed old-world elegance and taste.[10] Like Bobbie Lehman, Meyer drove Lazard into taking principal investment positions in companies the firm dealt with and conspiring, as in the case of Warner-Hudnut, to put the companies into the path of deal-makers or conglomerates much like the private equity activities of some investment banks today. He was much less interested in being an investment banker as Sidney Weinberg defined the role—there was little money in doing that—but he would provide the services when they were needed and charge as big a fee as he could. Meyer's financial acumen, his many important European contacts, and his reputation for having assembled great wealth himself provided a cloak of mystique that helped to attract the attention of many prominent figures, including Aristotle Onassis and his wife Jacqueline Kennedy Onassis, Fiat's Giovanni Agnelli, RCA's chairman David Sarnoff, David Rockefeller, French president Georges Pompidou, and U.S. president Lyndon Johnson. He was as secretive as he was complex, still active in business at the time of his death in 1979, at age eighty-one. He left an estate of only about $90 million, having spent a decade repositioning a fortune estimated at between $300 million and $800 million into family trusts or foundations. This made him one of the richest men in the country (far richer than anyone on Wall Street, except perhaps Bobbie Lehman), and almost all of it had been earned since his arrival from France thirty years before.[11]

Meyer operated behind the scenes and in the shadows, but he autocratically controlled everything Lazard did. He believed in a firm of "great men" famed for their connections, stature, and experience, men who would attract business and investment opportunities to the firm by their mere presence. He was one such man, of course, as were some of his French partners and European associates, but he needed some American great men, too, and for this he raided some of his competitors. But most important, he developed his own extraordinary protégé, brainy, Austrian-born Felix Rohatyn, who joined the firm after graduating from Middlebury College in 1949. Rohatyn's Jewish family lived in France before World War II and spent four torturous years from 1938 to 1942 attempting to immigrate to America. He was made partner in the firm in 1961 and worked on a lot of Meyer's deals. By the mid-1960s, Rohatyn had developed his own clients and reputation as a merger specialist. He was on the board of ITT and a close advisor to Harold Geneen. As a result of Geneen's active program of acquisitions, Felix became the most visible man at Lazard Frères in the merger business. Lazard was a smaller firm than the other main investment banks, with little interest in the traditional businesses of underwriting and brokerage. The merger boom of the 1960s was perfect for it. The conglomerates used such small firms, and so did mainstream companies, when they needed a second opinion or when their regular bankers had conflicts of interest. The main Wall Street merger firms would recommend Lazard if conflicted, because they knew that it wouldn't try to run away with their underwriting businesses. So Lazard received lots of referral business in addition to the considerable amount Meyer, Rohatyn, and a few others developed on their own. By the end of the 1960s, Felix Rohatyn was the industry's most visible go-to man for mergers of any kind, a reputation he maintained for another thirty years. He would also apply his skills to assisting the New York Stock Exchange in sorting out the wreckage of some of its member firms that collapsed under the weight of the paperwork crisis that nearly brought the industry to its knees at the end of the 1960s, and in guiding New York City through its financial crisis in the 1970s. Rohatyn was the only Wall Street figure to serve during five decades as a key player in the mergers business, in which he was the undisputed, all-time, hall-of-fame standout. But he never wanted to (nor did he ever) become chief executive of Lazard Frères, partly because signaling such an intention would have completely poisoned his relationship with Meyer and partly because he preferred being king of the deal jungle where he could be the Great Man, while dabbling in government and politics in his spare time. He strongly aspired (and lobbied) to be appointed secretary of the treasury, and although this didn't happen, he was named ambassador to France by President Bill Clinton in 1997, thus ending a forty-eight-year career at Lazard. Upon returning to

New York in 2000, he set up his own merger advisory firm, the Rohatyn Group, and became an advisor to Lehman Brothers.[12]

The takeover business changed profoundly in 1974 when the Canadian blue-chip International Nickel, represented by Morgan Stanley, launched an unwanted $157 million offer for Electric Storage Battery. This offer, which was ultimately successful, attracted a lot of attention and comment. Within months, other blue-chip companies (and their blue-chip investment banks) were justifying unfriendly offers to shareholders of companies they wanted to acquire. They were no longer waiting for a white knight opportunity to arise (though they still responded when one did); they were becoming more aggressive, seeking out the companies they wanted to buy, making an initial approach to suggest "discussions leading to a merger," then, if such were rejected, going directly to the shareholders with an offer. On the whole, the Electric Storage Battery deal loosened up the merger market for a lot more participants, expanding the amount of activity in it.

At first, the merger business did not look very promising at Goldman Sachs. Despite the Warner-Lambert deal, there had not been very many blue-chip transactions, but the firm thought it needed to be ready to advise on them if Weinberg's clients called to ask for help, as some did. A corporate mergers guy was hired to set up a Mergers Department, and he hired two others, a junior banker from Morgan Guaranty Trust, Corbin Day, and a young tax lawyer named Steve Friedman (who was recruited in 1966 and would rise to be co-head of the firm along with Bob Rubin, and then sole head after Rubin left to join the Clinton White House). But there just wasn't enough going on, so the corporate guy left the firm to join another corporate acquirer, and Day replaced him, with Friedman as his deputy in a two-man shop. Whenever they worked on a merger, they were allowed to raid the Buying Department for some people to staff the deal.

Day and Friedman soon came up with the idea of selling "anti-raid" services. "Hire us," they said, "and we will help you prepare a plan of what to do if you are the subject of a raid by a hostile bidder. We'll also help you to make yourself less attractive to raiders by communicating your plans to increase earnings and grow the company (thereby raising your stock price) and to lay out viable options that you might undertake to escape the raider altogether, or to at least find another buyer who would pay more, i.e., a white knight." The fear of raiders was sufficient to

ensure that this service sold well, and that companies would even be prepared to pay a retainer to keep Goldman Sachs available to them if they
should need them.

Indeed, Goldman Sachs already had a sales force in place to sell corporate financial services. John Whitehead, who joined the firm in 1947
and worked as Sidney Weinberg's assistant until becoming a partner in
1956, persuaded a reluctant Weinberg to let him set up a group to develop new business for the firm, which was otherwise far too dependent
on Weinberg's clients. By the mid-1960s this group (the New Business
Department) was in place and did indeed generate some new business,
though still nowhere near as much as Weinberg. But now they had something to sell that other firms did not, and the New Business group could
use it to get their foot in the door with companies that used other investment bankers. Long before the Electric Storage Battery deal, Whitehead
wanted to use the raid-defense product as a way of loudly advertising
Goldman Sachs's virtuous approach to client relationships. "We are on the
side of the target companies," Whitehead would exclaim, "not the raiders,
and would never assist a raider in a hostile takeover attempt." Other investment banks were reluctant to say this for fear of discouraging clients
who were acquirers, especially after International Nickel. Whitehead
made a calculated bet that more of Goldman Sachs's clients, and prospective clients, would fear raiders more than they wanted to be one, though
some business was lost. Corporations on the whole appreciated the policy and would use Goldman Sachs when needing a defensive merger
banker, and the firm's business picked up accordingly. But it meant that
other clients (i.e., some of Gus Levy's) would be turned away when they
wanted Goldman's help in taking over someone else. This created some
more tension, as both the Weinberg side and the Levy side wanted to be
able to represent their clients freely on the deals they did. Being virtuous
for the sake of pleasing the Weinberg side (the established companies that
often were targets for takeovers) was all well and good, but the clients
on the Levy side were the ones doing all the deals. Compromises were
made—we could represent a bidder, but if the deal turned hostile (i.e.,
was resisted by the target), we could not act as manager of the public
tender offer on behalf of the bidder. We could, however, manage the
debt or other financing for the bidder, if asked to do so. For Levy's clients, Goldman did not handle tender offers (Lehman Brothers did that
for Ling-Temco-Vought and some other conglomerates that were Levy's

clients), but it did participate in the underwriting of large amounts of takeover financing, then typically in the form of convertible debentures or similar securities.

After the Williams Act was passed in 1968, the takeover process was slowed and investors had more time to consider the merits of an offer and the possible alternatives for target companies wishing to escape the offer or replace it with a better one. Now that targeted firms were getting proactive defense advice (from both Goldman Sachs and, in time, some other firms), the range of tactical maneuvers was greater, and in a significant number of cases the offer was not successful, though most cases resulted in the target company being acquired by someone, usually at a higher price than the initial offer. A key element in evaluating an offer was to put a value on the securities that were to be issued to shareholders by the acquiring company. Some cash was used, but as deals got bigger, securities were substituted. There was no market for junk bonds then, so the equivalent at the time was a convertible subordinated debt issue (or a convertible preferred stock) that was junior to bank and other senior debt. Investors could look forward to converting the low interest rate debentures into common stock in the future (when the stock price had exceeded the price at which the bonds could be converted into stock; meanwhile, they received interest on the bonds greater than the stock's dividend payments) to provide a return adequate for the risk taken. These debentures were popular enough, but before long there came to be a lot of them on the market. Ling-Temco-Vought might be doing three or four takeover deals at once, each one to be financed by a different convertible debenture. Investors had to rely on complex pro forma calculations to show what the issuing company's earnings per share would look like if all or some of the deals were completed and all or some of the convertibles were converted into stock. Sophisticated traders and arbitrageurs would figure out how much they thought each of these debentures was really worth, and then buy and sell them when they could to make a profit. But most Americans found all this activity to be confusing and somewhat intimidating, and before long a journalist coined the term "Chinese money" to refer to all the acquisition currency then in circulation.

The merger business of the 1960s was something of a shock to the leading firms of the "new" investment banking business established in Wall Street after 1933. Many of Morgan Stanley's clients were too big to worry about takeovers and too stolid to think about acquiring other companies. Firms such as Blyth and Kuhn Loeb had too many of their clients in the utility or railroad businesses, which were not active in the mergers game then. Other firms were very active, however, and appeared to adapt their business modus operandi to accommodate mergers, on both offense and defense.

WALL STREET EVOLVES

The 1960s transformed the business of Wall Street more than anyone could have expected. The stock market had become institutionalized, performance-based mutual funds flourished, mergers and hostile raids and complicated ways to pay for them had displaced the steady business of issuing bonds for large industrial and utility companies, and all of this caused the trading volumes on the NYSE to soar. In 1970 the daily average number of shares traded reached twelve million, up from three million in 1960. Each one of these shares, according to NYSE rules, had to be physically delivered from the seller to the buyer in order for payment to be made. This represented an extraordinary amount of activity in matching trades, and in finding and delivering the share certificates and making all the settlements to all the right people in the right amounts. The system Wall Street used to do all this was primitive. It involved armies of clerks in dingy back offices (called "cages" because of the bars on the windows to prevent robbery) matching up trades and packing securities into large black boxes on wheels that elderly "runners" (often retired firemen and cops) would hustle from their cage to yours and back again. Inevitably this system couldn't support the weight that the rising volumes put on it. Computerizing did not help—at least not at once. Hardwick Simmons, a former partner of Hayden Stone, described the situation at his firm in the 1960s:

> Although we were new users of computers, our systems did not talk to one another. At Hayden Stone we had what we called a "wire" where all of our orders were carried. We switched those orders to the floor for execution. And then at the end of the day we had to dump all those orders into paper and resubmit them on a new computing system. We used Univac for the front end and IBM for the back end, and we had to dump them, retype them, keypunch them, verify them, and then put them into the back office system in order to get the whole thing up and ready by the next morning so everybody would know what his margin and account status was. We simply couldn't keep up.[13]

The Paperwork Crisis

By January of 1968 there were plenty of signs that the system was failing. If securities were not delivered on time (five days after the trade), the transaction would be labeled a "fail" (i.e., "failed to be delivered"). If a delivery was made but not recognized, it would be sent back labeled as a "DK" (i.e., "don't know this transaction"). In January both of these indicators were on the rise, and the NYSE advanced closing time to 2:00 P.M. from 3:30 P.M. Still, the number of fails rose. In April 1968 they exceeded $2 billion, and in May, $3 billion. By June, Lehman Brothers couldn't settle at all and had to close down until it could. It had installed a new computerized system earlier in the year, but it didn't work. Later in June, the NYSE ceased trading on Wednesdays in order to allow an extra day for the back offices to clear up past trades. It didn't help very much. Meanwhile, however, brokerage firms were running more ads, hiring more salesmen, and opening more branch offices to meet the demand for stock investments that had sprung up around the country. Many firms were lobbying the NYSE hard to cancel the Wednesday holiday so they could do more business. As one observer pointed out, "Wall Street had become a mindless glutton methodically eating itself to paralysis and death."[14]

Next the SEC got involved, announcing that firms that failed to deliver could be charged with fraud under the securities laws, but basically the SEC left the mess to the NYSE to settle. The NYSE had certain regulatory (self-regulatory, that is) powers that the SEC had in effect delegated to it, so the SEC was relying on the Exchange and its leaders to find solutions or face the possibility of being closed down. With fails at more than $4 billion by December and a study from the Rand Corporation indicating that 25 to 40 percent of all trades were DK'd at least once, it was clear that firms were losing money and eroding their capital, and would need to be rescued or closed down to prevent a widespread loss of customer money. Such an event would, of course, augur very poorly for the future of the stock market.[15]

The NYSE under a new leader, Robert Haack, formed a special committee to decide which among the worst-performing firms would live and which would not. Felix Rohatyn was the committee's key player and acted to force mergers among several different firms. The committee wanted to avoid liquidations, as customers' money would be lost if the NYSE emergency fund for such things weren't sufficient (which it would not be) if any of the big firms failed. Among such failing big firms was old, blue-blooded Bostonian Hayden Stone, the third-largest brokerage in the country. In 1970 it was losing money fast, and its capital had fallen below the amount required by the NYSE. It found itself in the arms of an unlikely rescuer, Cogan, Berlind, Weill and Levitt, a scrappy start-up brokerage firm (sometimes known as "Corned Beef With Lettuce") run by an aggressive group of New Yorkers that launched the four-decade career of Sanford ("Sandy") Weill.

Many other mergers occurred, including an improbable one in which H. Ross Perot, flush from the recent IPO of Electronic Data Systems, acquired a majority interest in F.I. DuPont, Glore Forgan and Co. in late 1970. This was a large but ailing retail brokerage firm that the salty and now very rich Perot figured he could turn around and make fly right by using his computer know-how and management skills. He had made a whirlwind entry into Wall Street earlier in the year by landing contracts to analyze the computer systems of the NYSE, and to assist DuPont in rescuing theirs. Perot rolled up his sleeves and went to work. He introduced several new ideas almost at once. The firm would be open on Saturdays. The perks of executives and top producers would be slashed. The employees would have to contribute to the rescue effort by foregoing bonuses and salary increases. Accounting and other controls would be introduced to tighten management's grip on the risks to which the firm was exposed. All of these ideas were good ones for turning around a troubled firm. But none of them was accepted by DuPont's resentful employees and managers. Much to Perot's surprise, the key employees rebelled. Most sought jobs elsewhere. Those who could not get new jobs retired to live on their savings and investments. These valued and senior employees would rather let the firm die than conform to Perot's humiliating regime. Perot was astonished, and horrified by such behavior, which he considered immoral, and he exited the industry a few years later still muttering under his breath. But the industry-wide back-office problem was improving by the time of the Perot investment, and the two-year crisis, in which one hundred member firms of the NYSE vanished or were forced into mergers, appeared to be over. The resolution of the crisis was aided by a nasty bear market that began in early 1969 and drove prices and volume down.[16]

At the same time, the NYSE and SEC pushed ahead with a plan for a central stock depository that would replace the need to run the certificates from place to place, and all firms accelerated plans to computerize their back-office operations. In 1970, Congress created the Securities Investor Protection Corporation (SIPC), which is now the investor's first line of defense in the event a brokerage firm fails still owing customers cash and securities that are missing from customer accounts.*

By 1970, firms had to face the fact that successful computerization of their controls and administrative processes was a requirement for staying alive in the securities business, and of course from then on many millions were spent to modernize and extend data processing systems.

The End of Partnerships

The back-office problem scared almost everyone. There was such a small margin for error that unexpected losses from the ancient payment and delivery system, or from anything else, simply ate away a firm's capital. And expanding, as many firms were doing to keep up with soaring volumes and the demand for new types of services (such as mergers), meant having to add more capital. But in Wall Street, capital was scarce. The firms that were members of the NYSE were proprietorships or partnerships, and partnership capital was not permanent. Partners retired, or died, and capital had to be withdrawn to pay them (or their estates) out. New partners coming in often did not have any capital and had to borrow it from the firm, i.e., from the senior partners, who had large capital accounts and would probably just as soon withdraw some. Partnership agreements rarely lasted more than a few years, and were renewed only when all the partners agreed to do so. This limited the investment horizons of many firms, when older partners were reluctant, for example, to invest in foreign markets because the investment would take many years to pay off. Nor did it encourage banks or other lenders to make longer-term loans to the firms. Also, partnerships in New York then were subject to unlimited liability: each partner had to stand for the others with all the money he had. This was not a structure that made any sense for firms engaging in enterprise expansion, block trading, arbitrage, and possibly risky mergers. The sensible thing would be to change the rules of the NYSE to allow member firms to raise capital from the market, just as the

---

* From the time Congress created it, through December 2008, SIPC has advanced $520 million in order to make possible the recovery of $160 billion in assets for an estimated 761,000 investors.

firms were telling their clients to do by issuing common stock. But the NYSE was a tradition-bound place, and changes to old ways were almost always fiercely opposed until finally some sort of catalyst pushed through the resistance.

In this case the catalyst was Donaldson, Lufkin and Jenrette, the new upstart firm that specialized in institutional research and brokerage. It wanted to grow, but was capital constrained. In 1969, Dan Lufkin was elected to the board of the NYSE and proposed changing the rules of the exchange so the firm could convert itself to a corporation and then sell shares to the public. According to Lufkin:

> The reaction I got was pretty nasty: old men screaming, "Who the hell do you think you are?" Felix Rohatyn compared me to Judas Iscariot. They felt that I was forsaking the rules and traditions of the exchange and forcing their hands, which of course I was. But I was also right. I remember that night there was a dinner for the governors of the exchange, and nobody would speak to me. I was standing by myself and Gus Levy came up to me and said, "I don't agree with what you did. I don't agree with how you did it and I don't agree with why you feel this way. But, I'll tell you this, I admire your guts for coming to this dinner."[17]

Donaldson Lufkin announced its plans to go public in May of 1969 and filed a registration statement with the SEC for an IPO. It took a long time for the NYSE to come around, and for the SEC to approve the issue, which it finally did a year later, in April 1970, deep into a bear market. The issue was priced much lower than the $35 per share that Donaldson Lufkin initially hoped for. They raised $12 million by selling 800,000 shares at $15 per share in a difficult market trending to worse. The after-market price dropped below the issue price and kept going. Within a few months the stock was trading at $5 per share, and it took a long time for it to recover. Within months, however, Merrill Lynch, never a firm to worry about the rules and traditions of the NYSE, would also go public, and after it, several other old-line firms. The access to public capital would change the industry in many ways. The firms could think expansively and plan accordingly. They could fund necessary improvements to their infrastructure and trading platforms. They could expand abroad. Within a few years of almost any firm's going public, the majority of its pre-IPO partners would retire, leaving room for promotions of younger colleagues to take their places. This, too, proved to be a significant benefit.

It also meant that firms could end the consensus-based governance structure of a partnership in favor of more decisive, if authoritarian, leadership arrangements. Perhaps no firm would benefit from that single change as much as Merrill Lynch, which would be run by Donald Regan as chief executive from 1971 until 1980, when he left to become secretary of the treasury in the Reagan administration.

There were, however, three firms that did not take up the opportunity to go public for many years, firms with large streams of income from trading activities that had conserved their capital for years: Goldman Sachs, Salomon Brothers, and Bear Stearns. These firms did not pay out any of their annual income to their partners (beyond a salary and interest on their capital accounts), nor did they allow partners to withdraw capital without permission of the firm's management committee. Partners, accordingly, did not have a lot to spend, and were dissuaded from high living or other such distracting activities. Everyone's nose was to the grindstone until death or retirement, and even then, retired partners were encouraged to remain as limited partners. As a result, and because none of these firms had retail businesses, they passed through the back-office crisis relatively unscathed.

Setbacks Before the Storm

The market had risen and propelled trading all though the early part of the 1960s, but the latter part was tougher going. The Vietnam War had become highly unpopular by early 1968, prompting riots and disturbances on college campuses that helped trigger both the announcement by President Lyndon Johnson that he would not run for reelection and the violent clashing of demonstrators and police at the Democratic National Convention in Chicago. In April of 1968 Martin Luther King, Jr., was murdered, setting off civil right riots throughout the country, and Bobby Kennedy was shot and killed a few months later. The Dow Jones index rose slightly to 943 by January 1969, up 4 percent for the year, then dropped 15 percent by January of 1970. In that year, four college students were shot and killed by troops of the Ohio National Guard sent to control student antiwar protests at Kent State University. Later in 1970, the Penn-Central Railroad went bankrupt, the largest bankruptcy in American history, and was taken over by the U.S. government. In 1971, to stop the rising outflow of American gold reserves, President Nixon closed the gold window to foreign central banks, thereby unilaterally ending the 1944 Bretton Woods Agreement that had established a fixed-foreign-exchange-rate financial system, which resulted in a rapid devaluation of the dollar and high levels of volatility in foreign exchange and fixed income markets. Nonetheless, the stock market climbed the "wall of worry" and on November 14, 1972, closed with the Dow Jones index breaking the 1,000 barrier for the first time. However, in 1973 a coalition of Arab states led by Egypt and Syria attacked Israel on Yom Kippur, leading to a full-scale war that lasted about three weeks. But afterward the Arab oil-producing countries declared an embargo on countries sympathetic to Israel, and OPEC followed with fourfold oil price increases. This "oil shock" plunged most Western economies into recession, and pushed inflation, already strained by the cost of the Vietnam War, sharply upward. The stock market dropped precipitously. In 1973, the Securities Industry Association reported that its members as a whole had lost money for the first time since the Great Depression. In 1974, Congress passed the Employee Retirement Income Security Act (ERISA), which set new standards for the management of pension funds and challenged the role of Wall Street firms in managing money for institutional clients. Also in 1974, Richard Nixon resigned the presidency after a prolonged struggle over Watergate that otherwise was destined to lead to his impeachment. Economic prospects were very worrying and markets reacted accordingly. The Dow Jones index reached its low point for the decade, 577 (down nearly 50 percent from its 1972 high) in December 1974, another year in which many Wall Street firms lost money.

The years 1973 and 1974 were two very difficult ones for investment banks. The capital-raising business was off, but for block trading with institutions trying to dump shares in a falling market, things were awful. At Goldman Sachs, there was no money for bonuses in 1973. The following year was only slightly better, so the partners provided a small bonus from their own capital. This was hard on employees, who then, as now, received most of their income from bonuses, but few people left and hardly anyone was laid off. Everyone weathered the storm with internal (and personal) cost-cutting, and hoped for the best. But it was hard to be optimistic—Goldman Sachs had been the sole commercial paper dealer for Penn Central when it went bankrupt with about $80 million in paper outstanding that had been sold to investors by the firm, and these investors were suing Goldman to recover their money. Those were big lawsuits for a firm with partners' capital then of only about $25 million. The investors claimed that Goldman Sachs knew, or should have known, about the sharply deteriorated financial condition of the railroad, and should have either disclosed what it knew or refrained from selling the paper. Goldman said it had stopped selling new paper once it concluded that the railroad was in trouble, but it couldn't do anything about the $80 million that had already been sold. There were several investors, and the lawsuits took nearly ten years to settle, but at the time they were very scary to general partners with unlimited liability, who risked losing everything they had ever made at Goldman Sachs, and perhaps more, if the suits were decided against them.

Gus Levy was senior partner of the firm and chairman of its management committee then. The management committee had been formed in 1969 just before Sidney Weinberg died. Weinberg apparently felt that some restraints should be placed on Levy, an aggressive trader with no banking experience, but who nonetheless had collected a group of rough-and-tumble entrepreneurial clients that Weinberg thought of as ragtag. Weinberg had the partnership agreement amended to provide for the committee and its powers, and Levy accepted the change graciously. But right after he took over, and the shadow of Sidney Weinberg no longer blocked him from view, he was confronted with the Penn Central lawsuits, some of which were brought by his own clients. (Once one commercial paper holder sued, all the others had to do so, too, to protect their interests in bankruptcy.) Levy was aided in dealing with the matter, which consumed a great deal of his attention until he died, by George Doty, a former senior partner of Coopers Lybrand who joined Goldman Sachs in the mid-1960s at Sidney Weinberg's prescient request to sort out and organize its financial systems and controls, and brought in a number of competent administrative and technology executives, who helped steer the firm through the back-office crisis. He also managed a battalion of lawyers advising the firm on Penn Central developing options and alternatives for each of quite a number of dangerous individual lawsuits. Doty was a very capable man, but he knew Levy had to make the key decisions.

Gus Levy was a larger-than-life character. He had come from New Orleans to Wall Street before the crash of 1929. He was educated only through high school (and two months at Tulane University) before heading to New York to make money, staying initially at the 92nd Street YMHA. He was smart, quick, and extremely intuitive. He was the most intense man most intense men had ever met. He couldn't sit still, or stand still—he constantly jiggled the coins in his pockets—or spend much time listening to others. He was tall and well built, and almost always clad in a white shirt and dark suit. He rarely smiled or joked, and was extremely rough on his subordinates (two or three quit the firm not long after becoming partners because of the incredible pressure they felt working under his constant gaze). He demanded to know what was going on with his various clients or deals, but he would give people only a few seconds to say what they had to say. Sometimes what had to be said was complex, so we used to write out whatever we wanted to tell him as succinctly as we could, with no excess words, and read it aloud to him. He always grasped everything immediately, even the complex parts. He was intimidating, and frightened most of us as no one else did. He was an unrelenting workaholic, arriving in the office before anyone else and calling clients all over the country before most of them got to work, leaving messages for them, then pacing back and forth, usually on the phone, in his cramped, glassed-in office in the center of the trading room, where he could watch the tape and yell at people for missing trades, without interrupting his telephone conversations. He had two secretaries in the office with him, who took incoming phone messages and simultaneously got someone else on the line for him. It was very hectic in there. If you had to see him about something, you just went down and stood around in his office until he noticed you, and you made your ten-second report and then left after it was clear you were no longer being noticed.

Levy was also incredibly active on the not-for-profit scene in New York, and would attend one or more black-tie events virtually every night. He was a generous contributor of time and money and a champion fund-raiser for dozens of organizations in New York and for the Republican Party. Many people commented that there must be two or three Gus Levys, because no one person could make so many calls, attend so many events, or be on so many boards. On most weekends, wherever he was physically, he called colleagues and associates to find out the status of things he was interested in. The calls were brief—"This is Gus. What did (so and so) say?"—and would end abruptly, without a goodbye. Once, he called me on a Saturday without seeming to realize he had called an hour or so earlier, about a different matter. He was totally focused, confident, and absorbed, all the time.

Though he was also awkward with some clients and in some social settings, there was yet another side to Levy that didn't show. He was insecure about leading the firm. He worried that he might not be able to handle all the responsibilities that he had sought and received. After his death, a prayer, handwritten on a yellow legal pad, was found in his desk drawer that asked God to help him manage and protect Goldman Sachs, which he feared he could not do alone. Apparently when he arrived in his office very early every morning he would recite the prayer by himself and gain comfort from it. He was especially humbled by the Penn Central affair, which he feared might do to Goldman Sachs what GSTC had done to it in the 1930s. That situation worked out much better than expected, partly because Levy decided to hang on to some certificates of beneficial interest in Penn Central's numerous real estate investments that were surrendered when settlements were made with particular litigants. Ultimately these proved to be quite valuable.

At about this time, soon after Penn Central, the back-office paperwork crisis and the public offering of Donaldson Lukfin, the NYSE began to consider rule changes that would abolish fixed commission rates and change the governance mechanism of the Exchange in order to increase competition in the securities industry. Levy was a member of the Board of Governors of the NYSE, and became its chairman in 1970. For the next several years he would struggle with an issue of enormous importance to the industry, to Goldman Sachs, and to the line of business that he personally ran there: the trading business, which had made him so successful and been the source of all his celebrity and notoriety.

MAYDAY

It started—explosively, as it turned out—when Robert Haack, president of the NYSE, addressed a 1970 meeting of the New York Economic Club and suggested that the Exchange was no longer "the only game in town," that it be reformed to become more competitive, and that across-the-board negotiated rates be an "ultimate objective" of the Exchange. Haack had expressed concern over the fact that 35–45 percent of trades of ten thousand shares or more were being executed on regional exchanges or in the OTC market, because some institutions were shopping around for lower commission rates. He also said that though he personally continued to support fixed rates, he thought that "it now behooves our industry leaders to rethink their personal judgments" about them. Before delivering the speech, Haack had shown it to the outgoing chairman of the NYSE's Board of Governors, Bunny Lasker, a leading and influential floor broker who was well connected to all the principal trading firms, and

Lasker was horrified that Haack should both have had such thoughts and want to state them publicly. But Haack went ahead anyway and shocked the industry. There was a huge uproar, and many members of the Exchange called for his head, and indeed his contract was not renewed when it expired in 1972. The members could not believe what they had heard. Fixed commission rates had been the practice of the Exchange since its beginning in 1792. They provided for "orderly markets" and what the members believed to be a fair and appropriate income for the members of the Exchange who made the markets in the shares of hundreds of great American corporations. Haack also said, "Whatever vestiges of a private club atmosphere still remain at the NYSE must be discarded."[18] This didn't go over very well with the members, either. But of course non-members thought it was right on.

Haack, a onetime broker who was previously head of the NASD, became the president of the NYSE in 1967, after the retirement of the popular Keith Funston. He arrived just in time to address the back-office crisis and the efforts to get Congress to pass the SIPC bill. Not long afterward he began to face the realities of the Exchange's minimum-commission structure, which had come under great pressure as trading volume surged. Institutions, then estimated to account for 50 percent of NYSE trading, were complaining that commissions were far too high and that the cartel-like rules of the Exchange prevented the institutions from becoming members to recapture them.

But the anticompetitive aspects of the cartel-like rules were not so clearly illegal. In 1953, Judge Harold Medina had ruled that the syndicate system did not violate antitrust laws, and in 1963, the Supreme Court had ruled, in *Silver v. The New York Stock Exchange*, that because the NYSE was an SRO whose powers were under the jurisdiction of the SEC, the NYSE's commission structure, however archaic and anticompetitive, must be considered to be approved by and acceptable to a federal regulator, the SEC, and thus could not be in violation of other federal regulations.* In other words, the beef should not be with the NYSE, but instead with the SEC.

So the SEC took up the issue of whether the commissions were acceptable, and convened hearings about negotiated rates in 1968, under the vigorous direction of Eugene Rotberg, a staff lawyer who would go on to

---

* Subsequent Supreme Court cases affirmed this antitrust position in 1975 (*Gordon v. NYSE*) and 2007 (*Credit Suisse v. Billings*).

be hired by Robert McNamara to become the treasurer of the World Bank. The high-visibility hearings drew out all sorts of other views, beyond those of the NYSE and its members, including those of Donald Weeden, who operated the so-called Third Market, which arranged for trading in NYSE-listed shares away from the Exchange, as a sort of competitive OTC market for institutional investors, public pension funds, and others.

Under pressure from the SEC, Haack announced in January 1969 that the NYSE would make one of the most complete studies of commissions ever undertaken, which would lead to new proposals to be made to the SEC. Before they were completed, however, there was a change in government as Richard Nixon replaced Lyndon Johnson as U.S. president, and the priorities of the Justice Department and of the SEC were altered. A new SEC head, Hamer H. Budge, a former district judge from Idaho who previously was an SEC commissioner, was appointed to replace activist SEC chairman Manny Cohen. With both Cohen and Rotberg gone, the SEC lost some of its momentum in pursuit of negotiated rates. In any event, the back-office crisis was revealing just how precarious the securities business was on Wall Street, and the time could hardly have seemed right to slash much of the industry's revenues. Richard Scribner, then a lawyer at the Securities Industry Association, recalls making a presentation to the SEC asking for permission to *raise* the minimum rates, because of the poor state of the industry. He and John Whitehead, who was a director of the SIA, went to Washington to make their presentation, taking with them a large copy of the published "tombstone" advertisement from the 1956 Ford Motor Company IPO in which the names of 772 participating underwriters, large and small, from all over the country, were printed. They had drawn a red line through the names of all of the firms that had since disappeared because of mergers and difficulties in keeping up with the changing economics of the business, and from a distance the tombstone looked as if it had been printed in red.*

The permission to raise rates wasn't granted, but the SEC did seem to back off on negotiated rates, and shifted instead to the private club atmosphere of the NYSE. Budge was replaced in 1971 by William Casey, a New York lawyer with many Republican and Wall Street connections, who later became the director of the CIA in the Ronald Reagan administration.

---

* This tombstone was kept in the chairman's office at Goldman Sachs until well into the 1990s, by which time virtually all the names on it but Goldman Sachs and Merrill Lynch had been crossed out.

The Stock Exchange was then indeed a club. It was owned by members, or "seat holders," who were free to trade on the floor and charge minimum commissions to non-members. Many seat holders just traded for their own accounts, commission-free, or executed trades for other members for a fee. Others made markets as "specialists" in specific designated stocks, at "posts" on the floor that you had to approach in order to make a trade on an open outcry basis. There were formalized rules that set out how orders were to be prioritized and executed. Brokerage firms owned seats and had their own people on the floor, but not as specialists. Since the Exchange was formed, minimum commission rules prevented one member from undercutting others, to preserve the integrity of the Exchange, the orderliness of markets, and to ensure that members' profits were not competed away. Haack and others believed that reorganizing the governance functions of the Exchange would take away some of the pressure, so in 1972, the NYSE announced a reorganization in which the offices of the president of the Exchange, who was a paid employee and not a member, and the unpaid chairman of the Board of Governors, who was a member, were merged. The Board of Governors itself, which had thirty-three members, all members of the Exchange, would be replaced by a Board of Directors with twenty-one members, including the chairman. Ten of these were securities industry leaders and ten were non-industry "representatives of the public." This move was intended to reduce the power of the active members, the floor brokers and specialists, who had dominated the Exchange since its beginning. It reduced their power somewhat, but because the so-called public members knew so little about the Exchange's complex, idiosyncratic policies and operations, and could easily be influenced by the members, not much really changed.

Haack's main point in his 1970 speech was that the NYSE had become uncompetitive because of its commission structure, which was driving business away. Don Regan believed that after Haack's speech some members would look ahead and start discounting commissions where they had not before, further undermining the system. Regan himself favored negotiated rates, and publicly began to separate Merrill Lynch from the rest of the members. But, just about everyone else from the major firms was dead set against negotiated rates. Why piss in your own soup?

Don Regan had been a tough scholarship kid at Harvard who dropped out of the Law School to join the Marines in 1940 and fought all the way through the Pacific War from Guadalcanal to Okinawa, finishing as a decorated, battle-hardened lieutenant colonel. He joined Merrill in 1946, and rose through the ranks rapidly. He became president of the firm in 1968, the youngest in its history; in 1971 the firm went public, and Regan became chief executive.

Merrill Lynch was founded in 1914 by Charles E. Merrill and his partner, Edward Lynch, and they made a fortune trading in the bull market of the Roaring Twenties. Merrill, however, became pessimistic in 1929 and withdrew from the firm, saving much of his money. Lynch lured him back in 1939, and they then created the foundation for the successful national retail brokerage serving the "little guy" that the firm became. When Charlie Merrill died in 1956, the firm had 6,000 employees, in more than 120 offices around the country, and $83.5 million in revenues, making it by far the largest securities firm in the country. It handled 20 percent of the volume of trades in small lots and about 15 percent of the rest. By the time Don Regan took over fifteen years later, the firm had increased its market shares further, and had become a clear leader in corporate underwriting and institutional trading. It had already become the "Thundering Herd" whose placing power (the ability to distribute stocks in new issues or in traded blocks on short notice) awed corporate America and made Merrill a preferred underwriter.

Don Regan, like Charlie Merrill, was an iconoclastic figure in Wall Street, caring nothing for the established ways and traditions. He decided to support negotiated commissions, over objections from his own colleagues, which he ignored, as much to be a troublemaker as to advance some sort of master plan he had tucked away. "We were practicing capitalists bragging about our free society and free trade and all that," Regan said, "but we wanted to fix commissions. It was like Carry Nation [the champion of Prohibition] being caught tippling in the basement."[19] Regan was very combative by nature, and he felt that anything that loosened Wall Street from its old roots and ways would improve Merrill's chances at increasing its market power.

Gus Levy, however, took an entirely different point of view. He replaced Bunny Lasker, as chairman of the NYSE, and fought hard to preserve it from change. He believed that it was a delicate institution that had been battered by the back-office mess and by the dissent that surrounded the rule change that had allowed DLJ to go public. He did not think the Exchange could survive negotiated rates—all the cohesion, discipline, and orderliness necessary to provide efficient market executions would be turned into chaos that would destroy the Exchange's ability to perform its function. He believed, as did most knowledgeable observers, that despite its commission structure, the NYSE provided the "best realized price" (i.e., after commissions) of any stock market in the world. Though he had to cope daily with soft dollars, give-ups, and rebates, he believed that the minimum commission was still the heart of the Exchange and needed to be defended. He was disgusted with Regan and others—non-traders who appeared to be willing to throw away the Exchange in order to appear more liberal or independent. On several occasions he said that if commissions were to be negotiated, Goldman Sachs might resign from the NYSE. He said it and he meant it.

As Gus Levy knew, the reality of the commission business was very different from what it seemed. Many institutions used commissions as soft dollars to pay small research shops such as H. C. Wainwright, Clark Dodge and Mitchell Hutchins, for their detailed reports and frequent contacts with star analysts. Levy thought these firms served a useful purpose, but probably would not survive negotiated rates and the end of soft dollars. Some of the gunslingers insisted on (and were offered) de facto rebates from their brokers, who would return commissions by absorbing some of the operating expenses (soft dollars), such as telephone lines and office equipment, of their hot, actively trading money-manager customers. Some institutions insisted on sharing commissions by being able to direct portions of the commission to different brokers who had been helpful to them in other ways. A Donaldson Lufkin idea might be paid for by Fidelity by diverting (giving up) to DLJ part of the fixed commission charged by Goldman Sachs for executing the trade. In 1970 an average minimum commission was about forty cents per share, but for large institutions that pushed hard, this could be reduced by 40 to 60 percent.[20]

The NYSE produced its ideas on the commission structure promised by Haack, and the SEC became reengaged. This led to interim arrangements being mandated by the SEC in 1974 for negotiation of commissions on orders above $300,000. The trial would be announced successful, and fixed minimum commissions would be set aside for good on May 1, 1975, a day Wall Street still remembers as "Mayday," which is either identified as the annual day of recognition for the Communist Party or the radio call put out by ships or aircraft in distress.

Commissions started to drop in a hurry. Early on, Goldman Sachs announced that it would offer discounts of 8 percent to large institutions, but the market quickly blew by that to about 15 percent. By the end of the year, however, the discounts were down more than 50 percent and they were still declining. Some aggressive firms cut rates by as much as 90 percent. Within a few years the forty-cent commission had dropped to a nickel. Hundreds of millions of dollars in revenues had been stripped from the industry. Trading volume, however, was increasing. In 1974, a hard year for the market, the average daily trading volume was fourteen million shares, down from sixteen million the year before. In 1975, the average daily trading volume was nineteen million shares, and within five years it would nearly triple. So for many firms, what they lost in price was offset by the increases in trading volume, and further offset by cost reduction and other efficiencies resulting from the forced computerization of the trading and delivery systems since the breakdown in the 1968–1970 period.

These two changes in the business, the need for systems technology and negotiated rates, created powerful, almost Darwinian incentives to change. By the year 2000, the average daily trading volume on the NYSE would exceed one billion shares, and information technology expense had become the industry's second greatest cost, after compensation. Every firm would have to learn to manage technology requirements and budgets, or risk being thrown out of control or descending into a black hole of cost that seemed to have no bottom. They would all have to hire a chief technology officer, someone whom most firms had to replace two or three times until finding the right person, and to commit to a particular system or vendor to meet expanding, unfolding needs that few could properly anticipate. At Goldman Sachs, a major commitment was made to a Honeywell system, which took years to convert to, only for the firm to discover that the system was inadequate soon after it was installed. This meant the process had to be repeated as the firm converted to IBM. For large retail firms, it was all the more difficult, and often a competitive advantage would go to whichever firm could develop excess capacity, which could be filled by clearing trades for others or by acquiring a rival broker at a knocked-down price. This was a feature that Sandy Weill would turn into a business strategy as he embarked on the long string of acquisitions of brokerage firms that would make his name.

But the biggest effect of the changes was seen in the economics of the brokerage industry. Merrill Lynch, long a proponent of negotiated rates, actually increased rates charged to retail investors by about 10 percent after Mayday, but it aggressively competed for institutional business at much lower rates. It would have been suicide, Merrill thought, to cut the rates to the retail sector, or so it seemed, but not doing so left the door open for future discount brokers such as Charles Schwab to contest for Merrill's customers. Merrill had developed a reasonably efficient back office by then, and could absorb other firms into it, and it had enough of a business flow at the retail rates to underwrite a vigorous effort to increase market share in institutional trading. Other firms, especially research boutiques, however, found this almost impossible to do as their share of soft dollars and give-ups faded away. There were no give-ups at four or five cents a share. Institutional research was very expensive when the product was given away, unless adequate commissions were generated from it, which increasingly, for many firms, was not the case. Block trading, once a gold mine, might only break even without fixed rates. At many firms, institutional commissions barely covered overhead, if they covered it at all. The institutions reduced the number of brokers they dealt with, no longer having a way to pay the marginal ones, and this created triage within the industry. Many firms faded away, were taken up in acquisitions, or simply disappeared.

But the main lesson from the experience of negotiated rates—a crucial, inevitable, but unplanned form of involuntary deregulation—was the experience of harsh, bare-knuckle price competition that replaced a predominantly relationship business. To compete effectively in such a market, firms had to offer better service, and give away a lot of know-how for free. Their clients had to get first calls, the best research, continuous follow-up, and good seats at Knicks games. The intensity of the industry picked up and set the tone for the future.

4

THE INDUSTRY REINVENTED

THE ANNUAL REVIEW published by Goldman Sachs for its clients and employees in 1980 contained a reflective note that had the partners known a decade before what they would be going through during the 1970s, they might have voted to disband the partnership and withdraw from the business entirely. The decade of the 1970s had brought Goldman Sachs the Penn Central bankruptcy and its lawsuits, the collapse of the Bretton Woods Agreement that held up the international financial system, the quadrupling of oil prices, war in the Middle East, Watergate and the resignation of Richard Nixon as president, negotiated commission rates on the NYSE, runaway inflation with double-digit rates on U.S. treasuries, the sudden death of Gus Levy in 1976, the ineffectual presidency of Jimmy Carter, the Russian invasion of Afghanistan, the weak dollar and gold priced at $800 an ounce, a stock market that ended the decade where it began, and, finally, the election of a B-grade movie actor as president of the United States. The partners could not have known what lay ahead, of course, including the fact that it was during those years that Goldman Sachs would break into the ranks of the industry leaders, in terms of both market share and profitability. The firm was able to turn adversity into opportunity during the 1970s, and position itself very well for the long, continuous bull market that began in the summer of 1982 and lasted, despite a few temporary setbacks, until the millennium.

FOUR LEADERS EMERGE

The decade of the seventies ended with four firms vying with one another for the industry's top positions: Morgan Stanley, Merrill Lynch, Salomon Brothers, and Goldman Sachs, in the order in which their underwriting businesses were ranked by *Institutional Investor* in 1977. For the other firms, however, the challenges of the 1970s and 1980s—mainly those of good leadership to manage transition to an increasingly more competitive marketplace—proved to be too much, so they sought refuge in mergers with stronger players. The process of transition began with Mayday, with commission rates being negotiated below the levels of most firms' economic sustainability, but it continued with deregulation, internationalization, and innovation that changed the role and functioning of capital markets profoundly. Indeed, the transition begun in the 1970s lasted for more than thirty years, as capital markets have grown steadily larger and more integrated and price sensitive.

Morgan Stanley

Morgan Stanley, the industry leader, had a lot to lose if it didn't make the right moves coming into the 1970s to ensure its competitiveness. The increasing volume of equity trading, the appearance of the gunslingers and other new investors, and the rising importance of big distribution firms such as Merrill Lynch and institutional specialists such as Goldman Sachs and Salomon Brothers, was surely going to affect Morgan's legacy client list in important ways. The firm, some thought, would have to change or face a serious risk of losing these clients and being unable to replace them. Some in the firm thought like this, but others did not. Morgan Stanley, they knew, had always been devoted to providing excellent service and maintaining impeccable relationships with clients. Surely if they focused on doing so in the future, the firm would be all right. Morgan Stanley, after all, was dedicated to serving users of capital, not the providers of it. To change would be to enter into risky transitions that they were not really prepared for. The firm had been capitalized with only $7.5 million in 1935, and when it partly incorporated in 1970, that figure was still $7.5 million. The stated reason for the incorporation of Morgan's underwriting and related businesses was to avoid the legal risks of unlimited liability associated with partnerships, but another reason was to provide some capital discipline for the first time in the firm's history. Profits had always been paid out; when additional capital was required, one of the Morgans would be asked to cough some up temporarily. Incorporation, however, required the firm to pay taxes on income, but the firm kept what was left, not paying dividends or even any interest on the former partners' capital.

Robert H. B. Baldwin, a three-sport athlete at Princeton, joined Morgan Stanley after World War II and became a partner in 1958. In those days, he said, "Morgan Stanley did not do business with institutions. It didn't have any individual customers. It didn't do research. And it wouldn't even sell common stocks, because stocks were too risky. Morgan Stanley did bonds."[1]

Baldwin was frustrated by the unwillingness of the older partners (some of the founders were still at the firm in the mid-1960s) to modernize the firm in response to market changes, so in 1965 he left to take a job in Washington, as undersecretary of the navy. He returned a few years later and picked up where he left off. It wasn't easy, as there was still an internal culture clash going on at the firm, but he organized a discussion group to talk about Morgan Stanley's future. He suggested an operations committee, which he would head, but the partners rejected the idea. Undeterred, he organized informal committees to consider particular subjects, with only limited effect. But in 1970, six new partners were named, including Harvard Business School graduates Richard Fisher and Robert Greenhill, and the internal debate tilted toward modernization. In 1971, Morgan Stanley, with two hundred employees, was incorporated, a respected senior partner, Frank Petito, became chairman, and Bob Baldwin became president. Baldwin later replaced Petito as chairman, a role he played until he retired in 1985. In keeping with the spirit of the partnership, there was no official CEO until the firm went public in 1986.

Baldwin recognized that the firm would have to become a full-service organization, or its powerful leadership position in the market would be eroded away. But that meant having to expand the firm greatly, against continuing resistance from many older partners, and to do so into several areas in which the firm had no experience at all, and indeed may have had some institutional disdain for. So he wasted no time. Assisted in dealing with internal resistance by Petito, Baldwin pushed ahead. He set up six "new enterprise" units to be implemented within the next five years, which would be fed and sustained by Morgan Stanley's basic corporate business: Mergers and Acquisitions (to be led by Greenhill), Sales and Trading (led by Fisher), Research (Barton Biggs, an early hedge fund analyst was recruited to head the effort), Private Wealth Management and Equities (Anson Beard, recruited from DLJ), and International Business (Richard Debs, recruited from the New York Federal Reserve Bank). Each unit was to do what it had to in order to shift into high gear and make an impact on the market. Each would have to hire people to fill key positions, develop a business plan, and execute it. Baldwin, direct, aggressive, and impatient by nature, used all his energies to support these units and to push them forward. Capital needed for the expansion would come mainly from retaining earnings, but other sources would be tapped from time to time. By 1979 all of the new businesses were established and doing well—all of the original leaders were still in place and their units were affecting the markets. It was an extraordinarily successful transition, done in difficult markets in the face of internal resistance at the firm.[2] Not many firms would have been able to pull it off, but it probably saved Morgan Stanley from a fate similar to Kuhn Loeb's.

During the 1980s, market conditions would reward Baldwin's strategic transformation with a major stock market rally, a merger boom, and an enormous increase in fixed income trading as the Treasury issued new bonds to fund the exploding federal fiscal deficit, while the Eurobond, foreign exchange, and international asset management businesses began to burst at the seams.

In 1984, Baldwin named Parker Gilbert, a popular, long-standing Morgan Stanley culture carrier, as his successor. By then, the firm's capitalization had risen from $7.5 million to $300 million, revenues were $1.79 billion, and it employed 4,100 people. Income from principal trading was $243 million. The firm had set profit records six years in a row, with much of the income derived from the mergers and acquisitions business, which funded the expansion of the other businesses, but they were all doing well. In 1986, a year after Baldwin's retirement, Morgan Stanley went public in an IPO that raised $257 million from outside investors. After the offering, Morgan Stanley managing directors and principals owned 81 percent of the firm's shares.

In 1990, Parker Gilbert retired and Dick Fisher, to whom Sales and Trading and Asset Management reported, replaced him as chairman, and Bob Greenhill (in charge of Investment Banking) became president. Fisher and Greenhill, rivals since their days at business school, clashed in various ways, and in 1993, Greenhill left Morgan Stanley to join Sandy Weill's new effort at Smith Barney to penetrate the top ranks of investment banking before setting up his own investment banking boutique.

Merrill Lynch

Don Regan became CEO of Merrill Lynch in 1971, the same year Bob Baldwin took over at Morgan Stanley. The two firms had little in common at the time, but their leaders were similarly aggressive and impatient in pursuit of the changes they thought were both necessary and opportunistic. Merrill was already America's largest and best known brokerage, with offices all over the country servicing the retail investor. Regan had risen to the top like his predecessors and successors by demonstrating skill as a branch manager and then as a manager of branches. Each branch had to produce commissions, meet quotas, and rule over the chaos of dealing with thousands of trades every day with an iron hand. The former Marine had been very good at these jobs and was widely known within the firm as tough, smart, and combative. Some of his colleagues claimed that he enjoyed conflict and would argue endlessly to win a point, any point. But he realized early on that Merrill could be a lot more than it was. Its strength was its enormous amount of placing power. He wanted to extend this advantage further, by using it to leverage Merrill's way into institutional sales and trading, to fixed income, and to expand into other services.

In the early 1960s, Regan was brought from Philadelphia (where he had been the local czar) to New York to be in charge of administration, a job he didn't want but agreed to take if it included long-term planning. He became executive VP in 1964 and president in 1968. By then, he already had unconventional and unpopular views on many subjects that would shape the future of Wall Street. He made hardly any effort to befriend or collaborate with other Wall Street leaders, who in general he thought were a bunch of stuffed shirts who looked down on mere "wire houses" and, in his view, were completely out of step with the times. Regan was for lots of competition in free and open markets, for negotiated commissions, for enabling financial firms to participate in various different types of businesses and be able to sell their securities to the public to raise capital. He was for expanding Merrill's services and activities into real estate, economic and securities research, and mutual funds, once considered taboo by Charlie Merrill. In the 1970s he described what he called a "financial firm of the future" that was modeled on the idea of the supermarket, an industry that Merrill Lynch had been especially powerful in since Charlie Merrill cut his teeth on it as an investment banker in the 1920s. People have financial needs, Regan thought, and they ought to be able to shop for them at a single place, where they could be offered bank accounts, investments, real estate, and insurance, all under one roof. But it was also important for this future financial firm to be able to acquire the products and services for the supermarket from the wholesale side of the market. To do this, the firm would have to be able to operate effectively as a market maker to pension and mutual funds and other institutional investors.

At a time when Glass-Steagall separated commercial bankers from investment bankers and commercial banks were many times larger than investment banks, Regan foresaw the end of this regulation and was eager (unlike everyone else on Wall Street) to compete with the big banks head on. He wanted to offer his clients a basic bank account (something everyone had to have) to collect deposits and to provide a variety of check-writing and lending services that present law prohibited. Regulations on the amount of interest that banks could pay on deposits in a rising interest rate environment gave Regan the opportunity he was looking for—the creation of money market funds to draw money out of the banks. As Robert Pozen, a later president of Fidelity Management and Research, put it:

> The fund industry really got pushed into the money-market mutual funds business because the seventies was such a lousy decade for stocks. You had these great years in the sixties and then it just died. It was very hard to sell stock funds in the seventies. And there was a ceiling on how much banks could pay in interest on deposits. So when interest rates started to rise it wasn't hard to see the compelling argument for the money fund. I don't think the mutual fund industry would've just decided to compete with banks for assets. It was simply a response to the economic conditions of the times.[3]

In 1975, Regan pushed Merrill into developing the idea of the "cash management account," or CMA, to make up for shrinking commissions. The CMA was an effort to attract funds to brokerage accounts at Merrill Lynch by offering a unified system for managing cash balances. Customers would be offered a marginable brokerage account (one that can be margined) that would sweep all the cash into a money market mutual fund managed by the firm, which would have check-writing privileges and would include a Visa credit card with borrowing limits set by the size of the assets in the brokerage account. But legally, this wasn't a bank account; it was just a brokerage account tied to a mutual fund with credit facilities. Merrill would charge a fee for managing the CMA, and would have the money in house to direct, if its clients agreed, into the large variety of investment options on offer by the firm. According to Regan, "I wanted us to be a bank because that's where the money was. At the time the banks basically had a monopoly. . . . The banks knew this and were taking advantage of their customers. They were charging for checking accounts; savings accounts paid 2 or 3 percent when they were lending it out again at 12 and 14. It was like shooting fish in a barrel."[4]

But of course, the banks opposed it and sued to require the CMA to be vetted by state and federal regulators. The process of getting everything cleared, in all fifty states and at the federal level, would cost over $100 million (a great deal of money in 1975) and take the better part of a year. There was much opposition within Merrill Lynch to the program— giving up free account balances and expending so much capital on an idea that might be rejected by regulators or by clients, many feared, could bankrupt the firm. The whole idea was based on the expectation of receiving billions in new balances (on which management fees would be paid) to offset the loss of the benefit of free balances on hundreds of millions in existing customer accounts. Regan, however, was an extremely forceful person and would not hesitate to push forward on things he wanted to do despite substantial opposition from his colleagues, as was the case with his position with the CMA. He apparently went into a meeting with his senior colleagues and was told, "Don, we're going to get killed on this one. And Regan said 'You guys want to take a vote on this, or is it unanimous?' They murmured that the majority was against it. So he said, 'Okay. I can see you are all against it. I'm for it, so we're going to do it. . . . As long as I'm here we're going to do it my way.' "[5]

Regan had to deal with the internal resistance and relied on two key associates, Tom Chrystie and Paul Stein, to help. Together they drove the project through. The CMA was introduced in 1977 but only caught on slowly. There was considerable resistance from the sales force, and perhaps that explains why no other firm introduced a similar product for three years. Stein recognized that the sales force would have to be educated in the product, which, once presented, should sell itself. Rapidly escalating interest rates in the late 1970s, that pushed money market rates to 15 percent, helped the effort, and by 1979, Merrill Lynch brokers were adding three thousand new CMA accounts a week, and by the early 1980s, six thousand a week. Merrill Lynch discovered a gold mine and had stuck a mighty blow against the banks.[6] *Fortune* called it "the most important financial innovation in years."[7]

Regan also pushed the idea within the firm that Merrill should be at the top of the research analysts and investment banking rankings, or "league tables," which were created and published by *Institutional Investor* magazine, beginning in the late 1960s. Though brokerages generally did not aspire to such high ambitions, nor did their salesmen naturally have access to CEOs and other top executives, Regan simply insisted that Merrill Lynch appear at or near the top of every league table the magazine published. Well-regarded analysts and investment bankers were hired away from other firms; at Merrill they either produced or were let go. Senior sales executives began to call on CEOs in their areas, offering investment advice and selling Merrill's distribution capabilities. These guys would often offer on the spot to do deals at what other banks thought were outrageously high prices, but the effect was to lock in a good impression of Merrill with the client. Merrill also began to approach pension and mutual funds with research advice and help on block trades. After Mayday, Merrill's share of the institutional market could be increased simply by lowering commissions, which in turn could be paid for by continuing to keep commissions high for their army of retail customers. It would also work on extending its presence into government and corporate and municipal bonds. Merrill Lynch would have to fight it out with its major competitors for the bond business of the largest institutions, but there were bond buyers all over the country, and local banks, insurance companies, endowments, and pension funds well within the reach of Merrill's sales force.

But Merrill lacked a deep bench in the corporate finance department—people who had been trained over the years to do analyses, valuations, and complex corporate deals. They were distributors, not financial engineers. Merrill was able to remedy this deficiency by acquiring White, Weld and Co. in 1978, at a price reflecting the distress the firm had fallen into since Mayday and its decision to focus more on smaller companies and venture capital. White Weld was founded in Boston in the nineteenth century, originally to finance overseas trade. It developed into a small, well-connected New York investment bank by the twentieth century and became a bastion of the establishment. For example, George Herbert Walker, Jr., uncle of the president George Herbert Walker Bush, became an executive of White Weld when his firm, G.H. Walker, was bought by them in the early 1970s. One of White Weld's most prominent transactions in its final period was the IPO of Wal-Mart in 1970. White Weld brought some useful contacts, but more import was the skilled corporate finance department that would enable Merrill to compete more effectively against its major underwriting rivals. Merrill's aggressive marketing and its White Weld acquisition would help it push to the top of these leadership tables in the next few years.

Salomon Brothers

Another firm overlooked by the Justice Department in 1947 was Salomon Brothers and Hutzler, founded in 1910 as a money broker and headed by a son of one of the three founding brothers, William ("Billy") Salomon, since 1963. The firm had no connection with the great Jewish banking houses of the nineteenth century, and indeed it had few corporate clients at all until the 1960s. Billy Salomon had engineered a coup to wrest control of the firm from an unpopular leader in 1956, but he had to wait a few more years before his partners turned leadership of the firm over to him. Salomon wanted to move up-market and recruited an eminent economist, Sidney Homer, to set up a bond research department in 1960 and Homer soon hired Henry Kaufman to assist him. The firm was active in utility competitive biddings and in market making in all forms of short- and long-term fixed-income securities. Salomon Brothers was not especially visible until the late 1960s, when it decided to expand into corporate bonds and stocks, using the firm's trading know-how to bid aggressively—it always bid aggressively—for large blocks of business with institutional investors or with corporate issuers. In 1965 it decided to apply its trading skills to the equity business, especially trading large blocks, where it soon became Goldman Sachs's leading rival. Michael Bloomberg joined this group directly from Harvard Business School in 1966 and was the first member of our class to become a partner of a major investment bank. In 1967, Salomon ranked fourth among all underwriters of U.S. securities; in 1977, second; and ten years later, first. In 1970 the firm dropped Morton Hutzler's name from the firm, Hutzler having retired in 1929. In 1974, a high visibility former Salomon partner, William Simon, who headed the government bond business and was assumed to be Billy Salomon's heir apparent, was appointed secretary of the treasury in the Nixon-Ford administrations, and never returned to the firm.

As the firm's trading skills increased, it became bolder. In September 1979, Salomon challenged Morgan Stanley by bidding aggressively for a $1 billion bond issue for IBM, a traditional Morgan client. Salomon offered to let Morgan retain the credit for leading the issue (by appearing on the left side of the tombstone advertisement, with Salomon on the more junior right side). IBM liked Salomon's rate and thought its proposal was reasonable, so it presented it to Morgan Stanley, who rejected it on the grounds that it never allowed co-managers on its deals. In the past, such a strong position about its position was enough to force the clients to back off and let Morgan have its way, but not this time. Morgan said IBM would have to choose between it and Salomon, and IBM chose Salomon (and then added Merrill Lynch as a co-manager). Not long afterward, Morgan Stanley changed its sole-manager-or-nothing underwriting policy. However, the deal was still in syndicate when the famous "Volcker Shock" occurred in October 1979 (when newly appointed Fed Chairman Paul Volcker pushed interest rates upward by as much as one hundred basis points in order to curtail the rampant inflation in the United States), threatening the deal and Salomon's bold effort. Salomon, though, came through very well because it had hedged the exposure in the futures markets.

Billy Salomon retired in 1978 and was replaced by John Gutfreund (he pronounced it "Goodfriend"), who had joined the firm in 1953 and become a partner ten years later. Gutfreund had been a literature major at Oberlin College, but he had adapted well to the rough-edged, paternalistic culture of the firm. Under him, however, the environment, described amusingly in Michael Lewis's 1989 bestseller *Liar's Poker* as a sort of Animal House for delinquent millionaires, would become rougher, tougher, and more political.

The firm was completely dominated by traders, and trading was conducted as a form of warfare in which bold moves and big victories became the stuff of legend. The firm's culture valued boldness, flare, innovation, initiative, and perhaps most of all, street smarts. It disparaged pedigree, affectation, timidity, and hesitation. The culture was binding, and almost all of the firm's senior people were lifetime employees. They believed that to make a mark you did something dramatic and worried about the consequences later. A trader completing a successful strategy would be called a "big swinging dick" by his admiring colleagues. Sometimes you would get it wrong and lose a bundle, but if you knew what you were doing you would make a bundle more often than not. If you knew your markets and had the courage to "bite the ass off a bear," as Gutfreund put it, then you could make it at Salomon.[8]

But it wasn't all luck and daring. Salomon's traders had a battery of Ph.D.s to advise them on their strategies, and many of their most successful positions had been carefully worked out ahead of time, but there were still plenty of trades that just had to be made to show the market who was boss. Gutfreund believed his job was to spot the talent, provide it with plenty of money to trade with, and let the chips fall where they may. This meant everybody had to deal with Gutfreund, and to stay in his good graces. He worked out different compensation deals with all sorts of people, and keeping track of them all was not his strong suit. There was a lot of chaos and a lot of arguments, but the system seemed to work. Salomon's trading skills became sharper, braver, and more innovative. Salomon made lots of money in the roaring bond markets of the 1980s, and used its newly recognized muscle to expand its penetration into investment banking. In 1981, Gutfreund orchestrated the merger of the firm into Phibro-Salomon, Inc., a lucrative but unusual and daring transaction. In December 1985 *Business Week* put Gutfreund's picture on the cover and called him the "King of Wall Street." Salomon's preeminence in bond trading caught the attention of the popular writer Tom Wolfe, who based his 1987 best-selling novel, *The Bonfire of the Vanities*, on the misfortunes of a bond trader, Sherman McCoy, who worked in an incredible trading room that "hummed" with the sound of money being made, and where he was one of the firm's "Masters of the Universe."

Goldman Sachs

From the time that Gus Levy became senior partner, the firm's basic wholesale business strategy was fixed in place: it would strive to be the best investment banker to corporate issuers of securities, and the best broker and market maker to financial institutions. To develop its investment banking business, it continued to pursue the full-court-press marketing strategy devised by John Whitehead in the 1950s, a strategy that had been successful by virtue of the firm's ability to offer commercial paper, anti-raid defenses, and a variety of other ideas to take advantage of capital markets developments. The key to this effort was in the high quality and determination of the marketing people (Hank Paulson, a later Goldman Sachs CEO, began his career doing this type of marketing in the Chicago office) and the ability to give undivided attention to the clients and prospects.

On the institutional front, however, there was a weakness. Goldman had virtually no fixed-income capability. Since the 1920s, Goldman Sachs had regarded bond trading as either too risky or insufficiently profitable, and accordingly had shied away. Gus Levy thought fixed income was likely to become an important business for his trading clients, and for Whitehead's corporate clients, too, so he commissioned a study in the early 1970s to look at setting up a fixed-income division. The firm decided to do so, but it was unsure how to implement it. Levy asked George Ross, the head of the Philadelphia office and a skilled sales manager, to head the new division, it being unthinkable to bring in someone from outside. Ross struggled with the job for a few years and set up a minimal structure for a fixed-income business, but he begged off, and John Weinberg took it over long enough to hire an outsider to get it right. The outsider was Frank Smeal, who had run the bond business at Morgan Guaranty Trust and knew what to do to get the firm properly into the business. One of his early hires was Jon Corzine, another future CEO of the firm, who rose to become the head government bond trader.

The big event for Goldman Sachs in the 1970s was the unexpected death of Gus Levy, sixty-six, who had a stroke at a meeting of the Board of Commissioners of the NY/NJ Port Authority. Knowing of Levy's habit of intense concentration on something else, the other commissioners thought nothing of the fact that he had slumped down in his chair and seemed to be staring straight ahead. After a while someone asked if he was all right, and finding him not to be, called for an ambulance. He died a few days later, without a successor, leaving behind a management committee that had been in existence for only a few years, and anyway had been dominated by him most of that time. Rummaging through his desk, his secretary found Levy's daily prayer and an envelope addressed to the management committee that said that if anything happened to him, the committee ought to consider appointing John Whitehead, fifty-four, and John Weinberg, fifty-one, as "co-heads" of the firm. The management committee appointed the two of them forthwith.

This was a very unusual move. Co-heads was not then a concept anyone understood. You couldn't have two leaders; each would constantly be struggling to displace the other. No one could think of a precedent for such a situation. Marvin Bower, the managing partner of McKinsey and Co., the blue-chip management consulting firm, called Whitehead to tell him that the idea of dual leadership was nice, but it would never work, and that Goldman Sachs ought to hire McKinsey to help them sort out a proper leadership structure. Bower's opinion was widely shared by other senior business figures. The firm's partners and employees, however, were not too concerned. "The Two Johns," as they came to be known within the firm, explained that they had not expected the designation, but they had talked about it at length and decided that they had been friends and colleagues a long time (between them they had been at the firm fifty-nine years) and would do their best to work it out. They thought that the best way to do it would be for them to share all the duties and responsibilities—not divide them—and to move to adjoining offices, where they could be in close touch daily.

Gus Levy's shoes would be very hard to fill, even with two sets of feet. *The New York Times* referred to him as "perhaps the best-known figure in the moneyed world of investment banking and brokerage firms" and "one of the country's top fund-raisers for philanthropic and Republican causes." He was on the board of sixteen major corporations and a number of important charitable organizations. According to John Whitehead, "every CEO used to say that Levy was his best outside director. It may be easy to be the best outside director for one or two companies, but to be the best director of all the companies whose board you are on is really quite remarkable."[9] It was Levy who expressed Goldman's famous philosophy of being "long-term greedy," which implies that as long as money is made over the long term, trading losses or other business development expenses in the short term were not to be worried about. Nelson Rockefeller, the vice-president of the United States and a former governor of New York State, gave a eulogy at Levy's memorial service, which was attended by nearly two thousand people. At the time of his death, *The New York Times* reported, "there were 47 general partners and 18 limited partners of Goldman Sachs, with total capital of $78 million and none of the partners owning more than ten percent. Goldman Sachs' average annual income before partners' taxes over the last five years was more than $25 million."[10] This number was a little misleading, because it included the two years of virtually no profits (1973 and 1974); the subsequent years had been very profitable for the firm, its best years ever. Gus Levy, a successful investor as well as the holder of the firm's largest partnership interest, left an estate estimated to be worth around $25 million.

On December 1, 1976, the partnership was opened for some retirements and additions, as it was every two years, and I was one of ten added then. Over the next several years, the two Johns forcefully drove the firm ahead along four fronts: beefing up fixed income, further expanding its growing list of investment banking clients, expanding internationally (offices in London and Tokyo were opened in the early 1970s), and solidifying the Goldman Sachs "culture" by developing and inculcating the firm's fourteen "business principles," which are still in use today, unchanged and taken seriously by the firm and its employees.

Gus Levy's intuition about his successors proved to be right. The two together turned out to be better than either one running the show alone. Whitehead, a navy veteran from World War II, was generally thought to be the more cerebral, and more management-systems oriented, if often cold, standoffish, and aloof. John Weinberg had been an officer in the Marines in World War II and Korea, had joined the firm right after Harvard Business School, and worked under his father's critical eye for more than a dozen years. Weinberg, who had been dyslexic as a child and not a good student, believed his position in the firm was purely the result of his father having brought him in and advanced him, and accordingly he had devoted himself to being a "people person," good with clients, colleagues, and employees, and, as it turned out, developing (like his father) an acute street smarts that stood him in good stead with everyone. He had many clients, such as Jack Welch of General Electric, who constantly sought his advice, and he was deeply liked and respected by his colleagues at the firm, whom he never put down or treated badly. He would remain at the firm until his official retirement, in 1990—he was active as a chairman emeritus until just before his death in 2006 at age eighty-one. His son, John S. Weinberg, by that time had also joined Goldman Sachs and risen to become a vice chairman of the firm.

Both Johns agreed that neither had a future trying to oust the other, and indeed neither had any interest in doing so, despite everyone's predictions to the contrary. The two worked together very well for eight years, until John Whitehead surprised his partners by resigning in 1984. In an interview with *Institutional Investor* three years later, Whitehead explained his departure:

> Part of the reason why I felt the time had come for me to step aside was that the business had changed so much from what I was used to, particularly the change from a relationship business to a transactional business. I worried about whether I was really with it anymore. After all, I was a relationship banker, and I thought that system was better for the clients than this wild bidding system in which relationships counted for nothing. . . . When you are only asked to decide whether to bid 7.22 percent or 7.24 percent, well, that didn't quite seem important to me anymore.[11]

Whitehead may have been among the first of Goldman Sachs's deep bench of investment bankers to feel the pressure from the "transactional business," but many (though apparently not John Weinberg, whose relations with clients only seemed to strengthen as things became more transactional) felt the same way as the business was changed by market pressures and innovation that were just beginning in the mid-1980s.

After leaving the firm, John Whitehead expected to work on a book for a while, but he was soon picked up by the Reagan administration, in which he served as deputy secretary of state, after which he continued to have an active career in investing, philanthropy, and government service. He even managed to write his book.

After the successful sharing of power, the firm repeated the co-head experiment many times at the department-head level and with two later sets of CEOs. The practice also appeared in other firms in Wall Street—if it worked, valuable senior executives would not be lost to the firm, and corporate actions would be more balanced and consensual than might otherwise be the case. Of course, outside of Goldman Sachs the shared-leadership idea didn't often work. Even within Goldman Sachs it didn't always work, but it was expected to, so the practice became sufficiently familiar as to impart an important piece of cultural DNA to the firm's future leaders.

CONSOLIDATIONS

Other transitions were occurring in Wall Street as firms struggled to find their places in the new capital markets environment. Many such transitions included mergers among retail brokerages and research boutiques trying to gain size and enough capital to manage in the post-Mayday markets. In 1977 the merger of Kuhn Loeb (founded in 1867 and an original member of the bulge bracket of underwriters) into a revitalized Lehman Brothers (founded in 1850) seemed to set a precedent for fading members of the old guard. The two firms descended from the German Jewish roots described in Stephen Birmingham's *Our Crowd*, and members of the families had intermarried and been connected in various ways for years. Kuhn Loeb, however, had failed to modernize itself and had fallen behind its peers. Unlike Morgan Stanley, it had not found internal leadership capable of grasping what it would need to do to remain competitive and appeared to be much like a deer caught in the headlights of an oncoming car, unable to avoid being hit by it. It had only 500 employees and $18 million in capital, as compared with Lehman's 1,200 employees and $60 million in capital, and it had recently suffered a fixed-income trading loss nasty enough to cause a loss of confidence among the partners. Most of its capital was owned by retired partners, and when merger overtures were floated (there were three or four other invitations), some of these partners were eager to take advantage of them, despite the fact that Lehman was not offering any sort of premium over the stated value of Kuhn Loeb's capital. As a partnership, Kuhn Loeb would have found it difficult to raise capital to pay out those wishing to withdraw, and those wishing to modernize to remain in business would have found it hard to do so without being able to get rid of the older partners. For them, the Lehman solution was perfect: the old guys get taken out, and the younger ones get to move in with some distant cousins eager to do business with them. Lehman could see only a no-cost way of adding clients and some useful talent.

Other mergers among major underwriters included the West Coast leader Blyth and Co., which was sold for $55 million to Insurance Corporation of North America in 1970, the first of what became several mergers of Wall Street firms with financial firms outside the industry. In 1972, Blyth combined with Eastman Dillon and Union Securities Co. (itself a recent merger); the surviving firm, Blyth Eastman Dillon, was then merged into Paine Webber in 1979. Paine Webber was a Boston brokerage firm that had expanded rapidly in the 1970s, acquiring three boutique firms—F.S. Smithers; Mitchum, Jones and Templeton; and Mitchell Hutchins—before springing for heavyweight Blyth Eastman Dillon, to add a major underwriting capability. But the string of acquisitions overwhelmed Paine Webber's back office, forcing it into a period of no expansion until it had brought all of its new acquisitions into line with its own systems. In 1980, Donald Marron took over as CEO and revived its aggressive pace of expansion.

OUT-OF-INDUSTRY MERGERS

There were many mergers and acquisitions within the industry in the 1970s and 1980s, but also a surprising number involving firms not from the securities industry (despite the unhappy lessons learned by Ross Perot a few years before).

Indeed, interest among the big dogs had been awakened. Wall Street was no longer seen as a specialized but local cottage industry, and other major nonbank financial service providers began to see opportunities for themselves to build out their businesses to include capabilities in a much larger and more robust capital markets industry.

These capabilities were important, the big players thought, for extending businesses in wholesale banking, retail services, and trading. For the time being, the big banks were precluded by law (the 1933 Glass-Steagall Act) from getting into these businesses in the United States, but someday, perhaps, they would not be. For now, nonbank financial players had an opportunity to move in ahead of the banks to buy up talent and capacity in the securities industry. Indeed, the combination of financial backing, synergies to be developed from cross-selling, and the introduction of sophisticated marketing systems, financial controls, and international linkages would greatly upgrade the quality and efficiency of the undermanaged investment banks. The resulting superfirms would be enough, many observers noted, to change the nature of the industry forever.

Within the industry, however, many firms saw these big players as golden opportunities, if not as pigeons waiting to be plucked. The buyers were prepared to offer record-level prices, and essentially to leave them alone to run things as they had before, without threatening management positions, compensation, perquisites, or prestige. They would be a source of the additional capital that all of the firms knew they would need, and a source too, they may have thought, of a public share price to be used for management and employee options as well as for an acquisition currency. If you were not sure about making it on your own, then selling out to one of these players might be the best outcome of all. Turning down such an offer just might leave you right where Kuhn Loeb or Blyth Eastman Dillon had been.

There was plenty of incentive on both sides to make these deals work, but all of them ended up as disappointments.

First Boston and Credit Suisse

One of the most original, complex, and heartbreaking of the tie-ups was First Boston's eleven-year joint venture with Swiss banking giant Credit Suisse. It began with an opportunistic situation that developed when Merrill Lynch acquired White Weld in 1978. Prior to that event, White Weld, under the direction of a talented Swiss partner, had created a European business (White Weld Limited) that was an early leader in the Eurobond business. In 1974, White Weld Limited and Credit Suisse (then led by

Rainer Gut, a former Lazard Frères executive who was very market-wise) formed a joint venture (Credit Suisse White Weld) to underwrite Euro-bonds (bonds denominated in a currency other than that of the country in which they are issued, such as Eurodollar or Euroyen bonds issued in the UK) and sell them to Swiss and other investors. This venture was instantly successful and became a market leader. In 1978, when White Weld's U.S. business failed and it was taken over by Merrill, Credit Suisse White Weld was reluctant to have large, lumbering Merrill Lynch take over the 40 percent interest in their firm owned by White Weld, so after a limited beauty contest, they offered it instead to First Boston, with the understanding that the company would be called Credit Suisse First Boston (CSFB) and would receive a 40 percent interest in First Boston, one of America's leading bulge-bracket investment banks. This was thought to be a very high price for First Boston to pay for a 40 percent interest in a Eurobond business, but that business at the time was doing very well, and First Boston was suffering from post-Mayday difficulties and poor results from its domestic business. The deal, actively pushed by First Boston's CEO, George Shin, who was credited with the first vision of a global investment banking firm, would both bolster First Boston's weak capital position and give it a new source of revenue.

During the next few years, CSFB ran itself with little interference from either New York or Zurich. It had become the leader of the Eurobond market by being bold and creative, but also because of the Swiss placing power at its disposal. But it was also brassy, disorganized, and often riven with internal strife. It fought often with First Boston over the division of turf, fees, and expenses and over who got the credit for deals. This was a natural result of the asymmetrical ownership arrangement, but it also reflected the high level of competitive aggressiveness on the part of both firms. In 1982, Jack Hennessey, a senior First Boston executive, was sent to London to take over CSFB, and the relationship settled down for a time.

Meanwhile, in New York, the bull market that began in 1982 had generated a great deal of corporate finance business, especially in mergers and acquisitions. First Boston had two outstanding merger specialists, Bruce Wasserstein and Joseph Perella, who had invented themselves during the early 1980s and become stars attracting a great deal of profitable business to the firm. Wasserstein and Perella wanted to expand their business further by offering high-yield bridge loans to their leveraged buyout clients in order to lock in their business and make even more money. This would require a greater allocation of the firm's capital to the mergers and acquisition area, something the management of First Boston decided it did not want to do. So Wasserstein and Perella left First Boston to start up their own firm, and First Boston, fearful of losing the firm's profitable merger business, went into bridge lending after all. Relations between First Boston and CSFB had deteriorated by this time, and First Boston, buoyed by its high standings in the various investment banking league tables at the time, largely ignored criticism or suggestions from its largest shareholder.

In 1988, Credit Suisse decided to end the agony and moved to buy up the rest of First Boston and make it a wholly owned subsidiary of a new holding company, to be run by Hennessey, called CS First Boston, which would be 44.5 percent owned by Credit Suisse (the maximum the U.S. Federal Reserve would allow at the time), and 31 percent by a wealthy Arab client of Credit Suisse's who was to be a placeholder until an appropriate partner from the Far East could be found. The remaining 24.5 percent would be set aside for management of the operating companies.

However, when the merger and junk bond businesses turned at the end of 1989, and the market for junk bonds and similar paper collapsed, First Boston was stuck holding $1.2 billion in virtually unsellable bridge loans to deeply troubled LBOs, and again faced serious capital constraints. In November 1990, Credit Suisse agreed to pump an additional $300 million into CS First Boston, and purchase more than $400 million in troubled loans from First Boston, which would report a loss for the year of $500 million. To assist in the rescue, the Federal Reserve allowed Credit Suisse to increase its ownership in CS First Boston to 60 percent, giving it absolute control over the firm. Shortly afterward, Credit Suisse, which had never been able to control its talented but unruly investment banking children, announced that its earnings for the year would be reduced by about a third, that it would be raising additional capital, and that Moody's had lowered its treasured long-term bond rating from Aaa to Aa1.[12]

Prudential Insurance and Bache and Co.

In 1979, Belzberg Brothers, a rough-edged Canadian group, decided to stake out a potential takeover position in Bache Halsey Stuart Shields Inc., a group of three once-prominent retail brokerages assembled by Harry Jacobs, its chief executive. Bache had been formed a hundred years before, had $151 million in capital, some 10,000 shareholders, and more than 6,500 employees, including 2,500 account executives. It was involved in practically every facet of the securities business and had 176 offices in 143 cities in 11 countries. By 1981, the Belzbergs had accumulated 22.6 percent of the firm and appeared threatening. Jacobs hired First Boston to locate a white knight to take over the company. After showing Bache to several potential bidders, First Boston settled on Prudential Insurance, a mutual company owned by its policyholders that was the country's largest insurer, and an offer was made at a 25 percent premium to the market, and quickly accepted. The deal immediately set off speculation about the ambition of the other insurance companies, the future of Glass-Steagall (which was under pressure for reform), and the general notion of combining large retail organizations selling different financial products under one roof. Prudential claimed that it was in the business of satisfying "the financial service needs of people," and thus "the deal made a great deal of sense."

The Bache acquisition may have been strategically sound for Prudential, but it was a disaster tactically. There were no appreciable synergies—the insurance and securities sales forces would not or could not cooperate—and Prudential lost control of its newest subsidiary almost from the beginning. Acknowledging that it knew too little about the securities industry to supervise it closely, and believing in the benefits of delegation, Prudential basically left it alone. Harry Jacobs retired in 1982 and was succeeded by George Ball, who had been president of E. F. Hutton, another large retail brokerage. Ball ran Prudential Securities, as Bache Halsey Stuart Shields was then known, until 1991. Soon afterward there were problems. During the 1980s and 1990s, approximately $8 billion in real estate and oil and gas limited partnership interests were sold to more than 340,000 retail investors. These investors lost over $1 billion in the partnerships, which were often sold without regard to whether the buyers were suitable purchasers for such risky investments. Prudential and its brokers shared up-front commissions and fees of 20 to 30 percent of the money raised by the partnerships, the marketing of which, the SEC said, involved outright lies and deception.[13]

When Robert Winters, the chairman of Prudential Insurance, referred to 1993 as a "very tough year," he wasn't kidding. In that year, Prudential Securities had concluded a landmark settlement with the SEC involving fines and restitutions of $1.6 billion, admission of criminal wrongdoing, and three years' probation. The settlement, the securities industry's first product liability case, is still the largest ever for a single firm.

Prudential Insurance was forced to write off nearly $3 billion against its relatively small investment in Prudential Securities. Similar difficulties arose in Prudential's insurance and real estate divisions, causing additional billions to be written off and Prudential's aloof and unobservant top management to be replaced. In 1990, Arthur F. Ryan, a hardheaded Chase Manhattan senior banker, became chairman and CEO of Prudential Financial, and of Prudential Insurance in 1994. My classmate Hardwick Simmons, who had run the retail business at Shearson Lehman Brothers, became CEO of Prudential Securities and made a mighty effort to turn things around before leaving to head NASDAQ in 2001. In the end, Prudential became totally discouraged with the business and sold Prudential Securities to Wachovia Bank in 2003.

Phibro-Salomon Brothers

In the autumn of 1981, a senior partner of Salomon Brothers met socially with a senior executive of commodities trader Philipp Brothers, who attended the same synagogue. One of them asked, "Since you guys are traders, and so are we, shouldn't we talk about doing something together?" The conversations were enriched by the fact that during the summer, Salomon Brothers had experienced some nerve-wracking losses in the bond markets. A few weeks later, Salomon surprised Wall Street (and many of its own partners) by announcing that it was selling out to Philipp Brothers (later Phibro, Inc.) for $483 million in cash and convertible securities. A new holding company, Phibro-Salomon, would be formed that would own Salomon Brothers and Philipp Brothers in two separate, independent subsidiaries. John Gutfreund and David Tendler, Phibro's CEO, would become co-CEOs of the holding company, which would be publicly traded. The deal was rammed through by John Gutfreund; Billy Salomon and the other retired partners were not told about it until it had been completed. These retired partners would not receive any of the $250 million premium over book value that Phibro was paying to acquire Salomon (all of the premium would go to the general partners), and many of them, including Billy, were considerably upset with the transaction.[14]

The two firms had no particular association before, and though both would try to make the case that the merger would integrate the skills of two similar trading houses, the reality was somewhat different. Salomon was totally focused on securities and operated out of an intense, close-linked, and very inside professional culture in which almost everyone was a homegrown Salomon product with a nickname. The Philipp Brothers people, equally inbred and secretive, with many of them joining the firm right out of high school, were totally unknown to the Salomon people, and virtually unknown to anyone else on Wall Street. They were exotics who traded in 150 raw materials, including crude oil, fertilizers, cement, grain, coke, and plastic. Their clients were in Russia, South Africa, Taiwan, and Kansas. They owned refineries and tankers and things like that. What kind of synergies could these two firms ever be able to put together?

Philipp Brothers had been a subsidiary of Engelhard Minerals and Chemicals, specializing in trading metals and ores. It had been spun off the previous year after a decade of expansion and diversification in which profits had grown from $27 million in 1971 to $467 million in 1980. A fear of falling commodity prices inspired the forty-three-year-old Tendler, who had begun in the traffic department and moved from there into trading, to act quickly to further diversity into the big time in finance. He offered Salomon twice its book value; about half paid in convertible securities, through Phibro's investment banker, Felix Rohatyn.

What was Gutfreund thinking? He was by all accounts as much of a hard-nosed realist as there was. He probably didn't put much value on the expectations of synergies. The money might have been attractive—twice book value (half in cash) was a very good price then for an investment bank—and it provided an opportunity for the firm to recapitalize as a publicly traded company and retire the limited partners, whose continuing capital in the firm (as Rohatyn may have reminded him) was a worry for the same reason that it had stymied Kuhn Loeb. Being a public company would mean having access to debt and equity markets, which could be essential to a trading house always in need of capital. And Tendler, despite being the acquirer, had been willing to let Gutfreund be a co-CEO (something tried only once before on Wall Street, at Goldman Sachs after Gus Levy died), and Gutfreund believed he could handle Tendler. What the hell, he might have thought, an offer like this doesn't come along every day; after what Wall Street has been through over the past ten years, let's take a chance on it.

Gutfreund, however, did not feel the new company could afford all of the existing partners of Salomon, so he decided to eliminate a few of them, one of whom was Mike Bloomberg, who had been displaced from his job as head equity trader (he left to found the Bloomberg Group with the money he had withdrawn from the firm after the Phibro deal was done*) and another was James Wolfensohn, who had been in charge of corporate finance and left to set up his own successful boutique investment bank before becoming president of the World Bank.

The Phibro deal did have one unexpected effect. The management committee at Goldman Sachs, constantly watching its competitors, became convinced that Salomon Brothers knew something that it didn't, and immediately went on the lookout for a commodities firm of its own to acquire. Without looking too hard, it found J. Aron, a coffee dealer that also dealt in gold and foreign exchange, and offered to buy it for $100 million. This proved to be a very controversial (and expensive) acquisition: within a few years, Aron's earnings had collapsed, virtually all of the senior people from J. Aron, including several who were made partners of Goldman Sachs, were gone, and former Goldman people were drafted to run the business. But it did provide a catalyst for Goldman Sachs to accelerate its entry into the foreign exchange and some other businesses that became very important to the firm a decade later, and it delivered a promising young gold salesman named Lloyd Blankfein, who twenty-five years later would become Goldman's chairman and CEO.

The arrangement between Salomon and Phibro came unstuck, however, when commodity prices, which had peaked just before the Phibro offer, started downward again and Philipp Brothers's profits went astray, while Salomon's earnings were soaring as interest rates continued to descend following the Federal Reserve's historic intervention in the markets in October 1979. The earnings disequilibrium enabled Gutfreund to force out Tendler in 1984 and to take control of the whole business himself, after which he would begin to disassemble the commodity unit, retaining the parts he liked but getting rid of the rest.

Three years later, Minerals and Resources Corp., a subsidiary of Anglo-American Corp. of South Africa, which as a former major shareholder in Philipp Brothers owned a 14 percent block of Salomon Inc. (the new name for Phibro), asked Felix Rohatyn to find a buyer for it. Rohatyn offered the block to corporate raider Ronald Perelman, knowing Perelman might be interested and that John Gutfreund, a rival of Rohatyn's, would hit the ceiling when he learned who might turn up as his new largest shareholder. Gutfreund had absolutely no interest in letting Perelman get hold of such a large block, so he approached Warren Buffett and worked a deal in

---

* Mike Bloomberg has often said that the two secrets to his early success were getting hired by Salomon Brothers and being fired by them.

which Salomon would repurchase the shares from Minerals and Resources at a premium over the market price and finance the purchase by selling $700 million in 9 percent preferred stock (which would be convertible into 12 percent of the Salomon stock) to Berkshire Hathaway, Buffett's insurance holding company. Buffett would agree never to own more than 20 percent of Salomon, and Salomon would agree that it would not appoint anyone to be CEO of Salomon except John Gutfreund without Buffett's consent. Buffett also had five separate opportunities to sell the bonds back to Salomon, which could be paid for in stock or cash. Perelman offered to top the offer, but was rebuffed. He was not about to go up against Buffett, one of the country's richest and most respected investors, so he withdrew.

Gutfreund thought he had made a good deal for Salomon in taking on Buffett as its largest shareholder. The 9 percent dividend rate was pretty steep, but Buffett would certainly be a long-term, hands-off shareholder as long as Gutfreund, whom apparently he admired greatly, was around. Buffett would see the deal as easy money made out of a panicky moment in someone else's life. Of course, after October of 1987, when the market experienced a 22 percent one-day drop, the investment made by Buffett just a month before never looked quite so good again.

Sears Roebuck and Dean Witter

In the late 1970s, Sears Roebuck, America's largest retail chain, was running out of gas. It had been one of the country's best-managed companies for years, but it was rapidly losing market share to specialty retailers and catalog marketers. Its old-fashioned style of merchandising was on the way out, so it did what many companies do in such situations: it brought in McKinsey to do a strategic study. Two years later a conclusion was reached by Sears's chairman, Arthur Wood, and the McKinsey team led by Philip Purcell: Sears should make a major acquisition of a great American financial services company to augment its Allstate Insurance and Coldwell Banker real estate businesses. Sears had twenty-five million active charge accounts, but while only 9 percent of the cardholders had brokerage accounts, 75 percent of households with net worth of $500,000 or more had a Sears charge card. "There is no reason," said Purcell, who had since joined Sears as its vice-president for planning, "why someone shouldn't go into a Sears store and buy a shirt and coat, and then maybe some stock."[15]

Federal regulation precluded Sears from buying a commercial bank, but a brokerage firm would be okay. In 1981, the Sears team met with Merrill Lynch, but was quickly turned away. They ruled out a hostile takeover effort, because they thought it would undermine the Sears image as "a trusted family friend." Next they focused on Dean Witter Reynolds, itself the product of a merger completed in 1978 to create the country's fifth-largest brokerage, and in October 1981 struck a deal, half in cash and half in Sears stock, to acquire 100 percent of the firm for $607 million. Sears would offer $50 per share, which represented a premium of about 100 percent over the price at which Dean Witter Reynolds's stock had traded the day before. Sears would leave Andrew J. Melton, sixty-one, and Robert M. ("Stretch") Gardiner, fifty-nine, in place as chairman and president, respectively. Edward Telling, Sears's chairman, said Dean Witter Reynolds "will get the support it needs to become an even stronger factor in its industry."[16] Sears was represented in the negotiation by its long-standing investment banker, Goldman Sachs.

After the deal was completed, Telling created a Dean Witter Division at Sears and put Purcell, then thirty-eight, in charge. He remained in a planning role, letting Stretch Gardiner, who had replaced the retiring Andy Melton, run things. Purcell did his best to try to install financial services booths inside Sears stores, where customers shopping for socks or screwdrivers could insure a car, or buy a house or some mutual funds, but it was hopeless. The stockbrokers considered themselves above such activity, sitting in a Sears store waiting for the screwdriver buyers to happen along looking for stocks. It was humiliating to them, they said, and in any event, they didn't want anything to do with the Allstate or Coldwell Banker salespeople, whom they assumed would only be after their lists of clients. But Purcell's deep knowledge of retail financial services did enable him to figure out how to launch the Discover credit card (the successor to the twenty-five million Sears charge accounts) and to create a variety of in-house mutual funds. The Discover card, which could be used as a charge card on which cash rebates were paid based on purchases, could access instant cash through ATM machines, accumulate savings balances, or open an IRA at Dean Witter for free, was an exceptional success. In 1986, Stretch Gardiner retired and Purcell was named chairman and CEO of Dean Witter Discover, Sears's new name for the Dean Witter Reynolds Financial Services Group.

But Dean Witter's success did little for an ailing Sears Roebuck, which was fading as fast as Dean Witter was expanding. It offered no synergies, no capacity for financial support—it was the reverse, really—and no improvement to Dean Witter's marketing, controls, or other systems. From Dean Witter's point of view, its Sears relationship had become a drag, though it didn't really slow it down much. In 1993, the Sears board decided that it would have to sell its financial services group in order to repay some of its burgeoning debt. Allstate and Dean Witter both went public in successful offerings, and Coldwell Banker was put up for sale as a management buyout. In 1992, Dean Witter Discover had earned $400 million on $3.7 billion in revenues. After a sale of 20 percent of the common stock to the public for $775 million, Sears spun off the rest of the Dean Witter stock directly to its shareholders.

Purcell, a dour, methodical, Midwestern corporate type who greatly preferred Chicago to New York, was then made chairman and CEO of an independent publicly traded company with a solid retail brokerage business specializing in the sale of mutual funds to middle-income people and a credit card business that had proven to be a formidable cash generator. From unusual outsider origins, Purcell's investment banking career that began at Sears Roebuck was launched. He would make his next big move four years later, when blue-collar Dean Witter would acquire blue-chip Morgan Stanley.

American Express and Shearson Loeb Rhodes

Of the many acquisitions of Wall Street firms by out-of-industry corporations in 1981, the one that caused the most attention was the $915 million merger of Shearson Loeb Rhodes into the classic branded products superstar American Express. The combined companies would be able to operate on a scale with the world's largest financial service providers, Citicorp or Merrill Lynch, and could operate in 130 countries with synergies being developed from offering Shearson's many retail brokerage customers American Express credit cards, traveler's checks, and luxury travel and accommodations, and vice versa. As Louis V. Gerstner, American Express's vice-chairman (and future IBM CEO) saw it, "In twenty years there will be a profound democratization of financial services. American Express cash machines will be located all over the world enabling customers to do their banking, financial planning, tax preparation, buy and sell stocks and insurance, invest in a money market fund or write checks on it all at home on a computer terminal."[17]

The deal was a dramatic moment in the extraordinary career of forty-eight-year-old Sandy Weill, who had come a long way since beginning his Wall Street career in 1955. The somewhat introverted son of Polish Jewish immigrants, he scrambled to graduate from Cornell, but couldn't immediately find a job, so he took one as a runner for Bear Stearns. This was about as low an entry point into investment banking as he could find. Sandy used the opportunity to talk his way into become a "boy" (a personal assistant) to one of the top traders, and in time he emerged as a licensed stockbroker. He then joined his neighbor Arthur Carter and Roger Berlind and Peter Potoma in forming a little firm of their own that would try to do what it could. Carter did some investment banking, Berlind and Potoma brought in some rich clients, and Sandy read research reports and developed investing ideas. Potoma later withdrew as a result of disciplinary proceedings brought by the NYSE, and Arthur Levitt joined the others in 1960 to form Carter, Berlind, Weill and Levitt.[18] In 1968, Carter was thrown out by his partners when he got too bossy, and Marshall Cogan, another investment banker, was brought in without having to change the firm's initials, CBWL, by which they had become known. Sandy decided they should set up their own back office, which he took charge of. Starting de novo, the clearing operation he put together was up-to-date and efficient. "This will be our pipeline for growth," he told his partners. The paperwork crisis that came the following year proved to be an enormous blessing to CBWL, because it suddenly opened doors for the firm to acquire larger, better-known firms in trouble. The pipeline made it possible.

First there was McDonnell and Co., an elite securities firm with close ties to the Ford family. CBWL bought its Beverley Hills office for pennies on the dollar. Then began a series of rapid-fire, opportunistic acquisitions that would become Sandy Weill's trademark. Elegant, stuffy brokerages with long pedigrees fell into ruin during the paperwork crisis, and CBWL was there to pick up the pieces at bargain basement prices. There was risk, but CBWL was buying the firms' blue-chip books of business for far less than book value. Meanwhile, Sandy and his skilled operations people learned how to turn things around quickly. Costs would be cut to the bone; the clients would be preserved but only the best producers could expect to be retained, everything else would be scuttled. Then Sandy would provide carrots and sticks to make the acquired salesmen produce at a higher level, and repeat the process with another firm. Starting in 1970, CBWL absorbed some of Wall Street's most respected names in retail brokerage: Hayden Stone, Shearson Hamill, and perhaps the most satisfying to Sandy,

Loeb Rhoades Hornblower, one of the last surviving Our Crowd firms, which had refused to clear for CBWL in its early days because the firm was only an upstart. CBWL also raised capital by going public in 1971 (as soon as it could, right after Merrill Lynch did) and changed its name several times to reflect its improving provenance before settling down in 1979 as Shearson Loeb Rhoades, the country's second-largest brokerage, just behind Merrill Lynch. Cogan left the firm in 1973, and Sandy became chairman and CEO. The other original partners also drifted off.

By then Sandy Weill was a made man on Wall Street. He was a New Man who had incredibly enough emerged from the back office to build an important retail brokerage business literally from nothing. The decade of trouble on Wall Street in the 1970s created the opportunities that Weill was able to capitalize on. The difference between Shearson and every other retail brokerage firm Sandy acquired was in the attention of management to costs and controls, with which Sandy was obsessed. Most of Weill's many talented underlings during this period—Frank Zarb, Peter Cohen, Jamie Dimon, Robert Druskin, and Jeff Lane, all of whom rose to high positions in Wall Street—were operations experts.

Sandy himself was developing from a shy, chubby, insecure Jewish kid from Brooklyn with an accent and poorly fitting clothes, into a dynamic, forceful, intimidating, and utterly focused leader of a publicly traded firm of thousands of smart, socially correct brokers and investment bankers picked up from some of America's snootiest WASP and German Jewish firms, who wouldn't have paid any attention to him at all only a few years before.

When Sandy read of the Prudential-Bache acquisition, he immediately saw a different future for his firm. The best of America's financial service firms, he thought, were going to follow Prudential into visionary tie-ups with large, efficient retail distribution machines. He began looking around for the right company for Shearson to partner with. He picked American Express as the best possible partner to bring prestige and wider market access to his firm, and asked a mutual friend to set him up to meet James D. Robinson III, American Express's chairman and CEO. Sandy was a good negotiator. Initially he proposed only a joint venture to do marketing together, watching as the concepts of the deal settled in with Robinson: Integrated financial services. One-stop shopping. Synergies and cross-selling. In the end, American Express bought in to the idea and offered a 60 percent premium over the last traded price of Shearson Loeb Rhoades on the day before the announcement. Weill and his deputy, Peter

Cohen, continued to run Shearson as a wholly owned subsidiary. Weill, who would become the largest individual shareholder of American Express, was appointed a vice-chairman, and chairman of the Executive Committee, of American Express in 1981, and president in 1983. Peter Cohen would become CEO of Shearson Loeb Rhoades, the name of which would be changed again, to Shearson/American Express.

Weill turned his interest at this point to American Express, leaving Cohen to manage Shearson. He was initially hopeful that he would be able to play an important role in American Express's affairs, especially in its acquisition policy and to become the successor to Robinson. Robinson, however, had no interest in either proposition, and Sandy grew frustrated. In 1985, Weill left American Express to start his second career, which would follow a similar pattern of acquisitions. In 1986 he made a pass at taking over a troubled Bank of America, without success. Then he discovered Commercial Credit Company, a finance subsidiary of Control Data, a large, troubled computer company. Sandy bought the finance company, then added Primerica, a conglomerate investment vehicle that was American Can Company before Gerry Tsai, the former Fidelity and Manhattan Fund gunslinger, acquired it after leaving the fund management business. Primerica had bought Smith Barney Harris Upham, another up-market brokerage and investment bank, in 1983. Weill was delighted to get back into Wall Street, but he surprised everyone in 1993 by arranging for Primerica, a firm that now was a mixture of different financial service companies, to acquire Travelers Insurance Group, one of the country's largest life and property and casualty insurers. By then he had insurance, brokerage, investment banking, and commercial finance businesses all under one roof. Primerica was renamed Travelers, and its stock shot through the roof. Buy the jockey, not the horse, many savvy investors were saying. In the same year, Robinson would be forced out at American Express after a series of missteps.

One of the missteps that brought an end to Robinson's career at American Express occurred in 1984, when Shearson/American Express jumped on an opportunity to acquire a failing and dysfunctional Lehman Brothers for what seemed at the time to be a bargain price of $360 million. The acquisition was set up and negotiated by Peter Cohen, with Weill playing only a background role. Lehman was attractive to American Express because of its great name and investment banking prowess, and no doubt because it was seen to have a place in the one-stop shopping notion of integrated financial services

Lehman's chief executive had been Peter G. Peterson, who was appointed in 1973 after the firm's difficulties following the death of Bobby Lehman in 1969. He had led it to recovery and several profitable years. Notwithstanding the firm's success, however, there were hostilities between the investment bankers and the traders (who were responsible for most of the profits). To address this, Peterson promoted Lewis Glucksman, Lehman's trading chief, to president and chief operating officer, and then to be his co-CEO in 1983. Glucksman introduced changes in personnel and in the methods that determined how compensation and partnership interests were to be decided. These changes had the effect of increasing tensions, which, when coupled with Glucksman's abrasive management style, dislike of Peterson (whom he considered to be an investment banking lightweight), and a downturn in the markets, created a bitter struggle for power later in 1983, in which Glucksman prevailed and Peterson was ousted.

Upset, several important investment bankers who had soured over the power struggle left the company. Lehman suffered under the disintegration, and Glucksman was pressured into selling the firm to Shearson/American Express in 1984. In 1988, Shearson Lehman/American Express acquired E. F. Hutton, and the firm's name was changed to Shearson Lehman Hutton Inc.

These two mergers turned out to be too much for American Express. The Hutton division was a very large organization that had been badly managed and demoralized. It was not so easy to chop it up and reshape it to fit into the smooth-running Shearson brokerage system, and accordingly indigestion resulted. Perhaps more serious, Lehman's investment bankers considered Peter Cohen and the Shearson people to whom they now reported to be arrogant, brassy, unprofessional, and ignorant of investment banking. Lehman had its share of prima donnas, and they were difficult subordinates at best. Those among the experienced bankers who could do so left to find other jobs. Lehman's share of the lucrative merger and LBO financing markets declined. This was offset, however, by the firm's turning up the heat and becoming more aggressive on deals.[19]

Cohen led an unsuccessful effort to bid for RJR Nabisco together with Salomon Brothers and the company's CEO, Ross Johnson. Lehman lost this competition to Kohlberg, Kravis and Roberts in a close decision, but Cohen was discredited in the press for the failure. Much worse was the exposure that the firm had developed to bridge loans in conjunction with uncompleted LBOs in 1989, which put Shearson Lehman under great strain.[20] The firm lost $966 million in 1990, largely because of the bridge loans. This was reflected in a sharply lower stock price for American Express, which ultimately led to the replacement of Robinson by Harvey Golub in 1993. Golub decided that Cohen and Shearson Lehman Hutton were unhealthy for American Express's price-earnings ratio, and as his first act as CEO, he decided to shed them both. In 1994, he broke the business up into two parts, retail (Shearson) and wholesale (Lehman), sold the Shearson business to Sandy Weill, who was three acquisitions into his comeback, and spun off Lehman to the public as a reconstituted investment bank under Richard Fuld.

Equitable Life and Donaldson Lufkin

Late in 1984, the Equitable Life Assurance Society of America, the third-largest life insurance company and a major manager of pension fund assets, announced an agreement to acquire DLJ for $432 million, a 28 percent premium over its book value, in a difficult market. Richard Jenrette, the last of the founding trio to remain at the firm, would resign as CEO of DLJ and become vice-chairman of the Equitable. He would be replaced by John Castle.

John Carter, chairman of the Equitable, said the deal was very different from Prudential's investment in Bache because "DLJ is far more institutional. The Equitable, he said, "would be a powerful ally given the increasingly capital-intensive nature of the securities industry."[21] DLJ at the time owned Alliance Capital Management, an institutional money management firm that DLJ had founded. The Equitable separated Alliance from DLJ and, in time, transferred the management of the investment portfolios of the insurance company to Alliance. Otherwise, DLJ was left alone. Subsequently it went public again by selling 20 percent of the firm in a second IPO.

The Equitable, however, began to fall on difficult times soon after the DLJ acquisition. It suffered from the diffused governance structure of a mutual company in which the equity of the company is owned by the insurance policyholders, and from an archaic regulatory system that used an out-of-date insurance accounting system instead of generally accepted accounting principles. There was virtually no accountability on the part of management. The Equitable therefore decided to de-mutualize the company (by going public), which required a de novo audit done in accordance with generally accepted accounting principles. While this was being prepared, the company experienced some serious losses on certain insurance products. The combination of losses and the change in accounting practices led to the Equitable's reporting a loss of $123 million, which left it undercapitalized and put the IPO in jeopardy. In 1992, the Equitable was bailed out of the situation by the French insurance group AXA, which invested $1 billion in the Equitable for a 49 percent interest. By 1998, this interest had been increased to 60 percent. Meanwhile, DLJ continued to prosper, and in 2000, AXA sold it to Credit Suisse for $11.5 billion.

General Electric and Kidder Peabody

In 1986, General Electric announced that it would make a $600 million investment to acquire 80 percent of Kidder Peabody and Co., a 120-year-old investment bank, and invest an additional $130 million into it. GE had been looking for such an investment for the past few years, to participate in the merger-and-acquisition and financing boom that was occurring at the time. It had been turned down by Goldman Sachs and Morgan Stanley, and in due course a deal was struck with Kidder. GE had a substantial investment already in financial services—in addition to the enormous General Electric Credit Corporation, it also owned Employees Reinsurance, a large insurance business. Kidder Peabody was a tiny business by GE's standards, and there is some evidence that Jack Welch lost interest in it as soon as he realized how small it was in relation to the rest of GE's businesses.

At first the business ran well enough, but in the turmoil that struck the markets after the end of 1989, when the market turned and LBOs were hung up and difficult to finance, GE put one of its own men, Michael Carpenter, in as CEO. Three things happened at Kidder that soured GE on it and ultimately resulted in its forced sale. First there was the arrest of Martin Siegel, Kidder's former head of mergers and acquisitions, recently departed to Drexel Burnham, on insider trading charges. Second was an absurd scandal involving a black government bond trader, Joseph Jett, who had misreported trades so as to overstate the firm's income in 1993 by $350 million. Some reports put the blame for this event not so much on Jett as on Kidder's accounting systems, which apparently didn't realize that the Treasury strip trades that Jett was making had to be recombined with the original Treasury security before profits or losses could be calculated. This episode caused no customers to lose money, but Kidder, and thus General Electric, was made the butt of jokes for months. Finally, there was the biggest problem: runaway losses in mortgage-backed bonds, a business that Carpenter had encouraged Kidder to enter aggressively just before a serious market break in 1994 that withdrew liquidity from these types of bonds and made pricing them very difficult. Kidder was caught holding positions of $12 billion in mortgage-backed bonds as 1994 began. That was the last straw for GE, which resented the amount of attention tiny little Kidder was demanding from its top officers, and the implications that could be drawn from GE's experience that it was unable to manage complex trading businesses. So Carpenter was fired, and GE sent in some heavy guns to sell it or close it.

So they sold it. In December 1994, GE gave Paine Webber the pick of Kidder's assets and personnel for a net payment of $170 million. Paine Webber would pay $670 million in common stock (25.8 percent of Paine Webber), $100 million in convertible preferred stock, and $250 million in nonconvertible preferred stock for all the assets of Kidder Peabody except its Tokyo office and its mortgage-backed securities business (once Kidder's elite trading unit), which it did not want, and GE would retain all of Kidder's long-term liabilities, including severance payments to Kidder employees. Ironically, GE would recover all of its losses together with a substantial profit within a few years when Paine Webber was sold to Swiss universal bank UBS in 2000 for $10.25 billion.

A FLAWED CONCEPT?

None of these out-of-industry deals worked out very well. The concept of adding capital market capacity to a different type of financial services business proved difficult to implement. Nor did the synergies that were supposedly the reason for doing the deals ever develop; indeed, it may be argued that negative synergies evolved instead. In four of the cases, the acquired investment bank over time turned toxic to the buyer, which got rid of the problem by selling the firm for a loss or, in the case of First Boston, by having to buy out the minority interest. These buyers, Credit Suisse, American Express, Prudential, and General Electric, did not appreciate the potential for harm that First Boston, Lehman, Bache, and Kidder Peabody, respectively, brought with them. From their point of view, the investment banks proved impossible to manage and were filled with uncooperative or disdainful employees who expected to be paid far more than they were worth and who took risks and engaged in conduct that threatened the market value of the buyer companies. In three other cases, Phibro, Sears, and Equitable, problems that developed with the buyers prevented any useful support or business enhancement from occurring, forcing the end of the arrangement. In all the cases, the senior managers of the investment banks resented being employees of large, dissimilar enterprises with little in common with them, and that prevented them from acting independently and from paying people what they thought they should. Nor did the new corporate structure permit the investment banks to participate in significant equity ownership of the acquiring firm—they were accustomed to sharing income and control among themselves to build loyalty and teamwork within the firm. Instead, something of an every-man-for-himself attitude developed, which further frustrated their corporate owners. So-called cultural differences may have reached their peak in 1987, when GE installed Silas Cathcart, the retired chairman of Illinois Tool Works and a longtime GE director, to become chairman of Kidder Peabody after GE made its investment. GE trusted Cathcart and relied on him to tell it the truth about what was going on and to begin a management overhaul along GE lines. From the Kidder Peabody point of view, however, the placement was seen as an ill-considered effort to send a "tool and die man" in to Wall Street to fix things up.

In none of these out-of-industry merger cases did a dreaded superfirm emerge to dominate markets or to grab up market share. In none of the cases did anyone benefit very much. Indeed, all seven of these supposed superfirm deals came undone, Salomon, Dean Witter, and Lehman returned to the market as independent firms, and were able to resume where they'd left off—strengthened from the reorganization efforts, but mindful, too, of the painful, sometimes nightmarish experience of being a part of a large corporate owner.

5

THE BANKS

THE MONEY CENTER BANKS, as the large wholesale lenders were then called, were pretty sleepy in the 1970s—all but one, that is. First National City Bank, under the leadership of Walter Wriston, CEO since 1967, was straining at its leash, eager to show its stuff. Wriston had been the head of international banking at First National City (called Citibank, later to become Citicorp, then Citigroup) and had managed to drive the bank's overseas branches and affiliates to such levels of achievement that by the 1970s, 80 percent of the bank's profits came from international activities. Wriston, the son of a legendary president of Brown University, was not the usual banking type. He was bright, impatient, aloof, and somewhat awkward socially. He didn't play golf and he hated the deep-rooted, orderly bureaucracy that typified most banks.

Tall, lean, and angular, with a stern visage (he rarely smiled) and a sharp tongue, Wriston was a driven man who might have been too forceful to be successful in banking at the time he started out. But he was taken under the wing of George Moore, an energetic, charismatic future president of First National City, who appreciated Wriston's ability to get things done. Moore was responsible for rebuilding the international business after World War II, and he rose to become chairman when Wriston was selected as president and CEO. According to Philip Zweig, Wriston's biographer:

Wriston built Citicorp into the world's mightiest banking power and established for himself an unchallenged reputation as the world's most influential banker. Along with J.P. Morgan and Bank of America founder, A. P. Giannini, he ranked as one of the three most important bankers of the twentieth century. During his regime, Citicorp flexed more financial muscle around the globe than most countries. By force of intellect, acerbic wit, and hobnail boots, he transformed Citicorp from a genteel utility, where golf scores counted for more than IQ, into a tough, arrogant, corporate meritocracy that dragged the rest of the industry out of the era of quill pen banking.[1]

Once in charge, Wriston developed into a totally original figure who forced enormous change on Citibank and its industry. He was constitutionally not happy with the way things were. He was confrontational and pushed the bank hard in all directions—to develop new markets, products, and customers; to use its freedom from U.S. regulation overseas to develop investment banking and other skills; and to challenge regulators almost constantly to work free of the confinements of the Glass-Steagall and McFadden acts, which prevented Citibank from competing in the securities business and in branch banking across state lines. He pushed technology equally hard and maintained the world's largest budget for computer applications in banking. He recruited and promoted the best of the brightest and most aggressive young bankers and set them all into competition with one another. Performance was king, especially performance arrived at through personal effort and innovation—if you produced, you rose; otherwise, you left. Wriston transformed the bank into a ferocious, combative organism in which the working environment became political and very stressful. The turnover of officers was huge, but the alumni corps was cohesive and much respected by all other banks.

In 1970, Citibank was America's second-largest bank, slightly ahead of Chase Manhattan and trailing the leader, Bank of America, by less than $5 billion in total assets. Citibank was also the second-largest bank in the world, employing more than 24,000 people in 148 offices and 93 affiliates overseas. Trailing Chase on the list of the world's top thirty banks were Manufacturers Hanover (sixth ranking by assets), Morgan Guaranty Trust (eighth), Chemical Bank (tenth), Continental Illinois (twenty-sixth), Security Pacific (twenty-eighth), and First National Bank of Chicago (thirtieth). Most of these banks were rated AAA by the two leading U.S. rating agencies. Without a doubt, U.S. banks dominated the world. It was a time of expanding world trade and financial innovation, especially in the area of offshore currency deposits and internationally syndicated loans, but the industry was not much changed from what it had been a decade or so before. Money was made by taking deposits from customers at little cost and lending to trustworthy borrowers with which the bank had strong relationships. Pricing was much less important than the relationship, and many of the banks' top officers were champion client schmoozers.

In the early 1970s, Wriston began claiming that Citibank was a growth company like many high-priced technology companies, and that therefore its stock price should be higher. Citibank was growing at 15 percent a year, he would say, and could keep it up indefinitely because of the enormous potential available to it from the vast international market—where stifling U.S. banking regulations did not apply—and by increasing its market share in the United States by working harder and being smarter and more aggressive than its competitors. This being the case, Citibank's stock should trade at a price-earnings ratio of 15 to 20, he claimed, not the measly 5 to 10 that the market awarded to public utility companies and banks.

By 1973 the market had bought into Wriston's line of thinking, and indeed Citibank's stock traded at twenty-five times earnings, a really exceptional thing to happen to a bank, hemmed in as it was by regulation, price controls (on interest rate levels), and bureaucracy. The huge leap in Citibank's stock price, of course, brought the other major banks into the game of being growth stocks, too, and they were soon all off to the races to demonstrate their ability to grow at 15 percent a year indefinitely. This meant, among other things, doubling the size of assets on the books every five years, something that proved to be extremely hard to do without losing control of credit standards.

Wriston and the other big banks had a break when the oil-producing countries of the Middle East embargoed oil shipments to the West after the Yom Kippur War of 1973, which quadrupled the price. Instantly all the world's oil-consuming countries were exporting cash to the oil producers, and the medieval kingdoms of the Middle East soon were awash in money. Citibank, with sizeable branches and joint ventures in the region, was in position to collect a lot of this money in the form of bank deposits, on which the bank paid only a very low interest rate. But low cost or not, the deposits had to be lent out or the bank would choke on them. Wriston's solution was to find borrowers hungry for large, costly loans to which he could lend these "petrodollars." In particular, Wriston favored lending to governments of large developing countries, such as those in Latin America and Asia and on Europe's fringes. These countries needed lots of money, he said, and Citibank was going to be doing business with them for a long time. "Countries don't go bankrupt," he said, "they just reschedule at higher rates." This phrase would come back to haunt him, but even so, Wriston always thought that the banks had saved the world from financial collapse in the mid-1970s by efficiently recycling the oil money.

Citibank also loaned money to voracious corporate borrowers—some in the same developing countries—but mainly in the United States, Europe, and Japan. These companies were run largely by New Men with big ideas and little money, who needed to borrow some. Real estate developers, Greek shipowners, Las Vegas casino builders, various corporate takeover guys trying to do deals, and anyone else who seemed a good enough risk. Citibank had to load up the balance sheet to grow at 15 percent, and these insatiable borrowers would do very nicely. Citibank's competitors, now in the habit of doing so, watched carefully and followed suit.

But all of the banks were heading into trouble. The rising price of oil generated increases in other commodity prices, and both inflation and interest rates began to follow upward. Three-month Treasuries traded at interest rates of around 5.5 percent until the middle 1970s, but then started a sharp upward trajectory, with rates exceeding 10 percent in late 1979. For the banks, the interest rate spike would slow economic growth and put great pressure on of the creditworthiness of their borrowing clients, especially developing country governments and highly leveraged corporations.

It would also cause the greatest American financial collapse since the 1930s, the Savings and Loan Crisis.

THE S&L CRISIS

The S&Ls were in the business of financing house mortgages, usually long-term fixed-rate mortgage loans to homeowners. They financed these loans, as they always had, with short-term deposits. In the 1970s, when interest rates rose to double-digit levels, the cost of deposits skyrocketed, while the interest rates on outstanding long-term mortgages remained the same, which brought the S&Ls into a structural loss-making situation they couldn't do much about. Before long, the S&Ls began to fail, at first just the weaker ones, but by 1980, three fourths of the S&Ls were deep into the red, and many had been taken over by their regulators. The whole structure of home mortgage lending was collapsing, so the industry's regulators and Congress stepped in to help. Starting in 1980, a series of reforms provided a new set of rules for the S&Ls that essentially enabled them to disguise their deteriorating financial condition; they could operate with lesser amounts of capital; merge with other weaker S&Ls; enter into interest rate swap contracts to exchange long-term, fixed-rate income flows for shorter-maturity, variable-rate flows; defer losses on sales of mortgage loans; and use the proceeds from the sales to buy other mortgage loans from other S&Ls at big discounts or otherwise invest in riskier, nonmortgage assets that would increase their income.

Many of these forbearing regulatory reforms, however, actually weakened the S&L industry further and worsened the situation, but they did enable the problems to be delayed, tolerated, and spread out over a variety of other institutions, so that the better companies in the industry could survive. Nevertheless, the scale of the S&L crisis was enormous, and ultimately presented a bill to the American taxpayer (because of deposit insurance obligations) of approximately $200 billion. Most money center banks, however, were relatively unaffected because they held little mortgage debt, but aggressive corporate lending in the 1970s and early 1980s came back to haunt them. The 1970s were tough times for lending money and getting it back, but the 1980s were worse. Still, banks were continuing to compete actively for market share despite rising interest rates and deteriorating credit conditions. Consequently, the money center banks generated their own banking crisis alongside, but partially hidden by the experience of the S&Ls.

THE BANKS ENTER THE PENALTY BOX

In 1984, Continental Illinois became the first major U.S. bank to be taken over by federal regulators since 1933, beginning a chain of banking failures, forced takeovers, and regulatory imprisonment that would capture almost all U.S. money center banks. Bad loans became the curse of the 1980s. There were over $100 billion in write-offs in the five years between 1986 and 1991—the principal offenders being developing country governments, real estate developers and investment trusts, and highly leveraged corporate borrowers—and they affected all the major wholesale banks, which had been aspiring to rapid growth.

Beginning in the early 1980s, banking regulators subjected all but a very few banks to a decade or more of defensive, no-growth strategies that turned over their dominant positions in providing finance to major corporations to large European and Japanese banks that had appeared to replace them, and to investment banks that quickly stepped in to find solutions to corporate financial needs in the capital markets. As the banks experienced sharp deterioration of their credit ratings, their cost of funds increased accordingly, and many of their corporate clients could borrow much less expensively in the bond market than banks could.

The major banks were effectively sidelined for a full decade while they fought to get their balance sheets under control. For example, in 1970, at the height of its powers, Chase Manhattan reported net income of $138 million, a 12.2 percent return on shareholders' equity. Its stock price traded at 11 times earnings and 1.7 times book value. Net interest income was 81 percent of the bank's total revenues; deposits made up 87 percent of its funding, and 57 percent of these were non-interest-bearing demand deposits. Loan loss reserves were 30 percent of shareholders' equity. Twenty years later, Chase reported the worst year in its history, losing $334 million because of increases in loan loss reserves to 60 percent of shareholders' equity. Moody's had dropped Chase's bond rating to Baa-3, just one notch above a junk bond rating. Deposits were down to 72 percent of total funding, and only 18 percent of these were interest-free demand deposits. Its stock had dropped to $9.75 per share, only 32 percent of book value, and its dividend had been halved.

The other top banks did just as badly; 1990 was the worst year for banking since the Great Depression. Profits of all commercial banks averaged a miserable 0.54 percent of assets.[2] A great many banks, in danger of failing, simply were steered by the FDIC into mergers, including most of the large independent banks in Texas, New England, and the Pacific Northwest. Of all the industries involved in public mergers after 1985, the banking industry was at the top. Many of these mergers required waivers of state or federal laws restricting interstate transfer of control of the banks; the waivers were granted in the interest of saving the banks. At the end of 1990, only one of the leading thirty banks in the world was American: Citibank, which was then ranked eighteenth.

Wriston, who started it all, retired in 1984, and Citicorp was turned over to a forty-five-year-old eccentric, retail-banking-oriented computer-jock, John Reed, who was selected by Wriston to replace him after a painful two-year shootout among potential successors.* Wriston was able to watch from the sidelines as Citibank's stock slid back to $8.25 in early 1991, a price-earnings ratio lower even than public utilities. Widely thought to be kept from bankruptcy only by the tough love of the Federal Reserve, Citibank was helped by a rich Saudi prince who bought a large block of stock and became the bank's largest shareholder.

In the mid-1990s John Reed announced that Citicorp would get out of the corporate lending business, except for a select group of real estate and private equity clients. The other large U.S. banks and the Europeans hung in there, but even so, by then the investment banks had largely taken over the global, large-scale corporate financing market by default.

This was not so evident at the time, but it is hard now to imagine a greater gift to Wall Street than the collapse of the entire phalanx of the hitherto dominant players in the wholesale finance marketplace. The big banks, whose enormous working capital and term loans had dominated this marketplace for many generations, simply got up and left. Certainly they were sidelined by regulators, but without them, many would have failed. They had been victims of a lending euphoria that the industry had never succumbed to before—a belief that the benefits of aggressive, lemming-like asset accumulation was manageable by their credit administrators and functionaries and that the strategy would make them all rich and more powerful. Instead, the lemmings went over the cliff and left the wholesale domain to a bunch of securities brokers and dealers, who managed to transform it in ways that would be irreversible for the banks.

THE INDUSTRY TRANSFORMED

The agonies of the 1980s completely transformed the banking industry. None of the ten American banks among the top thirty in the world in 1970 would survive as independent entities, as all would be recombined by 2008 into one of three multiple-platform, mega-banking groups, each with assets in excess of approximately $2 trillion.

A weakened Bank of America (which had acquired Security Pacific and a relaunched Continental Illinois in the early 1990s) was acquired in 1998 by an upstart from North Carolina called NationsBank, which was

---

* Tom Theobald, who lost out to Reed, was hired to be head of the reconstituted Continental Illinois.

formed over a decade by the mergers of several Southern banks under the auspices of North Carolina National Bank. NationsBank took over both the assets of Bank of America and its name, and the new Bank of America went on to acquire FleetBoston (an amalgamation of various New England banks) in 2004, MBNA in 2005, and U.S. Trust in 2006, before taking on Countrywide Financial and Merrill Lynch in 2008.

Chemical Bank, tenth ranked in 1970, acquired a failing Texas bank in 1986 and an ailing Manufacturers Hanover in 1991, and in 1996 it acquired a much larger, but by then dead-in-the-water Chase Manhattan Bank, and appropriated its famous name. The new Chase in turn acquired the elegant but faded JPMorgan in 2000, and Bank One (which had acquired First National Bank of Chicago) in 2004. This group, now called JPMorgan Chase, is headed by Jamie Dimon, formerly CEO of Bank One and president of Citigroup, who engineered the distressed acquisitions of Bear Stearns and Washington Mutual in 2008.

John Reed, after restoring Citibank to its leadership position by exploiting its retail and international strengths, merged it with Sandy Weill's Travelers Insurance in a landmark transaction in 1998. Travelers, a leading property and casualty and life insurance underwriter, had by this time already been combined with broker/dealers Smith Barney and Salomon Brothers, and Commercial Credit, a large Baltimore-based finance company. The combined enterprise, named Citigroup, would continue to make acquisitions, and for several years would reign as America's largest and most valuable financial service corporation. The Travelers-Citicorp transaction was made in open defiance of the Glass-Steagall Act, which the government chose to repeal the following year rather than enforce.

Glass-Steagall

In 1933, when the Roosevelt administration took office, both the economy and the banking system were in a mess. During the years of the Depression, $1.3 billion in deposits were wiped out as a result of some nine thousand bank failures (40 percent of all banks). Roosevelt's first action as president was to declare a bank holiday, or a temporary closing of all banks, to let things cool off, having advised all Americans in his inaugural address that they had "nothing to fear but fear itself," and promising banking reform and federal assistance to clear up the problems that were causing the fear. Among the many measures taken in the first years of the new administration was the passage of the Banking Act of 1933, containing the Glass-Steagall provisions, and the Securities acts of 1933 and 1934.

These acts had in common the theme that the banking industry, having succumbed to excessive levels of speculation, bore much of the responsibility for the Great Depression. Later studies have transferred some of this blame to the Federal Reserve and the Treasury, both of which were seen to have handled fiscal and monetary policy inappropriately after the financial crises posed by the market crash of 1929 and the banking crisis of 1932, but there was enough evidence at the time to encourage Congress and the administration to subject the financial system to strict regulation for the first time.

The Banking Act provided for a strengthening of the Federal Reserve System, federal bank deposit insurance, and the forced separation of the banking and securities businesses (the Glass-Steagall provisions, named for their two congressional sponsors), which most money center banks then conducted. The Securities Act of 1933 provided for extensive information disclosure for new issues of securities, and the Securities and Exchange Act of 1934 provided for fair trading rules in the secondary markets and established the SEC.

As a result of the Banking Act, banks had to spin off their securities dealing arms. JPMorgan was reconstituted as Morgan Stanley, and a combination of others became First Boston. For the following fifty years the boundaries between commercial banking and investment banking were well established and accepted. Wriston's manifold assault on banking regulation was aimed mainly at getting more freedom of action for bank holding companies and in knocking down the McFadden Act of 1927, which severely restricted banks from operating branches in states other than their states of incorporation, but Wriston had no love for Glass-Steagall, either. The first serious challenges to the Glass-Steagall provisions occurred in the 1980s, when Bankers Trust wanted to sell commercial paper and was able to gain consent to do so. Subsequently, the banks began a protracted effort to chip away at the law and began to lobby in Congress and at the Federal Reserve to be allowed at least partial access to the securities markets.

They were opposed in this by some of the investment banks which attempted to parry their efforts in Washington, but other securities firms were quietly exploring ways in which they might gain access to the deposit markets by securing a banking license.

One of the first to try this was Goldman Sachs, which in the early 1980s purchased a small London-based subsidiary of the First National Bank of Dallas, which was undergoing difficulties and wanted to shut down its European operations. I was the Goldman Sachs partner in London at the time and, under instruction from my colleagues in New York, negotiated the purchase and endeavored to get the deal approved by the Bank of England. But we were stonewalled. The Bank of England did not want to become involved in a controversial deregulatory struggle in the United States. They told us we would have to get the okay of U.S. banking regulators first. So we went to see the Federal Reserve, which was also reluctant to approve the purchase, fearing it would accelerate the Glass-Steagall issue for it, and Paul Volcker, chairman of the Fed at the time, was reluctant to see the law compromised or overturned. So the Fed sent us to the New York State Banking Commission—it had no visible jurisdiction in the case, but it was a way to continue the bureaucratic delay—which was then headed by political appointee Muriel Siebert, the first woman ever to be a member of the New York Stock Exchange. She was sympathetic, she said, but decided the matter should be approved by the New York Clearing House, an organization of New York–based banks, to ensure effective interbank clearance and settlement. The major banks were well represented on the Clearing House, so they got to have the final say. The board of the Clearing House took up the case (of our acquisition of a tiny bank in London with no New York settlement issues at all) and narrowly approved it, thinking that doing so might strengthen the big banks in their effort to undo Glass-Steagall. The whole process was then reversed. About eighteen months after our first discussion with the Bank of England, we received approval to close the deal. We used our new banking license as a means to access the London interbank market to fund trading positions and a new foreign exchange business. Soon afterward, Merrill Lynch also secured a London banking license.

As the banks recovered from their low point in the early 1990s, having either merged or worked through their portfolios of bad loans, they subscribed to a more pragmatic system of governance, one that emphasized sound, "back-to-basics" management. Results improved, and before long the new team of managers brought in after the debacles began to look around and assess the damage that a decade of absence from the main competitive fields of banking had incurred.

They first saw the fields well occupied by large European universal banks, those permitted by their regulatory authorities to engage in all forms of financial services, including securities and insurance. Some of these banks were grandfathered in the United States and were able to participate in all forms of financial transactions, but most were not. The large European banks, however, were very active in the Eurobond and other international securities markets and were active lenders to American companies, to whom traditional U.S. banks had been restrained from lending because of their balance sheet difficulties. As a result, by the middle 1980s, foreign banks (including several large Japanese banks) then with solid credit ratings when the U.S. banks were fading, had gained a 22 percent market share of domestic wholesale lending to U.S. companies (41 percent, if you counted overseas lending as well), which was a serious concern to the U.S. banks.[3] These integrated banking entities were the future, the U.S. banks thought, and the American banks lobbied hard to be allowed to be given the same universal powers as the European banks, in order to be able to compete with them.

The European Common Market had evolved into the European Union by 1992 with the passage of the Single Market Act, which was intended to withdraw all restrictions preventing the crossing of European borders by goods, money, people, and ideas. A banking directive issued by the EU established that banks active in one country in the EU could be active in all, and universal banking was to be accepted everywhere. U.S. banks with subsidiaries within the EU would be afforded the same rights as European banks, but they would be severely hampered at home, they said, if they could not be universal there, too.

Though House and Senate banking committee members of Congress were getting fat from a decade of campaign contributions from both the banks and the investment banks, they did little more than hold hearings. The Federal Reserve, after Paul Volcker was replaced by Alan Greenspan, began to fudge things by announcing that under Section 20 of the Glass-Steagall statute, the Fed could establish a limit on the amount of "prohibited" transactions permitted in "unassociated" (i.e., insulated or "firewalled") subsidiaries. The Fed started with a limit of 5 percent of assets and revenues that could come from prohibited transactions, such as underwriting securities or brokerage commissions. This was a major breakthrough for the banks, but at first it was too small an amount of leeway to be able to complete meaningfully. In time the banks overcame this by lobbying for an increase in the percentage of permissible transactions to about 20 percent, and by increasing the size of their banks' assets through a continuous stream of mergers.

THE INTERNATIONALS

In 1990, large banks and other financial players located outside the United States were settling in to be major competitors in the new global banking industry. During the 1980s, large Japanese banks and securities firms developed powerful overseas lending and underwriting businesses based in London and New York, where they mainly served Japanese companies eager to raise capital. There were four principal Japanese securities firms, and eight or ten "City" (i.e., money center) banks with serious international aspirations, but like the Americans, they were stuck with a law adopted during the postwar American occupation that separated banking from securities activities and had been modeled on the Glass-Steagall Act.

But after the crash of the Tokyo stock market that began in December 1989, when the Nikkei index was 39,000 and fell to a low of 15,000 in mid-1992, before leveling out at an average level of 18,000 for the remainder of the decade, the Japanese lost their appetite for international finance. After 2000, reflecting the difficulties in the U.S. market in the post-high-tech and Enron era, the Japanese market fell even further, to a low of 7,600 in 2003. This market decline produced cataclysmic effects on the Japanese financial system and economy, forcing it into a prolonged recession that extended into a fifteen-year period of little growth or progress. During this time there were record levels of bankruptcies and efforts to prop up old, uneconomic industrial corporations running big losses. The market effects immediately following the crash also revealed a lot of shady practices involving the heads of the large securities firms and banks, and just about all of them were forced to make CEO changes and pull in their horns to hunker down until better economic conditions returned. The Japanese banks were stuck with enormous amounts of non-performing loans that took many years to write down. The securities firms were even worse off. Nomura Securities, Japan's largest broker-dealer, survived, but the other three of the "Big Four" did not. Yamaichi Securities went bankrupt, Daiwa was absorbed by Sumitomo Bank, and Nikko was acquired by Citigroup.

Relationship-oriented Japanese banks carried large amounts of shares in client companies on their books at historical cost, and the difference between their cost and after-tax market value was permitted, under

Japanese regulations, to be counted as capital, as the banks did not maintain loan loss reserves. As share prices plummeted, so did the capital of the banks, just when they were experiencing heavy losses from margin loans, loans to real estate operators, and to dodgy corporations. The banks were rattled by these events and passively submitted to a massive government-led, forced banking industry consolidation into four mega-banking behemoths, in order to better absorb the titanic quantity of bad loans that the crash and subsequent recession produced. The mergers involved several awkward consolidations at once in a system that eschewed mergers or corporate combinations of any kind. The banks have now further consolidated these four groups into three. Sumitomo merged with Mitsui Bank, Sakura Bank, and others; Mizuho Group was newly formed from the merger of Industrial Bank of Japan, Dai-Ichi Kangyo Bank, and Fuji Bank; the Mitsubishi Bank was merged with the Bank of Tokyo and two trust banks to form the Mitsubishi Tokyo Group, which later merged with the UFJ Group (one of the original four mega-banks), made up of Sanwa Bank, Tokai Bank, and Toyo Trust. There are still a number of other, independent banks operating in Japan, but all of the major money center banks have been combined into one of the three giants. Along with these actions, the law separating banking and securities businesses was repealed, but the Japanese spent far too much time in the penalty box (and fell too far behind in developing their global financing capabilities) to capitalize on the new freedom to be fully competitive. They have a lot to learn about operating in modern, fast-changing financial markets before they will be able to do so.

European banks, on the other hand, entered the 1990s optimistically, with a new single market unfettered by borders or competitive restrictions. The Europeans figured the universal banking model would become the world's standard, and the largest universals considered they had advantages in the coming competition that U.S. banks did not.

One French universal bank, Crédit Lyonnais, run by a well-connected former head of the French Treasury, sought to become Europe's leader through a quick rush of acquisitions of other European banks, branches, and affiliates, but in doing so, it poisoned itself with enormous bad loan exposures that not only killed off the effort after a few years but also cost the French taxpayers nearly $40 billion in rescue and intervention costs. Indeed, the European banks would experience their own wave of bad loans much as U.S. banks had in the 1980s and the Japanese had in the early 1990s, and these losses would dampen the ambitions of many of them.

Some European banks chose to combine within their own countries to create a stronger competitive presence—ABN Amro Bank was such a combination in Holland, as was BNP-Paribas in France. Others, such as Barclays and National Westminster Bank (NatWest) in the UK, acquired investment banking arms, but trading losses and mishaps caused Barclays to scale back considerably to rely mainly on its retail banking business, and NatWest, weakened by its efforts in the securities markets, was ultimately acquired by a smaller, feistier bank, Royal Bank of Scotland. The two other large British clearing banks, Midland and Lloyds, disappeared into other mergers with mainly retail organizations. Just as in the United States and Japan, Europe also experienced a decade of bank problems and mergers that affected all countries and industry participants. Most of the mergers were to shore up banks weakened by heavy loan losses.

By the end of the 2008, three major European universal banks had appeared as survivors ready to challenge their American counterparts for market leadership: Deutsche Bank, Germany's largest bank, and UBS and Credit Suisse, Switzerland's two largest banks. All three had arrived at their positions having experienced a fair amount of pain and suffering. All had begun as large, dominant banks in countries that had little capital market activity of their own and had to adapt to markets outside their own countries, in New York, London, and Tokyo. This was not easy to do. It required shifting major operational responsibility to these locations where other languages were spoken and the business cultures were very different. It required either acquisition of existing businesses or of teams of trained professionals. Neither option was easy for them to manage. The British, Americans, or Japanese they might acquire or hire could not be counted on to be loyal to them, or willing to work for the modest compensation packages considered generous in Germany or Switzerland. Top investment banking producers were often very difficult to handle, like prima donnas, who walked off the stage when they were disappointed. Over more than twenty years, under four successive CEOs, Deutsche Bank hired a number of star performers or teams who walked out on them. In 1990 it acquired Morgan Grenfell, a merchant bank in London, which strongly resisted being told what to do by a bunch of Germans—and in turn, cost the Germans a fortune to settle lawsuits from a nasty mismanagement-of-money charge.[4] It also acquired Bankers Trust and Alex Brown in the United States in 1998, but soon experienced defections and discontinued their brand names. However, Josef Ackermann, a Swiss who has been a Deutsche Bank board member since 1996 and CEO since

2002, has transformed the bank by committing it to increasing shareholder value, a concept that was new to most Germans, by focusing on its international opportunities in capital markets. The bank has largely shed its cumbersome portfolio of postwar industrial holdings, has moved major decision-making units to London and New York, and introduced international (i.e., Anglo-American) business practices and cost-cutting methods, despite a fair amount of internal resistance to doing so. Ackermann is striving also to transform the bank into principally one for corporations and private investors, and to lessen its role in German retail banking.

UBS is the result of a 1998 combination of Union Bank of Switzerland and Swiss Banking Corporation, Switzerland's largest and third-largest banks after the smaller bank, headed by Marcel Ospel, managed a hostile takeover in the wake of Union Bank's weak performance and scandals related to alleged mishandling of accounts held by Holocaust victims. Under Ospel, a sophisticated and Americanized onetime Merrill Lynch managing director who rejoined the bank in 1987, SBC had already acquired a Chicago-based derivatives firm and Britain's leading investment bank, S. G. Warburg, and had used the skills acquired in the mergers to greatly enhance its own performance and capabilities. The merger established UBS as the world's largest private banking asset manager; the bank acquired Paine Webber in the United States in 2000.

Credit Suisse has survived thirty years of an up-and-down relationship with its U.S. affiliate, formerly called Credit Suisse First Boston, through which it has developed a lasting capability in, and commitment to, global capital markets, and from which it acquired its American chief executive, Brady Dougan. It ventured heavily (but briefly) into Swiss insurance and retail banking, but returned to focus on international markets in 2000, when it acquired Donaldson, Lufkin and Jenrette in an $11 billion transaction that proved to be very difficult for it.

In retrospect, the U.S. banks' urgent appeal to their regulators to be allowed the freedom necessary to be able to complete with Japanese behemoths and European universals seems now to be a case of mistaken role models. The Japanese have not been competitive at all since the early 1990s, and the European universals have had as much or more trouble adapting to a highly competitive and innovative capital market environment as the American banks have. But the European and the Japanese contenders, keeping up with the Americans, have certainly increased in size and complexity, all now being multi-product-line corporations with vast amounts of assets under their management. Citigroup was the world's largest banking entity in 2007 (before its current difficulties began), with $2.6 trillion in assets and more than 350,000 employees. This is more than twenty times the amount of assets that the bank held in 1990 (but with only about four times as many employees).

THE BIG BALANCE SHEET

In 1998, Sandy Weill stunned the banking world with his announcement that Travelers Insurance Group would combine with Citicorp for a minimal 8 percent premium in a so-called merger of equals. The new combination, to be called Citigroup, would be led by him and John Reed, as co-CEOs, with a board of directors equally represented by both companies. The new group, with combined assets at the end of 1997 of $700 billion and net revenues of $50 billion, would become the world's largest and most profitable financial services firm. The stocks of both companies rose sharply on the news, which was exciting but also confusing. This was because the acquisition would be illegal, a direct violation of Glass-Steagall. The deal could be closed only when it secured approval of banking authorities—the terms specified that the two entities would be kept separate for a period of two years (followed by three consecutive one-year extensions), and if Glass-Steagall were not repealed or the deal were not otherwise rendered legal by then, the deal would be unwound.

Immediately the buzz became deafening. This would be the deal of the century (which had only two more years to go). It would make Citigroup the premier financial institution in the world, would increase competition in capital markets, would better serve customers, and would lead the way into the future for all financial services companies. Citigroup would become the only financial service platform in the world operating in all sectors of the business—banking, securities, insurance, and asset management—doing so both globally and domestically, and in both wholesale and retail markets. It would develop its new platform further by intensive efforts to achieve cross-selling of products and services, by a major effort to reduce costs (though there were not many overlapping activities), by an exploitation of opportunities presented by technology, especially the Internet, and by further acquisitions to strengthen operating units.

This was certainly an exciting and ambitious undertaking, but as investors thought more about it, they developed second thoughts. How could such a large, complex organization be headed by two very strong and dissimilar personalities, Weill and Reed? How could they be so sure the government would allow the deal to be done? If the government didn't approve it, what would happen to the values of the two companies? What about the hidden costs that affected so many mergers—the departures and infighting; the long, painful selection of the new management team; and the delays in decision making caused by having to consult co-heads endlessly? These concerns caused the stock price to drop about 30 percent (and then another 20 percent as the group endured the financial storms of mid-1998), until most of the doubters had sold out and the stock began to recover nicely.

The government, however, did allow the deal to go forward as negotiated, and in November of 1999, President Clinton signed the Gramm-Leach-Bliley Act which repealed the Glass-Steagall Act. The two businesses were consolidated shortly thereafter, but management issues quickly surfaced. Friction developed between the two sides when they discovered that there is no such thing as a merger of equals, and this friction was reflected at the top. Clashes occurred, and various senior management changes were made, but difficulties between Weill and Reed emerged as insurmountable. Fifteen months after the deal was announced, co-CEO John Reed was ousted, leaving Citigroup in the hands of Sandy Weill as sole CEO. He would be assisted by Bob Rubin, who joined the company after leaving the Treasury in 1999 and who had supported Weill in the conflict between the co-CEOs.

The Citigroup deal certainly captured the attention of its competitors. It was a game-changing event, some thought, and others would have to respond accordingly. In 1999, Deutsche Bank acquired Bankers Trust, which owned Alex Brown, a midsize investment bank. In 2000, Chase Manhattan acquired JPMorgan, to gain its wholesale finance expertise, and Credit Suisse acquired Donaldson, Lufkin and Jenrette. All had to consider how they could keep up with Citigroup unless they, too, adopted a "big balance sheet strategy."

A big balance sheet strategy involved making very large loans to clients that were increasingly looking to capital markets and/or leveraged loans to provide facilities in the billions. A U.S. bank is restricted from lending to any single client more than 15 percent of its capital, so the bigger the bank's capital, the larger the loan that can be made. A bank with $1 trillion in assets, and a capital-to-assets ratio of 10, would have capital of $100 billion, of which as much as $15 billion could be loaned without security to a single entity. Not many banks want to go that far, but the ability to offer huge commitments has to be important to large corporations, LBO operators, and governments seeking financing. That sort of muscle will always get a big bank in the door to decide just how much it wants to lend and at what price.

But the strategy is not just of large loan making. Indeed, lending spreads, especially for high-grade credits, are fairly small. The bigger money is earned from management and other fees associated with large deals, which can involve large initial commitments, but these can then be sold down in the market and the capital returned to be used for another deal. It is important to keep the capital circulating as quickly as possible, to make the most on it. This, in turn, requires the ability to gain the mandate to do the financing (usually in competition with other banks, but often in cooperation with them) and the ability to resell the positions through the bank's distribution channels. Once these positions are sold, they constitute a considerable secondary market, which the bank's traders can then try to exploit.

Finally, and most attractively to the banks in the period after the Citigroup combination, banks can use their ability to extend credit facilities to clients as a quid pro quo to obtain mandates to perform other services, such as underwriting equity issues or advising on a merger or LBO. These mandates are where the real money is made in investment banking, and though the banks may have lacked experience and capabilities in these areas, they could insist on being added as co-managers of deals being arranged by others. This, in effect, means getting a share of the fees from unrelated business as a result of an aggressive offering of credit facilities. Of course the strategy was being pursued by several banks, so competition began to affect pricing, and before long the banks were thought to be offering low-cost, below-market credit facilities to clinch the biggest deals.

This part of the strategy soon became troubling to the investment banks. They did not want the banks horning in on their most profitable businesses, nor did they want to be put in a position where they, too, would have to offer cheap credit facilities from their own, much smaller balance sheets. Their corporate clients, however, were good at playing one bank or investment bank off another, and competition often meant that the banks would succeed in elbowing their way in, and the investment banks would have to extend credit from time to time. They protested, but figured they would have to learn to live with the banks as competitors in ways they had not before. One of those ways was to increase the size of their own balance sheets to keep up with the others. By 2007, Goldman Sachs, Merrill Lynch, and Morgan Stanley all had balance sheets with more than $1 trillion in assets. These assets were largely made up of trading positions, but they also provided the capacity to make loans to corporate clients, especially for leverage loans to support LBOs.

In 2007, eight years after the end of Glass-Steagall, a New York University ranking of global wholesale banking market share positions by volume of transactions originated showed that the top ten firms controlled more than 70 percent of the market.* The top five firms according to this ranking (with 43 percent of the market) were Citigroup, JPMorgan Chase, Goldman Sachs, Morgan Stanley, and UBS. Of this group, Citicorp and JPMorgan Chase originated by far the greatest amount of syndicated bank loans (more than $600 billion each) and were co-advisers in $1.4 trillion of mergers; Goldman Sachs, the long-standing leader of mergers and acquisitions, originated $1.6 trillion of mergers and $187 billion of syndicated bank loans. The next five firms among the top ten were Deutsche Bank, Credit Suisse, Merrill Lynch, Lehman Brothers, and BNP-Paribas. Six of the top ten firms were large U.S. or European universal banks. These ten firms have occupied these or similar positions in this ranking for many years.

The big balance sheet strategy seemed to be working for the big banks as they increased their overall market share by encroaching into the merger and underwriting activities. Since 1998, however, the most aggressive of the big banks have had more than their share of difficulties with lending activities in the corporate sector (Enron, WorldCom, Parmalat), mortgage-backed securities, and leveraged loans for LBOs. These difficulties, beyond the loan losses, have also included substantial exposures to litigation and regulatory penalties such that most of their profits from investment banking over the past decade have been wiped out by losses, settlements, fines, and legal fees.

These setbacks in earnings have extended into the realm of their stock prices, which have been unable to keep up with their growth stock ambitions. To be seen as growth stocks, the big banks need to demonstrate that they can grow at 15 percent or so a year, and keep this up indefinitely. This has proven to be difficult to do, not just because of their inability to

---

* The wholesale market for this study comprises syndicated bank loans, securities underwritten, and merger advisories, with full credit given to the book-running manager(s).

deliver the earnings behind the market shares, but also because of the huge amount of annual growth such an increment implies—"a fifteen percent growth rate for an outfit like Citigroup," said Arthur Zeikel, former head of Merrill Lynch's asset management group in 2006, "would mean that they'd have to add a Merrill Lynch every year." That's certainly a tall order; to meet the target, growth has to come from both organic earnings and mergers. Organic earnings growth from aggressive wholesale lending usually has to focus on higher-yielding, and therefore lower-quality, loans, made in very large quantities, but managing the various risks appropriately under competitive pressure has so far proven to be very difficult for the banks to do. Acquisitions are size-restricted: only very large deals make much difference if the bank is already very big, and the number of firms to be acquired in such a size range may be very limited. Even then, such acquisitions usually require significant takeover premiums, which detract from profit growth, and they have often been difficult to integrate.

There is also the question of whether such large, heavily risk exposed, and diversified businesses can be managed well by their executives. Being well managed in today's market environment means staying on top of several different types of businesses, gaining market share, sustaining profit growth, and staying out of trouble from a proliferation of regulators, class action and other litigators, or other events that can suddenly destroy shareholder value. Certainly since the repeal of Glass-Steagall, the big balance sheet banks had great difficulty doing all of these things, which called into question whether the strategy was executable. And this was before the mortgage crisis and market meltdown of 2007–2008.

6

INTERNATIONALIZING

AT THE END OF 1968, Henry H. Fowler, fifty-eight, the retiring secretary of the treasury in the Lyndon Johnson administration, was among a small group of men who joined the partnership at Goldman Sachs, the last such group to be selected solely by Sidney Weinberg, who died about six months later. Weinberg, who was a Johnson supporter, had known Fowler since their service on the War Production Board during World War II, and the two had stayed loosely in touch since.

Fowler, whom everyone called Joe, was a lawyer with no knowledge of banking, at least until he joined the Treasury, first as deputy secretary (1961–1964) and later as secretary (1965–1968). There he was known for orchestrating through Congress the Kennedy-Johnson tax cut (1964), used as a model by the Reagan administration in the early 1980s, and for successfully wrestling the federal fiscal deficit into a small surplus (after a modest tax increase) just before he left office in November 1968.

However, the U.S. balance-of-payments with foreign creditors was perpetually negative, and therefore there were more dollars leaving the country year after year than returning to it, and the books had to be balanced then (as now) by selling either gold or securities to foreign central banks and other overseas investors. As a result, there was a movement of gold from the great U.S. hoard in Fort Knox, Tennessee, to foreign destinations—not much of a movement from among all that was stashed there, but enough to frighten conservative economic commentators and, through them, the media, thus making it a political issue. Joe did his best to stop the outflow. He introduced an "interest equalization tax," which virtually precluded foreign borrowers from using U.S. debt markets, and arranged a system of "voluntary restraints" on capital outflows by U.S. companies—these later became mandatory—which had a more burdensome effect. These restraints required U.S. companies investing abroad in subsidiaries, factories, or any other capital acquisition to finance the project outside the United States, not within it. U.S. companies were expanding abroad very actively then, especially in Europe and Japan, where interest rates were higher than at home. Companies did not like being made to finance at higher rates, and of course Wall Street was annoyed by the government's actions to suppress bond issues in the U.S. market by foreign governments and corporations, and by making U.S. corporations borrow somewhere else.

Joe was tough, though, and made the measures stick. Partly as a result of Fowler's policies to preserve the dollar, and their forceful implementation, a new, alternative, financial marketplace, the Euromarket, emerged outside the United States. Within less than twenty years, the Euromarket would become one of the world's principal venues for capital market transactions, nearly equaling the United States in volume and pricing of new issues of debt and equity securities.

The Euromarket began with dollar-denominated deposits in bank branches in Europe, mainly in London. A convenient location for everyone, London was outside the reach of U.S. bank regulators (and thus deposits were free of reserve requirements), and accounts could be opened without being reported to U.S. or other tax authorities. Dollar-denominated deposits needed to be invested in dollar-denominated instruments by the banks that held them, but there weren't any such things in Europe until "Eurodollar" loans were created.

As dollars were not the local currency of any European location, an over-the-counter market developed between banks in Eurodollar deposits—you could buy or borrow Eurodollars, or invest in loans or other instruments denominated in them. This became the London interbank market, where daily rates were posted for both the London interbank offered rate (LIBOR) for loans and the London interbank bid rate (LIBID) for deposits. Citibank expanded the range of this market in the early 1960s by introducing large-volume Eurodollar certificates of deposit (CDs), and the first dollar-denominated Eurobond was issued in 1963, by the British merchant bank S. G. Warburg, for the Italian state highway authority, Autostrade.

This was a small issue, only $15 million, but it was monumental in importance. Warburg had painstakingly orchestrated a Europe-wide consensus that as long as these issues were marketed as "private offerings," they did not have to be registered with any of the many securities regulation authorities that existed in Europe, but they did have to be sold by banks to their clients. As a result, the issues were essentially unregulated and stateless in jurisdiction, meaning that they didn't really come under any country's legal or regulatory framework, or attract tax in any country. Furthermore, the bonds would be offered in a form that did not require that they be registered in the investor's name—they were "bearer bonds," payable only to the person presenting them for payment—so they could be held anonymously, a real treat for secretive European and other investors with money they did not want to be traced.

The new bonds also appealed to European private banks that managed large sums for clients, especially Swiss banks, which, through their secretive "numbered accounts," managed money for all sorts of people, a great many of whom were hiding the money from someone: tax authorities, family members, or foreign governments. Europe was only a little more than twenty years past World War II when great quantities of private wealth were lost or stolen because they were not sufficiently well hidden. And in the immediate postwar period, many countries were in the grip of ardent forms of socialism that worried many of those who had money. The banks would charge large fees for distributing Eurobonds to their clients, but the clients didn't mind. They valued anonymity more than investment returns, which, being salted away in numbered accounts, weren't going to be taxed anyway.

Sidney Weinberg didn't know much about any of this, but he knew his clients were arranging financing overseas and didn't want to lose them to other investment banks that were more active abroad than Goldman Sachs, especially Morgan Stanley, First Boston, and a smaller, blue-chip firm with a specialty in foreign finance, White, Weld and Co. Joe Fowler would be a door-opener in Europe and elsewhere, and would work with Michael Coles, one of the other new partners, selected in 1968 to build up a competitive entry into the international sector. Three years later, contrary to the advice of all my colleagues in the mainstream (domestic) corporate finance department, into which I was settling nicely and was a new vice-president, I joined this tiny but ambitious band of brothers seeking to open up the world to Goldman Sachs.

In 1970, Goldman Sachs had no foreign offices and virtually no non-U.S. corporate clients. There were some international brokerage accounts and a number of correspondent relationships with banks and merchant banks abroad, but only a trickle of so-called reciprocal business. The firm had few if any relationships with important central banks or finance ministries, and indeed was hardly known at all in Europe, or in high-growth Japan, which was then the latest economic phenomenon to splash on the scene, similar to China today. There was a lot of work to do. Mike Coles, an Englishman who had been the firm's man on the ground for such Eurobond transactions as it had done, was a Harvard Business School graduate who attended the school without ever going to college first; he had been a teenage fighter pilot in the Royal Navy and fought in the Korean War instead. Mike opened a tiny, four-man office in London in 1971, and when he moved there, I was asked to take his place in New York as the guy you talked to if you had clients with international business to be done. I was also the guy who was supposed to look after Japan, to visit the country periodically to try to drum up business there.

We were doing some international business then, and needed to be able to talk knowledgably about Eurobonds to domestic clients still operating under the controls set in place by Joe Fowler, the new chairman of our international affiliate. We were also interested in financing Japanese companies issuing convertible debentures (bonds convertible into stock) in either the United States or the Euromarkets, and in assisting non-U.S. companies seeking to make acquisitions in the United States. Just as we were getting started, however, the world changed.

THREE SHOCKS THAT CHANGED THE WORLD

The Japanese refer to great and sudden changes as "shocks" (they call them *shokkus*). During the 1970s, three such shocks occurred that particularly changed Wall Street and the business it did, even though at the time their impact was not well or fully understood.

The Nixon Shock

In 1944, the U.S. government had convened an international conference of all allied nations in Bretton Woods, New Hampshire, to seek agreement on an international monetary system that would help return the world to economic and financial stability after the war. The conference gave birth to the World Bank and the International Monetary Fund, and to an international exchange rate mechanism based on the gold standard. Financial stability essentially meant containing inflation, the big worry for the coming postwar world economic recovery. The system that was agreed upon was one in which the U.S. dollar would be pegged to gold at the official rate of $35 per ounce, and all the other countries subscribing to the international monetary system (i.e., the West and some developing countries) would fix their currencies to the dollar at an agreed-upon exchange rate. The exchange rates were to be vigorously defended by the governments of the subscribing countries, usually by adjusting monetary or fiscal policies.

However, this would mean imposing economic discipline on their countries. In reality, the system was bound to break down, because the initial exchange rates were set in 1944, when the economies of all the countries involved were essentially shattered or dislocated by the war. In postwar recovery, many of these countries would experience different rates of growth, inflation, and indebtedness, which would effectively require their exchange rates to change. But the system was designed to preserve the original exchange rates, not to adjust them frequently or gradually. Countries with high inflation would be required to raise interest rates or impose price controls; countries with successful export businesses would be required to suppress them or to encourage imports to stay within the agreed-upon currency ranges, but few countries could impose such terms on their economies without serious political repercussions. Sometimes adjustments were unavoidable, and countries devalued their currencies in a sudden, usually embarrassing, and economically painful announcement. Still, the system that wheezed along for twenty-five years, despite all its faults, seemed to be the best it could be.

By 1970, the Vietnam War had begun to increase inflation in the United States, and foreign confidence in and regard for the dollar began to sink. The war was as unpopular in Europe as it was in America. Several European governments complained to Secretary of the Treasury John

Connally* that U.S. inflation was heading out of control and was straining the international monetary system. Connally replied that the "dollar
was our currency, but your problem,"[1] which probably made the problem
worse—in the first six months of 1971, assets of $22 billion fled the United
States.[2] In response, on August 15, Connolly announced that the United
States would no longer exchange gold for dollars. Thus, the Nixon administration unilaterally "closed the gold window," making the dollar incon-
vertible to gold, except on the open market. This decision Nixon made
without consulting members of the international monetary system or even
his own State Department; it was soon dubbed the "Nixon Shock."

After the announcement, the value of the dollar and all other currencies would be set by the market, not by governmental efforts to maintain
often artificial exchange rates. This was not a form of deregulation the
United States commissioned; it was a forced and unexpected event, imposed on the U.S. economy by market and political pressures. That such
a thing could have happened was the real shock.

At the time, many statesmen and economists, including Joe Fowler,
feared that the floating rate system would shatter international financial
stability and endanger world trade, creating conditions that could bring
back the 1930s. They had confidence in the wise men guiding their governments and could not imagine a system controlled by no one but market
speculators. To their great astonishment, the market system worked better than the Bretton Woods system, though it took some years to see this.

At first, the price of gold moved only a little, up about 10 percent in
the wave of the shock. But it crept up to about $90 per ounce by the sum-
mer of 1973. By 1979, when most of the effects of the systemic change
had been absorbed, gold was trading at about $250 per ounce, reflecting
more than a sevenfold devaluation of the dollar against the metal, thus
demonstrating the dollar's overvaluation during the postwar period. Other
currencies had adjusted, too, especially the deutsche mark, the yen, and the
Swiss franc, which rose in value relative to the dollar. But the new equilibrium in foreign exchange rates provided a realistic platform from which
trade and investment decisions could be made.

World merchandise trade (exports plus imports) expanded at a rate of
20 percent between 1970 and 1980, more than double its rate of growth

---

*The Texas governor who was riding in the limousine with John F. Kennedy when he was
shot.

from 1960 to 1970. As exchange controls were removed (they were no longer needed in a floating rate environment), the volume of daily foreign exchange trading soared, reflecting financial investment transactions as well as those in goods and services. These financial transactions involved movement of funds for investing in the various financial markets of the world, especially at the time in the U.S. market, the Euromarket, and the growing markets of newly prosperous Japan.

The world pool of investment funds more than doubled in a decade, which allowed for arbitraging markets internationally and assisting integration of fixed-income markets. The new mechanism allowed for pressure to be brought on foreign exchange or interest rates that the market thought might be out of alignment. The transmission of this pressure also helped to increase volatility in both markets substantially. And increased volatility attracted the attention of traders.

The Nixon Shock took Wall Street by surprise, but didn't upset it very much. It seemed to be an appropriate way for tough old Nixon to show a bunch of ungrateful foreigners that they would henceforth have to deal with America differently and that the "bugaboo" (as Nixon called it) of official dollar devaluation "had been laid to rest."[3] But we in the tiny International Department at Goldman Sachs knew it would change our business, which was largely based on Eurobond issues, a great deal.

First, the mandatory restraints on capital exports would surely come off, meaning that our existing U.S. clients would no longer be forced to finance in the Euromarket.

Second, it would mean that non-U.S. issuers could return to the U.S. markets—but would they want to? The Eurobond market could supply what they needed, maybe at lower cost, because in Europe, Europeans would not be regarded as foreigners and required to pay a premium for money.

So the business that was to be our future was likely to involve issuers that were not among our existing clients, and markets in which we had little or no placing power. Our business plan would have to change to emphasize marketing to European and Japanese issuers and developing better international sales and distribution capability.

The Oil Shock

While we were struggling with our business plan, the Yom Kippur War started with a surprise attack by Egyptian and Syrian forces on Israel on

October 6, 1973. The war lasted only three weeks, but the effects of it were to politicize the price of oil, which was trading at around $2 to $3 per barrel before October 6. Afterward the Arab oil-producing countries followed Iran (while the Shah was still in office) in declaring they would no longer ship oil to countries that supported Israel in the war, and would substantially reduce production and increase prices. Prices quickly shot up to around $13.50, and then to $15 per barrel by the end of the year, long after a UN cease-fire agreement had ended hostilities. Stock markets around the world plunged, and forecasts were quickly revised to provide for more inflation and less growth in all the OECD countries and in most developing countries.

The immediate impact of this jolt was larger than the Nixon Shock because everyone could imagine the short-run consequences. The cost of production, transportation, and housing would rise everywhere by significant amounts, like a giant global tax increase. A recession would follow, and money would be flowing into the Mideast, which didn't need it, draining it from the world's economic growth engines that did. We, however, had to adapt to be able to capture a share of the reinvestment business. Goldman Sachs was not well known in the Persian Gulf, but Joe Fowler happened to know finance ministers and other officials there, which made a big difference.

The petrodollars flowed to the oil countries, where they were invested in banks' CDs and in short-term deposits, until the governments could figure out what else to do with the money. The deposits were accepted at a discount from LIBID, making them very valuable to the banks if the banks could lend them back out again. But who wanted to borrow when business was headed so far south? Following Walter Wriston's lead at Citibank, the banks quickly rounded up the developing countries and other hardscrabble borrowers to whom they could lend at large spreads over LIBOR, locking in very large lending profits, at least until the loans became "nonperforming."

We found a former high-ranking World Bank official, an Arabic-speaking Iranian, to work with us to line up some business for Goldman Sachs, and managed to help keep the firm off the "Arab Blacklist," which blocked those with known or suspected Israeli ties from doing business with any of the Islamic governments. We figured that a lot of the petro-dollars would find their way to Switzerland (where they would benefit from the secrecy), and therefore the Euromarket might be flooded with surplus cash for a while, which suggested American or Japanese Eurobond deals might be done at good prices. This turned out to be so, at least for a little while, but deteriorating market conditions in the United States, and the lack of need for financing by major American corporations, frustrated our plans. Nevertheless, the oil shock, which induced runaway inflation around the world and caused a great deal of financial distress, put a premium on innovation and adaptability that had not existed before, and competition for business in financial services began to reflect that premium. The 1970s were trying years for Wall Street, and as a result, many traditional client relationships were changed.

The Volcker Shock

Inflation soared throughout the Carter years, from 1976 to 1980. The Iranian Revolution, in which the Shah was overthrown, occurred in 1979, pushing the price of oil from an already difficult-to-manage $15 per barrel to over $40. Also in that year, the Soviet Union invaded Afghanistan and gold hit a peak of $680 per ounce, nineteen times what it had been before the Nixon Shock. Short-term U.S. government interest rates were over 10 percent and rising. Despite this level of rates, however, real interest rates (i.e., actual interest rates less the inflation rate) were still negative—there was still a lot of money in the markets looking to be loaned or invested. In October 1979, Federal Reserve chairman Paul Volcker, appointed by Jimmy Carter and in office for only a few months, decided that inflation, which had reached 13 percent, had to be reversed no matter what it took. He cranked up interest rates to prohibitive levels. This was accomplished by dramatically shrinking the money supply and, in doing so, affecting a change in monetary policy, according to Federal Reserve historian William Greider, "without precedent in modern experience":

> In a few short months, the Fed had nearly doubled the price of money. Despite the technical complexities, that was the essential meaning of Volcker's operating shift—the dramatic ratcheting upward in interest rates. A few months before, the governors had been arguing over half-percent increases. Now the Fed was pushing the Federal Funds rate from 11 percent towards 20 percent. And other short-term rates followed in step.[4]

All this, the first really forceful use of monetary policy by the Federal Reserve in its history, affected the economy immediately. The stock and bond markets plunged—the 1970s were full of such plunges—unemployment rose sharply, and by the early part of 1980, recession set in just as Jimmy Carter was trying to run for reelection. Real interest rates soon turned positive, reaching 4+ percent by 1981, and the inflation was checked. By the end of 1982, gold had dropped to $300 per ounce, nominal interest rates were declining, the dollar was rising, and America's new president, Ronald Reagan, had reappointed Volcker as Fed chairman.

For our little group at Goldman Sachs, the Volcker shock was profound. It enabled Reagan to be elected, for the market to gain confidence as economic indicators began to look better, and for foreign investors in U.S. securities to be soothed. Perhaps it also assisted Reagan in getting his tax cut through Congress, which he did with very little opposition. But it certainly teed up a great bull market in stocks and bonds that both enabled and symbolized the 1980s. Nowhere, however, did it have more impact than in the Euromarkets.

THE EUROMARKETS COME OF AGE

The Swiss banks were engorged with cash, partly from the oil-producing regions but also from Japan and other regions in which they had invested during the 1970s, giving the troubled United States a pass. With interest rates falling and the dollar rising, they were more than ready to get back to acquiring dollar-denominated stocks and bonds. But the Swiss have strict rules on preserving client secrecy, and will not buy bonds unless they are in bearer form and free of withholding taxes imposed by tax authorities of the issuers' countries. Client names were not to be given out to bond registrars or tax authorities requesting investor identification. The U.S. Treasury does not issue bearer bonds, so the Swiss could not buy Treasuries, which they might have preferred. They could, however, buy double- or triple-A-rated bonds of well-known U.S. corporations instead, but only if these were made available free of withholding tax, which domestically issued bonds are not. So American companies issued Eurobonds through a guaranteed subsidiary located in a tax haven with no withholding, and that seemed to work for everybody. But the 1970s had not generated a lot of U.S. corporate Eurodollar bonds, and the secondary market was fairly illiquid, so there weren't many Eurodollar bonds of U.S. corporations to buy, which gave those that were in existence a scarcity premium.

A Feeding Frenzy

Some of the Swiss began to reach out to large creditworthy American companies to do business with them at low interest rates; they were effectively making them offers they couldn't refuse in order to create a supply of bonds sufficient to meet their clients' demand. For example, if Procter and Gamble, an AAA-rated household-name client of Goldman Sachs, wanted to raise $100 million in the New York market, it might have had to pay 8 percent—say, 50 basis points over the comparable maturity U.S. Treasury bond, after all costs and expenses. We might have gone to a large Swiss bank and offered to co-manage with them a $100 million Eurodollar bond at an all-in cost to P&G of, say, 7.85 percent. The Swiss would share in the underwriting fees, charge its clients its usual high brokerage commission, and the client would be delighted to own the bonds, which were rising in value relative to Swiss francs, because of the strengthening dollar. These deals set off a feeding frenzy in London that not only had the Swiss running around trying to get in on all the deals, but also telegraphed the investment appeal of the bonds to other, somewhat similar non-dollar investors, such as the large government-owned investment funds in the UK, Norway, Kuwait, Singapore, and elsewhere; European pension funds; and Japanese insurance companies, which had large amounts to invest. Before long, AAA-rated U.S. companies (and some well-known names with less than AAA ratings) were tapping the Eurodollar bond markets at rates reflecting not a premium over U.S. Treasuries, but a discount—something that could never happen in the United States.

In 1982, I was in charge of Goldman Sachs's European business, and based in London. In that year, more new issues of high-grade corporate debt were made by U.S. companies in London than in New York. My partners in New York were astonished when I informed them of this statistic: nothing like that had ever happened before. "How could it be?" they asked. "London is just a backwater business for us. How did all this happen?"

The "Bought Deal"

In the late 1960s, a few American firms began to participate as underwriters in the Eurobond market, and a leadership role was forged early by White Weld, which created an innovative though complex joint venture with Credit Suisse, the second-largest bank in Switzerland. This venture combined White Weld's new-issue expertise with Credit Suisse's extensive placing power. In 1978, when White Weld was acquired by Merrill Lynch, Credit Suisse arranged for First Boston to replace White Weld in the partnership. After some management turmoil in which several senior people were replaced at the new firm, the investment banking arm was headed by Michael von Clemm, a colorful American onetime anthropologist and restaurateur who covered the world in search of new business. The Eurobond syndication and sales business of CSFB became the preserve of Hans-Joerg Rudloff, a talented young Eurobond salesman who was rescued from Kidder Peabody's European syndicate desk in 1980, just as the market began to explode. Rudloff knew everything about the Eurobond market, which he had been in since the mid-1960s. Though he was German, he hung out with the reclusive Swiss bond traders, spoke "Schweizerdeutsche" (the Swiss German dialect of Zurich) with them, shared their inside jokes, and became one of the boys.

From the beginning, Rudloff had the confidence of Rainer Gut, Credit Suisse's Americanized chairman, who had great ambitions for the bank in the Eurobond business. Rudloff was a bold innovator who would carefully plot his next moves with Gut to be sure he had the necessary backing to protect him from second-guessers if the schemes went wrong. He also had the placing power of the Credit Suisse portfolios on his side, as long as he stuck to doing business with clients the Swiss portfolio managers approved of.

Rudloff and von Clemm soon became famous for making offers to issuers—U.S., European, and Asian blue-chip companies—to buy large quantities of their Eurobonds at what the rest of us in the market thought were extremely low interest rates. Rudloff, while at Kidder, had astonished the market by offering to buy an entire bond issue from the government of New Zealand in 1975, thereby committing the firm to a huge underwriting risk without syndication, in order to pressure the issuer into accepting his aggressively priced terms on the spot, which New Zealand did in a flash. This was the first "bought deal" to appear in the Euromarket, and there was some indication that Kidder's New York partners were horrified by it, but when Rudloff relocated to CSFB, bought deals reappeared in a flurry. Once he had the mandate to control the bonds, he would call in favors, twist arms, and make aggressive promises to sell them, but mainly he would rely upon the cover that his relationship with Gut provided for him, and the eagerness of Credit Suisse's portfolio managers to load up on high-grade dollar-denominated Eurobonds at almost any price. Their wealthy, secretive, tax-avoiding customers were not very familiar with market rates, and didn't seem to worry too much about whether they were getting the best rates. Anyway, where else could they go if they were unhappy?

This was a tough business for investment banks without captive Swiss clients and forgiving chairmen. Goldman Sachs, for example, could not sell Eurobonds to an institutional investor unless they were discounted to yield market rates, and the discount had to come from our share of the commission. This left us with a pretty small margin to apply to markets that could be very volatile, and where the actions of other underwriters to dump unsold bonds as quickly as possible could spoil whatever secondary market there was.

But Rudloff or his colleagues could call up well-known companies they liked, offer them below-market financing without any waiting to test the market, seize the mandate, and then start to call other prominent European banks (but not CSFB's Swiss competitors) seeking to establish their reputations as managers of Eurobonds and invite them into the deal to take two thirds or more of it. Many of these banks could stuff the paper into their managed accounts, or sell it in the market as soon as they committed themselves to taking it on, or hold it for a while, hoping for market prices to rise as the dollar strengthened and interest rates declined further, a trend that prevailed from 1983 to 1986.

The effect of this was to tighten the wires on the market and force bankers to bid to purchase deals at even lower interest rates, then lower still. The market had started to come up with further innovations to help deliver low-cost financing deals to eager issuers. Bonds were issued with warrants attached to enable the investor to buy more of the same bonds, or of something else. Warrant pricing was inexact then, but there was nevertheless plenty of demand in those days of rising markets. Or a bond could be bought with a coupon of zero, with all of the interest appreciation in the bond to be repaid at maturity with a higher principal amount (like a U.S. savings bond). In Japan, tax authorities did not count accrued income as taxable ordinary income, so for Japanese investors, zero-coupon bonds (the appreciation on which was taxed as capital gains) could be low-yielding but still provide a superior after-tax investment return. The flow of innovation was impressive, and steadily new issue rates declined in Europe for U.S. corporations with A ratings or better. From 1983 to 1986, Eurobond new issues tripled, and most investment banks had to scramble to hang on to their corporate clients, who were getting unsolicited calls from Rudloff and von Clemm, and their U.S. colleagues Paul Downey and Charles Murphy, who were offering them deals they could not refuse. CSFB originated a large percentage of Eurobond deals and dominated the league tables for Eurobonds for many years. Corporations of course took advantage of the competition for their business, the low rates, and the ability to enter the market instantly and fix the cost of funds over the telephone after a short auction process.

Rule 415 Europeanizes America

This was something they couldn't do in the United States. Securities laws required the filing of a registration statement with the SEC, beginning a processing period while the SEC reviewed the registration, which ended when the SEC permitted the issue to be sold to the public. The entire process took about thirty days, and there was no way to avoid a waiting period, during which time markets could deteriorate; nor was there an opportunity to select underwriters based on the lowest cost bid for the issue; the underwriters couldn't bid before they were allowed to sell the securities. As a consequence, corporations saw no advantage to maintaining relations with multiple underwriters; they had their main, exclusive investment banker and possibly a co-manager, and these were rarely changed. But once they started getting calls from London, they changed their tune. They were interested in lower-cost deals and competition for their business, so they encouraged the competition as much as they could.

In time, the SEC realized that a great deal of the corporate bond business was leaving U.S. markets, and sought to attract it back by offering similar conditions for issuing new securities as prevailed in Europe. This meant, in effect, a deregulation of U.S. new issuance rules to match a more liberal regime existing in another market, one that had grown to be a significant competitor to the U.S. corporate bond market. The SEC didn't want to admit that there was anything wrong with the way it had regulated markets for the past fifty years, but it had to find a way to justify a major change to its new issuance rules that would allow it to match the easier, quicker, and cheaper market access features of the Euromarket. So it conceived the idea of an "integrated disclosure" system, in which it relied on the "perfect market" notions advanced by finance academics, which asserted that once information was released to the market, it was fully absorbed and distributed and its effect on prices was immediate.

This being the case, the SEC said, once a registration statement containing information about a new issue is filed, it can be assumed that the information is distributed, and therefore a lengthy review process for already regulated companies was unnecessary. This was a good, if involuntary move to protect the competitive relevance of U.S. corporate bond markets. In 1984, the SEC approved Rule 415, the so-called "shelf-registration rule," that enabled companies to register securities in advance of issuing them, and then, when they were ready to go, to issue them "off the shelf." This had a huge effect on U.S. investment banking relationships, because it meant that companies could auction off their new issues of bonds to the highest bidder, and of course many companies did just that, which ended the days of exclusive banking relationships and introduced an era of priced-based competition (as opposed to the relationship-based system that had existed for years) for all forms of the investment banking business. This also lowered the cost of new debt issues for companies by making the underwriting commission negotiable or, in fact, making it disappear, as new bond issues began to be sold to underwriters in the United States on a bought-deal basis at an all-in interest cost.

With Rule 415, much of the value added in creating a new security moved from its manufacturer to its issuer. But it had a further, equally important effect. It encouraged corporations to search international as well as domestic markets for the best offer for their bonds, setting up an auction between not just bankers in the same market, but also bankers in all markets—the Eurobond market, and national markets in countries such as Japan, Australia, or Switzerland, in which local currency bonds could be issued with currency swaps or other forms of derivatives contracts that effectively created a synthetic dollar liability at a lower cost. This effort to search all the world's debt markets for the best financing opportunities based on tax, foreign exchange, regulatory, or other market changes helped to integrate these global markets, with pricing anomalies and similar inefficiencies being arbitraged out.

Another rule was introduced by the SEC in 1990 that permitted foreign issuers of debt and equity to issue securities in the United States without having to register them with the SEC. Rule 144a provided for "private placement" treatment of these, or any other issues of securities, as long as the investor was a "qualified institutional buyer," or QIB. Private placements are exempt from registration requirements, but they must be sold only to sophisticated investors: qualified institutions and wealthy individuals. Rule 144a, however, allowed such investments to be resold to other QIBs, which the previous private placement rules did not. Thus the securities could be traded among QIBs, where a reasonably liquid market soon developed that priced the securities at about the same level as an issue of registered securities sold by the same issuer. This was an especially useful breakthrough for emerging market securities, for which an appetite developed in the United States in the early 1990s. Subsequently, debt and equity issues by companies from China, Brazil, or Russia, for example, could be sold in the United States even though the issues had been registered only in their own countries.

THE BIG BANG

On October 27, 1986, what seemed to be an earth-shuddering event took place in the City of London, the square-mile financial center of Britain that dates back to the time of the Norman Conquest. The event, called "the Big Bang" by British wags, was one that would change forever the lives and the businesses of almost everyone who worked in the City, and indeed had already done so in anticipation. City life would never be the same. The rules of the stock exchange had been changed, and because of this, the old cliquish ways and traditions had been blown away and swept into the Thames. New rules, appearing like little green shoots, were now in force, but these innocent-appearing new rules would change British financial markets beyond recognition.

As a result, nineteen of the twenty largest stock brokerage firms in the UK were sold, and so were all of the principal "jobbers," or dealers, whose function was most closely paralleled in New York by Stock Exchange "specialists." Stock exchange transactions in London would now occur through a brand-new, just-installed, electronic market-making system that closely resembled NASDAQ. As in New York, brokerage commissions would be negotiated, not fixed, and membership of the stock exchange would be open to any qualified applicant: bank, broker, jobber, or foreign investment bank. These simple reforms destroyed the capital market system that Walter Bagehot, the editor of *The Economist*, described in 1873 as one of the crown jewels of the British Empire. What would replace it—a new, robust and more competitive marketplace—would be efficient, effective, and still located in the City of London, but it wouldn't be British. That is, after a few years there would be no British-owned firms among the market leaders.

This all started innocently enough. In 1976, a Labour government, mindful of the Mayday reforms in New York, passed a law extending the application of laws affecting restrictive practices in business to the service sector. The London Stock Exchange, along with travel agents and real estate brokers, were asked to present their "rule books" to the Office of Fair Trading (OTF) for inspection. The OTF found 150 of the Stock Exchange's hundred-year-old rules to be in violation of restrictive-practices laws and brought a lawsuit against the Exchange in 1979, just before the selection of Margaret Thatcher as prime minister. The Stock Exchange regarded the whole matter as a nuisance, and assumed that the new Conservative prime minister would call off the dogs. But they didn't understand their new leader very well. She turned out to be a dyed-in-the-wool free market advocate, and figured the OFT had a point. She had big plans to privatize many of Britain's state-owned enterprises, accumulated during nationalization binges by Labour governments of the past. To do that, she knew, would require a lot of support from capital markets, which would need to be brought up to world-class competitive form to do so. She sent a junior minister to the Exchange with instructions to negotiate a settlement, which ended up bringing about three main rule changes: commissions would be negotiable, members could act as brokers or jobbers or both (but would no longer be restricted to acting in only one such capacity), and membership would have to be opened to anyone qualified who wanted to join. It seemed simple but proved to be anything but.

In 1980, the London Stock Exchange was the largest and most active of all stock exchanges in Europe, of which there were many. Since Bagehot's day, London had been the financial capital of Britain; and the Stock Exchange, the principal market for securities. Also since Bagehot's day, Britain had been Europe's leading practitioner of market economics, and the location of most of Europe's publicly traded corporations. British companies engaged in IPOs, other new share issues, and mergers and acquisitions far more than companies from other European countries. Because the London Stock Exchange had initiated a NASDAQ-like trading market, it was easy for it to extend this market to other large non-UK European companies in which UK and other international investors traded. This extended market-traded shares in French, Dutch, German, and other companies. Most of Europe's institutional trading in these shares was done on the London system, and volume had been increasing as cross-border capital controls were withdrawn following the collapse of the Bretton Woods Agreement. Britain's own foreign exchange controls, in place for sixty-five years, were removed by Mrs. Thatcher in 1979.

The old rules of the Stock Exchange, however, had turned the City of London into a rabbit warren in which there were many different types of players, and these players were kept separate from the others, presumably to protect livelihoods from excessive competition. Brokers could be only brokers (they could not trade); jobbers could be only dealers (and thus they could not be brokers); merchant bankers (similar to investment bankers) were underwriters of stocks and bonds, but could not be either dealers or brokers. Commercial banks and insurance companies could be none of these things. Compared with Wall Street after Mayday, most of the firms were quite small, held very little capital, employed a lot of people for relatively little money, and were not very profitable. They had traditional, long-standing clients who had dealt with them for years, without much regard for performance. Brokers, jobbers, and merchant bankers in the City all knew each other professionally or socially (from schools or university—usually Oxford or Cambridge) and were from upper-middle-class families. Some were from the nobility or higher classes. They did little marketing, enjoyed long wine-filled lunches and the opera, and left early on Fridays for their weekends in the country. But they were also smart, quick-witted, and charming, and could be innovative, untiring, and thorough in the service of their clients, who were loyal to them.

But the deal with the OFT, which was announced in 1983 with a three-year delay before implementation, changed the economics of the Stock Exchange and shook it all apart.

An English broker faced with having to negotiate rates and increased competition only had to look to the United States for a picture of what was likely to happen. Rates would be negotiated to a level much lower than present rates. Competition would become dog-eat-dog and he would lose some clients and have to compete to get others to replace them. The firm's ability to pay for research, entertainment, and other necessities of a more competitive universe would be diminished by the reduced cash flow. Unless it could find another business, such as jobbing, to supplement revenues, it would be unlikely to survive. So brokers had to arrange to become dealers, and vice versa, though there were far more brokers serving the market than there were jobbers. Mergers would perhaps help, but mergers with whom? Other firms like theirs might not be able to offer enough capital support and know-how to be able to put together a full-service firm quickly. Joining a merchant bank might be a way out, but would they want them? Only S. G. Warburg was talking about building a new, integrated firm to become the Morgan Stanley or Goldman Sachs of the UK. It had already agreed to a three-way merger with a leading broker and a top jobber. The rest of the merchant banks seemed to be confident that they could continue to survive on their own, as they had before, by "living on their wits." Some large UK and other commercial banks were in the market to acquire some broker-dealer capacity, but would they be a competitive platform once put together? One thing was clear: brokers and jobbers had to join together to survive, and competition was going to get a lot worse, including increasing competition from the Americans, who were already broker/dealers/investment bankers/underwriters and had had at least a decade to sort our negotiated rates before Big Bang became effective.

Integrated Investment Banking

We were offered a number of brokers and jobbers to buy if we wanted to. We didn't bite because we didn't have to. The rule changes favored firms such as Goldman Sachs greatly. We could become members of an exchange that had previously excluded us. We could become market makers in British stocks and offer to trade with British institutional investors in blocks of stock, position their orders, and provide them with high-grade research on British stocks, which would enable us to develop a share of the UK market comparable to our share of the U.S. market. Indeed, we had a big advantage during the three-year waiting period before Big Bang went off. We had been trading with UK institutions in UK stocks for some time—through American ADRs* traded in New York, where negotiated commissions were lower and the British stamp tax on stock trades could be avoided. In fact, we traded with these institutions in the morning in Japanese stocks, and in the afternoon in U.S. and UK and other European stocks, something the UK brokers were incapable of doing. Our market share was already increasing, well before Big Bang actually took place. In the longer term, Big Bang legitimized us in the London market beyond being broker-dealers, by removing our foreign identity. If we could offer other ideas and services that were better and more user-friendly, we could earn a lot of business that would establish

---

*American depositary receipts, representing a specified number of foreign shares, are held in the United States and traded there in dollars.

our reputation. We could be as British as anyone else by hiring and promoting British employees—which we did—but also, by becoming members of the Exchange and trading in their securities, we would become in time no different from any British firm. This identity shift took a while to work through, but it made a huge change in our business strategy, and its economics. In time, as reforms similar to Big Bang were also adopted by necessity in France, Germany, Japan, and ultimately most of the rest of the world, the world securities markets became more integrated, more competitive and efficient, and more remunerative as we and other American firms who were willing to spend the money, time, and effort to become global players found ourselves welcomed in the indigenous business of our clients as well as their international business.

PRIVATIZATIONS

In 1979, when Margaret Thatcher became prime minister of Great Britain, the economy was a mess. The last prime minister from the Conservative Party was Edward Heath, who left office in 1974 after caving in to a coal miners' strike that had paralyzed the economy into a state of "stagflation," or stagnation with high inflation. Heath was succeeded by two different Labour governments that continued their party's policy of turning Britain's economy into a welfare state by, among other things, nationalizing several industries with high employment, such as coal, railways, steel, shipbuilding, aerospace, aviation, energy, communications, and parts of the automobile industry. In 1975, expenditures by the government sector, central and local, reached 50 percent of gross domestic product.

The Conservative Party needed a change, and selected Thatcher, a youthful and feisty free market advocate, over several older, more experienced men, to succeed Heath as party leader in 1975. Four years later she became Britain's first (and as yet only) woman prime minister. She served as prime minister until 1990, the longest tenure of continuous service of any prime minister for more than a hundred years. She was a disciple of Milton Friedman and an economic soul mate of her American opposite number, Ronald Reagan. She set her course and stuck to it, challenging unions, local governments, even the City of London on her way to rescuing the nearly socialized economy of Britain in order to fling it into the powerful and frightening jaws of free market capitalism.

Her grand vision of Britain's future included cutting taxes, removing foreign exchange controls, denationalizing the many nationalized sectors of industry, reforming old institutions (from the stock exchanges to the universities), and making everything work in a fully competitive, open environment. She took over at a time when the great British voting public, mostly working class, had lost confidence in the policies and governing abilities of the Labour Party and believed that even a conservative woman with the management style of an old English nanny would be better than more of the same from Labour. She believed that if her policies were allowed breathing space for five to ten years, they would be able to demonstrate success and no one would want to turn back to socialism again. She was right.

The key to her program was denationalizing British industry. But it was not going to be easy to implement such a program—yes, there were political problems in selling the program to the people, and in getting the necessary legislation passed, but even then the burden on capital markets was enormous. Big Bang would take time to implement, but even with its reforms, a vast quantity of stock in numerous large, often poorly performing British companies, valued at many billions of pounds, would have to the sold on the market.

Such concerns did not deter Thatcher. Her driving instinct was to set the large industrial enterprises owned by the state free of featherbedding, subsidies, concessions to unions, and general inefficiency, to turn them into profitable, growing, tax-paying, wealth-creating private-sector companies that would lead Britain into another economic renaissance. She knew that her opposition would charge her with selling the real crown jewels of Britain to fat cats and foreigners, and forcing wave after wave of layoffs and job losses to pass through every town and village in the realm. It would be a tough sell, she figured, but she never hesitated to get on with it. The process, soon to be called privatization, would involve selling shares in the companies to be denationalized in large public offerings in British and overseas equity markets.

The first such issue occurred in November 1979, when £280 million in British Petroleum (BP) shares were sold in a coordinated global underwriting. BP was already a well-performing public corporation (majority owned by the government), so a new market for its shares did not have to be created. This issue, though large for the British market, was easily sold, with a modest portion being allocated to overseas investors. A number of similar issues of smaller companies followed, and their shares were substantially oversubscribed, resulting in the share prices popping up above the offering price when trading was permitted. Some critics focused on this as an indicator that the government was giving the shares away at below-market prices. The next issue was much more ambitious, a £549 million issue—Britain's largest ever stock offering—for British National Oil Company (its North Sea oil franchise). The government pushed back against the underwriters on the offering price, and the market was weak when the issue came, so the share price dropped after the offering, indicating that it had been overpriced, not underpriced. The government continued to march right along, regardless of market conditions or anything else, and in November 1984 it successfully sold £3.9 billion in British Telecom shares.

This was an enormous deal, one that could not have been done without huge participation from the British general public, which had little history of share ownership. The offering was supported by a massive marketing effort supported by television advertising. Retail investors could pay in installments, and were offered bonus shares for holding the shares they bought. About 20 percent of the issue was allocated to institutional investors in the United States, Europe, and Japan, the rest being aimed at retail investors. The issue was oversubscribed and did very well. Thousands of British families bought shares in the company to have a stake in its future for their children. All of the privatization issues since 1979 were trading above their offering prices, and many British families were enjoying the benefits of a rising market for the first time. Indeed, the public was enjoying being investors, the new supply of shares had greatly increased trading volume on the London exchange, and opposition to privatization began to fade away.

Meanwhile, the deals continued and got even larger. Six weeks after Big Bang went into effect, a £5.4 billion issue of shares for British Gas hit the market. This time, the foreign tranche was made part of the UK underwriting effort for the first time. This was different from U.S. underwriting, in which the deal was filed with the SEC, marketed, then priced and sold. In the UK, issues are sold through front-end underwritten subscription offerings. Underwriters announce their commitment to purchase the entire deal at a set price, after which a subscription period of about two weeks begins, during which time investors are invited to subscribe to the offering. At the end of the subscription period, the subscriptions are counted up and if there is a shortfall, the underwriters take up the difference; if an excess, the subscriptions are reduced pro rata. But such offerings are exposed to market risk during the subscription period. If the market drops, investors will hold back, preferring the buy the stock after the underwriters start selling off the shares purchased by them. The British Gas deal came off without a hitch, setting the stage for the next jumbo-size privatization issue.

This was a £7 billion issue by British Petroleum, designed to sell off the last of the government's shares, 31 percent of the company. This was the first British privatization issue valued at more than $12 billion, which was then more than twenty times the size of the largest ever U.S. stock offering.* It was huge, but the market seemed to be willing. Unfortunately, this deal had the bad luck to have the middle of its subscription period occur on October 19, 1987, the day the Dow Jones Industrial Average plunged more than five hundred points, or 22 percent, affecting stock markets everywhere. The price of BP shares dropped about 30 percent, so when the subscription period ended, there were no subscriptions whatsoever; the entire issue went back to the underwriters. As only about one third of the deal was actually underwritten—the other two thirds were set aside to be purchased by investors under deferred purchase arrangements designed to provide a financing advantage to subscribers—the damage was less than it could have been, but even so, the four Wall Street firms sharing the underwriting burden for the $1 billion U.S. allocation of the deal, Goldman Sachs, Morgan Stanley, Salomon Brothers, and Shearson Lehman Brothers, together lost about $250 million.[5] The underwriters appealed to Thatcher to recognize force majeure and either call off the deal or modify it in some way, but they underestimated her tenacity. "A deal's a deal," she said, and refused to change anything, though later the Bank of England offered to put a floor on the stock price to prevent further losses. It was a hard lesson, but the underwriters, including the forlorn Americans, stuck it out, and it closed on time. The following year the privatization parade continued in the UK, with no changes in the front-end underwriting method that determined how the deals would be done.

Thatcher's success with privatizations, which included some pretty quick turnaround results for some of the industrial companies released from the government's stable of state-owned enterprises, caught the attention first of Britain's European rivals, who adopted the same policies for their state-owned companies, of which the French seemed to have the

---

* In February 1987, Nippon Telephone, also valued at about $12.5 billion, was privatized in Japan.

most. All of these governments needed to raise cash, reduce the government's borrowings, and stimulate economic growth with greater competition. Subsequently, privatization spread as well to Japan and, during the 1990s, to the rest of Asia and emerging-market countries. During the 1980s, privatization issues totaled about $100 billion, and expanded several times beyond that in the 1990s. These issues were great windfalls of opportunity for the investment banks, but to win positions as lead underwriters of the global or U.S. placement tranches they first had to adapt their businesses to be able to market their capabilities to senior officials in ministries of finance and central banks all over the world, to be able to adapt their distribution capabilities to handle large IPOs from all sorts of foreign countries, and to be able to support these issues in the secondary markets with research coverage and market making. Investment banks might have done all these things in due course anyway, but the privatization wave that started in 1984 and lasted for about fifteen years certainly justified doing it sooner and to a greater extent, thus accelerating the organic internationalization of Wall Street.

THE RISING SUN

In 1969, Joe Fowler, another senior partner, and I made a three-week trip to Japan to scout out opportunities there for Goldman Sachs. Joe was well known in Japan, having struggled with the government on balance-of-payments issued when he was U.S. secretary of the treasury, and he was respected and well liked. The other senior partner, Charles Saltzman, had made an annual pass-through to show the flag, but had not generated any business. I was assigned at random to accompany them, take notes, and assist them in making a report to the management committee suggesting the firm's future actions. Japan then was bristling with promise and opportunity, much of it fairly far down the road. Several of our competitors had been active in Japan since the 1960s, when the World Bank declared Japan capable of raising funds from international markets—First Boston had done a bond issue for the government, and Morgan Stanley, ever the darling of the prestige-conscious Japanese, was closing in on the major industrial groups. We had done an equity issue in the early 1960s for a small motorcycle manufacturer named Honda, and other firms had pulled off occasional deals for Sony and other high-growth electronics companies.

Japan had returned to life economically during the Korean War (when U.S. purchases of supplies there created a boom) and had continued to grow at more than 10 percent a year through the 1960s, thanks to an extraordinarily high domestic savings rate and a combined cooperative effort between government economic planners, business, and labor that pundits at the time called "Japan, Inc." Japan was a low-cost manufacturing site with a high level of technical and industrial know-how that had been developed before the war. It copied things, made them cheaper, and exported them in droves to the United States and elsewhere, but mainly to the United States, which was the world's largest consumer market for everything. This created decades of tensions between U.S. and Japanese trade officials, but Americans appreciated the low-cost textiles, consumer electronics, automobiles, and other increasing high-tech products made in Japan. This process, we believed, would continue for many years, and Japanese companies would need financing from abroad, though their own equity market, infused by foreign investment, had developed surprisingly well. Joe Fowler and the rest of us recommended that Goldman Sachs join the group of foreign investment banks competing for business in Japan, and the management committee designated me as the point man for this effort, a position I would occupy for about ten years.

Japanese companies mainly relied on Japanese banks to finance their continuous need for funds for new plants and equipment. Most Japanese companies had little equity and a lot of debt on their balance sheets and were not looked upon as good credit risks by foreign investors. Japanese companies seeking to issue bonds could do so in the early years only by having a bank guaranty the debt. But their stocks were attractive, so before long, companies began to issue convertible debentures in the markets overseas, while continuing to use their domestic markets for new stock issues.

The oil shock was hard on Japan, which imported almost all of its oil, and afterward its growth rate was cut approximately in half. After the shock, Japanese companies began to increase their overseas financings, and most of these ended up in the Euromarket, where access to the markets was quicker, cheaper, and less subject to complex and burdensome SEC regulation. Goldman Sachs opened an office in Tokyo in the early 1970s to chase after corporate financing, principally Eurobond issues, in competition with investment banks from the United States, merchant banks from the UK, and universal banks from Europe. Most issues were convertibles debentures, in the early days, then straight (bank-guaranteed) debt with detachable stock-purchase warrants became more popular. Occasionally a brave company would elect to try a registered issue in the United States.

Japanese companies were not very sophisticated financially in the 1970s and 1980s. When they needed money they would ask their "main" bank for it. The bank would usually just send it over, but sometimes they might suggest that the firm raise some additional equity to support the growing amount of debt. Then the company would speak to its "main" investment bank, and it would decide what the company should do: issue stock in Japan or something else overseas. Sometimes the process would change a little if the company wanted to keep up with its competitors (by doing similar issues) or showing off that it could do better. Still, the process put a lot of the power for deciding in the hands of the Japanese investment bank with which the company had a close relationship. So, before long, all the foreign investment banks had to beat a path to the doorsteps of Nomura, Nikko, Daiwa, or Yamaichi securities firms to get or confirm a mandate.

During the 1980s, the situation changed in many ways, but essentially was much the same in a supercharged sort of way. It was supercharged because during the 1980s, the Japanese stock markets went through the roof during a feeding frenzy in the markets that drew in surplus funds from Japanese corporations, new pension accounts, and scads of money from abroad. During the decade, price-earnings ratios were boosted to average over 70 in 1989 (the average price-earnings ratio in the United States then was 14). Japanese companies could raise capital for overseas investments (such as the purchase of Rockefeller Center, Firestone Tire Company, Pebble Beach Golf Course, and Columbia Pictures, among many other high-profile and expensive acquisitions, including a surprising $500 million investment in one eighth of Goldman Sachs—with no votes—acquired by Sumitomo Bank in 1987; this last proved to be a terrific investment for Sumitomo and very low cost capital for Goldman Sachs, but the deal was difficult to complete because it intruded on the Federal Reserve's notions about the Glass-Steagall and the Bank Holding Company laws, though these were resolved by limiting the scope of interaction between the two firms).

The Japanese issued more Eurobonds in the period 1984–1989 than did companies from any other country. Altogether, they issued approximately $330 billion in equity-related debt securities in Europe, and another $294 billion in the domestic Japanese markets, far more than U.S.

companies issued at the time. In 1987, 1988, and 1989, the market capitalization of stocks listed in Japan exceeded the dollar value of stocks listed in the United States, and in 1988 and 1989, the value of shares traded in Japan exceeded the value of shares traded in the United States, even though more than half of all Japanese shares were held in institutional crossholdings and never traded. In the 1980s, Japanese stock prices increased sixfold (reflecting a compounded growth rate for a decade of 18 percent), compared to a mere threefold increase in the United States during the best of the Reagan years. In December 1989, the Nikkei Dow Jones index closed at an all-time high of 38,916.[6]

During this period, the stock market underwrote Japanese corporate expansion and overseas investments everywhere. Sumitomo's investment in Goldman Sachs was financed by the issuance of $500 million in new shares in the bank at a price-earnings ratio of 100, suggesting a cost of capital of about 1 percent. But also, the rising stock prices added capital to the Japanese banks, because Japan had allowed its banks to count the after-tax value of their holdings of shares in client companies as capital.* The banks held a great deal of these shares, which were bursting in value. The increased value of the banks' capital encouraged them to make more aggressive loans to borrowers in Japan (collateralized by stock or real estate holdings) and to foreign corporations and governments.

In December 1989, the whole thing blew up. The bubble burst, and share prices plunged to a fraction of what they had been before. Japan's financial system broke apart as margin loans were called, bankruptcies proliferated, and shady deals were uncovered everywhere. All of the securities firms and most of the large banks were involved in various ways in scandals that required the resignation of CEOs and, in some cases, the failure of their firms. Yamaichi Securities went bust, and Daiwa and Nikko had to be rescued. Banks suddenly found themselves facing a mountain of loan losses that effectively shut them down for a decade and forced most of them into one form of merger or another, which over about a fifteen-year period ended up rolling all the major banks into three megabank successors. Japan's role as a financial powerhouse of bank lending and securities issuance suddenly came to an end, though its high savings rate continued to attract the attention of investment managers. The chaos that descended on Japanese financial markets was increased by the pressure

---

* Japanese banks did not have loan loss reserves, so their holdings in these shares were deemed to be an equivalent.

on Japan to effect a Big Bang to reorganize and open up its capital markets to foreign competition. During the entire 1990s, and most of the 2000s, Japan was occupied sorting out and restructuring its financial markets, with the result that large foreign banks, such as Goldman Sachs and its usual competitors, are now able to play much more extensive roles in institutional markets on both the new issue and investment sides.

EMERGING MARKETS

The first time I heard the term "emerging market," it was applied to Germany. It meant that in Germany, capital markets had begun to emerge from their inactive past to become a serious source of finance for corporations and opportunity for investors. Germany and the rest of continental Europe experienced the transition to active capital markets in the 1980s, but the phrase continued to live on based on the progress being made by several developing countries seeking to adopt free market economic policies and governance so as to increase growth and the viability of their own capital markets. These countries initially included the so-called Asian Tigers (Korea, Taiwan, Singapore, and Hong Kong) and later were expanded to include other countries after the latest round of third world debt restructuring, which occurred in the later years of the 1980s.

Third World Debt

After the lending binge of petrodollars in the 1970s, many borrowing countries fell behind in their payments of interest and principal on their loans. Economic conditions were difficult, but much of the money borrowed by the countries was poorly invested, wasted, or stolen and the borrowings produced less growth than the cost of the money. The banks, buoyed by their confidence in being able to reschedule as necessary to avoid default, began to advance additional loans by capitalizing interest. The total amount of this debt to developing countries—by 1988, Brazil owed $82 billion; Mexico, $78 billion—began to loom ominously over the banks, and their regulators began to show concern. At the end of the 1980s the U.S. government put forward a plan by which borrowing countries could purchase a long-term zero-coupon U.S. Treasury note (all of the interest and principal would be paid to investors only at maturity) to use as collateral for new long-term bonds to be offered in exchange for outstanding (defaulted) bank loans. The new bonds, called Brady bonds in honor of the U.S. secretary of the treasury at the time, Nicholas Brady, a former senior partner of Dillon Read, were priced to reflect a substantial discount in the value of the bank loans being exchanged—i.e., reflecting the estimated market price of the defaulted loans—so the banks participating in the exchange had to realize substantial losses in doing so, but if they didn't exchange, they might be left with loans that would be nearly worthless. The banks accepted the exchange offers rather than wait endlessly for government-to-government negotiations that might pay them something many years in the future. This was the first market-based exchange offer to resolve excessive third world debt.

The exchange offers involved a vast amount of new Brady bonds, which most banks were eager to sell when they got them. These bonds began to trade actively in New York and London, and soon market prices for the credit of the various countries involved began to appear, and the spread (or difference) between the yield to investors of the bonds could be compared to U.S. Treasury bonds of the same maturity. Salomon Brothers and Shearson Lehman were early leaders in making markets in the Brady bonds and, in time, in the distressed bonds of developing countries not backed up by the Brady collateral. With bond trading active in such debt, a demand immediately surfaced for bond ratings, and the rating agencies (Moody's and Standard & Poor's) complied and began to publish ratings.

The market for third world bonds was speculative, but so was the market for junk bonds. However, bond prices could rise because the credit ratings improved, liquidity increased, or because governments promised new reforms that would set the country on the path to free market economics. Defaulting bonds, however, were not protected by bankruptcy laws because of the sovereign status of the borrowers, but if countries encountered financial distress, investors might look to some form of international bailout to minimize the damage, or otherwise expect another restructuring exchange offer. Both occurred periodically during the 1990s and 2000s.

Sobered by their experiences as loan defaulters shunned by the capital markets, and pressed at home to produce more economic growth, a number of countries decided to attempt to adopt real market reforms that would produce price stability and attract capital investment. Mexico was one of the first to try this approach, under the leadership of the Harvard-trained economist Carlos Salinas, who became president in 1988 (though he left office in disgrace in 1994). This new pathway for economic development, called the "Washington consensus" by some economists, opened the door for price improvements in the Brady bonds and attracted investment interest by corporations and institutional investors. If the Washington consensus helps bond prices, they wondered, won't it help stock prices more? First mover investors could jump in to take up positions in these countries and wait for the markets to discover them. And if this happened, wouldn't there be room for some even larger reforms, such as privatizing some of the state-owned enterprises?

Indeed all this happened, and the third world came to be known as emerging markets. There was a substantial boom in stocks and bonds of companies from emerging markets from 1991 to 1994, as foreign portfolio investment, as well as foreign direct investment, in the area soared, encouraging a wave of privatization share issues. The concept of the Washington consensus appealed to many countries that had been reluctant to allow market economics to replace the firm hand of government control, and the boom expanded to include countries such as Peru, Indonesia, Pakistan, and others that had had reputations for extremely poor economic governance.

The boom became a bubble as the euphoria continued. It was further encouraged by economic reforms in China, the fall of the Berlin Wall in 1989, and the subsequent collapse of the Soviet Union and its empire of satellite countries. Virtually the entire Communist world had voluntarily chosen to reform its system of governance to improve economic conditions by adopting some forms of market economics. In a few years, India would be added to this list of once-socialist countries that bloodlessly effected a change in economic governance to improve their citizens' lives and futures. These countries represented almost half the world's population. If the reforms were successful enough to be continued, the addition to the pool of investing and developmental opportunities in emerging markets would scale beyond anything ever experienced by capital markets before.

But just as the proponents of emerging markets were singing this tune, the bottom fell out again, and the markets plunged into disarray. The collapse of the Mexican peso in late 1994 brought an abrupt end to the euphoria. Emerging market equity securities crashed in a simultaneous pattern all over the world. The IFC Emerging Markets Investable Composite Index, measured in U.S. dollars, dropped by 12 percent in 1994, having risen by 80 percent in 1993, but by the end of January the damage had become much greater. Measured against its level as of January 1, 1994, the stock market in Turkey was down 57 percent; in Mexico, 56 percent; in China, 54 percent; in Poland, 50 percent, and in Hong Kong, 41 percent; with plunges of 20 to 30 percent common in most countries.[7] The stampede for the exits was caused by large U.S. and European institutional investors, especially dedicated country fund managers who were shocked to discover politically motivated, deceptive, and misleading reports of questionable financial practices in Mexico—where the Washington consensus had begun—and decided en masse that it was time to get out.

But the markets came back. The economic reforms had begun to pay off in terms of higher growth rates, and this sustained foreign direct investment, especially in China. The reforms came gradually, and sometimes fitfully, in Russia, China, Latin America, and India, but they did come. These countries realized that growth depended on investment, and that the best and most reliable source of capital to provide for investment had to come from private-sector investors, not from foreign aid or from international development agencies such as the World Bank. Those sources had been unreliable and inadequate for fifty years,* but investment from private investors would continue as long as the countries played by the rules the investors expected: reforms that protected private property in the law, openness to investment and ownership, privatization, and the reduction of the size and role of the state's involvement in the economic sector. These did not have to happen all at once, but there had to be confidence that they were occurring and that the economy was increasingly responsive to market forces. Disappointment could be expected, but the game would be over if the countries reverted to the extremes of socialism or totalitarianism.

In 2003, Jim O'Neill, an economist at Goldman Sachs, published a research paper noting that if the high rate of economic growth in four large emerging market countries, Brazil, Russia, China, and India (called the BRICs), continued, it would overtake all of the largest Western economies by 2050, making them the most important economic powers on the planet, with many interesting consequences. A few years later, O'Neill added another eleven countries to his list of important emerging market countries that had gotten the word about the reforms and were trying

---

*Indeed, net official payments to emerging market economies have been negative since 2003.

hard and doing better. O'Neill could point out that in the eight-year period from 1999 through 2006, the average economic growth rate of emerging market economies as a whole was 5.9 percent (Russia, India, and China averaged 6.5 percent, 6.6 percent, and 9.0 percent, respectively) compared to an average growth rate for the same period of 1.5 percent in Japan, 1.9 percent in the European Union, and 2.8 percent in the United States.[8]

The leading investment bankers have been scrambling to position themselves in emerging markets since the early 1990s. They have seen many ups and downs and have been frustrated by what often seems to be a very slow pace at which their business develops. But without a doubt, countries such as China, thirty years after Deng Xiaoping's "Four Modernizations" policy (which got it all started), have paid off for them. Goldman Sachs, for example, has led several Chinese privatization stock issues, including one for a large denationalized bank (in which the firm had made a substantial private equity investment); invested in real estate; advised on mergers; transacted with the central bank, which manages reserves of more than $1 trillion; and has opened offices and joint ventures in China. Former Goldman president John Thornton has become a professor of management at Tsinghua University, one of China's best schools. To support the initiative, Henry Paulson, who became CEO of Goldman Sachs in 1999, made seventy visits to China over an approximately ten-year period before becoming U.S. secretary of the treasury in 2006.

MANAGEMENT CHALLENGES

In 2007, the market capitalization of the world's stocks and bonds was $144 trillion, about half of which was in stocks. The U.S. markets represented 36 percent of global stock market capitalization, and 49 percent of bond market capitalization. Emerging markets represented 19.3 percent of global stock market capitalization, up from 6.4 percent in 1990. Less than half of all assets under management by professional institutions were located in the United States. Since the Nixon Shock in 1971, and subsequent reforms and (mostly involuntary) deregulation due to the pressure of market forces in the United States, Europe, and Japan, capital markets around the world were drawn toward an integrated whole allowing for vast flows of investment dollars (in various currencies) to cross borders to find attractive investment opportunities wherever they were. Today the markets are highly interconnected and efficient. They are also better regulated, more transparent, and cost less to use than a decade ago. They are dominated now by skilled professional investors, traders, and managers who have exported their talents and capabilities to wherever they are needed. All of the changes that these developments represent were initiated by forces beyond the control of the investment banking industry. They occurred as governments shifted important policies, deregulated old practices and procedures, and reacted, perhaps reluctantly, to economic and market forces that could no longer be denied. This extraordinary, sudden whirlwind of social, political, and economic change is the sort of thing that occurs in financial arenas only every century or so, creating great hazards for some and great opportunity for others, placing an enormous burden of adaptability on all the industry's players. As a result, industry leadership shifted greatly as firms expanded well beyond their borders and their own expectations in pursuit of one new opportunity after another.

As of the end of 2007, nine large, global investment banks each accounted for more than $1 trillion in originated transactions involving syndicated bank loans, global debt and equity, and mergers and acquisitions. Together these nine firms accounted for two thirds of all global transactions of these types. Six of the firms were American (Citigroup, JPMorgan Chase, Goldman Sachs, Morgan Stanley, Merrill Lynch, and Lehman Brothers) and three were European (UBS, Deutsche Bank, and Credit Suisse); five were universal banks and five were stand-alone integrated investment banks without deposit-taking businesses. The events of the last months of 2008 will not change this hierarchy very much. Bank of America will stand in for Merrill Lynch, and Barclays for Lehman Brothers, but the rest of the group is likely to remain much the same. These firms had been at the top of the league tables for many years. Most of them had more than half of their total revenue from operations outside their home countries, and foreigners represented half or more of their total number of employees. Many of these employees, born in many different countries representing many cultures and religions, do not speak English fluently.

These large investment banks have seen the market for their services double in the last twenty years, and can well expect that, with the effect of the growth of emerging markets and the continuing disintermediation of financial transactions into capital markets from the balance sheets of banks and insurance companies, it may double yet again over the next twenty years. There will be great opportunities for those firms willing and able to take advantage of them. In most areas of the world, these firms can operate as indigenous banks, performing local transactions in Italy, Brazil, Australia, and China, as well as participating in the large cross-border deals that make the headlines. They can take advantage of fast-breaking events around the world, such as a surge in investment power in the Middle East following sharp oil price increases, and benefit from other trends and developments that enable them to add value in one way or another. Goldman Sachs's third largest office in 2008 was in Bangalore, India, where it maintains its own in-house IT-outsourcing business. It also had thirty other international offices, as compared to a total of fifteen located in the United States.

These firms have increasing freedom and capability to allocate resources and talent to where it is most needed or best used. However, to develop these capabilities effectively, and to knit them together with values and principles and control systems adequate to the tasks at hand, takes time, patience, and a lot of investment. Many firms have set out on the path to full internationalization and fallen by the wayside. Crédit Lyonnais a leading French bank with major international ambitions, went off the rails after a binge of hasty foreign acquisitions and had to be taken over by the government in 1993. S. G. Warburg, after emerging as Britain's leading investment bank following Big Bang, was stunned by international bond trading losses in 1994 and forced into selling itself to a Swiss bank; also in 1994, Goldman Sachs was implicated in fraud charges brought against a rogue British entrepreneur named Robert Maxwell, who looted his pension fund, went bankrupt, and committed suicide, leaving Goldman Sachs to pay fines for its carelessness; Baring Brothers, a distinguished 233-year-old British merchant bank, went bust in 1995 after a rogue trader exploited loopholes in its Singapore back-office systems to create massive losses on arbitrage trades; in 2004, Citigroup lost control of its Japanese private banking business, which had defied regulators, and was forced to close the business, and in 2005, it engaged in a massive bond-shorting scheme in the Euromarket, which was exposed and caused it much public humiliation and criticism. There are many other examples of mistakes that occur in international business that, though not always fatal, nonetheless involve costs and embarrassment that can contribute to a lowering of the reputation of the firms involved that weaken their longer-term survivability.

Nevertheless, the international dimension to investment banking is now dominant—firms cannot satisfy large and thirsty corporate and institutional clients by operating in only one marketplace; they have to scour the world for the best opportunities at the lowest cost. The barriers to entry into this world of the top nine banks are very high, and so far these barriers appear to be insurmountable except through acquisition. However, in a highly competitive, price-sensitive, fast-moving environment, the best teams are usually not those that have just been crunched together by merger.

7

THE INNOVATION DECADES

THE ELECTION OF RONALD REAGAN as president of the United States in 1980 began and inspired a series of changes in the U.S. economy, and in the world of investments, that had profound effects on the capital markets industry. The first change was one of supplying calmness and optimism to a society that had become depressed by a decade of economic disruption, recession, inflation, and uncertainty. After his first year in office, with a recession still lingering, Reagan introduced his famous debt-financed tax cuts. Nominal interest rates, which had begun to fall in 1979 after Federal Reserve chairman Paul Volcker brought a sudden end to the escalating inflation of the latter years of the 1970s, continued in a decade-long decline, and the dollar, weak for several years, began a sudden climb. Stock prices rose and rose, and rose further, igniting a seventeen-year period through to the end of the Clinton administration at which the compounded annual growth rate of the Dow Jones Industrial Average averaged 16 percent. This was the greatest seventeen-year period of wealth creation the world had ever known, and the stock market was the principal vehicle for it. Wall Street exploded with activity, innovation, and riches. Changes in the underlying economic environment helped pave the way for all this financial market activity, which itself effected continuing changes in the capital markets and the investment banking business.

Financial markets in the 1980s took everyone by surprise. Stock and bond markets exploded as they institutionalized, securitized, and internationalized. Technology made some of this possible as desktop computers began to appear everywhere and programmatic trading and hedging activities proliferated. Some of it was the result of regulatory changes that loosened things up in areas of currency controls, antitrust enforcement, and securities issuance and trading. A lot of the growth in financial market activity, however, was the result of a continuing chain of innovation as market solutions emerged to meet challenges and opportunities.

The numbers tell some of the story: During the decade, the real growth of U.S. GDP was a bit less than 4 percent. The government deficit grew from $73 billion in 1981 to $277 billion in 1990, reflecting a 14 percent compound growth rate. Most of the deficit was financed by the issuance and rollover of new Treasury securities—a total of $13.5 trillion in marketable securities were issued by the federal government from 1981 through 1990. This volume contributed to the development of new hedging and speculating techniques. The volume of futures and options contracts traded during the 1980s nearly tripled.

Corporate financing through public offerings and private placements was also very active, growing from $74 billion in 1980 to $500 billion in 1989, reflecting an annual growth rate of about 20 percent. The Dow Jones index nearly tripled then, and the volume of trading on the NYSE increased three and a half times. Financial institutions came to dominate markets, accounting for 70 percent of all stock trading and 90 percent or more of bond trading. Mutual fund assets increased nearly tenfold, to more than $1 trillion in 1990.

The decade was also the first when capital markets became closely integrated. The exuberance of the U.S. markets was shared in Europe, Japan, and in some emerging market countries. The global market value of stocks increased from $4.6 trillion in 1985 to nearly $10 trillion in 1990, though the U.S. share of this sum declined to 32 percent from about 50 percent. Japan had been the star performer in the global market surge, and cross-border investment flows increased accordingly. In addition to all this, the United States experienced a major merger boom in which corporate transactions totaling $1.5 trillion were completed in 1985–1990. About 20 percent of this volume involved foreign participants, and about 15 percent involved leveraged buyouts (LBOs), often financed by the issuance of below-investment-grade fixed-income securities, called junk bonds.

During the 1980s investment banks learned to be traders, if they were not already traders, and to compete for business on the basis of the best idea or the best price rather than on the basis of the longest-standing relationship. They learned how to borrow money, to raise new capital, and to manage risk and mollify public investors. And they learned how to invent new products, services, and roles for themselves.

DEBT

Whatever else the 1980s and 1990s is remembered for, in finance they will be known in particular as the debt decades. In 1981, the first year of the Reagan administration, $1.3 trillion in U.S. government securities were outstanding; in 1999, government securities outstanding exceeded $7.6 trillion. Similarly, corporate bonds outstanding expanded from $540 billion to $4.5 trillion. Medium-term notes, an expansion of the commercial paper market, grew from virtually nothing in 1980 to more than $1 trillion outstanding in 1999. The following year, the aggregate market capitalization of global bond markets was $35.6 trillion, of which only $16.3 trillion were U.S. government and corporate bonds. This two-decade increase was partly the effect of surging government deficits that had to be financed by issuing government debt, partly because capital markets had displaced the banks as the primary source of corporate capital, mortgage finance, and below-investment-grade debt, and partly because Wall Street threw so much of its energy into creating new fixed-income products and making markets in them.

In 1982, Salomon Brothers and Merrill Lynch developed a product to be sold to bond mutual funds and other aggressive fixed-income investors that involved buying Treasury bonds, stripping them of their interest coupons, and then selling the principal payments and the coupons separately at appropriate discounts to reflect the different levels of risk involved. The principal-only part would trade as a "zero-coupon" bond and the interest-only part would be sold to investors seeking volatility. Salomon called its product CATS for Certificates of Accrual on Treasury Securities, and Merrill's were known as TIGRs, for Treasury Investment Growth Receipts.[1]

The issuance and trading of fixed-income securities became a major focus of all the major securities firms, even those that had been cautious about it, such as Morgan Stanley and Goldman Sachs. The fixed-income market was huge, and growing, and for traders such as Salomon, which still dominated all but the junk bond markets, it could be very profitable.

But the markets were also very volatile and extremely competitive, and the advantages went to the firm with the best information. The best-informed firm was one that saw the whole order flow and saw it early. Sources, speed, and global reach were essential. But so was knowing what to do with the information once you had it. There was no money to be made in brokering a trade of government securities between two investment banks—success in this business would depend on knowing which institutions around the world wanted to acquire particular risk exposures and putting the opportunities in front of them before someone else did. This was a market-making function that all major Wall Street firms understood; the major firms tried to establish profitable trading spreads for hundreds of different instruments differentiated by credit, currency, and maturity, and to drive, with the help of an active sales force, as much volume through the spreads as they could.

Securitization

Nothing changed the competitive landscape in the field of corporate finance more than securitization, the process of transforming a financial asset held by a bank or other institution into a security that could freely be traded in the market, where it would be subject to competitive pricing discipline. This discipline involves bids and offers in an over-the-counter marketplace in which prices, and thus interest rates, are set continuously by market interaction. Frequently the market price for a security will be more favorable to the issuer than a transaction negotiated directly with a bank. When this is the case, all other things being equal, transactions will be disintermediated, or will flow to the lowest cost of financing.

A simple example is the substitution of commercial paper for short-term working capital bank loans made to corporations, usually under revolving credit facilities. These facilities require some modest standby fees during times when they are not needed and utilization fees expressed as a spread over a base rate, effectively reflecting a premium over the banks' own cost of funds. The rates banks could quote were affected by regulatory limits on the interest rates they could pay for deposits until 1980, which drove depositors to money markets for higher returns, and by their own cost of funds, which reflected the banks' demand for funds and any change in their credit ratings. During the 1980s, banks were committed to strategies of rapid growth in lending, which by the end of the decade (especially after their credit ratings began to erode) put a lot of pressure on their cost of funds; many of their corporate clients with access to the commercial paper market could borrow at much lower costs, and indeed chose to do so.

Commercial paper is a short-term, one-page promissory note issued by a corporation and bought by other corporations or institutional investors. Though a great deal of commercial paper is issued directly to investors, who hold it until maturity, some of it does trade in the market, and prices are available daily both for new issues and for secondary transactions. Commercial paper rates closely track federal funds rates, and the market is usually very liquid. During the 1970s, while interest rates soared, commercial paper outstanding increased fourfold to $124 billion, and four more times in the 1980s, to $570 billion. By contrast, the Federal Reserve reported that the commercial and industrial loans of all money center banks in December 1990 were only $322 billion. Thus the growth in commercial paper represented a big loss of profitable, low-risk lending business to the banks. The banks tried to get back into this business by offering to purchase commercial paper from their clients and resell it on the market for small processing fees, but this was not nearly as attractive to the banks as the business they were losing.[2]

The problem for the banks was actually worse than that, because the growth in commercial paper investments was funded substantially by money market mutual funds, which had attracted funds otherwise deposited in banks (or used to purchase certificates of deposit). Both sides of banks' balance sheets were being eroded by market-based alternatives. Deposits were lost to money market funds that financed commercial paper loans to the banks' clients.

Another form of securitization came to the rescue of the stressed-out S&L industry. Starting in late 1981, regulators offered the S&Ls irresistible conditions for selling their mortgage loans and replacing them with other assets, including mortgage-backed securities. Suddenly there was an enormous demand to sell "whole loans" (individual mortgage loans), and to convert these into securities. But Wall Street was wary of the S&L industry, and most of the firms backed away. But not Salomon Brothers, which had been trading with the S&L industry for years, thinking that whatever happened to it, the government would have to lend it support, perhaps a lot of support, to keep the home-financing industry together. Salomon had the only fully staffed mortgage department on the street in 1981, which was then headed by an overweight, disheveled thirty-year-old named Lewis ("Lewie") Ranieri, a college dropout who had begun his career at Salomon in the mail room in 1967, while training to become an Italian chef.

Ranieri showed some promise in the mail room and was promoted to supervisor before worming his way first into the back office, handling bond trades, then onto the utility bond trader's seat on the corporate bond desk. Salomon was extremely unstructured and informal then: if a trader quit or was absent, the other traders on the desk would reach out to whoever was standing nearby and say, "Hey, kid, you're pretty smart. Sit here and start trading." If you were as smart and unaware of your limitations as Lewie was, you would soon make a mark, and indeed might even take over.

Sliding into the head trader's seat on the mortgage desk when he did was an exceptional stroke of luck for Ranieri. But also, once the floodgates opened and the whole loans were swamping the market, it meant that he had to swim against the current. According to Ranieri, "The Executive Committee said I couldn't trade whole loans [it wanted only to trade mortgage-backed securities]. So, I just went out and did it anyway. They told me I was going to jail. But the whole loans were 99.9 percent of the entire mortgage market. How could I not trade whole loans?"[3]

He bought up everything he could, at deep discounts, and either sold them off again at a quick profit or packaged them up as securities to sell to institutions. Soon he was sitting in the middle of a very profitable monopoly, and he heard little more from the Executive Committee.

Collateralized Mortgage Obligations

Salomon had maintained close ties to many S&Ls, and once their troubles began, it was ready to help. So was First Boston, whose mortgage desk was headed by Larry Fink, a trading phenomenon in his twenties, who later, in 1988, would found and head BlackRock, Inc. In 1977, Salomon and Bank of America came up with a way to package a number of whole loans into a single, larger unit in which security interests could be sold to institutional investors in the wholesale market. This was the first securitized mortgage product, a "pass-through," in which a group of several hundred individual mortgages were segregated and sold to a trustee, and the trustee sold bonds collateralized by the mortgages and guaranteed by one of the government mortgage insurers. All of the cash flow from the mortgages was passed through every month to the investors, who considered the securities to be both collateralized and government-guaranteed.

When Ranieri began to buy whole loans in 1981, he planned to convert them as quickly as possible into pass-through securities and sell them, but the market wasn't big enough to buy all the whole loans he was acquiring. Though the pass-through securities traded at interest rates that reflected substantial premiums to the Treasury market, the problem was that mortgages were subject to prepayments, especially in declining interest rate environments, and therefore an investor could never know for sure what the maturity of the bond being purchased would turn out to be. This made such a security extremely awkward to own. So Ranieri set out to do something about the problem. He had a lot of loans to sell. He organized a research department of math and science Ph.D.s to help him understand the mortgage loans better.

In 1983 a breakthrough occurred when Ranieri and his team invented the collateralized mortgage obligation (CMO). This was a securitized mortgage bond that was offered initially in three or more tranches, i.e., pieces with maturities of two, five, and ten years, plus a residual. The cash flow from the mortgage pool serviced all three tranches, and what was left went to the residual security. Investors could expect prepayment risk to be of relatively little consequence for the two-year piece, somewhat more for the five-year, and mostly confined in the ten-year and residual pieces. Each piece would be priced differently to reflect the different risk of prepayment, so investors could choose the risk exposure they wanted. The two-year tranche, for example, would have a lower risk premium relative to U.S. Treasuries than the others, because the investors' return was fairly certain—though not certain enough; nor were the securities liquid enough to make them equal to Treasuries. The farther-out tranches would carry much larger risk premiums, because of the greater uncertainty of prepayment, but if they were not prepaid, these tranches would have greater value. These features provided a much greater variety of investment choices to sophisticated fixed-income fund managers. Before long, the variety and complexity of CMOs extended to include bonds with as many as fifty tranches, bonds that are "stripped" by further diverting cash flows into two or more new securities with different investment characteristics, and even bonds with entitlements to only interest or principal, and thus containing greater volatility. CMOs became a playground for bond mathematicians and hedge fund managers, who could create whatever interest rate and volatility exposure they wanted.

Demand for CMOs exploded and continued steadily throughout the 1980s and 1990s. Before long they were being created by their guarantors, Ginnie Mae (Government National Mortgage Association), Fannie Mae, and Freddie Mac, and by large banks and investment banks. CMOs made an enormous difference in the market for mortgage-backed securities, which blossomed into a whole new component of the fixed-income market. In the first year after Salomon introduced them, Freddie Mac created and sold approximately $10 billion in CMOs, with Salomon accounting for about 65 percent of the total, and First Boston a good part of the rest.[4] The net effect of all this, of course, was that a competitive market, not a group of banks holding assets on their balance sheets, set the prices (and thus the interest rates) for home mortgages, and the average of such rates declined significantly.

In 1984, Salomon increased the variety of CMOs on offer, and included mortgages backed by commercial real estate for the first time. In time they would include adjustable-rate mortgages (ARMs) and subprime loans to borrowers with impaired credit. The CMO business soon became a gold mine, and Ranieri plunged into it with little restraint. Mortgage-backed securities grew at a compounded annual rate of 67 percent from 1978 to 1987, when total volume reached nearly $100 billion. By 1991, the volume was over $250 billion. Salomon's profits from CMOs alone totaled several hundred million dollars,* or more than 25 percent of Salomon's net income during its most profitable years in the mid-1980s.[5] Salomon completely dominated the market for CMOs in their early years, and Lewie Ranieri was promoted to the Salomon Executive Committee and made a vice-chairman of the firm. But he was an ungovernable force and either he proved to be too difficult to handle or claimed too large a share of the firm's profits, so he was let go in 1987, just about the time that the CMO market began to develop signs of commoditization as other firms dove into it and bid away the juiciest business. Undeterred, Ranieri acquired his own S&L and made another fortune as a mortgage industry entrepreneur and private investor.

---

* Much of Salomon's profits then were calculated from the difference in yield on its inventory of mortgage-backed securities less its firm-wide short-term borrowing costs, which were not adjusted internally for risk or maturity.

The CMO business finally receded in profitability as competitors piled into it, and Salomon seemed to lose interest in it. But the firm had learned several valuable lessons from its experience. It could exploit its strong market access in fixed income by developing new products designed to satisfy the immediate needs of issuers as long as in doing so the new products appealed to its sophisticated, institutional clients. Complex computer modeling and a battery of brainy Ph.D.s combined with aggressive trading practices would be a dynamite combination that could make far more money than anything else the firm could do in already established markets. But expertise in such new products would only offer a comparative advantage for a few years, until the juice was squeezed out by competitors and they would have to move on to the next new thing. They also learned that a technique that works on the basis of one type of collateral might also be used with other collateral. In the 1990s, collateralized mortgage obligations morphed into a large family of asset-backed securities, in which the assets backing up the bonds would include car loans, credit card receivables, corporate loans, and a variety of miscellaneous items such as airplane parts and rights to rock-and-roll royalties. By 2005, the asset-backed securities market produced $1.8 trillion in new issues in the United States, a little less than half of all new debt issues in that year.

Junk Bonds

In the 1970s (before CMOs), four types of taxable bonds were traded in the United States. There were U.S. Treasuries, the gold standard, with high volume and tight trading spreads—often no more than a couple of sixteenths of a point separated the bid and asked prices quoted. Then there were corporate bonds, issued by large creditworthy companies that traded at larger spreads of one quarter to three-eighths of a percent. There were also the bonds of foreign governments, often rated lower in the U.S. market than at home because of uncertainties in making foreign exchange payments, but also affected by low volume and liquidity and by their exotic nature. Spreads were greater for foreign bonds.

The last category of bonds included those rated below investment grade (i.e., below a rating of BBB-, which many thought to be the minimum rating for investment in bonds by conservative U.S. insurance companies). Below-investment-grade bonds were mainly bonds that had been issued with investment-grade ratings but had fallen on hard times. Such bonds were called "fallen angels." They were not of much interest to bond

buyers in general, though occasionally they were looked at by proprietary traders or hedge funds. The bonds were thought to have value if they
had been discounted in price more than they should have been, but the
trouble was, in order to make money on them, someone else would have
to want to pay a higher price for them. The market, however, was very
illiquid, so there wasn't much chance of that happening.

Fallen angels became something of an obsession to Michael Milken, a
young student at Berkeley in the 1960s, when and where student radical-
ism was at its peak. When everyone else was smoking pot, burning bras
and draft cards, and using foul language in public, Milken was absorbed
in the works of W. Braddock Hickman, whose enormous, multivolume
Corporate Bond Quality and Investor Experience analyzed bond performance and default rates from 1900 to 1943. Milken was fascinated to
learn that throughout this long period in which a depression and two
world wars had occurred, the prices of lower-grade bonds had reflected a
lot more defaulting than actually happened. Later he found a follow-up
study by T. R. Atkinson covering the period 1944–1965 that reached the
same conclusion. The studies revealed a powerful systemic bias in the
market that underpriced below-investment-grade bonds, suggesting that if
you bought a lot of those bonds and held them to maturity you could
make a lot of money. After graduating, Milken carried his obsession with
him to Wharton, where he finished two years later and joined a once-
prestigious investment house, Drexel Harriman Ripley, which was soon
thereafter bailed out by the Firestone family and renamed Drexel Firestone. There he was made head of fixed-income research and soon migrated to trading, where he was free to locate and trade fallen angels. He
studied the market thoroughly and knew all there was to know about
who owned the bonds and what they ought to be worth.

Milken began to trade fallen angels actively, but Drexel Firestone was
not a trading firm and was reluctant to allow him the capital to build the
business up as much as he could. He was rescued from this situation when
Drexel was acquired by Burnham and Co., whose principal owner, I. W.
("Tubby") Burnham—a contemporary and good friend of Gus Levy's—
was an old-time trader. Burnham immediately spotted Milken and substantially increased the capital he could use for trading. Neither one ever
looked back.

Michael Milken is often referred to as the father of the junk bond, but
that statement is not actually true. The fallen angels already existed; he
just began to trade them as a specialty. What he is, is the father of the junk

bond market. Milken identified a supply of high-yield bonds, but he also developed whole new batteries of buyers and sellers, and as a result, he expanded the market enormously, while still retaining very large trading spreads that made the business extremely profitable.

He started with buyers. Whom could he persuade to invest in the high-yield bonds? He developed a relatively simple sales pitch: you could build a diversified portfolio of the bonds at low prices that overcompensated for their risk. Milken's knowledge of the bonds available in the market would be used to cherry-pick the best, the least risky. He knew that the statistics had consistently demonstrated that the portfolio yield on the junk bonds less the comparable maturity U.S. Treasury rate (the "risk-free rate") would be one hundred to two hundred basis points (1 to 2 percent) greater than the expected default rate on the portfolio, adjusted for recoveries in bankruptcy. But he also believed that junk bond prices could rise if their creditworthiness improved, or if more investors began to realize the inherent value in them. So the downside risk was much less than the upside potential. Milken looked for investors who would be responsive to this sales pitch: hedge funds, fixed-income mutual funds, aggressive insurance companies that needed strong investment performance, distressed savings-and-loan associations desperately searching for increased investment yields to shore up their mortgage loan portfolios, and a variety of financial entrepreneurs who were sitting on cash waiting for their next takeover move to develop.

There were a lot of these investors, and Milken sold the fallen angels to them. But he worried that he was going to run out of bonds to trade, so he set out to find ways to increase their supply. This he could do by offering to raise debt capital for risky borrowers who would be willing to pay the high rates required, but who believed that they could put the capital to good use anyway. He found some airlines, some oil and gas wildcatters, some weaker conglomerates, and he found the takeover artists, the "greenmailers" * and the rough and eager New Men of the 1970s and 1980s, who otherwise had little access to capital. Milken drove a hard bargain with these issuers. They would have to give up equity warrants in the companies they were taking over with the bonds to be issued, and they would have to agree to use some of the proceeds from selling new bonds to buy the bonds of other of Milken's clients.

---

* A term applied to payments made by companies to purchase significant minority stakes in their companies from potentially hostile investors who had accumulated the positions.

In the middle 1970s, Drexel Burnham, as the firm was then known, was struggling in Wall Street's worst bear market since the 1930s. But Milken's junk bond operations were prospering, and were responsible for most of the firm's net income. Milken was allowed to retain 35 percent of his unit's profits, which netted him $5 million in 1976, during a time when no one (well, hardly anyone) made that amount of money. By 1978, Milken had made himself into the financier most sought out by the country's rogue capitalists, and decided to move his operation to Beverley Hills, far away from the managerial disciplines and controls of Drexel Burnham. He developed the habit of starting to work very early in the morning, often requiring his supplicants to show up for meetings at 5:00 a.m. He issued letters to clients saying he was "highly confident" that he could sell bonds to raise money for prospective takeovers, and his clients could borrow from their banks on the strength of these letters. He also organized a lavish annual meeting of current and prospective junk bond issuers and investors that came to be called the "Predators' Ball." He was the unquestioned king of the junk market.

Tubby Burnham wanted Milken to be more closely tied to the firm and asked him to acquire a major ownership interest in it, which he did. By 1983, Milken's direct compensation and profit sharing in the firm exceeded $45 million; in 1984 it would total $123 million, twenty times what many high-producing partners earned at firms such as Goldman Sachs. In 1985, when junk bonds appeared in the market as the crucial ingredient of financing packages for large, publicly contested leveraged buyout deals, Milken earned $135 million. In 1986, $33 billion in junk bonds were issued, 45 percent of the market being controlled by Drexel Burnham; mostly to finance takeovers and LBOs, and in 1986, Milken earned $295 million. In 1987 his take from junk bonds rose to $550 million (more than the entire firm would earn) and his ownership in Drexel Burnham stock was worth another $98 million. By the end of 1988, the year in which the RJR Nabisco LBO was financed, the total amount of junk bonds outstanding was about $200 billion. Approximately $62 billion of these were thought to be held by insurance companies (including some of the stodgy ones that had come around), $50 billion by mutual funds, $20 billion by pension funds, $20 billion by individuals, $12 billion by S&Ls, and $36 billion by a wide variety of others, including numerous foreign investors. Drexel had come from nowhere to become one of the leading U.S. underwriters, and Milken had made himself into one of the country's richest men in little more than a decade, the first billionaire to emerge from a major firm. But the market had reached its peak and was beginning to lose speed, and the world Milken had dominated for more than a decade was closing in on him.

EQUITIES

However adaptive, innovative and expansive debt markets were in the two decades at the end of the twentieth century, the star performer of the period, by far, was the stock market. The market capitalization of all American stocks on December 31, 1999, was $16.7 trillion, up from its twenty-year low of $1.3 trillion in 1981. The gain for the period reflected a compounded annual increase in the value of stocks that was over twice the 7 percent nominal rate of the U.S. GDP growth, indicating the extent to which this nearly fourteenfold increase in stock market capitalization had created wealth in excess of underlying economic activity. The long bull market survived eight-year presidential terms of Ronald Reagan and Bill Clinton (with four George H. W. Bush years and the first Gulf War in between) and indeed experienced significant setbacks in 1987, 1990, 1994, and 1998, and ended in 2000 with three consecutive years of negative returns to follow. It was the longest sustained bull market in American history, one that created many new millionaires and was opened to most of the members of American society. In 1998, a Federal Reserve study reported that 48 percent of American households participated in the stock market, most indirectly through mutual and pension funds, and thus in the wealth that its growth created. Demand for stocks predominantly came from pension funds, mutual funds, and foreign investors.

Pension Funds

Pension funds are divided into (private) corporate funds and those (public) funds maintained by states, municipalities, and trade unions. Corporate funds in particular are evolving away from "defined benefit" funds (in which a pensioner is paid an agreed amount annually for life) and toward "defined contribution" funds (in which pension contributions are agreed upon and invested on a tax-deferred basis, often through mutual funds—and the principal plus appreciation is returned to the employee on retirement). All types of pension funds have recognized that long-term gains are more likely to accrue from a portfolio that is heavily weighted to stocks, and as a result most funds have a majority of their funds, and invest a majority of their annual premiums, in stocks.

Mutual Funds

Mutual funds proliferated over the 1980–2000 period such that there were many more mutual funds than there were stocks. In 1982 there were approximately 860 mutual funds in the United States, representing assets under management of $287 billion, of which only $47 billion was invested in equity securities. By the end of 1998, there were more than seven thousand mutual funds managing $5.5 trillion in assets (nearly twenty times the 1982 total), of which $3 trillion were invested in equities. Mutual fund managers, however, have consolidated through acquisitions, and as a result, the great majority of funds are managed by a relatively small number of highly competitive firms, which include banks, investment banks, insurance companies, and international financial firms. The fund management companies have developed large marketing capabilities for their funds, and have a great variety of new funds to offer. These included real estate investment trusts (REITs); "country funds," in which all the investments are in stocks from a particular country, such as Brazil or Korea; and a variety of different international funds with investments in stocks of different countries. Some fund managers also offered a series of "index funds," in which the managers use computer programs to duplicate certain stock market indices such as the S&P 500. In the mid-1990s, some fund managers began to offer "exchange-traded funds" (ETFs), low-cost indexed mutual funds that focused on a particular investment theme and were traded on national stock exchanges. By 2000, approximately 20 percent of all equity mutual funds by value were index funds or ETFs.

Despite the industry's growth, competition, and increasing transparency of fees and performance, the performance of most stock mutual funds has been unimpressive. When fees, which have not declined much despite the enormous increase in volume, are subtracted from gross investment returns, relatively few funds outperform the stock market index to which they should be compared. Between 1986 and 1996, Morningstar, a mutual fund tracking enterprise, noted that no more than 26 percent of stock mutual funds beat their indices during four different time periods. Fewer yet outperformed their indices over a longer, eleven-year period. The ordinary mutual fund investor, of course, selects funds to manage stock market investments for him and may not be concerned about whether the fees are too high, as long as the performance realized is good enough. He could shift to index funds instead, but then he would give up any upside above the index that some funds achieve from time to time. Most fund investors were happy with the way things were, and did not object to the relatively high fees and expenses, but if they did they could shift to a low-cost index fund. Either way, the fund managers did very well.

In 2000, Fidelity Management and Research Co. (FMR), the management company for the Fidelity Group of mutual funds, was America's largest single money manager, with over $1 trillion in assets under management. It is a family-owned and -managed business, acquired in 1946 by a legendary figure, Edward C. Johnson II (Mr. Johnson). A Boston lawyer who specialized in investment companies, Mr. Johnson acquired FMR when it had assets of only $13 million. He was not a portfolio manager himself; he hired others to do that for him, and the most celebrated of his protégés was the most famous of the 1960s gunslingers, Gerald Tsai. When it became clear that he would not succeed Mr. Johnson as head of the firm, Tsai left to set up his own fund, which was not particularly successful, and Johnson took over, found Peter Lynch in 1969, and groomed him to become one of the most famous American fund managers ever. Lynch, a shy, towheaded workaholic who was committed to researching everything and investing in the best 2 or 3 percent, took over a small nonpublic fund called the Magellan Fund, with $22 million in assets, and when he gave up running it himself in 1990, the Magellan Fund was the largest mutual fund in history, with $12 billion under management and more than a million shareholders. Other portfolio managers came and went, and Fidelity's competitors struggled hard to catch up to it, but by the end of 1999, FMR managed more assets than any other independent financial services firm in the world and was 60 percent larger than its closest rival, Vanguard. Nearly one in five dollars invested in U.S. mutual funds were in Fidelity's hands, and Fidelity's funds owned more than 5 percent of seven hundred public companies.[6]

International Investors

International investors were the third-largest source of investment funds to the U.S. equity market in 2000, after pension and mutual funds, with a total of $1.6 trillion, representing 11 percent. In the 1970s, most countries had foreign exchange controls that limited the ability of institutional investors and wealthy families from transferring funds abroad to make portfolio investments. After the adoption of the floating-exchange-rate system, most of these countries realized that they no longer needed to maintain their foreign exchange controls, and gradually they began to come off. By 1980, investors in Western Europe, Japan, and the Middle East were free to invest in the U.S. market, and of course many did. In the United States, after Ronald Reagan took office, nominal interest rates were declining and the dollar was rising against the principal European currencies and the yen, and U.S. stocks looked especially attractive.

Wall Street Becomes an Asset Manager

The bull market of the 1980s played into the hands of the mutual fund companies, such as Fidelity and Vanguard, which had products galore and mighty sales organizations to move them. During the 1970s, they sold money market mutual funds to customers with low-yielding bank deposits, and when the market recovered, they persuaded their customers to switch to stock mutual funds. The passage of the Employee Retirement Income Security Act of 1974 (called ERISA) provided additional opportunities for investment managers seeking to service pension funds. ERISA was passed to curb abuses in the corporate pension fund area during the late 1960s and early 1970s, when many large industrial concerns appeared to be on the brink of bankruptcy with serious amounts of underfunded pension funds still outstanding. The law addressed these problems by insisting that corporations not allow their obligations to their funds to fall into arrears, and that they provide a decent array of diversified assets in the fund (and not just a lot of the company's own stock). The government agreed to act as guarantor of the defined-benefit funds (but not of the defined-contribution funds, which technically were not pension funds but deferred retirement income funds). The act required a lot of shifting about, and many corporations decided to switch to defined-contribution funds if they could get the proposal through their labor unions. One thing was clear, however, most corporate pension or retirement funds would have to be more professionally managed and be more accountable for their results. This would create a large new business for institutional money managers and mutual fund companies, and Wall Street pondered what to do about it.

Fidelity and other mutual fund managers began to solicit corporations with defined-contribution pension funds, suggesting they include a mutual fund among the menu of investment options offered to their employees. The companies thought this was a good idea, and they negotiated lower fees and costs from the fund managers for setting up such funds, but the fund managers made up for these discounts in the volume of new assets turned over to them.

At Goldman Sachs and a few other trading firms that serviced institutional investors primarily, the decision after ERISA was to forego this investment management business rather than be in it competing with their large mutual fund clients. Indeed, this decision resulted in Goldman Sachs's spinning off its small Investment Management Department. This seemed like a sound decision at the time, but it was not the same strategy pursued by Merrill Lynch, which also had an active institutional trading business.

Merrill already managed some not-very-well-performing mutual funds in the mid-1970s, when Don Regan decided that the firm was going to take on a much bigger profile as an asset manager and, in typical Regan style, said he wasn't going to worry about offending some institutional clients along the way. It already had a large money market fund, called the Merrill Lynch Ready Asset Fund, or "the RAT," which could be used to attract new investments in stock funds, and of course Merrill had its vast array of branches taking in small investments from millions of retail investors daily. In 1976, Merrill hired Arthur Zeikel, a seasoned investment manager with experience at Oppenheimer and Co. and a founder of Standard & Poor's/Intercapital Inc., a diversified investment-management concern representing a joint venture between several investment managers and Standard & Poor's, the investment information company that is a subsidiary of McGraw-Hill.

Zeikel has said that when he interviewed for the job at Merrill, he had only one question: "Who's name is going to be on the door?" By this he meant to ask if Merrill Lynch was going to put its own well-regarded name on the funds or continue to use the names of the funds it had acquired, as it had been doing. "When I was told that Merrill was eager and willing to build a business they would be proud to have their name on, I accepted on the spot." Zeikel managed this business for twenty years as president and chairman of Merrill Lynch Asset Management, during which period client assets grew from $300 million to $500 billion, making Merrill the third-largest active asset management firm in the world.

This expansion caused others to look at the fund management business. Most funds charged management fees of around 1.5 percent and also charged their investors for various administrative and other expenses that were really just the costs of the fund. These amounted to another 1 percent or so, and therefore the total cost for management and administration was about 2.5 percent. But there were other costs, too, in terms of the affect on returns to be realized. The funds had to maintain sufficient cash reserves to accommodate redemptions, which could occur daily. This diminished the amount of the funds' assets that were at work in the stock market. There was also a tax bill that had to be paid by investors once a year based on the realized gains of the funds—the funds that traded actively, which many active managers were inclined to do, generated short-term gains that were taxable as regular income, rather than long-term gains that might be treated as capital gains. Overall, for some funds the total, all-in cost paid in terms of the returns received were closer to 5 percent, and over a period of time, a 5 percent discount could suppress the actual realized return for mutual funds considerably. It became clear from actual results that after fees and expenses, very few mutual funds beat the returns posted by the market indices, such as the Dow Jones Industrial Index or the S&P 500.

This awareness began to cause some bright people to wonder whether traditional stock mutual funds made any sense for average investors. Charley Ellis, a prominent consultant to institutional investors and investment banks, decided that it was a "loser's game" and that investors should develop their own investment strategies and horizons and work with successful investment managers to achieve their goals. In 1975, Ellis published a widely read book, now a classic, explaining his methods, called *Winning the Loser's Game*. In the same year, the Vanguard 500 Index Fund was established to create a synthetic representation of the whole market, which investors could purchase to hold indefinitely. The fund was entirely computerized—it bought and sold the stocks it needed to have to maintain parity with the S&P 500—there was no effort to manage a portfolio to "beat the market," which research by Ellis and others had indicated was rarely achieved by active mutual fund managers. As a result, the Vanguard Fund aspired only to passive management efforts to track, or equal, the market, and thus involved only very small fees and expenses, around ten basis points. In passive funds all the money would be invested, and there would be relatively low turnover; therefore the tax bill would also be low.

The index fund was developed by Jack Bogle, a hard-driving, cantankerous, dyed-in-the-wool mutual fund executive who had written a senior thesis at Princeton on the development of the mutual fund industry in 1951. After writing his thesis, Bogle joined Wellington Management and rose to become its CEO, but he was fired for what he called an "extremely unwise" merger he put into place. According to Bogle, "The great thing about that mistake which was shameful and inexcusable and a reflection of immaturity and confidence beyond what the facts justified, was that I learned a lot."[7] Bogle moved on to found Vanguard in 1974. By this time Bogle had become a fanatic about the high level of management and administrative costs mutual fund investors were required to bear. He thought these costs drained away too much of the return that investing in the stock market could offer ordinary investors, and he spent his time and effort developing the country's first low-cost index fund, the First Index Investment Trust. Upon its release on December 31, 1975, it was immediately derided by other fund management companies as being "un-American," and seen as "Bogle's folly."[8] Mr. Johnson said he "couldn't believe that the great mass of investors is going to be satisfied with receiving just average returns." Bogle's fund was later relaunched as the Vanguard 500 Index Fund, which tracks the Standard & Poor's 500 Index. It started with comparatively meager assets of $11 million, but crossed the $100 billion milestone in November 1999; this astonishing increase was funded by the market's increasing willingness to invest in such a product. The Vanguard 500 propelled the Vanguard Group into becoming the second-largest mutual fund company in the world, behind Fidelity, with assets of over $1 trillion. Bogle, now in his eighties, and a survivor of an early heart transplant, has parted with Vanguard and set up his own research center, but he is still very active pointing out the flaws in actively managed mutual funds and showing his support for index funds.

In the 1980s, the rising market, the increasing need of corporate pension funds for independent managers, and the oil wealth accumulating in the Middle East led other Wall Street firms into active asset management for institutional clients. Morgan Stanley hired Barton Biggs in the early 1970s as research director, and before long he was pushing the firm into investment management, which he also headed. Morgan Stanley made great inroads in Kuwait, Abu Dhabi, and other parts of the Middle East and the Far East, gathering up large, prosperous clients at a time when Goldman Sachs still eschewed the business.

Goldman reentered the asset management business in the 1980s, through a back door. A midsize money market fund called Institutional Liquid Assets (ILA), which was managed by Salomon Brothers, stumbled on a mistake made by Salomon and the fund's board of directors, quite unusually, found itself it the position of having to locate and hire a new manager. The board came to Goldman Sachs and asked the firm to take over from Salomon, without having to pay anything. This seemed like a good deal—the mistake was mended quickly, and the several billions already under management seemed an easy way to get started in asset management. Managing money market funds for small institutions did not upset any of Goldman Sachs's large institutional clients, so the firm went ahead, cautiously expanding its product line and offerings until, in the mid-1990s, it looked like all the rest of the firms offering a full range of debt and equity fund management services for pensions and its own stable of mutual funds.

Though Goldman Sachs wasn't seeking to compete with its institutional clients in managing money in the early 1980s, it was interested in providing products and services to pension funds and others that reflected the latest developments in modern portfolio theory and financial economics. In 1984 the firm hired Fischer Black, a well-known financial economist from MIT, to develop such products and services for it. Black was co-author of a seminal paper with Myron Scholes (who joined Salomon Brothers in 1990), "The Pricing of Options and Corporate Liabilities," which appeared in 1973 and set the standard used by Wall Street for the valuation of traded options. He was also active in developing the new field of portfolio insurance, a method of guarantying the value of an entire portfolio of stocks at any point by a strategy of selling a mathematically determined number of futures contracts on the S&P 500. The methodology of portfolio insurance was developed by two professors at Berkeley, Hayne Leland and Mark Rubinstein, who set themselves up in business in 1981 to provide the insurance product to pension funds with large stock portfolios. Other academics such as Black and Scholes were tinkering with the methodologies to make them more user-friendly to pension funds and more adaptable to the real-world conditions they lived in. By the mid-1980s there were several competitors to Leland O'Brien Rubinstein Associates, and both the stock and the futures markets had become well aware of the portfolio insurance product and how it worked.

By the end of the 1980s, the investment management business had changed in many ways that made it attractive to investment banks. The pension fund industry had been significantly restructured as a result of ERISA, the wider adoption of modern portfolio theory, and the use of high-power academic talent to produce new techniques and methods that could establish comparative advantages among money managers. At the same time, the mutual fund industry was exploding with a proliferation of different types of funds, the addition of corporate 401k and other retirement funds to the customer base, and the appeal of low-cost index funds and an increasing variety of ETFs. These developments all suited investment banks having a wide range of corporate connections and the ability to develop new intellectual property related to asset management. Some banks with large retail customer bases, such as Merrill Lynch, Dean Witter, and Shearson, were drawn to offering mutual funds to them, a business they all deemed to be potentially very profitable. Asset management became a new line of business for investment banks, joining corporate finance and sales and trading, offering potential for high growth and a stable source of income to firms otherwise subject to high volatility from trading and market changes.

The Crash of 1987

By the end of August 1987 the Dow Jones Index was up substantially over the past five years and well above the previous year's closing. According to Michael LaBranche, chairman of NYSE specialist firm LaBranche and Co.:

> The market was up a lot in 1985 and 1986. You'd had these really good years, and by August of 1987 the Dow was up about 35 percent for the year. In those days 35 percent was unheard of. Just a few years earlier it seemed the market hadn't gone up 10 percent in a while. Suddenly it was up 35 percent on a lot of speculation. And all this was happening in the face of rising interest rates.[9]

The market traded off from its August high, but on the whole it held up despite growing concerns that it had become overheated. Economic issues were added to the concerns, with reports of a breakdown in discussions with the G7 countries over monetary policy and an overvalued dollar. The Commerce Department reported an increased U.S. trade deficit in October, and there were reports that Congress might eliminate tax benefits associated with financing mergers. On October 14, the Dow Jones Index dropped 95 points (then a record), fell another 58 points the next day, and fell again on Friday, October 16, by 108 points on record volume. The market had fallen 10 percent from its August record high in just three days. Investors had a lot to think about over the weekend.

So did the portfolio insurance people. With the market starting to fall off a record high, this seemed a perfect time to apply the new principles. In the 1973–1974 market, many pension funds had sold during the fall-off, but did not return to the market in time to enjoy the post-slump recovery. Market values were still high—an insurance program could lock in the values and ride out any adjustments at only a relatively small cost. However, to implement the program, the fund managers would have to sell market index futures in fairly large amounts. The effect of large volumes of sell orders on the index futures would require selling in the cash markets of the underlying stocks.

The pension funds and other U.S. institutional investors were not the only ones studying the markets over the weekend, however. On the morning of Monday, October 19, in Hong Kong, stock prices plummeted, triggering similar moves in Australia and New Zealand, and these market actions were picked up a few hours later in Europe, where selling was heavy. By the time the market opened in New York, there was widespread selling of both stocks and the index futures, which triggered more sales of stock. This is turn caused the portfolio insurance models to sell more futures, in a downward spiral that seemed limited only by the fact that the market would close at the end of the day. Leo Melamed was CEO of the Chicago Board of Options Exchange (CBOE) at the time:

> There were absolutely no bids for the S&P 500 futures contract. The prices that emerged from the S&P 500 futures pits that afternoon were really only from a smattering of orders. Then there was this enormous vacuum before there were any other prices. After that there was another vacuum before there were more prices. It was unprecedented. The market was in pure shock. I had never seen that before. There were no limits, just this abyss heading down. I have few memories of my life where I would describe myself as petrified. This is one of them.[10]

When the stock market closed in New York, it was down 508 points, or 22.6 percent. Even greater drops occurred in Hong Kong (45.8 percent.),

Australia (41.8 percent.), Spain (31 percent), and the UK (26.4 percent). In New Zealand the market was hit especially hard, falling about 60 percent from its 1987 high. October 19, 1987, has been known ever since as Black Monday. The only worse day on the New York Stock Exchange was December 12, 1914, the day the Exchange opened again for trading after being closed for four months following the outbreak of World War I, when the Dow Jones Index declined 24.4 percent.

Black Monday is a day no one who lived through it on Wall Street will ever forget. I was secreted away in my office in New York with the top executives of a large British company that was planning to announce an offer to acquire a large California insurance company in a transaction we expected would be resisted by management. It was to be a very large deal—many billions of dollars—and the deal would do a lot to make my year. But as the market plunged—I was checking it often—it became clear that we could not go ahead with the deal. A hostile deal for a state-regulated big-name company in unpredictable California wasn't going to work in a collapsing market. We would have to wait until the markets recovered, if they did, and no one knew when that might be. My clients seemed to think I had arranged the market collapse just to frustrate them, and they returned to London in a heavy sulk. After they left, I was able to turn my attention to what was happening to the rest of the firm, with its many hundreds of trading exposures and its open underwriting position in the enormous privatization sale of British Petroleum shares by the British government.

Altogether Goldman Sachs had to pull everything together to see where it stood and whether there was enough capital to endure all the market write-downs that would have to be taken. Everything I owned was hanging in the balance, and there was very little I personally could do about it. That night I was teaching a class at NYU on global equity markets. I had already announced my plans to join the faculty at the end of the year, and this class was a warm-up. I got through it as best I could, but returning home late that evening I could only think about how much things had changed in just one day. If I wasn't petrified that night, I should have been.

Several things happened then, at end of the trading day on October 19. The Federal Reserve announced it would provide liquidity to banks sufficient to assist broker-dealers in meeting their credit obligations; other central banks echoed the sentiment, and some placed their exchanges on restricted trading so as to be able to sort out the as-yet-unmatched trades of the day before. The NYSE announced that it would stay open, no matter what, despite some rumors that it might close. Meanwhile, investors considered what had happened and whether enough was enough. The next day, the market opened still weaker, and around midday the CBOE suspended trading to preclude the further computer-programmed selling of index futures (it reopened the next day). Later in the day, the market recovered and gradually returned to normal. Later, President George H. W. Bush appointed his friend, former senator Nicholas Brady, who was chairman of Dillon Read (the future secretary of the treasury), to chair a presidential task force on market mechanisms, which was directed to find out what had happened to cause Black Monday and how such things might be prevented in the future. On December 31, 1987, the market closed 2 percent higher than the beginning of the year. In January 1988, the Brady Task Force issued its report. The report fingered the portfolio insurance managers as being principally responsible for the "frenetic five-day market drama of October 1987." This came as no surprise, and the data the report contained on the volume of sales of futures contracts during the five-day period was convincing.[11] The report proposed a few recommendations, but the most important lessons learned appeared to be that the portfolio insurance schemes really didn't work—the losses on the stocks held far outweighed the gains on the futures sales (the futures markets were not robust enough to handle all the volume, which slowed things down, but in any case the futures sales in turn triggered cash market sales that further depressed stock prices), and as a result, portfolio insurance has since gone by the board.

Second, the market administrators realized that there had to be some symmetry between the operating rules of the cash and the futures markets so as to prevent situations of one market being open while the other is subject to trading restrictions. The NYSE developed a series of "circuit breakers," which are activated to stop trading for brief periods when price changes exceed certain limits, and the CBOE has mirrored these as closely as practicable. This was supposed to stop the widespread dumping of futures contracts in runaway markets. Third, and perhaps the most important, the crisis forced the close cooperation of the principal regulators to take coordinated actions that helped prevent major liquidity difficulties from exacerbating the problems of a frightened market trying to sort itself out. In 1987, Alan Greenspan had only been on the job as chairman of the Federal Reserve for two months when the crash occurred, but he was an experienced economic policy-maker and had an equally experienced

Gerry Corrigan, as chairman of the New York Fed, to help. They recognized (as their 1929 counterparts had not) that infusing liquidity into such market crises is essential to keep them going and to minimize damages. These lessons were followed both in 2001, after September 11, and during the 2007–2008 mortgage-backed securities crisis, though in both cases, criticism has arisen that too much liquidity was injected for too long, which led (or might lead) to subsequent runaway asset prices setting up another bubble.

DERIVATIVES

Much of the new intellectual firepower accumulated by Wall Street was devoted to securities "derivatives." An official, if not particularly helpful definition of a derivative is "a security whose value is based on, or derived, from another security." Another definition might be that, like a derivative in calculus, the value of a derivative instrument is a function of the change in the value of an underlying security to which it is connected. As an example, the value of a financial futures contract changes when interest rates change. Before 1970, derivatives were confined to commodities and foreign exchange contracts that came in the form of forwards, futures, and options on designated instruments.

In 1864, the Chicago Board of Trade created the first futures exchange, to standardize contracts, and subsequently established the CBOT Clearing Corporation, to guarantee trades made on the exchange. The Chicago Mercantile Exchange, a rival institution, began to trade financial futures contracts in seven foreign currencies in 1972. CBOT introduced interest rate futures based on Ginnie Mae securities in 1975; CME offered Eurodollar and stock index futures in 1981; CBOT introduced options on financial futures for U.S. Treasuries in 1982; and so on. The two exchanges demutualized after 2000 and became public companies that merged in 2007 to form the CME Group, Inc., the world's largest and most diverse derivatives exchange. There is also a London International Financial Futures and Options Exchange (LIFFE)—a European equivalent of the CME Group—which was acquired by Euronext in 2002, and which in turn was acquired by the NYSE in 2007. Also, equity options, index options, and currency options are traded on the Philadelphia Stock Exchange (acquired by NASDAQ in 2008), and stock options are traded by the American Stock Exchange, which was acquired by NYSE-Euronext in 2008. Exchange-traded derivatives have grown considerably over the past twenty-five years as futures and options contracts have become important components in investment strategies and risk management programs, but they comprised only a small percentage of all derivatives outstanding in 2008. The rest are over-the-counter contracts in interest rate and currency swaps, and credit default swaps, which exploded on the financial scene in the early 1980s and grew at an average rate of 45 percent per annum through the early 2000s.

Swaps

In August 1981, a significant transaction took place in which IBM and the World Bank agreed to exchange (or swap) the future liabilities associated with borrowings in Swiss francs and U.S. dollars, respectively. IBM, with an AAA rating, was regarded in Switzerland as one of the best names in America and was able to borrow there at rates very close to those of the Swiss government. The World Bank, which had borrowed often in the Swiss market but was thought to be too associated with third world credits to be a solid AAA in Swiss eyes, had to pay a premium over the Swiss government rate of about twenty basis points. In the United States, the World Bank was thought to be a top credit (backed by the United States and other governments) and could borrow at a modest premium to Treasury rates, which IBM, a mere corporation, could not do. So each party borrowed about $100 million in the market in which it had a comparative advantage, and then swapped their respective borrowing obligations (interest rates and principal repayments) with each other and shared the benefits. IBM ended up with dollar financing at a rate less than it would otherwise have been able to attract, and the World Bank did the same in Swiss francs. This was perhaps the world's first "currency swap" involving the issuance of "swap-driven Eurobonds" in a "notional" amount, in this case, $100 million (or its equivalent in Swiss francs). The swap arrangement involved offsetting default conditions and some sort of payment from one party to the other to reflect a difference in the present value of the future payments being exchanged. It was a little complicated, but the value in arranging the swap was worth it, and banks soon learned how to arrange similar transactions and came to rely on a standard set of documents and procedures to do so. The currency swaps helped to close out market pricing aberrations between currencies and interest rates and could be used by both borrowers and investors to squeeze additional value from market transactions. Also, for countries with foreign exchange or market-issuing controls still in place, a "synthetic" market in Eurocurrencies created competition with their domestic markets (enabling their national foreign exchange or market controls to be avoided), which migrated business away from the national market and encouraged the countries to withdraw the controls. The swap was a technique that enabled markets to create viable, often lower-cost alternatives to domestic financing outside the country's borders. The currency swap business expanded rapidly after the IBM deal, with swap-driven bond issues ultimately accounting for approximately a third of all Eurobond issues.

Soon bankers began to experiment with other forms of swaps, including exchanging same-currency interest payment obligations (for example, swapping a future fixed-rate obligation for a variable, or "floating," one). This turned out to be just what the ailing S&L industry needed: a way for S&Ls suffering from rising short-term rates used to fund fixed-rate mortgage loans to exchange their future fixed-rate income streams into variable-rate streams that could be financed with variable-rate deposits. Not everyone wanted to enter into swap deals with shaky S&Ls, however, so banks that were already heavily involved with S&Ls (e.g., Salomon Brothers) stepped in between the swapping parties so each would have Salomon (or some other bank) as a "counterparty." Salomon wasn't too worried about the risk—the S&Ls were just passing along the income paid to them from the home mortgages, which were better credits than the undercapitalized S&Ls—and in any event, if there were a default, Salomon wouldn't have to pay out on its obligation (which was offset), though there were risks associated with replacing the defaulting party in the transaction. Thus the "interest rate swap" business was born and became enormous. In 1982, about $3 billion in notional value of currency swaps, and $2 billion in interest rate swaps, occurred in over-the-counter markets in New York and London. In 1984, First Boston flooded major newspapers with an ad featuring a large picture of a baby, captioned "The $40 Billion Baby That the World Hasn't Adopted Yet," which the text explained meant interest rate swaps. By 1988, more than $500 billion in interest rate swaps and $175 billion in currency swaps were completed (according to the International Swap Dealers Association, an organization that developed along with the business). By 1994, the notional value of interest rates swaps exceeded $4 trillion, and currency swaps, $1 trillion. These swaps were being used to hedge risk exposures in a great variety of ways, usually by intermediaries, market makers, and proprietary traders, but also by the end users of the instruments. Swaps are often customized to suit the needs of particular counterparties, and thus are not sufficiently standardized to trade on exchanges. By 2000, the notional value of interest rate swaps outstanding was nearly $50 trillion (currency swaps were only $3.2 trillion). By 2008, the combined notional value of interest rate and currency swaps exceeded $400 trillion.

The over-the-counter market in interest rate and currency swaps represents about three times the value outstanding of exchange-traded instruments, which consist of interest rate, currency, and stock index futures and options. All of these instruments, collectively, are called derivatives, and their effect on financial markets since the early 1980s, in terms of enabling risk redistribution and the elimination of market pricing anomalies, has been profound.

Wall Street jumped into the business feet first. Salomon Brothers and First Boston were early to apply interest rate swaps to S&Ls and other businesses. Before long, most Wall Street firms had several finance Ph.D.s on staff helping to find clever new ways to do things with derivatives that would create trading opportunities. Myron Scholes and fellow Nobel laureate Robert Merton both joined a hedge fund, Long-Term Capital Management, in the 1990s to do the same. The derivatives business was a catalyst for opening the industry to quantitative finance in all of its many applications; in the process, it raised the average IQ of traders by a considerable amount, but at the same time it exposed overmotivated derivative traders to some new kinds of risk.

The Ordeal of Bankers Trust

In the early 1990s, Bankers Trust was a star among American banks. It had gained this reputation because of its successful transition from a fifth-ranking New York City retail bank into a powerful trading and wholesale finance operation with commendable margins and high risk-adjusted returns on assets. Under Charles Sanford, the banking industry's first trading executive to become a CEO, the bank announced and implemented ambitious plans for repositioning itself in the investment banking industry and for specializing in risk management services. Frequently referred to as America's best-managed bank, it was a favorite of banking industry analysts. Indeed, Bankers Trust became a model for the modern wholesale banking enterprise. Loans had been reduced to no more than 30 percent of total assets, of which about 45 percent were devoted to securities and trading inventories. The loans the bank originated were complex, sophisticated precursors to the leveraged loans developed a decade later and used to finance leveraged buyouts and similar transactions. Bankers Trust would retain the management fees and syndicate or sell down most of the loans, retaining only small amounts. It developed ways for banks to be involved profitably in commercial paper and other money market instruments, and developed substantial trading businesses in government securities, foreign exchange, and derivatives. Noninterest revenues were 75 percent of the bank's total revenues in 1990, about half of which were from trading. Its traders were subject to tough capital allocation rules, but they were highly incentivized and well compensated. Charlie Sanford began to talk about the bank's changing relationship with its clients: "We don't have any clients anymore, we have counterparties. We don't coddle them, we trade with them. Whatever they want to do, we'll find a way to do it with them. And, of course, we expect to make money doing it."[12]

In the economic slump that followed the collapse of the junk bond market in late 1990, Bankers Trust's trading activities focused more on derivatives of various types. It specialized in complex, customized swaps worked out directly with individual counterparties. However, by the end of 1994, Bankers Trust found itself in the middle of several messy lawsuits involving the sale of unusually toxic derivatives to supposedly unsuspecting counterparties, including Procter and Gamble, which claimed to have been fleeced by the bank. The derivatives involved complex swaps that enabled the companies to make leveraged bets on the future direction of interest rates, which went in the wrong direction. The problem was the counterparties thought they were clients of the bank and hence entitled to some old-fashioned coddling. In late 1993, P&G had accepted an offer from Bankers Trust to sell it two customized interest rate swaps involving five-year Treasury notes and deutsche marks. By April 1994, after a substantial unexpected rise in U.S. interest rates, the swaps were in trouble. P&G took a $157 million write-off and fired its treasurer, the person responsible for the purchases of the swaps. It also very publicly and angrily sued Bankers Trust for fraud and deceptive practices, under the auspices of the federal Racketeer Influenced and Corrupt Organizations (RICO) Act, which could triple damages. Once this lawsuit was filed, it was copied by other disappointed Bankers Trust counterparties unhappy with the losses they, too, had been forced to take. Such losses were estimated to amount to about $500 million.[13]

As part of the disclosure efforts undertaken in connection with the lawsuits, Bankers Trust's trading room tapes of conversations among traders were subpoenaed, and trader talk entered into the case. Traders were then notoriously blunt and aggressive in their chatter with one another, in explaining how they had pulled off this or that killing at the expense of a less intelligent competitor or an uncomprehending counterparty. A trader who worked with me used to refer constantly to how, in getting someone else to accept his price on a trade, he had "ripped his eyes out." Mostly it was just macho talk. In this case such talk was soon leaked to the press. The Bankers Trust man working the P&G trades was recorded saying he had "lured them into the calm, and then really fucked them."[14]

That was all it took. Bankers Trust's stock price dropped like a stone, losing more than $2 billion in market capitalization. Client surveys taken by newspapers ranked Bankers Trust at the bottom of all customer satisfaction surveys (they had previously been at the top). The board of directors went ballistic, looking for those responsible for having done such harm to the company's good name. The board forced Charlie Sanford to retire early, passed over his designated successor, and hired someone from outside the bank to come in and clean things up.[15] Bankers Trust generously settled the suits without going to trial (their lawyers had expected the suits to be withdrawn, as trading losses occurring after the contract was signed were not its responsibility), and the bank took a substantial write-off. It later withdrew from the derivatives business and let go 1,400 employees, to save costs. A few years later a shorn and humbled Bankers Trust was sold to Deutsche Bank for $9.8 billion, its name was dropped, and Bankers Trust disappeared as an independent supplier of wholesale banking services.

Credit Derivatives

In the latter 1990s, a new form of derivative instrument, a "credit default swap" (CDS), a form of insurance against default on loan payments, was introduced and rapidly adopted into use by banks and other credit intermediaries and investors. Credit default swaps are entered into by two counterparties in which a payment is made annually by one party to be able to transfer the risk of the credit obligation to the other party in the event of default. There is now an active market for credit default swaps in which the cost of insuring debt exposures can easily be obtained. Such cost information has become an important information-signaling element in credit markets as it reflects on the creditworthiness of individual companies.

The cost of credit derivatives vary with those factors that can affect the market value of credit exposures from bonds or loans, including changes in expected default or recovery rates, actual or perceived changes in credit ratings, changes in the liquidity for debt instruments as a whole, and changes in the perceived value of debt insurance or guarantees. The volatility in the cost of credit derivatives can be seen in the subprime mortgage crisis in 2007. In June 2007, the cost of insuring $10 million in debt of Merrill Lynch against default was $25,000; nine months later it was $150,000.

In 2008, the notional value (i.e., the principal amount protected) of all outstanding credit derivatives as reported by the International Swap Dealers Association was $38.6 trillion.

TECHNOLOGY

Few of the innovations that so transformed the financial markets in the 1980s and 1990s could have occurred without a parallel development in what simply has to be called financial information technology: information gathering, display, analysis, dissemination, and application. Before 1980, traders relied on information they might pick up from talking to others, or from analyses based on published (usually out-of-date) financial statements or research reports. Fixed-income securities traded in a relative hierarchy of "risk premia," or the difference in yield between the risk-free rate (i.e., U.S. Treasuries) and other bonds. To trade such bonds, you would want to know what the historical risk premia were, and what they were at the exact moment you wanted to trade. Gathering this information was not always easy, and the information was not always accurate, standardized, or up-to-date. And even when you had the right information, you might need a sophisticated quantitative analysis to determine if the risk premia was worth betting on right then. Compound this by trying to apply the method to hundreds of different bonds, some quoted only in London or Tokyo, with markets constantly changing, and you can appreciate the difficulty in expanding a trading book by relying only on the trader's intuition. New tools needed to be developed that could gather real-time price information about all kinds of securities, and trading analytics had to be created that would enable traders to find the best places to put their money.

The Bloomberg

Michael Bloomberg, then at Salomon Brothers, understood the problem and was thinking about it when he was fired. Bloomberg had been a trader who was pushed aside in one of Salomon's typical periodic brutal reshufflings, and he resurfaced as the man in charge of the firm's computers, then an undisputed transfer to oblivion. This was a back-office function, where no self-respecting Salomon partner was ever to be seen. But Bloomberg figured that computers could be used to help traders, for example, by comparing risk premia of two essentially similar securities trading at different prices. A clever trader would buy the cheaper of the two and sell the more expensive, locking in a differential that was essentially free of market risk. When the mispricing corrected itself and removed the otherwise unjustifiable differential, the trader could cash in the profit. But Mike was fired just about then. As part of the merger with Phibro Corporation in 1981, Salomon had agreed to thin out its rank of partners and Bloomberg, then not considered essential, was let go.

He was surprised, and his feelings were hurt, but Bloomberg recognized the opportunity that being fired by Salomon presented—he would get all his capital back—around $10 million, which he could use to set up a business of his own. The business he wanted to start was one that would use new, small, desktop computers (the IBM PC was introduced in 1981 and soon appeared everywhere) to assemble and compare prices for two or more different bonds in ways that would enable traders to gain a leg up on the market. He hired some programmers and got to work. About a year later he had a machine (a minicomputer with a program) that could do the job—he called it "the Bloomberg"—and he set out to lease it to firms on the Street. Merrill bit first, and the rest, as Bloomberg said, "was history." Once Merrill was seen to be using the Bloomberg, all the other traders had to have one, too. Bloomberg had plenty of competition, from Reuters, Telerate, and Dow Jones, but his machine, constantly upgraded and continuing to reflect the trader's point of view, pulled ahead of all the others.

In its wake came a revolution in quantitative analysis techniques that enabled all of this pricing data to be put to even better use. Early market "quants" such as Fischer Black and Myron Scholes were put to work making models of how markets work, where equilibrium pricing should occur, where arbitrage opportunities could be found, how hedging strategies should be constructed, and how sophisticated risk management programs could be administered and controlled. This involved an ocean of mathematical analysis—surely a very far cry from the methods used by Gus Levy and his contemporaries in the 1960s—and opened many new career pathways for traders, fund managers, research analysts, and internal systems and management personnel. By the end of the 1990s, Wall Street was competing effectively for the best minds from academia in mathematics, economics, and finance.

8

RESTRUCTURING

IN OCTOBER 1988, RJR Nabisco's chairman, F. Ross Johnson, suddenly announced to his board of directors that he had tried everything he could since becoming chief executive two years earlier to boost the stock price of the company, without much success.[1] The market, dominated by institutions looking for something else, just wasn't responding to his efforts. No matter how well the foods and other brands of RJR Nabisco did, the market still valued them as risky tobacco company assets. Therefore, he thought it best if he and a group of colleagues, including the investment bankers Shearson Lehman Hutton, put together a bid for the company at $75 per share. The stock had previously been trading at $55, so the offer represented a 36 percent premium.

Several bankers had proposed an LBO to Johnson, though he had been noncommittal until late in 1988. Shearson Lehman Hutton and Drexel Burnham Lambert seemed to be the most aggressive. Each firm was willing to follow Johnson's lead into the deal, or at least they told him they were. Finally, Shearson was picked, and Johnson submitted his version of a management agreement, which he claimed was not negotiable. Shearson (joined later by Salomon Brothers) would put up about $3 billion in equity, but Johnson and six management colleagues were to get 8.5 percent of the company, together with a loan from Shearson to pay for it. There were several earnings performance bogeys identified, which if management met them all, would push the group's stake up to 18.5 percent. The management package might be worth as much as $2.5 to $3 billion over the coming five years. In the meantime, the group would share annual income of $100 million. Johnson would also receive a veto and control over the board, unlike any major LBO ever completed.

The agreement was an illusion, thought Peter Cohen, Shearson's chief executive, something Johnson claimed he had to have in the early stages of negotiation. Cohen badly wanted to manage the transaction, as any investment banker at the time would have wanted to do. It was the sort of mega-transaction on which reputations could be built, which would attract many future deals, and could be enormously profitable. However, if Cohen had sat down with Johnson in the old-fashioned way and said, "Look, Ross, there's no way the people putting up the money for this deal can let you take so much out of it; you'll have to do it our way, or get someone else," he knew what the answer would have been. Maybe Johnson would have heard the same story at the next place, but then he'd have been talking to somebody else, not Shearson. So Cohen said, "Fine, Ross," only he held out that the agreement would have to be renegotiated if their group had to bid more than $75 a share, their opening shot, as he thought it quite likely they would.

Johnson, thinking $75 was a full price that would be hard enough to raise the money for, was satisfied. Thus he could argue that he had extracted an unusually favorable deal for the management group. Cohen could equally argue (as indeed he did when Salomon challenged him on the agreement) that it was all meaningless: once the company was in play, Johnson would have to go along with whatever Shearson and Salomon wanted to do; if higher bids had to be made, they would be paid for by squeezing Johnson's deal. If no one else appeared on the scene, there was enough juice in the $75 price for the investors to pay Johnson what he wanted and still have a lot left over. By the time of the final bidding, the interest of the management group (then covering a greatly expanded group of managers) in the company was down to 4 percent from the original 8.5 percent.

The Nabisco board, surprised by Johnson's and Shearson's proposal, announced it to the public and appointed a special committee of its non-management directors to consider the proposal and any alternatives. The committee promptly hired its own legal and financial advisors to consider all options. Though it had not previously had any intention of doing so, the board's actions put the company in play, making it fair game for any and all other bidders to approach it.

Henry Kravis explained his view of the initial bid by the Johnson group in a later interview in *Fortune*:

> I think Ross Johnson made a number of mistakes. When he made his first offer, a management buyout at $75 a share, my first reaction was to think that RJR was in play—and at a price substantially lower than its real value. Was he actually putting up a For Sale sign on the company? Or did he really want to own it? If the latter, the one thing we were very certain of was that the management group was stealing the company.[2]

A few days later an alternative was presented when KKR, which also had discussed an LBO with Johnson within the last couple of years, offered to pay $90 per share in cash for 87 percent of the RJR Nabisco stock. The special committee then solicited bids from any other interested party, and a few tentative proposals came forward.

It wasn't long after the announcement of the buyout offers before the terms of Johnson's management contract were leaked to the press. The contract became the focus of concentrated media attention, which then grew into greed-bashing hysteria. *Time* magazine ran Johnson's picture on a cover announcing a story about greed in America. According to *Time*, "Seldom since the age of the 19th-century robber barons has corporate behavior been so open to question. The battle for RJR-Nabisco seems to have crossed an invisible line that separates reasonable conduct from anarchy."[3] *Time* never did make clear how "anarchy" fit into the transaction, but according to Kravis, "Ross Johnson turned out to be the best thing we had going for us because of all the adverse publicity he was collecting."

The board committee said it was considering the different bids and certain self-recapitalization and restructuring moves. It then asked for all final and highest bids to be submitted by November 18. On that day, three bids were received: from KKR, the Johnson group, and a group organized by First Boston Corp. A group of industrial corporations assembled by Forstmann Little, another buyout firm, and advised by Goldman Sachs, joined together for the purpose of bidding, but in the end chose not to. The bids were all quite different: the Johnson group valued its bid at $100 in cash and securities, the highest of the three. The special committee, advised by Felix Rohatyn of Lazard Frères, met often with each group to clarify features of the bids, and then decided to ask each to bid yet again.

The last and final bids received from the two sides were effectively the same—the Johnson group's bid had a face value of $112 per share, but it had to be discounted because the terms of some of the securities offered in the package were inferior to the securities offered in the KKR group's package, valued at $109 per share. Rohatyn, explained after an all-night effort to value the two bids, "Both bids are between $108 and $109. When you get that close, and you are dealing with securities in amounts that have never been dealt with before, in my business judgment, these offers are essentially equivalent. They are both fair from a financial point of view. They are close enough that we can't tell you one is clearly superior to the other."

The directors made their decision to accept the KKR proposal based on their assessment of the intangibles, by no means the least of which was the outraged reaction of the press to the Johnson group, which had deeply colored general public opinion of the deal. The board was certainly leery of being seen as a captive of Johnson, whose many favors to the outside directors had been fully reported, at some embarrassment to them.[4]

The accepted bid was nearly double the stock price of RJR Nabisco before the original Johnson proposal. The whole deal had been put together and concluded in less than three months—such a large deal, nearly $25 billion, and done so quickly. There was a great deal of fierce competition among the groups, and personal animosities were often evident. Ross Johnson, who had become CEO of RJR Nabisco only in 1987, acted at times as if the board would do whatever he wanted, at other times as if he were the single most important party to the transaction and without him any other bidder would be at a serious disadvantage. KKR offered at one point to allow Johnson to join their group, but he rejected this offer. Johnson knew that no other large LBO had been done without management on board and well taken care of. After all, management not only could point to some success at having already run the company, which would be an important comfort to the lenders, but it also had the benefit of inside knowledge of the company to use in shaping its bidding strategy—it would know just how much cash could be squeezed out of operations to service debt. Accordingly, Johnson believed that he could call his own shots in the deal. He could dictate the terms, and the investment bankers would have to take it or leave it. Still, his bid was turned down in favor of one without him, and he was shocked.

The transaction would generate $700 million in fees to bankers and lawyers involved in the transaction, 2.8 percent of its total value. Some of these fees were for legal and financial advice in structuring and negotiating the deal, but most were for arranging and providing commitments for the substantial amount of financing that was needed. It was a difficult and complicated transaction, and the technical advice was necessary—the financial engineering had to be exact for the highest bidder to have any chance of making money on the deal—and organizing financing of almost $25 billion in short order was a large and crucially important task that only the most experienced banks could handle.

In the end, the RJR Nabisco shareholders received a large premium on the value of their holdings and retained a small carried interest in the new company. Capital gains to the pre-buyout shareholders would exceed $13.3 billion. The KKR group would have the opportunity to restructure the company, which, though founded in 1875 by an itinerant goods trader, had been put together in its present form only in 1985, when R. J. Reynolds Tobacco Co. acquired Nabisco Brands (itself the result of a 1981 merger of Nabisco and Standard Brands) to become the nineteenth ranking company on the Fortune 500 list, with 1988 sales of $16.6 billion. It was a very profitable corporation, with a 1988 expected operating cash flow of about $3.5 billion. The tobacco business generated a substantial surplus cash flow with which to service debt, and the hundreds of branded food products could be sold off for high prices as part of the restructuring that would follow the acquisition.

The KKR group, however, had to stretch its bid to the group's outermost limit in order to win. After the tender offer and subsequent merger had been completed, the new company (that is, RJR Nabisco after KKR had financed its acquisition) would have $23 billion in interest-bearing debt outstanding, and only $7.8 billion in equity and equity-like securities holding it up. Total debt would account for 80 percent of capitalization, and annual interest costs would only just be covered by cash flow.

The complex capitalization structure of the deal described the times. There were three tiers, each designed to appeal to the investment interests of particular types of investors. Banks would supply the largest piece of the financing, a commitment of nearly $15 billion, of which 65 percent was provided by Japanese, European, and Canadian banks. The bank facility would be senior debt and have first claim on the assets of the company in the event of a bankruptcy. In addition to the banks' debt, the existing debt of RJR Nabisco that was outstanding before the acquisition, about $5 billion, would be included in this senior tier, for a total of $17.5 billion. Before the acquisition, the book value of all of the company's assets was slightly in excess of this amount, and the market value was very much higher.

After the expected issuance of bonds to replace the short-term notes and bridge loan facilities (offered from two investment banks) to finance the tender offer, and some immediate sales of assets, bank debt was expected to be reduced to less than half of the total capitalization of the company. The bank loans would have a six-year life and be subject to rapid mandatory repayment. The bank facilities were designed to provide substantially more asset and cash-flow coverage to the banks than most leveraged buyouts, and the interest rates payable on the loans, and the fees paid to the banks for providing their commitments, would be somewhat higher than what was normally received in large LBO transactions. The banks would also share arrangement fees of $380 million.

The next tier in the capital structure was $5 billion in subordinated debt, which was junior to, and therefore ranked behind, the senior debt. The subordinated debt was provided by the sale of several issues of long-term, high-yield, noninvestment-grade junk bonds (in the largest such offering ever done). These bonds were sold to pension funds, insurance companies, mutual funds, and savings-and-loan companies all across the country, and some were sold abroad. They, too, offered generous interest rates, approximately 5 to 6 percent more than U.S. Treasury securities at the time they were issued.

The final tier consisted of even-more-junior-ranking securities—two types of "payment-in-kind" (PIK) securities—and common stock, the latter of which involved less than $2 billion, or less than 8 percent of the total capitalization of the company. The PIK securities, one a convertible debenture, the other a preferred stock, paid interest and dividends not in cash but in more of the same kind of securities for several years. Investors in this tier could make money only if future operations succeeded, through either growth or the sale of properties at higher prices and/or further recapitalizations at more favorable financial terms.

Altogether the KKR group invested less than $2.5 billion in the transaction, approximately a tenth of its market value. And the $2.5 billion was not KKR's own money; it came from investment funds managed by KKR, whose investors were state and corporate pension funds, college endowments, insurance companies, banks, and savings institutions, most of which had invested in other KKR deals and done very well.

In the final analysis, KKR had put up virtually none of its own money, but had secured control of one of the largest and most profitable companies in America in a little over three weeks. From control of such a company, the opportunities to reshape the business to improve its performance, and its value, would be very considerable. The RJR Nabisco deal, the largest in contemporary valuation since the U.S. Steel merger put together by JPMorgan in 1901, would become the landmark of the restructuring deals of the 1980s. Nonetheless, this deal, however famous it may have been, was bought at too high a price, and in the end it would make very little, if any, money for KKR's investors.

MERGERS AND LBOS

The real impetus for the 1980s merger boom occurred in the mid-1970s with the buildup of significant cash reserves in "strategic" buyers (industrial companies in the same industry) during a time of depressed price-earnings multiples, when many companies had readily sellable assets on their books. It was triggered by the hostile takeover of Electric Storage Battery by International Nickel (advised by Morgan Stanley) in 1974, which legitimized such tactics for blue-chip companies and set up other similar deals. As interest rates declined, the availability of money increased and "financial" buyers such as KKR were able to enter the fray. The revival of strong economic growth and a recovering stock market in the early 1980s sped things along, expanded the use of leveraged buyouts, and saw the birth of a below-investment-grade corporate bond market and record levels of debt and equity financings in the United States and in the Euromarkets. The iconic American corporation, AT&T, was broken up into seven regional telephone companies, which were to compete with one another. This began a lengthy unwinding of the structure of the old telecommunications industry, and created a huge new one to replace it.

These events led to a massive restructuring of American publicly owned corporations, to increase their competitiveness and performance, and to increase the value of their shares, though the restructuring was generally to be imposed on target companies by their buyers. In time, the would-be targets recognized the value of self-initiated restructurings of their own.

The idea of a restructuring included making a lot of big changes in a company's capital structure, management, business plan, and incentives for the restructurers to perform well. It involved increasing leverage, cost cutting, selling nonessential assets, streamlining operations, and providing a working environment that was highly focused on results. Restructurings were intense events, and many were successful in turning companies around and making them more productive. As a result, lots of money was made from them. But with all this—the mergers, the LBOs, restructurings, and the determined pursuit of profits—came some scandals and the bankruptcy and liquidation of the firm that pioneered the junk bond market, an emblematic representation of Wall Street during the 1980s, Drexel Burnham Lambert.

The large merger boom of the 1980s was the fourth one of the century. Merger booms are periods of abnormal volumes of corporate mergers, acquisitions, spin-offs, divestitures, and related transactions. They usually last four or five years. The volume of mergers and acquisition transactions has followed a rising (but fluctuating) trend line from 1974 to 2007, with boom periods in the middle 1980s, the late 1990s, and from 2004 to 2007. Merger booms spark a great deal of corporate finance activity while they last, and this activity has the effect of raising the standards of performance for all publicly traded corporations, even those not directly affected by mergers. Market forces are released that seek to identify suitable targets for takeovers and to make financial resources available to aggressive and dynamic companies to gain control of them. Between 1982 and 1988, more than ten thousand merger transactions were completed in the United States alone, aggregating over $1 trillion in market capitalization. Another thirty-five hundred international transactions, totaling $500 billion, also occurred during this period. This boom ultimately played out and was followed by a recession, but another and much larger merger boom would succeed it in the period 1996–2000.

Merger booms occur for a variety of reasons, but some common triggering factors need to be present. These include a change in the regulatory or tax environment that permits strategic moves to be made that were not possible before; a misalignment of values in the sense that the market price of the company's stock does not reflect its underlying value; the availability of abundant and low-cost financial resources to finance merger transactions, some of which are always risky; and a supply of skilled entrepreneurial risk-takers willing to wager on their ability to realize opportunities from the transactions.

These triggering factors came together first at the turn of the twentieth century, from 1898 to 1902, as corporate combinations were made to enable companies to operate on a national as opposed to a regional basis. They came together again in the 1920s, when new technologies and market opportunities appeared, especially in electric power and the automobile industries. They appeared again in the 1960s, as corporations reorganized for growth in the postwar era and discovered conglomerates; and they reappeared in the 1980s, with the Reagan stock market boom and deregulation (especially the liberalization of antitrust policies) and an increase in cross-border investment and the spread of indigenous and often hostile merger activity in the UK and in other countries in Europe. The U.S. investment banks, using the know-how developed during the 1970s, played a very significant role in these transactions.

The regulatory environment of the 1980s permitted same-industry mergers in the oil and gas, foods, drugs, finance, and other industries that might not have been allowed at any time since the beginning of enforcement of antitrust laws early in the twentieth century. But mainly, the boom of the 1980s was initiated by recognition that the troubled political and economic conditions of the 1970s were over and a new set of policies that encouraged economic growth had emerged. Indeed, many large American companies had come through the difficult 1970s worn down and much more conservative than when they had entered them—in 1980, corporate leverage was down to levels not seen since the Eisenhower days, returns on equity were low, and the price-earnings ratio of the S&P index was below 10, versus a long-term average of 16.

The market moved into boom status with the recognition that the values of many corporations (especially some of the conglomerates) were less than they could be (some were less than their break-up values), and the fact that only a change in control could release this latent value to shareholders. Or as Carl Icahn, one of the leading takeover players in the 1980s (and still at it thirty years later), put it, "The takeover boom is a treatment for a disease that is destroying American productivity: gross and widespread incompetent management. Takeovers are part of a free-market response, working to unseat corporate bureaucracies, control runaway costs and make America competitive again."[5]

Soon the market recognized that a new type of CEO was necessary to guide major corporations to realizing their full economic potential. No longer could companies tolerate dull, cautious, bureaucratic CEOs—they now sought out young, dynamic, transformational leaders who would accelerate the pace of change and capture the value of all the opportunities out there. In the early 1980s, figures such as Jack Welch (General Electric), Steve Ross (Warner Communications), and Rupert Murdoch (News Corp.) emerged and successfully transformed their corporations, with mergers playing an important role in the process. These corporate tycoons were cheered along by their counterparts from the professional investing communities. This broad community of respectable business leaders did not fear being stigmatized by hostile takeover transactions—hostile deals, which reached a peak of 25 percent of all U.S. merger transaction in 1987, became progressively less controversial—and mergers, sometimes ruthlessly pursued, became part of the program for strategic development of successful corporations. The hostile deals, however, led to the development of a new legal environment in which courts would intervene to establish a whole new set of rules for maintaining a level playing field to balance shareholders' rights against those of corporate executives exercising fiduciary duties.

Established corporations were joined in the 1980s for the first time by a collection of financial acquirers or entrepreneurs seeking to use financial resources in a different way to enable them to acquire companies with the intention of managing them differently in order to create value for their investors. These transactions, known as "leveraged buyouts," or LBOs, developed initially by Jerome Kohlberg of Bear Stearns, had been around for some years, but only in the 1980s did they begin to play a significant role in the overall market for mergers and acquisitions, of which they comprised as much as 30 percent during the boom years between 1982 and 1988. LBOs grew to play such an important role in the merger market because the entrepreneurs behind them were able to exploit a new publicly traded debt market for subordinated junk bonds sold to a variety of nonbank investors.

Merger Wars

Thus in the 1980s a merger boom was formed, based on the usual triggering factors, but it was enhanced and extended considerably by a new set of players: aggressive CEOs of large establishment corporations (not just the raiders and dice rollers), who were prepared to launch hostile transactions to enlarge and empower their own enterprises, and LBO operators who were able to obtain crucial low-cost financing from the market for junk bonds. Transactions were both strategic and financial, hostile and not, and involved efforts by all sorts of companies to effect internal restructuring and new leadership so as to release otherwise unrealized shareholder value. Deal tactics and countermoves had to be developed, and these became rough and confrontational. Lawyers had to be involved, and public relations people and credit analysts, in addition to your ordinary corporate finance investment bankers trying to broker a fair deal between two willing parties. There was indeed a lot going on, and it was all going on intensely, on a large, unprecedented scale.

This intensity was reflected in the growing activity of risk arbitrageurs, who would buy large positions in target companies when deals were announced and then do all they could to urge the deals to go through. They would agitate as activist investors, publicly urging the defending management teams to come to terms with the bidder, and they were prepared to vote in favor of the deal in any proxy contest that might occur. Altogether, quite a few arbitrageurs were active in almost every deal, and collectively these investors controlled significant percentages of the trading float in the companies involved. They had the effect of forcing the deals to an economic conclusion that would reward their efforts, making it increasingly difficult for defenders simply to repel the bid and return to the status quo ante.

At Lazard Frères, Morgan Stanley, First Boston, Salomon Brothers, and Lehman Brothers, huge efforts were launched to assist buyers in finding targets and then helping them execute the transactions. This began with high-level contacts between dynamic CEOs and star merger bankers of the 1980s, who headed the teams at the major firms: Felix Rohatyn of Lazard; Robert Greenhill of Morgan Stanley; Eric Gleacher of Lehman Brothers; Ira Harris of Salomon Brothers; and Bruce Wasserstein and Joe Perella of First Boston. These men were all close to their corporate clients, participated in their inner circles, and mastered the process of fielding teams that could launch and negotiate takeovers on short notice. As the merger business brought in considerable revenues during the 1980s, these intense, charismatic merger men rose in power and influence within their firms, though none of them became the head of the firm they worked for during the merger years, and all of them moved around among firms and/or settled down in their own boutiques. Greenhill became number two at Morgan Stanley, lost out in a struggle for the top position, went off briefly to Smith Barney, and thereafter formed his own small firm, which later went public, making him a very wealthy man. Gleacher migrated to Morgan Stanley and moved on later to set up his own successful boutique. Harris left Salomon for Lazard, where he thrived for a while before leaving. Wasserstein and Perella left First Boston when the firm declined to make bridge loans to their LBO clients, and they set up their own firm, which they later sold to a German bank, with Perella going on to join

Morgan Stanley (and later his own firm) and Wasserstein successfully working out a scheme to take over Lazard Frères.

CEOs believed that the star bankers were skilled and connected and would help them do whatever they wanted to do. In the boom periods, these bankers received a great deal of press attention that built them up even further: Rohatyn was the subject of numerous cover stories in business, finance, and society magazines that helped propel him to celebrity status, but the same was true for other merger stars from time to time.

This publicity seemed to be good for business. A senior merger banker was transformed into a trusted consigliere, a relationship that involved a lot of hand-holding and strategy sessions in which he would propose and debate particular deals with celebrity CEOs. These bankers had to spend the time it took to know what their clients really wanted (it was not always easy to know this) and to develop a network of contacts with other CEOs, so as to know who the real players were and who they were not. They had to know what the merger market was doing and to anticipate its next moves. They had to be able to analyze potential transactions to see how they might create value and be financed, and how the stock and credit markets might respond to them. They had to anticipate moves the target companies would take to escape their efforts, all the while staying within the increasingly complex rules and guidelines from the courts and the SEC. They also had to be sure they got paid for their efforts by getting clients to retain them and to agree to pay the fees they asked for if the deals they recommended were completed, which many were not. They also had to be sure they would be indemnified against the costs and consequences of litigation and to ensure they were not exposed to conflicts of interests with or between clients.

All of this involved a great deal of work, much of it tedious number-crunching and checking on legal procedures. As an example, assume an investment banker wanted to propose to its client, General Soap, that it acquire a rival business, Soaps Incorporated. First the firm would have to find out if it had any conflicts of interest with the target company, or with any other company interested in it. Did it contain in its files any privileged information about Soaps Incorporated that would preclude its acting for General Soap? If not, an analysis would have to be made of the financial statements, operating record, and market price information about Soaps Incorporated, to compare it with General Soap and its other competitors, and to see what the two companies would look like if combined under different assumptions about the purchase price. Such analyses would indicate whether the idea made economic sense. These calculations were painstakingly performed by hand with a calculator and an accountant's spreadsheet until the introduction of desktop computers, LOTUS 1-2-3 software, and computerized analytical tools that began to appear in the late 1970s. Automation and the availability of databases containing corporate financial information sped up the process, but there was still more to do. An analysis of how General Soap could finance the transaction and the effect of the transaction on General Soap's balance sheet, credit rating, and stock price would also have to be made. Sometimes this would require speaking to one of the firm's stock analysts in a way in which the analyst was sworn to secrecy, to preclude any direct or inadvertent trading in the shares of either company. Another analysis would be made of how the approach might be made to Soaps Incorporated that might begin negotiations on a friendly basis, or otherwise how it should be handled if it were not to be friendly. And finally, an analysis had to be made of what other companies might enter the fray as possible white knights, or different bidders welcomed by the defenders.

No single merger star could perform all this work in the short time between getting the idea and presenting it, so large support teams of analysts, associates, and junior partners were needed to be able to put the whole package together before trying it out on the client. Even then, it may have all come to nothing. The client might reject the idea, or start out with it only to abandon it later, often without any fee being paid to the banker. As the thoroughness of the required analyses needed to put deals together increased, the importance of the support teams did also. The truth is that the merger stars were good client schmoozers, but without their support teams, they couldn't function at all. By the late 1990s, the star-quality component of the merger business began to fade as clients realized that it was the teams that really mattered.

As LBO operators became more active, the bankers also had to be able to know what sort of things they were looking for and to help in arranging the leveraged finance for the deals. Multiple teams had to be formed that could do all these things for many deals simultaneously, avoiding conflicts of interest, and complying with various forms of more complex insider-trading rules that were starting to be enforced for the first time.

Often on the other side of their deals were teams from Goldman Sachs, which had always preferred representing the "seller" side in mergers, and who used that experience to specialize in assisting defenders against unwanted or inadequate takeover efforts. This business was developed and polished during the 1970s by Steve Friedman, a highly competitive Cornell wrestling champion, and Geoff Boisi, Peter Sachs and Mike Overlock, his principal protégés. Steve moved up within Goldman Sachs (and together with Bob Rubin, who headed risk arbitrage during the early 1980s) was named as co-CEO of the firm when John Weinberg retired. Boisi replaced Steve as head of Mergers, but left Goldman Sachs to form his own firm, which was later sold to Chase Manhattan Bank, in which he subsequently rose to a high position and helped engineer the bank's acquisition of JPMorgan, before leaving to set up another venture. The Goldman teams were expert in blocking moves, demonstrating unrealized values in companies that made takeover offers appear to be too low, and in negotiating better arrangements than were originally offered. They worked with buyers, too, when the deals were friendly enough, or where the buyer wanted only advice and counsel, not public identification with a hostile takeover effort. Merrill Lynch, Lazard Frères, and a few other firms were also involved as frequent advisors on merger transactions, on either side of the deal; seven or eight firms controlled the bulk of the large merger business in the 1980s.

Battlefield Tactics

An early hostile tactic developed in the early 1980s in which an activist potential buyer would announce that it had acquired a significant minority position in a target company and was considering making an offer for the rest. The potential buyer might also announce that although it had not fully arranged financing for the transaction (which might be quite a large amount), it had received a letter from a Wall Street firm (usually Drexel Burnham) saying that the firm was "highly confident" that the financing for the takeover could be arranged. That might be enough to frighten the board of the target company into making an offer to buy out the investor at a premium price (one that was not paid to any other stockholder), in order to get it to agree to go away. Such transactions were soon dubbed "greenmail," and became highly unpopular with institutional investors. Nonetheless, even such large companies as Texaco and Disney were subjected to successful greenmail attacks.

Normally, however, hostile takeover attempts would be announced by buyers seeking to acquire control of the target companies. In many such cases the prospective buyer would send a letter to the CEO of the target company suggesting that the two companies get together to discuss a merger, offering a significant premium over the market price, and noting that the letter would be released to the press if a positive reply were not soon received. Such a letter, called a "bear hug" ("we love you but can crush you"), in effect put the target company in play (i.e., forced the board to respond publicly to the offer), and set the market in motion to expect the company to be sold. The stock price of the target company would rise as a result of the announcement and some shareholders would sell to take advantage of the higher price. Arbitrageurs, seeking to tender the stock in an offer, would buy huge numbers of shares. This put more pressure on the board, which might be sued by shareholders or the prospective buyer for blocking a bona fide offer that was in the best interests of shareholders. If the offer was in cash, as many offers in the 1980s were, the only deterrence would be to demonstrate that the buyer was unable to raise the money, which was hard to do. Very few offers that put companies in play resulted in the target escaping a merger with someone.

The game was changed, however, when Martin Lipton, an imaginative lawyer who headed a small corporate law firm in New York, introduced a radical new idea called the shareholder rights plan (otherwise known as the poison pill), which returned control of takeover situations to the boards of the target companies. Lipton designed the rights plan to be something a board could authorize without shareholder approval. It would provide that in the event that an independent party acquired an ownership interest in the company greater than a threshold level (e.g., 30 percent) without the consent of the board of directors, then all shareholders except the threshold-crosser would automatically be issued rights to acquire additional shares in the company at an exceptionally low price, such as 50 percent of the market value. Thus the threshold-crosser would in effect be swallowing a poison pill if doing so without board consent. No one has ever digested such a pill; all have deferred crossing the prohibited threshold in an effort to obtain board consent through negotiation or litigation. Often consent would be granted, but only at a higher price. The first shareholder rights plan was created for Household Finance in 1984. The would-be acquirer challenged the action of the board in Delaware Chancery Court—Household was incorporated in Delaware; the Chancery Court there hears all disputes related to corporate governance, control, and fiduciary duty—but the Chancery Court, and the Delaware Supreme Court on appeal, upheld the board. Thereafter, many hundreds of other Delaware corporations (and many from other states) incorporated shareholder rights plans of their own. The poison pill plans, like staggered boards and the removal of cumulative voting, were not intended to prevent takeovers, but to slow them down and require bidders to negotiate with the board of the target companies, rather than just drop an offer on the shareholders while bypassing the board. Since the poison pill's inception, deals continued, but they were done differently.

The next several years were spent challenging the applicability of poison pills under different circumstances. In theory, a board with a pill in place could "just say no"* to any takeover threat. But the Delaware Chancery Court ruled that poison pills could not be used unreasonably: boards could not use them to block actions that might otherwise constitute a breach of fiduciary duty, and in cases in which important ownership issues were at stake, boards would be required to meet enhanced standards of fiduciary duty. But boards' abilities to issue shareholder rights plans were upheld. Over time, the court's hundred or so rulings provided a volume of case law that brightly illuminated the pathway of what would and would not be permitted. Many of the rulings were controversial, but rulings are rulings, and they were upheld. The court disallowed poison pills, and the sale of "crown jewels" (i.e., large important assets of a company) on a number of occasions, enabling hostile takeover deals to be completed. The result was a much higher standard of corporate governance and fair play in takeover matters that balanced the interests of owners and managers in a sensible way. Hostile deals could occur, but they would be delayed until boards could consider them appropriately, which was another way of saying that the boards could extract a higher price for their consent if no better offer came along as a result of the company's being put in play. During the merger boom that followed in 1996–2000, when more than $3 trillion in U.S. deals were done (and another $3 trillion in non-U.S. deals), hostile takeovers declined to less than 5 percent in the United States, while in Europe they still comprised around 10 percent of all deals.

In one 1985 case involving Trans Union Corporation, the Delaware Chancery Court provided a great service to the investment banking community. In this case, a bidder made what seemed to be a fully priced offer and said it would expire in a few days. The board accepted the offer, thinking that if a higher offer were received once the news was out, the

---

* Named after Nancy Reagan's high-visibility program to encourage young people not to take drugs.

board would be free to accept it. So it accepted the offer without having had time to review expert advice as to what the company was worth at the time. A shareholder sued that the board had violated its fiduciary duties of care to shareholders by not securing advice from investment bankers or other experts, and the Chancery Court ruled in favor of the plaintiff.[6] Thereafter, all contested deals had to have expert advice from investment bankers, even if the advice was limited to providing a "fairness opinion." Bankers were thought to be willing to write fairness opinions about anything if it involved receiving a fee, but in reality, the fairness opinion could be challenged in court and bankers held responsible if their opinions were not defensible. Thus the bankers had to be prepared to face the risk and expense of litigation (though these were always covered by indemnification from their clients). Some were more willing than others to stick their necks out. Bruce Wasserstein, who represented many hostile bidders in the 1980s, developed the nickname Bid-'em-up Bruce for his willingness to urge clients to increase bid prices in contested deals, knowing he would have to be the one offering the fairness opinion, which often turned out to be very creative.

LBOs

The basic concept of a leveraged buyout was to find a company that was seemingly undervalued by the stock market or by its owners; to purchase the company for the purpose of rejuvenating it with strong incentives for operating management; to borrow most of the money with which to make the purchase; to run the company to maximize cash flow and repay debt, and then to resell it after a few years either through an initial public offering or in the merger market. The business to be acquired did not have to be especially successful—ideally it would be an unglamorous, mundane, noncyclical business that threw off a steady cash flow and did not require a lot of new investment. Banks would often lend around 50 percent of the purchase price, secured by a lien on the company's assets, and finance companies or insurance companies might lend 30 percent on the cash flow in the form of high-yielding subordinated debt, with a small equity participation. The LBO operator would put up the remaining 20 percent of the purchase price in the form of equity (in the mid-1980s, when this market was really hot, the equity components were often as low as 10 percent). All the borrowing reduced taxes and leveraged the investment's return, but of course it also greatly increased the risk. So it was essential that as soon as the LBO operator assumed control, he acted to reduce the risk by making changes, sometimes drastic ones, that could increase cash flow, and then used the cash to lower the debt exposure. After a few years of this, the debt would be reduced to a more normal level and cash flow increased to supply a comfortable margin against default.

Jerry Kohlberg developed transactions of this type (then called bootstrap acquisitions) while head of corporate finance at Bear Stearns in the 1960s. They were initially rather small deals involving family-owned companies without an heir apparent. Kohlberg invited the sellers to stay on as managers with a small continuing ownership interest and to cooperate in finding ways to reduce costs and increase cash flow. This lowered the risks of such deals considerably, and enabled him and his partners to make significant returns. One of his first deals was for a dental supply and precious metals company called Stern Metals (later Sterndent), which he bought for $9.5 million in 1965 together with some members of the Stern family, with an equity investment of $500,000 and the rest borrowed from banks and finance companies. Kohlberg offered strong incentives to management, and a few years later he sold Bear Stearns's equity stake for $4 million.

Soon afterward he added two young associates at the firm, first cousins Henry Kravis and George Roberts, to the unit handling LBOs. In 1976, the three of them left Bear Stearns to form their own firm, Kohlberg Kravis Roberts and Co., with capital of $120,000. The following year they bought a small truck suspension maker, A.J. Industries, for $25.6 million. They sold this company in 1985 for $75 million. KKR raised its first LBO fund for $30 million in 1978 by selling limited partnership interests to some state pension funds and other institutional investors. In 1979, KKR surprised all of Wall Street with its announcement of a $355 million buyout of Houdaille Industries, a maker of pumps, machine tools, and auto parts. By far the largest LBO transaction ever done, it utilized a capital structure similar to RJR Nabisco's and it opened everyone's eyes as to what could actually be done. By 1984, KKR had completed its fourth fund, this one for $1 billion—it had several other competitors at the time, but it was the first to market LBO funds in large size to major institutional investors and thus they were the first to compete for large, high-visibility public deals of which the $25 billion RJR Nabisco transaction in 1988 was by far the largest.

In 1980, LBOs aggregating about $2 billion in capitalized value were completed. By 1984, the volume had swollen to 76 deals totaling $11.8 billion; and in 1986, 212 LBOs totaling $37.6 billion. In 1988, 239 were completed worth $81.2 billion. Kohlberg was no longer an investment banker; he had become a money manager charging an annual fee of about 2 percent of assets under management and 20 percent of profits, just like a hedge fund.

The LBO business became a bonanza that turned all three of the initial partners into billionaires,* and attracted many new competitors, including several others that migrated from Wall Street, especially the Blackstone Group, founded by Pete Peterson and Steve Schwartzman after they were pushed out of Lehman Brothers. Some Wall Street firms also began to invest in LBOs, at first with their own money and subsequently through private equity funds similar to KKR.

The LBO boom fizzled out in 1990, along with the market for junk bonds, and most of the focus in the 1990s was on strategic mergers between companies in the technology, finance, drugs, and communications industries. LBOs declined to less than 1 percent of all mergers in the United States in 1996, but they began to revive in Europe, where they became 15 percent of all merger transactions by 1999.

Large LBOs reappeared in the United States in the early 2000s under the label of "private equity" investments, a general term referring to private placements of illiquid equity investments of various types, but principally comprising LBOs—and, combined with a soaring activity in Europe, constituted another boom period in 2004–2007 (totaling $1.9 trillion in transaction value), before declining again in 2007. This time the financing of LBOs was arranged differently. Banks still provided senior loan facilities, and junk bonds of subordinated debt were still sold, but a new form of subordinated "leveraged loans" appeared that provided much of the financing for the LBO transactions, often with the loans being made by the investment bankers arranging the transactions. These banks advanced their own money to enable their clients to act quickly and confidentially to tie up their deals, but they didn't insist on tight covenant structures to constrain the borrower. The banks received attractive loan spreads and fees for doing this, but they didn't intend to hold them for long—the loans would be resold in the market as soon as the deal was

---

* Kohlberg had a brain tumor in 1985, which proved to be benign but took a year or more to be treated. While he was away, the firm was run by Kravis and Roberts, who departed somewhat from Kohlberg's more conservative investing principles. They separated, as a result, with Jerry Kohlberg leaving to set up a new firm, Kohlberg and Co., in 1987.

completed, or combined with others into collateralized debt obligations (CDOs), or be refinanced by junk bonds as soon as they could be.

By midyear 2007, after a very robust, record-setting six months of LBO activity in the United States and Europe, banks and investment banks held more than $300 billion in such loans on their books. At that point, the credit markets began to close up, frightened by fears of defaults and illiquidity in the market for collateralized mortgage debt. The market for collateralized mortgage obligations (CMOs) became very illiquid very quickly, and the problem spread to CDOs, leveraged loans, and junk bonds. The leveraged loans couldn't be sold in the market or as CDOs or refinanced with junk bonds. Loan spreads shot up sharply, and the value of loans carried on the books of banks had to be marked to market, requiring large loan loss write-offs to be taken. In aggregate, these write-offs exceeded approximately $30 billion before the storm passed, and most of the write-offs were concentrated in only a few major banks—the same ones that had been forced to take large write-offs in the mortgage market—which led to a collapse in the stock prices of those banks and numerous senior management changes. In this credit environment, several LBO deals arranged before the crisis were canceled, despite threats of litigation. New deals could not attract financing, and the LBO business (and much of the non-LBO merger business) came to a sudden halt and did not reopen again for years.

THE BREAKUP OF MA BELL

American Telephone and Telegraph Co. was formed in 1887 and soon became a monopoly by consolidating dozens of local or regional telephone companies that used the Bell System, invented by Alexander Graham Bell in 1877. The government was eager to see the system expand at first, but by 1912 it realized that the "natural monopoly" that had evolved might nonetheless need restraining. It required the company to sell off its Western Union telegraph affiliate and to refrain from acquiring any more telephone companies without the government's consent. In time, the government's restrictions increased—AT&T could not be in any business but telephones and had to submit to rate regulation by the Federal Communications Commission. However, the company had managed to present itself as a very benign monopoly by heavily investing in technology that was essential during World War II and afterward, which enabled it to lower costs while still expanding capacity. "Ma Bell" was the nickname that "the phone company" developed; no one but government lawyers appeared to object to the monopoly, and millions of Americans owned its stock.

By 1974, when the Nixon administration's Justice Department made the government's most serious effort to cause the company to be broken up, it had more than one million employees and $300 billion in revenues, and it totally dominated the local and long-distance telephone businesses in the United States. The government wanted the company broken up into separate pieces that would compete with one another but also allow other competitors to enter the business. The suit worked its way slowly through the system for eight years, until it was settled by the Reagan administration in January 1982 (a long-running antitrust suit against IBM was dismissed on the same day). The settlement with AT&T provided that the company would retain its long-distance business, its Western Electric equipment manufacturing subsidiary, and Bell Labs, its R&D unit—these two units were combined to form Lucent Technologies—but divest itself within eighteen months of all of the rest of its businesses, including twenty-two local telephone operating companies and two partially owned operating companies. In return, AT&T would no longer be restricted from entering nonregulated telecommunications businesses, such as computerized information and cable television systems.[7]

The announcement set off an explosion of activity on Wall Street, as firms began to consider what the breakup would mean to financial markets, future investment banking business, and to them. Immediately demand for AT&T stock went through the roof— trading was halted on the NYSE because of a huge influx of buy orders. When trading resumed, volume was intense, and the price rose 3.5 percent on a day on which the market as a whole was down more than 1 percent. Some of this demand was from institutions happy with the outcome—AT&T would be free to enter new technology areas and would have to give up only its low-growth operating companies, which made up about 70 percent of its revenues, to do so. Some thought this was a good trade for AT&T. But surely the bulk of the demand pouring in the day after the announcement of the breakup was from arbitrageurs expecting that the market value of the various parts would prove to be greater than the consolidated whole, as had been the case with the forced breakup of Standard Oil Company in 1911. Those who had bought shares of Standard Oil on the announcement of the breakup made a significant profit when they sold the shares of the thirty or so individual enterprises into which the company was divided. The same thing was likely to happen again, the arbitrageurs thought, when one of the largest companies in America was divided into a slew of separately managed, more competitive units. Because of discrepancies in valuation between the pricing of the "old" AT&T shares and the new "when-issued" shares, investors were theoretically able to make risk-free profits.

But the deal was not without risk: it would be at least eighteen months before the breakup actually occurred—and legal issues or other delays could extend this occasion further—during which time markets could change drastically, new events might occur that could affect the value of the companies, or interest rates on finance positions could rise. Also, it was not easy to determine when to acquire an initial stake, or how much of one to take on. There were many investing strategies in play, and these would change over the course of the waiting time until the shares in the operating companies were finally issued. Goldman Sachs, under chief arbitrageur Bob Rubin, took a big position in the breakup and nursed it along until the shares were sold profitably.

In the meantime, AT&T had a huge task to decide how to prepare the companies for their spin-off. The twenty-two operating companies would be split into seven independent regional Bell operating companies, or "Baby Bells." But, in addition, management teams had to be selected, decisions made as to how much of AT&T's debt should be allocated to each operating company, and information that would meet SEC standards prepared on all the companies. Investment bankers were eager to capture a share of the bonanza, giving advice on breakup values and ultimately representing either the Baby Bells or AT&T, which were expected to be large capital market users in the future. Previously all this investment banking business had belonged solely to Morgan Stanley; now it was all up for grabs. And there were also the future business strategies of other companies to consider; AT&T would want to acquire computer, cable, or information companies to develop its business into newly permitted areas, and the Baby Bells would probably have similar aspirations to acquire other operating companies to the extent that they were permitted to. There was also the effect all this would have on independent telephone companies—they might be hampered in competing with the newly independent Baby Bells, or they might not. In any case, the breakup of AT&T would comprise the largest single opportunity to compete for top-quality investment banking business that the market had ever seen, and the banks were all over it.

The breakup did lead to a surge in competition in the long-distance telecommunications market, and to extensive diversification of AT&T into new technologies and businesses. Efforts by companies such as Sprint and MCI (WorldCom) were successful, and many new long-distance companies (which absorbed the Internet when it came along) prospered. AT&T's strategic gambit into computer systems (AT&T Computer Systems), cable, and high-technology equipment in exchange for its divestiture failed, however, and after spinning off its manufacturing operations (Lucent) and several misguided acquisitions (NCR and AT&T Broadband), it was left with only its core business, AT&T Long Lines and its successor AT&T Communications. At this point AT&T was purchased by one of its own Baby Bell spin-offs, SBC Communications, which started as Southwestern Bell and subsequently acquired three other of the Babies (Pacific Telesis in 1997, Ameritech in 1999, and BellSouth in 2006). The other Babies have also since been taken up in mergers: Bell Atlantic acquired NYNEX in 1996, and GTE, a nonregulated business, in 2000, and then changed its name to Verizon; and U.S. West was acquired by Qwest in 2000. Whatever good the breakup did to increase competition—and it surely did a lot—it certainly created a lot of business for Wall Street.

SCANDALS

The huge volume of corporate acquisitions and restructuring in the 1980s created with it temptations on the part of those who had access to information about deals to find a way to trade on it. This was illegal, though the law of insider trading was complex and indeed was still being shaped as various cases slowly made their way through the federal courts and the SEC. There was quite often a run-up in the stock price of target companies of mergers a day or two before the deals were announced. The SEC was fully aware of this and doing what it could to bring charges against offenders, but the progress it made was slow going and did not appear to be effective in deterring other cases of improper trading.

An insider is an officer, director, or important stockholder of a company who could be presumed to have information the market did not have about future events or results. It is illegal for insiders to trade on such information until it becomes public. It is also illegal for others to trade on information received directly from insiders, though sometimes the information is passed on or discovered and further passed along by third parties, making its "insiderness" unclear. In 1981, John Shad, a street-smart former vice-chairman of E. F. Hutton, became chairman of the SEC and publicly resolved to bring an end to insider trading, which he claimed had become rampant. In those days, the SEC and the NYSE lacked the technical tools they have today for identifying suspicious trades and tracing them back to their origins. Much effort was put into trying to curtail insider trading, and many new cases were opened, but lacking definitive evidence, they were often resolved with just minor penalties and little publicity. In 1985, however, Mr. Shad was handed a gift-wrapped box that would enable him to carry out his resolution. Inside the box was a suspicious-looking character named Dennis Levine, a thirty-three-year-old managing director of Drexel Burnham with a lot to say about insider trading.

Levine was an ambitious kid from Queens who'd scrambled his way into investment banking after graduating from Bernard Baruch College. After two or three earlier positions, he had become a mid-level mergers specialist at Drexel Burnham, earning about $1 million a year. He was a deal-spotter, someone who nosed around for business using his contacts and networks, and was thought to be reasonably good at it, if sometimes regarded as something of a loose cannon. For the past six years, however, he had been trading secretly in small amounts of shares of companies involved in mergers. These included companies known to Drexel, but in addition he had formed a ring of young associates from other firms who funneled information to him about other forthcoming deals. He had opened an account in the Bahamas with Bank Leu, a Swiss Bank with a branch there, which executed the trades for him through various brokers in the Caribbean area. In all, Levine made $12.6 million in profits from these illegal activities.

In March 1985, an anonymous letter arrived in the Caracas, Venezuela, office of Merrill Lynch suggesting that two employees there had been trading on inside information. The firm investigated and found that the two had been copying trades a third broker was making for Bank Leu, and it notified the SEC. Bank Leu was asked to identify its client, but it refused to do so, claiming that Swiss banking law prohibited it from providing such information. The SEC had noticed that many of the suspicious trades it identified went through Swiss banks, and it took the matter up with the Swiss government, which also protested that the law was what it was. The issue escalated to higher levels, and a year later the Swiss decided to cooperate in order to prevent the United States from canceling the banking licenses held by Swiss banks in the United States, and Bank Leu was compelled to give up its client: Dennis Levine. The SEC (which is limited to bringing civil enforcement actions) turned the case over to the U.S. Attorney for the Southern District of New York, Rudolph Giuliani, for criminal prosecution, and Giuliani not so nicely asked Levine if he wanted to reduce his otherwise considerable jail time by cooperating with the government. Levine decided he would like to do so.

He pointed the finger at his hapless yuppie informers from the other firms, and they were quickly rolled up. But Giuliani was not satisfied and pressed for more. So Dennis gave up Ivan Boesky, New York's most flamboyant risk arbitrageur, to whom Levine secretly had been passing tips. Boesky was a very rich and well-known figure on the New York financial scene, a shameless self-promoter who gloried in the attention he received, and used it to attract investors in his funds. Originally from Detroit, he'd dropped out of school repeatedly and amounted to very little until he appeared in New York and began to work in the risk arbitrage business for a series of small firms. He did very well in the 1970s, sometimes producing returns of 90 percent or more, and became very visible as merger activity resumed in the 1980s. In 1986, Boesky gave a speech at the University of California, Berkeley, in which he offered the now-famous line "Greed is good." He was thought to be the model for the disreputable character Gordon Gekko, played by Michael Douglas, in the 1987 movie *Wall Street*. He wrote a book at the peak of his fame called *Merger Mania*, in which he described what he did as a special art form, not just a regular business. He put a lot of pressure on himself to produce high returns for his investors, and in the end his approach was revealed to be less artful than crooked. In November 1986, Boesky admitted his misdeeds and agreed to cooperate with Giuliani in exchange for a prison term of three and a half years (he would serve only two) and a fine of $100 million, at the time the highest fine ever charged a financial offender for anything.

When it came time for Boesky to cooperate, he implicated Martin Siegel, Drexel's merger head, who had recently joined the firm from Kidder Peabody, where he had headed both the firm's merger and its risk arbitrage businesses. Siegel was a precocious thirty-eight-year-old Rensselaer Polytechnic and Harvard Business School graduate who had become an investment banking star at Kidder Peabody and was subsequently poached by Drexel Burnham. He provided Boesky with inside information on large deals he was involved with in exchange for briefcases stuffed with cash, handed off in laughably clandestine ways. No one knows why Siegel would do such a thing, but some trace it back to the fact that his small-businessman father had been forced to struggle for years against big store competitors when Siegel was a young man, and this had made him feel compulsively insecure about money.

Siegel, confronted by Giuliani, also quickly became eager to cooperate. Giuliani, on a roll, took what Siegel had to say at face value, without checking into the charges very deeply, and immediately acted on it, arresting Richard Wigton and Timothy Tabor, Siegel's two assistants at Kidder Peabody, and Robert Freeman, then Goldman Sachs's partner responsible for risk arbitrage. The arrests were staged to be public events—the accused men were frog-marched out of their buildings (one in handcuffs) by U.S. marshals in front of photographers. Charges against the two Kidder associates (one of whom was a Rhodes scholar) were subsequently dropped, but Freeman was pursued solely on the basis of Siegel's testimony, most of which was ultimately found to be false.[8] After two and a half years of maintaining his innocence, and still with no active indictment, Freeman learned that the government threatened to use the RICO Act against him. Under RICO, a defendant must put up an enormous bond and could have his assets seized, which makes one's defense strategies far more limited, with the penalties far more severe if the person is convicted. With the threat of RICO charges against him, he agreed to plead guilty to a single count of mail fraud. He was sentenced to a fine of $1 million and four months in jail, and of course he resigned as a partner at Goldman Sachs.

Boesky, Siegel, and Freeman were very prominent names that made headlines for Giuliani, but the three of them together did not equal the weight of the catch that Michael Milken, the hugely rich king of junk bonds, represented. Boesky provided Giuliani with crucial information needed to prosecute Milken and Drexel Burnham, which Giuliani regarded as effectively being controlled by Milken. Neither Milken nor Drexel would agree to cooperate, and instead both vigorously resisted Giuliani's charges.

Giuliani again responded by threatening to bring the charges under RICO, which substantially increased the stakes, and as a practical matter, this forced Drexel to agree to plead guilty to criminal charges, pay a $650 million fine, and to sever its ties to Milken and cooperate in his prosecution.* Milken, despite Drexel's betrayal, fought on a few months longer,

---

*During the 1990s, the federal courts, guided by the U.S. Supreme Court, substantially limited the applicability of RICO in civil cases.

but eventually (after a promise to leave his brother out of the lawsuit) agreed to admit to six felony charges involving market manipulation, for which he was fined $600 million (an amount later increased by civil litigation to about $1 billion) and sentenced to ten years in jail, a term that stunned Wall Street, though it would be reduced if he cooperated with the government. Milken provided some cooperation and was paroled after less than three years. Despite the fine and damages he paid, Milken was still worth more than $1 billion when he was released.[9]

The story of these insider trading cases, starting with Dennis Levine and lasting nearly five years until the guilty plea of Michael Milken, was told by James Stewart, a Pulitzer Prize–winning *Wall Street Journal* reporter in a bestselling book, *Den of Thieves*. Stewart had covered the insider trading stories as a reporter for the *Journal*, and reportedly had received information about Siegel's testimony and other matters that was leaked to him by Giuliani's office and which he accepted without challenge.

Illegal Wall Street trading naturally attracted a lot of attention in the media, and did much to persuade the public of low moral standards of even high-grade Wall Street firms, and Giuliani was able to parlay his role as a defender of the public interest into becoming the mayor of New York City. During all this, most of the major firms simply kept their heads down and waited for the storm to subside, but inside the firms, Wall Streeters were of at least two minds about the events. Some were upset that as widespread as the charges seemed to be, only a tiny percentage of Wall Street professionals had been involved, but the whole industry was taking the blame and paying the consequences. Others were more defensive, claiming that the law was unclear in many areas and that Giuliani had bullied people and been unfair in his self-advancing zeal to get convictions. Indeed, there was a very vocal group of Milken supporters (backed by extensive public relations efforts) who maintained that Milken had done nothing wrong but had been forced by the indiscriminate use of the exceptional powers of a federal prosecutor to admit to some technical violations in order to get the matter behind him. Others claimed he had been victimized because he had been so successful operating outside the established system and that those inside it had wanted to see him brought down.

One credible source on the Milken matter is Fred Joseph, Drexel's president at the time and its lead counterpart to the government's actions. Drexel had resisted settling with the government, and the negotiations dragged on. At one point the government said it was prepared to show

Joseph what it had in order to persuade Drexel to negotiate, even though this was not something it usually did. According to Joseph:

> They showed me spreadsheets with the calculations [justifying a] $5.3 million payment to Boesky, some trading tickets with signatures on them, and other incriminating documents. They also had me listen to tapes where you could hear people trying to affect the price of the stock, which is by definition manipulation. All I can say is, it was troublesome. It was a powerful batch of information . . . With the accumulated information they showed me, and new stuff I learned, it became clear that some things that shouldn't have been done were done. As you can imagine, it had an enormous impact on the way I was thinking.[10]

In fact, the government brought nearly one hundred counts of illegality against Milken. Some may have seemed trivial to the defendants and their supporters, but trivial or not, if charges are brought and presented to a jury, the jury may decide to convict. Facing a jury is always a big risk, whatever one's own perception of his guilt may be, and may cause someone who believes he did nothing wrong nevertheless to accept a plea bargain. This may seem unfair, but the government would probably just say, "Look, our job is to bring these charges when we believe things you did might have broken the law, and your job is not to do these things so as to avoid doubt about the outcome and the risk of conviction."

To be sure, this message did get through. Prosecutors may seem to be unfair to those caught up in charges, but the public does not want its prosecutors to be wimps. If a public official or prosecutor smells public support that will lift his or her own image, you can expect a vigorous effort to besmirch the accused parties and to apply all of the considerable powers that prosecutors have to drive home a settlement or, in criminal cases, an admission of guilt. Fairness may not have anything to do with it. In fact, many years later, Giuliani commented that the arrests of Freeman, Wigton, and Tabor should not have been made and that he owed those arrested an apology, which he never provided.[11] This disregard of fairness was repeated by Eliot Spitzer, attorney general of New York, in his pursuit of firms he thought were wrongdoers on Wall Street almost twenty years later.

These events should lead anyone considering insider trading or market manipulation to realize that you can't do these things by yourself— there is always someone else you have to trade with or deal with in some way who will know what you have done, and if those people ever come into the grasp of prosecutors, you can be sure they will give you up in a flash to save themselves. The consequences of being in such a situation are too grim to consider, but they are likely to be ruinous, almost regardless of the degree of guilt involved.

One other result was the erection within merger and arbitrage groups of high walls to protect the leaking of information, tough internal compliance standards, and major efforts to enforce them. However, despite the best efforts of the firms, there still have been instances since the Siegel case of investment bankers and others being arrested and convicted for insider trading, so the deterrent may not have worked as well as it was intended to. Certainly the technology for detecting insider trading has improved considerably, and the penalties for those convicted or admitting to insider trading have increased, making the whole proposition very dubious, but apparently it still goes on.

The Death of Drexel Burnham

Drexel Burnham entered into its plea bargain agreement with the U.S. attorney in December of 1988. The agreement required Drexel to sever its connections with Milken and to cooperate with the government in its effort to bring a case against him. This was very hard for Drexel to do, because Milken was held in such high regard—idolized, really, by many of those who worked closely with him. Shortly afterward, Milken resigned and devoted his efforts to his defense, and Drexel began the struggle for its survival. It had to face three major challenges: to hang on to its sources of financing from banks and other traders, to hang on to its key producing personnel, and to undertake an emergency cutback of expenses that would involve laying off almost half of the firm's employees. Drexel was severely weakened by its ordeal, but Fred Joseph believed that it could pull these things off and survive, and the firm nearly did so. It completed the underwriting of the massive RJR Nabisco junk bond offerings in 1989, for which a $250 million fee was involved, and it actually made money in that year.

But the market in junk bonds was beginning to weaken as some of the earlier issuers struggled to make their debt service payments. Economic conditions were tightening up, and bankruptcies and loan defaults were increasing. By the end of 1989, the junk bond market had suffered a large-scale loss of confidence. Many of Milken's earlier clients had declared bankruptcy, and junk bond prices everywhere began to sink rapidly during the first quarter of 1990, and later fell into freefall. This situation trapped Drexel—to maintain the credibility of the firm's main franchise, its domination of the junk bond business, it had to be willing to buy in all the bonds that its clients wanted to sell, yet having had its capital position and its access to credit so seriously eroded by its legal difficulties, the firm could scarcely expect to survive if the markets didn't turn up, which they didn't.

The junk market collapse was the final blow to Drexel, which, unable to roll over its commercial paper or induce others to rescue it, threw in the towel and declared itself bankrupt in February 1990. When it folded, Drexel had more than a billion dollars tied up in dealer inventories worth much less than it had paid for them. No one stepped in to help, neither the Federal Reserve nor any of its competitors, which were also suffering from the harsh conditions in the markets, so the firm was liquidated. There was no question, however, of Drexel's being too big to fail, and therefore needing government support. By comparison to the major firms of Wall Street in the late 2000s, Drexel was neither large enough, nor sufficiently interconnected with other major firms for its bankruptcy to threaten the solvency of any other firm. All that would come twenty years later.

Milken had made the firm but had also brought it down. However, many of his people—bright, scrappy, and driven, like New Men everywhere—survived and flourished in the 1990s, in hedge funds or as activist, takeover entrepreneurs. Milken, a survivor of prostate cancer discovered after his sentencing, served his prison term and devoted himself to medical research and philanthropy. The junk bond business recovered after a few years and returned to duty, providing financing for takeovers and distress situations, and indirectly extending itself into the leveraged loan market that flourished in the 2000s.

9

POWER SHIFTS

AFTER A RUN OF ABOUT EIGHT YEARS, the great LBO boom of the 1980s came to an end, leaving an exhausted junk bond market in the trembling hands of an embattled Drexel Burnham, which had been fending off federal charges of market manipulation and insider trading. By then the junk bond market had run its course, and during 1989, prices began to sink, then plunged as more and more of the lowest-grade issuers that had taken advantage of a hungry market in the years before 1988 began to default.

As the prices slumped, many of the bolder LBO bankers of the late 1980s were left holding bags of unsellable "bridge loans," loans extended to an acquirer to enable it to assemble the funds needed to purchase control of a target company, after which a full merger of the two companies would take place and the bridge loan would be refinanced by a bond issue, usually a junk bond issue. Investment banks acting as merger advisors would often extend the bridge loan from their own funds to facilitate the transaction, preserve its confidentiality, and participate in the lucrative fees that could be charged. However, as the market for junk bonds deteriorated, the refinancing of the bridge loans could not be completed. First Boston, in particular, suffered a lot of damage from a $1 billion portfolio of bridge loans to such ill-fated deals as the buyouts of Federated Department Stores and Ohio Mattress. Shearson Lehman Hutton and Merrill Lynch also had large bridge loan exposures, and in the end Credit Suisse had to take some of First Boston's positions on its own books to ensure the solvency of the firm. Without their deep-pocketed parents, First Boston and Shearson might well have followed the unhappy path of Drexel into bankruptcy.

The idea behind bridge lending was that the high fees and interest earned would provide a pool of profits sufficiently large to absorb normal risks from delays in refinancing the bridge loans with permanent debt. The concept, used moderately to support creditworthy transactions, proved to be sound. But it was not sound when used immoderately or in connection with shaky deals, or during market conditions that virtually shut off all opportunities for refinancing. Boom periods too often tend toward excess—especially in their late stages—and the excesses always seem to lead to trouble. Just as the excesses are underestimated, so are the consequences from them.

PROPRIETARY TRADING

Taking positions in bridge loans was a form of "proprietary trading," which most large Wall Street firms had begun to adopt in the 1980s. Previously many such firms had resisted trading as being too risky, but with the expansion of the debt markets, securitization, and the high level of activity in the merger and LBO markets, most of the more traditional investment banks, such as Morgan Stanley, First Boston, Merrill Lynch, and Lehman Brothers, began to regard trading as a major line of business, much as Salomon Brothers, Bear Stearns, and Goldman Sachs had done for years.

Traders can make money by market making, in which they provide prices at which they will buy or sell securities to clients and counterparties, or they can invest their own money in a trading position conceived or originated from their proprietary resources of skills, know-how, or information. Market making, which can include block trading, usually involves only modest amounts of capital and risk; proprietary trading, however, which can offer substantial profit opportunities, can involve great quantities of both. Money could be made, for example, by positioning the firm for an expected market shift, say, by borrowing $5 or $10 billion to invest in government bonds and making an informed guess that the prices of the bonds will go up within a few days. Buying on margin, you can control $5 billion in Treasuries with only $50 million in capital. If the price goes up fifty basis points (.50 percent) and you sell out within a week, you've made $2.5 million, before your financing costs. This would be a very high annualized rate of return on your investment, even after financing costs. Exposure of this type, however, can be very expensive if it goes wrong (what if prices instead go down by .5 percent?), so new ways of managing risk by hedging positions had to be found.

Salomon Brothers led the way in exposing itself to huge trading risks, developing new hedging techniques, and broadening the range of instruments traded. The firm made markets for its clients in all sorts of fixed-income securities, all over the world. It also developed proprietary trading to entirely new levels. John Meriwether headed Salomon's fixed-income arbitrage desk in the early 1980s, seeking ways to profit from market inefficiencies. He and his traders developed "spread trades," in which investments were made in the difference between the yield in a bond and that of another, reference bond, such as a U.S. Treasury security. If a spread is large, relative to historical amounts (i.e., an apparent aberration), it may be a good bet to assume it will narrow over time, and the change would be the trader's profit, which might be leveraged several times. You could apply the spread trading idea to hundreds of different instruments, but to do it safely (or more safely than otherwise) you would have to have good and timely information about the two bonds being compared. Providing such good and timely information is what the first Bloomberg machine did; there was much demand for it because it enabled Merrill Lynch, the first buyer of the machine, to keep up with Salomon, which either seemed to have better information than everyone else or simply acted, unhesitatingly, as if it did.

Meriwether used Salomon's Ph.D.s to help model markets he was interested in, and to find apparent aberrations. He would bet on the aberrations, sometimes very heavily, and wait for them to disappear (i.e., for the bonds to be repriced correctly) then liquidate the position. It was inherently rational and it worked most of the time, though sometimes an unexpected market event would occur to ruin things. Still, on balance, this kind of investing was expected to make returns far higher than market making or indeed from almost anything else Salomon did, such as underwriting. It worked for Meriwether, whose substantial contribution to Salomon's earnings led to his appointment as a vice-chairman of Salomon, replacing Ranieri, in 1988.

Spread trading got around in Wall Street, and soon nearly everyone was doing it, which meant that the industry as a whole had followed a path into highly leveraged, capital-intense trading activities that would drastically change the risk profile of the firms and create a requirement for increasingly sophisticated risk management capabilities. Not everyone learned how to master these new skills as they needed to, and some turned opportunities into failure. But on the whole, following Salomon into the trading arena shifted the axes of power within the firms to favor traders at the expense of bankers and to greatly increase the importance (and the cost) of effective risk-control systems. It also meant that firms would have to develop access to much greater amounts of capital than in the past, and this led to all of these firms becoming publicly traded corporations.

A Squeeze at Salomon

Salomon's tough-talking chairman John Gutfreund was at the peak of his career in 1985 when he was declared the "King of Wall Street," by *Business Week*. But he was tested when a large block of Salomon shares was put up for sale in 1987 by one of Phibro's largest shareholders. Ronald Perelman, an aggressive billionaire takeover specialist of the 1980s, wanted to buy the stock, but Gutfreund moved quickly to block it. He persuaded Warren Buffet to invest $700 million of Berkshire Hathaway's money in a new convertible preferred stock, and Salomon would use the money to buy the block of stock back itself. Buffett had a lot of confidence in Gutfreund, though he might have thought differently if he had been able to read Michael Lewis's 1989 bestselling *Liar's Poker*, about the realities of life inside Salomon Brothers. Gutfreund had, however, committed himself to better management and control procedures at Salomon, though the markets were difficult in 1990 and 1991, and some of his plans had to await a return to better cash flows. Earnings declined sharply in 1990 and top officers, including Gutfreund, took pay cuts. Some of the traders, however, cleaned up anyway, based on their one-off compensation deals negotiated directly with Gutfreund to reward individual performance. By the end of 1990, Salomon has pushed its trading revenues to 80 percent of total, up from 57 percent in 1987. But not all of the traders were happy.

At the center of Salomon's trading effort was its Government Securities

Department. This group personified Salomon at its best and its worst. Its brilliant, aggressive, dedicated young professionals were devoted to preserving Salomon's number one position and powerful reputation. But they were also arrogant, ruthless, and so obsessively focused on beating the competition and making money that they lost sight of everything else. As Floyd Norris of *The New York Times* put it, "At Salomon Brothers, trading has always been a form of war in which the opponent is entitled to no pity and rules are viewed as impediments to be side-stepped, if possible."

Before any government securities auction, the firm's traders endeavor to estimate what the winning rate level will be and how much paper could be sold at that rate. They try first to build a book of orders from customers and then make their bid. At the time, only firms designated by the Federal Reserve as "primary dealers" could submit bids for new Treasury issues. There were about forty such dealers, who could benefit from pre-bidding discussions with the Treasury to exchange views about the market. The dealers would aggregate their own bid for bonds with those of their large institutional customers that had authorized them to do so, in order to present the largest possible block of orders to the Treasury. To minimize their position risks, dealers would sell (short) the as-yet-unissued bonds to customers at a price that they hoped was a good bet. The dealers would then have to count on being allocated bonds in the auction in order to supply these customers with the bonds they had sold; any shortfall would have to be covered by purchasing bonds in the market.

Aggressive traders often bid for more bonds than they have orders for, and at a higher price. The more orders they have at the highest price, the more bonds they are allocated. The more they are allocated, the more they control. According to one former Salomon trader, "If you build a book of $3 billion, $5 billion, $8 billion, then you really control the situation. Then you use your muscle, your big war chest of dollars, to force the thing with a drop-dead bid."[1]

The idea is simply to try to control, or corner, the market to make those who want bonds come to Salomon to get them. However, cornering the market in Treasuries isn't allowed, though it seemed to be until July 1990, when the Treasury imposed new rules limiting the size of a single bid, after Salomon bid for, and purchased, 75 percent of a two-year issue in March. A few months later, Paul Mozer, Salomon's thirty-six-year-old managing director heading the Government Securities desk, astonished Treasury officials by bidding for 100 percent of an issue of thirty-year bonds. The Treasury rejected the bid and imposed a new rule limiting bidding to 35 percent of any single issue.[2]

In August 1991, Salomon admitted that its trading activities had become too aggressive and that it had made several illegal bids in auctions for Treasury securities between December 1990 and May 1991. A Treasury official had been suspicious about these auctions and had commenced an investigation of Salomon's bidding activities. When Mozer learned of the investigation, he came clean with his boss, John Meriwether, and in April admitted to falsifying a customer order that Salomon had presented at a February auction.[3] This and other phantom orders had put more of the notes being auctioned into Salomon's hands than the 35 percent rule allowed.

Meriwether was Salomon's top trading boss, the now-legendary character who supposedly (according to Michael Lewis) countered John Gutfreund's 1986 challenge to a hand of liar's poker—"one hand, one million dollars, no tears"—with an offer to play for "real money instead, ten million, no tears." Gutfreund apparently thought ten million was too much to bet on the serial numbers on a dollar bill, so he backed off. Salomon folklore uses this event to illustrate the "right stuff" of the trading floor, to show that even powerful, high-placed executives can't really measure up against the Cool Hand Lukes of the trading room. As cool as he was, Meriwether knew this was a big problem, so he reported it to John Gutfreund and Tom Strauss, Salomon's president. These three, plus the firm's general counsel, decided that Mozer's bidding practices had to be discontinued and reported to the Treasury. But no one actually reported them. A month later, Salomon violated the rules again, securing de facto control of 94 percent of that auction and cornering the market, causing market prices to spike (something that could be seen by anyone looking). Other dealers complained, the Treasury investigation was turned over to the Justice Department, and in June, subpoenas were issued. Salomon's admission of false bidding practices became big news.

The Treasury and the Federal Reserve were outraged and suspended Salomon from future auctions. Salomon's board of directors, whose lead outside director was Warren Buffett (Berkshire Hathaway was Salomon's largest single shareholder), called for the resignation of Gutfreund, Strauss, Meriwether, Mozer, and some lesser figures, and began pleading with the government not to put the entire firm out of business for the misdeeds of a few. Many of Salomon's customers announced that their relationship with the firm was under review, and Salomon's stock dropped 30 percent.

Buffett went to Washington to offer his personal intervention to restore faith in the firm's integrity and ethical conduct, and he succeeded in persuading the Justice Department not to bring criminal charges against the firm (lying to the government is a crime) that might put it out of business.

Buffett returned to New York and began interviewing potential replacements for Gutfreund as chief executive. He selected forty-three-year-old Deryck Maughan, who, until a month prior to these events, had been the head of Salomon's highly successful Tokyo office. He was not a trader, and had nothing to do with government securities. An Englishman, he had been at the British Treasury for ten years, received an MBA from Stanford Business School, and later decided to join Goldman Sachs in its London office (which I then headed). Salomon recruited him away, and he rose rapidly there, being sent to Tokyo as general manager. Maughan was presentable, well-mannered, articulate, and he seemed to be something other than the trading room animal the Salomon's senior people were then thought to be.

In time the scandal died down, Salomon survived to continue in the same businesses it had been in before, though now more carefully controlled. Maughan did well enough as chief executive, but it was tough—he always had to deal with the abiding attitude among the big producers that he would never have been selected by them to head the firm, so therefore they really didn't have to do what he said. Gutfreund ended his thirty-eight-year career and reign as Wall Street's king in typical fashion. A tough guy to the end, he reportedly told his top executives in a closed-door meeting, "I'm not apologizing to anybody for anything. Apologies don't mean shit. What happened, happened."[4]

LTCM and Other Trading Mistakes

John Meriwether was the only one of the fired Salomon executives to make a comeback. In 1994 he founded a hedge fund, Long-Term Capital Management (LTCM), which would reproduce the proprietary trading strategies that he had been executing for Salomon. He recruited a number of his former colleagues and two distinguished Nobel Prize–winning economists, Myron Scholes and Robert Merton, to join him in forming the fund. In 1990, Scholes had decided to get involved more directly with the financial markets and he went to Salomon as a special consultant, then becoming a managing director and co-head of its fixed-income derivative group.* LTCM, which started operations with $1 billion in investor capital, was extremely successful in the first years, with annualized returns of over 40 percent. However, following the 1997 East Asian financial crisis and the 1998 Russian government's default on its foreign debt, the highly leveraged fund lost $4.6 billion in less than four months and failed, becoming one of the most prominent examples of risk from proprietary trading in the history of the investment industry.

The LTCM episode was famous for another reason. As it began to fail, the Federal Reserve Bank of New York began to worry that because of the total size of the assets in the fund, around $100 billion, its collapse could affect the integrity of the world financial system. The fear was that in liquidating the assets, prices would be driven down sufficiently to panic the markets, adding to the considerable disruption that was already taking place in the markets then. As the New York Fed was charged by the Federal Reserve as being the principal market watcher for it, the New York Fed was certainly justified in trying to find out as much as it could about LTCM's deteriorating situation. So, alerted by Meriwether, William McDonough, the president of the New York Fed, called a meeting of the senior-most officers of the banks and investment banks thought to be exposed to LTCM to encourage them to work out some way of stabilizing the fund or otherwise taking it over. The New York Fed never intended to do anything like that itself, which would have constituted a "bailout." While the bankers were meeting, an offer from Warren Buffett (ever opportunistic where Wall Street is concerned) was received to buy all of LTCM's assets at a discounted price that would leave nothing for its partners. Cool-handed Meriwether, however, was trying to play his side of the game for as much as he could; he bet that he could let the Buffett offer expire unaccepted and that some sort of deal in which he and his partners retained some interest in the fund could be negotiated with the others that would be preferable to being left with nothing. Meriwether refused the offer, but knowledge of it caused the assembled banks to decide to fund a joint effort to buy up the assets for themselves and to resell them as market conditions improved. After a certain amount of haggling, with Bear Stearns refusing to participate, the rest decided on a deal that

---

* Scholes received the Nobel Prize in Economics for his work in formulating the Black-Scholes equation for valuing options. He was joined in this effort by Fischer Black, who joined Goldman Sachs in 1984 and later became a partner, much in the same way that Scholes had joined Salomon Brothers. Fischer Black died of cancer in 1995, before the Nobel Prize was awarded to Scholes. The Nobel Prize may not be granted posthumously.

did in fact leave the LTCM partners with a small interest. The deal calmed the markets somewhat, and in time the buy-up group profited from the effort. No money from the New York Fed or any other government agency was involved, but the New York Fed did bring the group together and encouraged them to work something out.

The episode did establish, however, that even the best and the brightest of proprietary traders can have their heads handed to them when markets lurch and then dry up in response to unexpected events, in this case the Russian default, which affected many of the bond markets in which LTCM had positions leveraged as much as a hundred times. One thing the story of LTCM showed was that you could not assume that liquidity was a constant in the markets, a lesson that would have to be relearned a decade later.

Other Trading Mishaps

There were other lessons to Wall Street firms from the trading experiences of their brethren in the 1990s.[5]

Kidder Peabody, a distinguished American investment bank with roots going back to 1865, was embarrassed by having to restate its earnings for 1993, removing $130 million in trading profits that were never earned. Kidder's head government bond trader, a Harvard Business School graduate named Joseph Jett, who was a star at the firm and received a $9 million bonus in 1993, was fired. Jett was accused of exploiting a loophole in Kidder's accounting system that incorrectly accounted for Treasury securities that had been stripped into interest-only and principal-only components, creating an illusion of trading profits. Jett apparently believed the illusion, but apparently everyone else at Kidder did, too. Such an error is hard to explain, but even more difficult to understand is how the very large positions that Jett put on the books were not questioned and the economic reality understood for what it was. Obviously Kidder's controls were not up to standard; the firm had also failed to detect rising losses in its Mortgage-backed Securities Department, which led to really large losses. These problems, which ultimately caused Kidder to look for a buyer (it found General Electric), were the result of an ambitious business plan to build market share in a particular trading area before having built the infrastructure to control it.

A similar incident occurred in 1995, when Baring Brothers, one of

Britain's oldest and most prestigious investment banks, suddenly failed when it found itself horribly overexposed and unhedged in the Japanese equities market. The 233-year-old firm had lost control of a rogue trader, Nick Leeson, who was located in its tiny Singapore office, and was forced to sell the firm to ING, a Dutch bank, for a mere £1. To save money, Baring allowed Leeson, a young back-office employee, to both trade and to manage the settlement process. He had opened a hidden "error" account in Singapore that he managed. He began to make arbitrage trades in Japan, in which the firm saw the profits, but losses went to the hidden account. This worked well for him for a while (he got credit for the profits), until he decided to be more aggressive and took large directional bets on the Japanese Nikkei index and on Japanese bond prices and the yen. On January 17, 1995, his market strategy collapsed when a large earthquake hit Kobe and caused stock, bond, and currency prices to plummet. Soon regulatory authorities began to question Baring's books, and it all came out. ING took over and fired the top twenty-three officers on the grounds that they either knew about the exposures that Leeson was putting on (and should have done something about them) or they should have known. Leeson was arrested by Singapore officials, tried for fraud, and sentenced to six and a half years in Changi Prison. He was released from prison in 1999, having been diagnosed with colon cancer, which he has survived, despite grim forecasts at the time. While in prison he wrote a memoir, *Rogue Trader*, which back-office managers have been urged to read to see what they are up against.

In 1995, S. G. Warburg, Britain's most fully integrated investment bank, experienced substantial trading losses that forced the firm to search desperately for new capital. The search was probably necessary; the desperation may not have been, but the non-trading CEO of the firm at the time, Lord Cairns, known throughout the City of London as Simon (Viscount) Garmoyle before he became the sixth Earl Cairns in 1989, may have panicked. He resigned suddenly, leaving the firm in the hands of its chairman, Sir David Scholey, a former Warburg CEO and member of the Court of Governors of the Bank of England, who put the firm up for sale and, after flirting with Morgan Stanley, made a deal with Swiss Bank Corporation, which later merged with Union Bank of Switzerland to form UBS.

POWER SHIFTS

Stung by the financial downturn of the early 1990s, the economy slipped into a recession that many observers said caused the defeat of George H. W. Bush in the presidential election of 1992 that was also contested by Texas entrepreneur Ross Perot but won by Bill Clinton. By the time the new president was sworn in in early 1993, the recession was over and the economy was beginning a recovery that would be uninterrupted until the end of the millennium, the longest continuous run of economic expansion in the nation's history. The stock market rose with it, throughout the whole of the Clinton administration (with a few short interruptions), during which the Dow Jones quadrupled.

The market was soaring for a number of reasons. Communism had come to an end, the cold war was over, and American military might had been awesomely displayed in the Gulf War of 1991. Japan was in the grip of a nasty economic slump, which removed it from the list of America's most threatening economic competitors. The European Union had adopted the Single Market Act, which removed barriers to trade and investment, harmonized economic policies, and set the stage for monetary union, which improved economic prospects and buoyed financial markets. The United States was the world's only superpower, with little to fear from China, which was embarking on a semi-liberalized pathway to achieve economic growth through trade and investment with foreign partners. Liberalization of foreign exchange regulations enabled savings, billions of dollars of them, to flow into U.S. financial markets, where they kept interest rates low and supported stock prices. The U.S. economy meanwhile was enjoying low inflation, relatively high employment, and a boost to productivity from the massive amount of corporate restructuring that occurred in the 1980s and from the widespread introduction of desktop computers and other technology improvements.

The Princes Depart

Among those enjoying the market expansion were two Wall Street veterans who joined the Clinton administration at its outset, Roger Altman, of Lehman Brothers, a former Carter administration official, who reappeared as deputy secretary of the treasury, and Bob Rubin of Goldman

Sachs, who was appointed director of the newly created National Economic Council.

To take this assignment, Rubin resigned as co-chairman of Goldman Sachs, after only two years in the position, an action that surprised many at the firm but not those who knew of Rubin's long-term interest in politics and public office. He had sought out Joe Fowler when the former treasury secretary joined the firm in 1969, to advise him on how he might involve himself in Democratic Party politics. Joe put him in touch with Robert Strauss, one of the Democrats' more visible and important behind-the-scenes players, and Strauss introduced Rubin to political fund-raising. Rubin became an important New York fund-raiser for all subsequent Democratic presidential nominees, especially Walter Mondale and Michael Dukakis, as well as helping with the campaigns of all sorts of other Democratic office seekers. By the time Bill Clinton offered him the job of being his chief economic policy coordinator, Rubin, then fifty-eight, was ready to take it. In 1995 he was selected to become treasury secretary after the retirement of Lloyd Benson. That position might have gone to Altman, one of Bill Clinton's classmates at Georgetown University, but Altman had been forced to resign after passing information to the Clintons on a Resolution Trust Company investigation into the Whitewater affair. Rubin would serve with distinction as treasury secretary for four and a half years, retiring in July 1999 and being succeeded by his deputy, Larry Summers, later the president of Harvard University and chairman of the National Economic Council for Barack Obama. On Rubin's retirement, the Reagan-Bush deficits had disappeared and the U.S. fiscal account was in surplus for the first time since Joe Fowler gave up the office more than thirty years earlier.

Rubin had always been on a very fast track. A graduate of Yale Law School, he joined briefly the New York law firm of Cleary Gottleib, Steen and Hamilton before becoming an associate in the Risk Arbitrage Department at Goldman Sachs in 1966, working with Gus Levy and L. Jay Tenenbaum as an arbitrage trader. He became a partner in 1971, and a member of the firm's powerful management committee in 1980. In 1984, after John Whitehead retired and John Weinberg was running the firm by himself, Rubin and Steve Friedman were appointed co-heads of the firm's Fixed Income Department. Friedman is a Columbia Law School graduate who also joined Goldman Sachs in 1966, after a short tour of practicing law, and who previously had headed the Merger Department. In 1987 the two were made vice-chairmen and co-chief operating officers of the firm, where it was widely accepted that they worked well together, Rubin being somewhat more the Mr. Outside and Friedman the inside guy. In December 1990, John Weinberg decided to retire after fourteen years as chairman or co-chairman, and after carefully having chosen and groomed his successors, the management committee appointed Rubin and Friedman, to become co-chairmen of the firm.

Both Rubin and Friedman were top producers, deep thinkers, and ready to make major changes to improve Goldman Sachs's profitability, risk management skills, and market position. They were eager to have a free hand to reexamine policies and procedures they believed had been made obsolete by changing markets that had increased the need for intensity, innovation, and assertiveness. They were ready for the transition to a harsher, faster-paced transactional business from the more genteel relationship-based one remembered by John Whitehead. Partners and employees needed to feel the pressure to produce results, to fight internally for the resources they needed to produce those results, and to understand that those thought to be underperforming would be let go. The highly valued culture of teamwork and cooperation inculcated by the Two Johns was brought under pressure by the new, more demanding attitudes of the new co-chairmen, though most of the firm believed that the heightened intensity imposed by the new leaders was justified by competitive conditions in the market.

Weinberg understood this and went along with it. However, he also believed, almost above all, in the importance of true dedication and loyalty to the firm on the part of its top leadership, and in this respect both Rubin and Friedman were major disappointments to him. He could understand why Bob Rubin might feel the pull of the siren song from Washington, but he was dismayed that he would forego the chairmanship of Goldman Sachs after only two years to follow it. Rubin, of course, had calculated his probabilities and assumed that if Clinton lasted eight years and Rubin did too, then he was likely to get one of the big jobs, after which he would be sixty-six and ready to slow down and enjoy some of the riches he had accumulated at Goldman, estimated then at around $100 million. Rubin was thinking about himself, Weinberg felt, not the firm, and the firm, to Weinberg, was far more important.

Steve Friedman took over as sole chairman in early 1993 and lasted less than two years. A domineering, intensely competitive, very physically fit man with seemingly boundless energy, Steve was into everything that happened at the firm. His first year set record profits, but in the second—one of Wall Street's few really bad years since the Depression—profits plunged, mainly on the back of rising interest rates and fixed-income trading losses. Other firms suffered then, too, as trading losses were rampant all over the Street. After sizeable losses in August, Friedman suddenly announced that he was resigning in order to keep a promise made to his wife to reduce the stress and strain of the job, which she thought was affecting his health. The news was explosive at Goldman Sachs—numerous general partners announced their retirements too, to get out when they could before the roof fell in, which is what many partners and employees thought Steve's action signified he was doing.

John Weinberg was horrified at the news and stepped in to help smooth things out. The management committee hurriedly appointed Jon Corzine, a co-head of Fixed-income to replace Steve, and Henry (Hank) Paulson, a co-head of Investment Banking, to be his deputy. The decision, however, did not sit well with Mark Winkelman, an extremely talented fixed-income trader who was Corzine's co-head, and he resigned, too. Corzine and Paulson spent the first few months after their appointments trying to calm the fears of partners and employees, to keep them from leaving, and for those selected for partnerships that year to accept them.

Steve Friedman's departure shocked the firm, but it recovered as the markets did. Profits returned, and Goldman Sachs bounced back almost as if nothing had happened, participating in all the many new business areas and opportunities that the 1990s presented. Steve would spend his time developing private equity businesses, and he became chairman of the board of Columbia University, but he kept a very low profile at Goldman Sachs, until Hank Paulson, who had once been a protégé of Steve's, invited him on to the board of directors of Goldman Sachs after it went public in 1999. Ironically, in 2002, Steve was appointed by President George W. Bush as head of the National Economic Council, the job Bob Rubin had accepted a decade earlier, where he served for two years in a relatively low-visibility capacity.

Jon Corzine grew up as a farm boy from Illinois, attended the state university at Urbana, and drifted to Chicago, where he joined Continental Illinois Bank in 1970. He attended the University of Chicago MBA program at night, where one of his finance professors was Fischer Black, later a Goldman Sachs partner, who gave him a grade of C. In 1975 he moved to New York and joined Goldman Sachs as a bond trader. He developed into a fiercely competitive trader, one who was comfortable with mind-numbing amounts of risk, and took over the government securities trading desks, which handled substantial proprietary trading accounts for the firm. He was selected by Friedman and Rubin, along with Mark Winkelman, a Dutchman who managed the firm's commodity businesses, to head all of the fixed-income and commodity activities. Though every bit as intense as he needed to be, Corzine, like Meriwether, was essentially a low-key trader, usually found hanging around trading desks wearing a gray cardigan sweater, which, with his balding head and full grayish beard, made him look more like a college professor than a Wall Street killer. Corzine was well liked and thought to be sympathetic to people issues in the firm to such an extent that some actually thought he might be "too nice a guy" to be able to be an effective leader of the firm. Corzine was also largely ignorant of investment banking, still a vital part of Goldman Sachs's business, so the management committee, in selecting him as senior partner and chief executive, also selected Hank Paulson as his deputy and chief operating officer.

Paulson, also from Illinois, was a year older than Corzine. He joined Goldman Sachs in its Chicago office in 1974, as a client relationship officer, responsible for bringing in new business for the Investment Banking Division. One of his colleagues there, who admired Paulson, referred to him as being "pathologically competitive." He was certainly good at what he did, and rose to become a co-head of the Investment Banking Division before being tapped as chief operating officer. Paulson moved to New York and settled in as Corzine's alter-ego, following him around closely as if he were number 1.5 rather than number 2. He took over a number of tasks that Corzine was disinclined to do, such as visiting clients overseas.

In 1996, Goldman was lead underwriter of the Yahoo! IPO, and in 1998 it was global coordinator of the large Japanese DoCoMo IPO. Pretax income from 1995 to 1997 grew at a compounded rate of 48 percent. In June 1998, Corzine, appreciative of Paulson's contributions and hard work, and also aware that Paulson expected it, appointed Paulson as co-senior partner.

Corzine personally took leadership of the effort to take the firm public. He foresaw a major need for new capital to fuel the firm's growing trading activities, and though he recognized that substantial limited partnership investments from Sumitomo Bank and Hawaii's Kemehameha Activities Association had enabled the firm to defer going public until then, the event could not, Corzine thought, be avoided any longer. The firm had discussed going public several times in preceding years, but had always rejected the idea.

Going public was controversial both because it presupposed a future of the firm being heavily involved with risky trading ventures that would greatly change the comfortable, private partnership culture that it had developed over the years, and because there would be disagreements over how to divide the considerable premium over the firm's book value that a market value of three or more times book would create. This would create an enormous windfall effect that would disproportionately favor current general partners, especially those who had been partners for several years. What about the many limited partners who had retired after long service and continued to leave their capital at risk in the firm but who were entitled to only a fixed-income return on it? And what about all the young vice-presidents and associates, who were vital to the firm's success but who would never have the chance to become partners?

While this was being considered, Corzine and Paulson were struggling with some other issues that increased tensions between them and among other members of the management committee. One of these was related to the collapse of Long-Term Capital Management in the summer of 1988. Corzine played a big role personally in trying to salvage the situation either by offering to join in bidding to purchase the assets of LTCM together with Warren Buffett, or when that initiative failed, by taking a large piece of the exposure that would have to be underwritten by the group of firms that ultimately acquired LTCM. The situation called for quick decision making and resolute action—conditions with which trader Corzine was comfortable—but because of the amount involved in the commitment ($300 million), Corzine needed the approval of his management committee, which he did not have before he acted to commit the firm. This upset some of the management committee members who might have been willing to back Gus Levy in such a situation, but then they didn't think Jon Corzine was a Gus Levy. Around the same time, Corzine was criticized by his partners for agreeing to meet with the heads of one or more major banks, who had apparently asked to talk about a merger. The meetings came to nothing, and Corzine disclosed them to his partners, but in a firm with many merger experts, senior deal men such as Paulson knew that casual, unscripted meetings can create complications and result in losing control of a situation, and therefore they should never happen without careful consideration and preparation. Corzine of course thought he was just doing what CEOs do, and it was not that big a deal, but he had appointed Paulson co-CEO in June, and here he was acting as if he hadn't. Apparently Corzine was rebuked by his management committee partners, and he resisted, which led to what was in essence a vote of no confidence, which Corzine lost. It was agreed that he would step down as CEO and resign from the firm after its IPO, which was scheduled for the fall of 1998, though market conditions were such that the firm deferred the offering until May of 1999.

The IPO was agreed upon after Goldman decided to set 10 percent of the value aside for future compensation and pension awards, 10 percent for limited partners, and 10 percent for the special limited partners (such as Sumitomo), leaving about 57 percent for the 220 general partners to divide among themselves. The windfall was indeed enormous. The offering was of 69 million shares (about 15 percent of the firm), priced at $53 per share, about 3.5 times book value, valued the whole firm at $33 billion, as compared to a market capitalization value at the time of $60 billion for Morgan Stanley Dean Witter and $30 billion for Merrill Lynch. The issue rose 33 percent on the first trading day, despite a 128-point drop in the Dow Jones Index. The issue made thousands of people at Goldman Sachs into millionaires. By the end of the 1999, the stock was at $92 per share, Jon Corzine, whose shares were worth about $340 million, had left the firm and announced his candidacy for the Senate in New Jersey, and Hank Paulson was sole chairman and CEO of a sizeable public company. In September 2000, Goldman Sachs used its new stock, its "acquisition currency," to acquire Spear, Leeds, and Kellogg, one of the largest specialist firms on the New York Stock Exchange, for $6.3 billion.

Lehman Escapes AMEX

James D. Robinson III was an Atlanta boy who had made it big in New York in 1977 by replacing American Express's chairman and chief executive, Howard Clark, Sr., when Robinson was only forty-one. Since then, as a master of brand management, he had devoted his efforts to the idea of the financial supermarket. The acquisition of Shearson Loeb Rhodes in 1981 was the beginning, followed by a subsequently contentious purchase of the non-U.S. assets of Trade Development Bank from Geneva financier Edmund Safra in 1983, then the purchase of troubled Lehman Brothers in 1984, and E. F. Hutton in 1987, all with an understood commitment to link the American Express credit card and travel services, and its international bank, into a multitier financial services delivery platform for wealthy investors.

But the idea never worked, Sandy Weill quit in frustration in 1985 (at not being given more to do), and Robinson never gained control of the disparate and unconnected financial businesses he had assembled. In 1987, American Express International Bank was required to add $950 million to reserves for third world loans. In 1990, according to American Express's corporate history, Shearson was "rocked by a series of serious missteps and setbacks that ultimately became so dire that in 1990, American Express was forced to repurchase all of Shearson's remaining publicly traded stock [it had gone public again just a few years earlier] for more than $1 billion and to provide a critically necessary capital infusion."[6]

Fireman's Fund, an insurance company owned by American Express before Robinson took over, had started to lose money and the travel and related businesses were in a slump. After years of disappointing performance that halved American Express's once high-flying stock price, the board decided it was time for "Jimmy Three-Sticks," as Robinson was known on Wall Street, to move on. He was replaced by Harvey Golub, the former CEO of AMEX's money management business, who took over in early 1993 as Robinson's replacement.

A few months later, Golub announced that the Shearson Lehman businesses would be sold or distributed to stockholders. In March 1993, the Shearson–E. F. Hutton brokerage businesses were sold to Primerica for $1 billion plus a share of future profits, where they would return into the hands of Sandy Weill. In January 1994, American Express announced that it would invest about $1 billion in Lehman Brothers, the new old name for the remnants of the Shearson Lehman Hutton investment bank after the brokerage part had been disposed of, and then distribute its shares in the company to American Express stockholders. This was to be accompanied by an earnings-sharing agreement in which American Express would recoup as much as $400 million over an eight-year period, plus certain other payments.[7] But mostly, American Express shareholders looked ahead to avoiding the volatility of earnings from Wall Street firms, and their increasing uncertainty due to an ever-rising reliance on trading income. Such strains on earnings had greatly diminished the price-earnings ratio that the high-growth, consumer brand leader American Express was used to, and therefore the shareholders were glad to shed its last remaining interest in the investment banking business.

The separation was awkward. Golub felt the investment had been a disaster, and he wanted to squeeze as much cash out of it that he could, but doing so might threaten the balance sheet and capital position of a newly independent firm that would be forced to compete with firms much larger than it. In addition, Lehman had been through a series of leaders before settling on Richard Fuld. Fuld began his career under Lew Glucksman, Lehman's rough-edged head of Fixed Income, and prospered there despite the organizational chaos that dominated the firm until its sale, in distress, to Shearson American Express in 1984. Fuld's subsequent ten years as an executive of an investment bank owned by a non-banking parent taught him all he needed to know about financial supermarkets and the glories of growth by acquisition—and he became extremely skeptical of both. Under his leadership (based on nearly twenty-five years of seeing how things ought not to be done), Lehman Brothers's stock price performed very well for many years, even relative to liberated American Express—thus the shareholders of both companies did well by the divestiture of the securities businesses from the travel and credit card services business, two businesses that were never compatible. Fuld made Lehman, Wall Street's fourth-largest independent firm by 2000, a symbol of "go-it-alone" determination, ready to compete with all the bigger players on the basis of its talent, work ethic, and entrepreneurial spirit.

Morgan Stanley and Dean Witter

Bob Baldwin retired as senior partner of Morgan Stanley in 1984, after thirteen very successful years during which the firm completed the difficult transition from stuffy, know-it-all blue-chip investment banker for only the best corporations and governments, to a full-service firm equipped to slug it out with the toughest competitors in mergers or underwritings, or in sales and trading. It had blossomed into a firm of 4,100 people, with $300 million in capital. Baldwin, however, was troubled by the prospect of selecting a successor.

Two of the most likely candidates—the stars of the firm—were Bob Greenhill, who headed Investment Banking and the profitable Mergers group, and Dick Fisher, who had developed and headed Sales and Trading, an increasingly important part of the firm's business. The two men had been classmates at Harvard Business School and each had attempted to outdo the other ever since. Greenhill was robust, proactive, and relentless in pursuit of objectives. Fisher, who had had polio as a child and was crippled by it, was quiet, cerebral, collegial, and very popular with his subordinates. Baldwin was convinced that if either were selected, the other would leave, something he wished very much to avoid. So he chose neither, instead picking a forty-nine-year-old Morgan Stanley blue blood, Parker Gilbert. Gilbert, whose father had been an original Morgan Stanley partner, headed the firm for five years, then selected Fisher to replace him as chairman and CEO of a now publicly traded corporation, and Greenhill to be president.[8]

In September 1985, the firm celebrated its fiftieth birthday by running a full-page newspaper ad announcing that the partners had agreed to remain as a private partnership dedicated to serving its clients as they had in the past. The ink was hardly dry on the newsprint before the partners had to eat their own words. They decided to go public following a successful share issue by Bear Stearns in the fall of 1985 and earlier offerings by Merrill Lynch and Donaldson Lufkin. First Boston was already public; Salomon Brothers had gone public by virtue of its acquisition by publicly owned Phibro. Morgan's partners saw all of its most formidable competitors, except for Goldman Sachs, having access to public markets for capital to support their trading positions and general growth efforts. They felt, despite some reluctance to give up the mystique of the Morgan partnership, that they could not afford to allow Morgan Stanley to become the only firm among its competitors with limited access to capital, so in March of 1986, Morgan went ahead and completed its initial public offering of 24.2 million shares (19 percent of the firm), offered at $56.50 per share, thus raising $1.37 billion and capitalizing the firm at $7.2 billion. On its first trading day, the stock leapt to $70, making every Morgan Stanley partner far richer than he might ever have dreamed of.[9] The former partners that hadn't expected to be able to withdraw capital from the firm until they died or retired, and even then only at book value and at a measured pace, were suddenly owners of shares worth a multiple of book value that traded in the market and could be sold as soon as restrictions following the offering (and those maintained within the firm) were lifted. There were setbacks, of course, especially after the market crash of October 19, 1987, and the difficulties that occurred in the LBO and junk bond businesses after 1990. But by then, Morgan Stanley had invested heavily in asset management and trading and had developed into a large, free-standing investment bank with international offices in Frankfurt, Hong Kong, Luxembourg, Melbourne, Milan, Sydney, and Zurich, with important regional headquarters in London and Tokyo.

Fisher was ascending through all this, but Greenhill, a quintessential deal man, was not. He and Fisher clashed and disagreed, and Greenhill was forced out by Fisher and the firm's management committee in 1993. Greenhill was replaced as president by a hard-driving fixed-income lieutenant of Fisher's, John Mack, the son of Lebanese immigrants. Mack had attended Duke on a football scholarship and joined Morgan Stanley in 1972 as a bond trader. Fisher also recruited Joe Perella to leave the merger advisory firm he had founded with Bruce Wasserstein to head up Morgan's important Merger unit.

Thus Greenhill came to the attention of Sandy Weill, now reassembling a brokerage empire after having acquired Smith Barney, and Shearson Hutton from American Express, and then added Travelers Insurance. Sandy was looking for a way to break into the leadership ranks of investment banking and figured who better than Greenhill, a prestigious Morgan Stanley man, to do it for him. So he made a deal that the frustrated Greenhill couldn't refuse, and Greenhill decamped to set up shop as CEO of Smith Barney Shearson. He had little regard for those already there and shoved them aside with an orgy of new hiring, offering large signing bonuses and guaranteed annual bonuses to attract big-name players to join him at the no-name shop. All the money available for the bonus pool for the Smith Barney Shearson investment bankers was diverted to the new guys, much to the disapproval of the folks who had been there for some time. Morale deteriorated, business was slow anyway, and the new Greenhill-empowered enterprise was a flop, so Greenhill left in 1996 to set up his own firm. Sandy rebounded the following year by acquiring Salomon Brothers to fill out his investment banking niche.

In 1995, Morgan Stanley revealed a hot hand in the technology field by leading the initial public offering of Netscape, the first company to attempt to commercialize the Internet. This issue set off a roaring bull market in technology stock IPOs. These were solicited and promoted by Morgan's technology banker Frank Quattrone, who soon left to join Deutsche Bank, then Credit Suisse First Boston. Quattrone became a high-profile player, allegedly making $150 million a year during the bubble for his ability to attract new business such as Cisco Systems and Amazon.

But Fisher and Mack, both sales and trading people, seemed to be looking for something else. Investment banking and mergers were fine, but there were always people who could do that sort of work quite well, and Morgan had developed a good many of them. Fisher and Mack were attracted by trading, something historically opposite to the firm's blue-blooded origins, and by asset management. Trading could be enormously profitable, but was of course risky. Asset management could also be very profitable, but not by running money for pension funds, which had the bargaining power to be tough negotiators on fees and which tended to switch their accounts if they were not satisfied with the last couple of quarters' performances. Managing mutual funds, on the other hand, could be very profitable and involved rather small amounts of risk to the firm. If funds did poorly, investors might withdraw their investment, but they might not. In any case, they could market the funds to new investors to replace any dissatisfied ones and charge everyone a full fee. In 1996, Fisher and Mack decided to enter the "asset gathering" business by acquiring the eleventh-largest U.S. mutual fund management company with $57 billion under management, Van Kampen American Capital, for $1.18 billion. The deal was thought to be a good way to acquire customers for their investment products and deals they were distributing, but the real reason was to launch the firm's first venture into the retail (mutual fund) business. This was a huge departure from the old Morgan Stanley—the elite investment bank serving only large, sophisticated, and successful wholesale clients. The retail business, the old guys thought, would involve a large, tawdry sales force of cold-callers chasing down blue-collar investors for a few hundred dollars of purchases at a time. Not their thing at all.

A year later, Fisher and Mack plunged all the way into the wholesale-retail cultural abyss by merging the firm into Dean Witter Discover, the publicly traded retail brokerage and giant credit card company spun off by Sears Roebuck in 1993 and headed since then by a reclusive ex-McKinsey, Midwesterner Philip Purcell. Fisher and Mack had met Purcell at the time of the Dean Witter IPO, which Morgan had co-managed, and liked him very much. Later they proposed that their companies consider a merger, and Purcell was delighted to have a chance to acquire such a prestigious franchise as Morgan Stanley. Fisher said the deal was intended to preempt the wave of consolidation in financial services that he and Mack saw coming: "If you believe that consolidation is inevitable," he said, "then it makes sense to pick your partner."[10]

The merger was a shock to Wall Street. The deal was described in the press as a merger of equals, but on Wall Street, where everyone knew there is no such thing as a merger of equals, the deal was seen as a sellout of Morgan Stanley to a second-tier firm, Dean Witter, which would control the combined enterprise with Phil Purcell as CEO. Fisher would retire after the deal was done (and the Street assumed many other Morgan principals would leave then, too, as many did), but the new firm's number two would be John Mack, who was devoted to the concept of the combination and who trusted in his friend Purcell to treat him right. Apparently Mack believed that this meant turning over the CEO position to him in a few years, but that thought was never documented. The combined firm would have a market capitalization of $24 billion, making it then the most valuable securities firm in the United States. With nine thousand retail brokers, it would field the third-largest sales force of retail brokers, behind Merrill Lynch and Smith Barney Shearson. It would also become the sixth-largest mutual fund business in America, with $120 billion in assets under management, and the manager of the largest credit card company, with thirty-six million customers.[11] The old Morgan Stanley was now a part of a vast retail-wholesale financial conglomerate that would involve entirely new managerial requirements.

The new firm of forty thousand employees was briefly known as Morgan Stanley Dean Witter Discover and Co., until 1998, when it was changed to Morgan Stanley Dean Witter and Co. In late 2001, to foster brand recognition and marketing, the Dean Witter name was dropped and the firm again became Morgan Stanley. There was little effort, however, to integrate the two components of the new firm; they were largely left alone, with Purcell managing the Dean Witter businesses, and Mack, the Morgan Stanley ones. The stock price of the new firm performed very well, rising by about 200 percent from the time of the merger until mid-2000—much more than its principal competitors, Merrill Lynch and Goldman Sachs—before it began to reflect the collapse of the technology market and the post-Enron recession.

John Mack, however, was impatient to replace Purcell as CEO, and said so to him in late 2000. Purcell denied having any kind of timetable for his succession by Mack, so after heated discussions, Mack decided to resign, which he did in January of 2001. He joined Credit Suisse Group in 2002, as co-CEO (with German-born Oswald Grübel, a career Credit Suisse employee), helped it turn around some troubled U.S. operations, and then proposed a merger (a sale, really) to Bank of America or Deutsche Bank. The board of Credit Suisse was horrified by this idea and quickly rejected it. It also did not renew Mack's contract when it expired in 2004.

In December 2004, Dick Fisher succumbed to prostate cancer, and his well-attended January 2005 memorial service attracted many senior Morgan Stanley veterans, most of whom had left the firm, and several of these agreed to meet later at the apartment of Parker Gilbert to express their grievances and discontent at the way Morgan Stanley was then being run by Philip Purcell. The "Group of Eight," as the attendants became known, decided to undertake a public campaign to discredit Purcell, and to have him replaced. They claimed to be unhappy about the stock price, which was recovering (but this time not as rapidly as the stocks of Goldman Sachs and Merrill Lynch), but the real reason was a passionate dislike of Purcell for what had become of their old firm and its key representatives in management.

They were outraged that Mack had been forced to resign because Purcell failed to honor the understanding they all thought he had had with Mack. They were unhappy, too, with the loss of the Morgan prestige and elite standing that they had been used to, and by the disagreeable circumstances of seeing their once-elegant franchise being run by mutual fund salesmen. They were prepared to shell out several million of their own money for legal and public relations advice to mount their offensive.

Purcell, however, had a lot of support from his board—many of the members were Midwestern industrialists or former Sears Roebuck people—and in the original merger contract (in what should have been a telling signal to Mack), it was specified that a vote of 75 percent of the directors would be required to change the CEO. Purcell, therefore, seemed invincible, but the Group of Eight campaign was spearheaded by so-called "activist" institutional investors disappointed with the relative performance of the stock, and after several months of high-visibility sparring and bad publicity, Purcell was informed by his friends on the board that in the best interests of the company, he would have to retire. In June of 2005, he did so, arguing that he should be succeeded by "anyone but Mack" (or any of the Group of Eight). There was an effort to appoint one of Purcell's co-presidents as his successor, but in the end Mack was recalled and took over as chairman and CEO on June 30, 2005.[12]

Among the many coups that have resulted in the ousting of Wall Street CEOs, this was one of the oddest. Purcell was very well entrenched, supported by his board, and protected by the 75 percent vote needed to replace him. His performance as CEO had not been so bad—all of the Wall Street stocks dropped significantly after the technology market collapse, the disturbances that followed 9/11, and the bankruptcies of Enron and

WorldCom in 2001 and 2002. The stock market produced negative returns for three years in a row between 2000 and 2002 (for the first time since the 1930s), and Morgan Stanley's heavy retail exposure adversely affected its earnings during the period. In 2003, its stock began to recover, along with those of its competitors, but both Morgan Stanley and Merrill Lynch lagged well behind the recovery of Goldman Sachs's stock. This really annoyed the Group of Eight, who saw Goldman as their real competitor, whereas in reality, because of Morgan's large retail businesses, Merrill Lynch was. Purcell was criticized for not having spun off the Discover credit card business, which Mack later did, but that business had been a lovely cash cow for years and helped finance much of the firm's expansion. The Group's case for removing Purcell was in fact a weak one, but the close association of the Morgan Stanley alumni to the hedge fund and activist investor communities gave the group access to many investors willing to listen to their complaints, and the Group, in typical, smooth, self-confident, old Morgan Stanley style, was good at making its case for the replacement of Purcell.

The Morgan Stanley board, in the meantime, was feeling the heat and found itself buried in the details of complying with the new corporate governance provisions of the Sarbanes-Oxley Act, passed in 2002, carefully maneuvering to avoid shareholder lawsuits, and trying to recover from its low corporate governance rating provided by the nonprofit governance watchdog the Corporate Library (which gave it a grade of D). After months of siege, the board must have figured that it would be better to get the controversy behind it by encouraging Purcell to retire honorably after twenty-four years as chief executive. Very, very few Wall Streeters serve as CEO of public companies for even half that time. The irony is that three years after taking over, John Mack had not changed the performance of the Morgan Stanley stock very much relative to Merrill Lynch (Morgan Stanley was ahead a little, but Merrill had just had a forced CEO replacement) or Goldman Sachs (behind which it lagged substantially).

Sandy Weill and the End of Glass-Steagall

Not long out of American Express, Sandy Weill offered to organize a group to acquire an ailing Bank of America, then suffering from the banking crisis of the early 1980s. His offer was rejected, but Sandy was not deterred. Always on the lookout for good businesses that he could buy cheaply because of some temporary distress or difficulty, he took a call from the CEO of a midsize Baltimore-based finance company called Commercial Credit, who invited him to take a look at the company with the idea of buying it from a troubled parent, Control Data Corporation. Assisted as he had been since 1982 by one of his many his protégés, Jamie Dimon, Weill acquired Commercial Credit in 1986, and met a young lawyer on the staff there, Charles Prince, who would become another protégé. Weill's idea of acquiring companies was to hang on to the customers, subject the firms to down-to-the-bone cost-cutting, search through the management and professional ranks to find the keepers, and let the rest go. By 1986 he had perfected the technique of acquiring brokerage firms, a technique that had a very heavy operational, back-office component to it, and was ready to go again.

The following year he noticed that a company called Primerica had acquired Smith Barney Harris Upham, a large retail brokerage at the top of the soon-to-crash 1987 market, and had borrowed a lot of money to do so. Primerica was formerly American Can until acquired by onetime Fidelity gunslinger Gerry Tsai, who sold off the container business and acquired a group of retail store companies with the proceeds. The acquisition of Smith Barney was to be the keystone in a move into financial services, but the market crash had squeezed Tsai's plans considerably. So Weill bought Primerica from Tsai in 1988 and converted it into a holding company for his own financial services combine. For the next several years he streamlined Primerica and its two principal subsidiaries, Commercial Credit and Smith Barney, into a low-cost, fast-growing company that became a Wall Street favorite. In 1992, Weill was introduced to another opportunity, Travelers Insurance, which had been suffering from real estate losses in the 1990–1991 market slump, and from large losses after a devastating hurricane in Florida. Travelers was seeking a minority investor, nothing more.

Weill quickly figured that he was Travelers's last best hope, and he drove a hard bargain to acquire 27 percent of the company for $722 million (which was about 50 percent of book value), with four board seats and Weill being given significant management responsibilities. Travelers consumed most of Sandy's ample energy for several months: he pushed hard for cost reductions and business improvements, and things turned around. By August 1993, the Travelers stock had risen 80 percent and Sandy had fallen in love with the red umbrella logo. He decided he had to have the rest of the company, and a year after the initial investment, Primerica acquired the 73 percent it did not own in a stock swap, and rolled all of its other businesses into it.[13]

Sandy Weill was an acquisition machine. His job was to find opportunities to acquire more and better businesses at decent prices, then squeeze them into shape while watching the stock price rise. He looked at Kidder Peabody when General Electric was trying to sell it, but balked at the price being asked. He looked at JPMorgan, but turned it down, too, because the price at which it was being dangled was too high. There were also unpleasant moments in the pursuit of things when Sandy was reminded that he and the new Travelers culture were just too dissimilar to the posh, WASP establishment ways of firms such as JPMorgan for a merger ever to work. While regretting a missed opportunity with Morgan in 1997, he received a phone call from another prospective seller, Deryck Maughan, Salomon Brothers's CEO, who was convinced that Salomon should be folded in to a larger organization that would enable it to compete effectively in the future.

Salomon had never fully recovered from the 1991 Treasury auction experience that cost it John Gutfreund, John Meriwether, and other top managers, and put its future into the hands of a disillusioned Warren Buffett, who had selected Maughan to replace Gutfreund, something that almost certainly would never have happened if the Treasury scandal had not occurred. Maughan had done his best to manage the wild animals at Salomon, but it was a difficult task at best. He held things together in 1994, a terrible year for the bond market, in which Salomon lost a fortune, but he was afraid Salomon's future was very unclear in the coming world of large, multi-platform financial service conglomerates with big balance sheets. Like Dick Fisher of Morgan Stanley, he thought the time might be right to merge Salomon into something bigger, and to try to get a premium price in doing so. Besides, Salomon's earnings had fallen short over the past few years, and its global investment banking business for the past twelve months was showing a loss of about $300 million.

The acquisition of Salomon was agreed at $9 billion in Travelers stock. The price would reflect only a small premium—it was acquired for less than two times book value in the middle of a bull market. Salomon would be consigned to a new securities division of Travelers to be called Salomon Smith Barney, which would be co-headed by Maughan and Jamie Dimon, the still-rising protégé, who was disappointed to be sharing the role with Maughan. Salomon would befall the standard Sandy Weill treatment for acquired companies and have to cut costs and shed employees not thought to be keepers. Sizeable trading losses soon after the merger caused Weill to reduce Salomon's proprietary trading activities sharply—what he really wanted from the deal was the prestigious investment bank. Travelers stock continued to rise rapidly, gaining almost 80 percent in 1997.

Without doubt, Sandy Weill's greatest deal, and maybe the most ambitious of all Wall Street deals, was Travelers's acquisition of Citicorp in April 1998. The deal was (as usual) cast as a merger of equals in which each party would be equally represented on the board, and Sandy Weill and Citicorp's CEO, John Reed, would become co-CEOs. The offer was valued at $70 billion, and both stocks quickly went to a premium, with Citicorp's shares rising by 26 percent and Travelers's by 18 percent, something that almost never happens in share-for-share exchange deals in which the buyer is often seen as having paid too much. The new company, to be called Citigroup, would create the world's largest financial services company, with assets of $700 billion, combined 1997 revenues of $48 billion, operating profits of $7.5 billion, and 162,000 employees serving 100,000 customers in 100 countries. Nothing this big had ever been imagined in the financial services industry before.

But there were many questions about the deal that could not immediately be answered. The deal, technically, was illegal because it would be prevented by the Glass-Steagall Act, which, though much eroded in practice, was still on the books. The parties agreed to unwind the deal if the law weren't changed within three years to permit the merger to occur (which it was). It was subject to approval by banking, insurance, and securities regulators in countless jurisdictions—federal, state, and foreign. It presented a management structure of co-equal CEOs that few thought would succeed, and would involve a variety of cost-cutting efforts, layoffs, severance payments, and other confusions typical of a large merger but on an unprecedented scale. And it greatly confused the competitive environment for the banking, securities, and insurance industries, which was already deeply engaged in strategic consolidation mergers within the industry sectors, but not as yet across them. Was Citigroup to become a behemoth that would dominate these industries that others would be compelled to follow, or would it prove to be the one acquisition too many that would turn the dream of Sandy Weill into a bloated bureaucracy? No one knew for sure, but later in that month of April 1998, two more mega-mergers between banks were announced: Bank of America's acquisition by NationsBank, and the combination of Bank One and First Chicago.

Even before these questions could be addressed, there was the matter of just what the two co-CEOs had in mind for the new combination. Sandy Weill's vision of the future always involved more acquisitions, more size, and more aggressive efforts to shake firms up to make them more productive. He certainly believed in cross-selling, without perhaps quite understanding how you pull it off without incurring incremental costs greater than any incremental income. He particularly wanted to put the investment banking capabilities of Salomon Smith Barney together with the corporate lending capabilities of Citibank, to increase investment banking market share and prestige.

John Reed's motivations for the deal were harder to understand. Reed, a technologist supported over traditional bankers by Walter Wriston, was about as unlike Weill as one could be: cerebral rather than impulsive; quiet, articulate, and tidy rather than boisterous, rude, and messy. Whereas Weill surrounded himself day and night by his acolytes and protégés, Reed was a loner. Reed eschewed acquisitions as a source of growth (he had made none of importance since becoming CEO in 1984) and had recently told most of the bank's wholesale customers that Citibank was dropping them to specialize in consumer-related businesses. Reed was fascinated by technology and wanted to perfect new techniques of data mining and information science to automate the banker–customer interface as much as possible. Weill wasn't interested in spending money on such far-out things. And Weill had an aggressive reputation that led one of my Goldman Sachs partners to comment that "Sandy has never shared an office with anyone who lived to talk about it."

The Citigroup merger forced a resolution of the long-standing debate in America over the role of banks, the deposits of which were guaranteed by the U.S. taxpayer, to participate in the riskier securities business. This debate had been going on for a decade or more, with an increasing acceptance by regulators, banks, and brokers that the separation put into effect in 1933 was no longer necessary and that greater competition in financial markets, which the banks would surely bring to bear, could make the markets only more efficient and could lower the cost of capital. In 1999, Congress repealed Glass-Steagall and freed banks up to participate in the investment banking business if they wanted to, which only a handful did, but these were determined to carve out important roles for themselves. The merger unquestionably established Citigroup as one of the leading investment bankers by market share of deals done, and it encouraged others to make similar moves to keep up, which some did.

In October 1999, Bob Rubin joined Citigroup as a member of the executive office and chairman of the executive committee of the board. He had left the Treasury in August and had been thinking about what he would do next when Weill recruited him. He would insist on not having any line responsibilities and would serve mainly as a consigliere to the co-CEOs and others at the company. He was of course a prized door-opener and a wonderful client schmoozer, but Rubin, who had already risen to the top of two prestigious organizations, did not want to be involved with anything too abrasive or threatening to his reputation. For this he would be paid well over $100 million over nearly a decade, perhaps more than any other nonexecutive director in history.

Weill believed that Citigroup could continue to compound earnings growth at 15 percent or more indefinitely, and the growth would come from cost management, cross-selling, and new acquisitions, of which several important ones were made over the next few years. Even at sixty-five, Sandy had lost none of his drive and ambition to rise ever higher, though Reed seemed to think that both his and Sandy's future best lay in retiring within a year or two and passing leadership to a commonly selected successor. Sandy had already become a billionaire, and a much-respected philanthropist, but he had no interest in slowing down. Rubin attempted to mediate between the two, but in the end it came down to the board accepting the resignation of one CEO and keeping the other. Another casualty of the Citigroup merger was the departure of Jamie Dimon, the most durable of Weill's many protégés, who had nonetheless run into conflict one time too many with the boss. Jamie would reappear within a few years as CEO of Citigroup's longtime principal rival, JPMorgan Chase.

10

THE NEW ECONOMY BUBBLE

THE BUZZ FROM THE VALLEY was that Netscape was the newest new thing: a real "killer app." It would popularize and democratize the Internet, allowing anyone to have instant access to Web sites that would connect to all the world's information sources. True, the Internet had already existed for a while, but it was mainly confined to universities and the military. Now, by making this new form of communication available to anyone with a personal computer, it could change the way business was done—all business: wholesale, retail, services—because everything depended on information, and now information would be delivered differently, in an architecture available to everyone. Netscape offered a free "browser" to let you "surf" the Internet over the telephone lines, and was building a network that would attract millions of users, and businesses would pay to access it.[1]

Netscape was offering shares of stock to the market in an IPO to be priced in August 1995. All of the proceeds would be new money to be invested in the business. No shares were being offered by existing investors—who included Jim Clark, a founder of Silicon Graphics, a previous Silicon Valley money-maker, and the famed venture capitalists Kleiner, Perkins, Caufield and Byers. All the right people were involved. And the deal was to be underwritten by Morgan Stanley, with a team headed by Frank Quattrone, the industry's star technology investment banker.

Morgan Stanley, however, was really taking a chance. Agreeing to underwrite this deal would violate all of the firm's traditionally conservative quality standards. Netscape was less than two years old. It had no profits and no immediate expectation of profits. Its most recent twelve-month revenues were less than $25 million. It was run by an unknown twenty-four-year-old Illinois computer science graduate, Marc Andreessen. But Quattrone hoped the deal would jump-start the technology stock market, which had been listless for a year or so. Total U.S. IPOs had amounted to only $46 billion in 1994, down from $64 billion in 1993, and technology deals had hit a three-year low of $8.5 billion—only 18 percent of all 1994 IPOs. Morgan Stanley had a new technology stock analyst, Mary Meeker, who was enthusiastic about Netscape but admitted that valuing such companies was very difficult. It was really a "concept stock," she said. Morgan said it expected to offer stock at about $12 per share, which would make the Netscape offering the third-largest IPO in NASDAQ's history.

A BUBBLE FORMS

Netscape aroused a broad range of interested investors, notably the most aggressive, performance-driven mutual and hedge funds and the technology-investing world as a whole. Some investors would plan to acquire shares from the underwriters and sell them later the same day if the stock spiked, although such immediate IPO gains as a whole had averaged only about 15 percent in recent years. Others, such as Microsoft, watched carefully as a new player ventured into its PC software domain. The buzz fed on itself, and huge indications of interest flowed into Morgan Stanley. Afraid the deal would be greatly oversubscribed, the large institutional investors tried to exert pressure on Morgan Stanley, reminding it of what good brokerage clients they were. Netscape and its advisors saw what was happening as well, and pressed for an increase in the offering price. Morgan Stanley, recognizing the huge unexpected demand for the new company, agreed to more than double the price, to $28, because of the unusually strong order book. But the firm knew that the market was overheated and that it had endorsed an almost indefensible price for the stock based on classic valuation approaches. It also knew that a great deal of Netscape stock would be sold immediately (or "flipped") by many of the IPO investors as soon as a significant price premium was reached, and Morgan Stanley might have to buy those shares back and resell them to maintain the offering price, essentially having to sell the offering all over again to keep it from collapsing entirely under the post-offering selling pressure.

Morgan Stanley's worries proved unfounded. The stock opened at $58 and rose from there. At the close of trading on the first day, the tiny, profitless company was valued by the market at $2 billion, and its young CEO was worth more than $80 million. Those allocated shares by Morgan Stanley had made a profit of more than $30 a share on a one-day investment that required putting up no money of their own since both their purchases and sales would close on the same day. According to Michael Lewis, author of the Internet bestseller *The New New Thing*, it wasn't only Wall Street that changed, "Netscape [was] what introduced the Internet to investors. It also [was] what captured the attention of the Silicone Valley engineer. When the Netscape IPO happened in 1995, a lot of smart people said, 'Whatever we do next is going to be Internet related because the market has this incredible appetite for it.' "[2]

The technology business had previously been ignored by the larger firms; the deals were too small and too risky. But Netscape changed this, too. William Hambrecht, the founder of Hambrecht and Quist, a small, technology investment bank, observed that:

> What the Netscape offering did was attract a lot of capital. It allowed a lot of companies to get very high valuations, which also attracted the very large investment banks. We operated out there for a long while without the big banks. It was Robertson Stephens, and Montgomery Securities, Alex Brown and us. But suddenly, when $20 million deals turned into $200 million deals, all the large firms came charging in.[3]

Suddenly, the financial community—investment bankers, analysts, brokers, mutual and hedge funds, and venture capitalists—began a rush to find other Internet companies. If it could work for Netscape, it could work for perhaps another one hundred companies that could similarly capture the imagination of investors. The Internet could change the world, as other important new technologies (radio, television, personal computers) had done before. Besides software suppliers, it would turbocharge demand for various types of computer and telecommunications equipment, including digital high-speed networks, or "broadband," which could carry data and audio and visual information, including motion pictures and cable entertainment. A new economy would be fashioned by fusing data, telecommunications, technology, and media and entertainment, and it would not be long before the market would have other Internet stocks to consider. Search engine companies came next—Lycos, Excite, and Yahoo in 1996, followed by a seemingly endless series of "B-to-B" (business-to-business) and "B-to-C" (business-to-consumer) companies. Virtually all had hot, wildly oversubscribed IPOs.

About the same time as the Netscape IPO, another new concept company was making a move. LDDS (Long-Distance Discount Services) was formed following the breakup of AT&T to take advantage of the newly deregulated long-distance telephone market, by offering steep discounts in rates. LDDS acquired several similarly entrepreneurial telephone service companies and, as a result of one of these acquisitions, had become publicly traded in 1989. Four years and several additional acquisitions later, LDDS operated the fourth-largest long-distance network in the country. In 1995, after further acquisitions of network companies and components, it acquired the voice and data transmissions company Williams Telecommunications, for $2.5 billion in cash. Later that year, LDDS, based in Jackson, Mississippi, and run since 1985 by Bernie Ebbers, a former high-school basketball coach who had owned a string of local motels before joining the company, changed its name to WorldCom.

Within the next three years, WorldCom would make several more large acquisitions of local-access facilities, digital fiber optic cable networks, and Internet access providers for businesses, culminating in a $40 billion acquisition of MCI Communications in 1998. The acquisitions were made possible by a rising stock price— from $8 in early 1995 to $50 after the MCI deal—and access to substantial credit facilities from banks.

Ebbers was assisted in developing and executing his strategy by an enthusiastic Paine Webber telecommunications analyst, Jack Grubman, a former AT&T engineer who understood the basic model of challenging the behemoth and enthusiastically recommended, first, LDDS and, later, WorldCom shares to investors. In 1994, Grubman left Paine Webber, a retail brokerage, to join Salomon Brothers. He was soon encouraged to do both stock analysis work, as he had before, and to assist Salomon's investment bankers with their mergers and corporate finance activities. Soon thereafter, Salomon Brothers became the principal investment bank to WorldCom, advising on various mergers and arranging the financing for them while continuing to recommend the stock to investors.

In 1997, Salomon Brothers was acquired by Travelers Group and merged with Smith Barney, a large stock brokerage business. Travelers was controlled by Sandy Weill, who the following year engineered the merger of Travelers and Citicorp, to form Citigroup. A major objective of the merged businesses was to cross-sell products and services across the banking and investment banking units. Citigroup soon formed a corporate banking division that combined the lending capacity of Citibank with the investment banking and brokerage ability of Salomon Smith Barney. It was a merger made in heaven for Jack Grubman, who now had enormous financial resources to offer to one insatiable client, WorldCom, and for his other telecom industry favorites, including Global Crossing and Qwest.

As one observer of the 1990s put it, it was the "greatest flood of liquidity since Noah,"[4] and people all over the world plunged into the water in search of investments in the "New Economy," which was also being called the second industrial revolution. The technology component of the boom was dominant. A nearly seventeenfold increase in the market capitalization of technology-laden NASDAQ stocks occurred from 1991 through 1999, changing what was a mere bull market (as represented by the fourfold increase in the market capitalization of all NYSE-listed companies) into a "bubble," a runaway euphoria about the future of the technology sector that drove speculation to extraordinary levels.

The NASDAQ index was a little over 900 in August 1995, and it would close the decade, the century, and the millennium, on December 31, 1999, at 4,069, on its way to an all-time high of 5,048 in March 2000. Much of this rise in the index occurred in 1999, when it suddenly jumped 85 percent. In 1999, the S&P 500 index, much less concentrated in technology stocks, rose only 19.5 percent. So-called technology IPOs increased fivefold from 1995 to 2000, and represented 77 percent of all IPOs in 2000.

But these developments were not based simply on speculation and to be dismissed lightly, many investors thought. These were indeed times, they said, when the forces of economics and history combined in an unprecedented period of disintermediation, deregulation, globalization, and of optimism and confidence in market-oriented economic policies. These were also times when financial markets, not banks or insurance companies, came to be relied upon to supply the bulk of the world's finance, and these markets were attracting capital at a record pace.

Financial Markets Expand

During the last two decades of the twentieth century, financial market activity expanded at a pace nearly twice that of nominal economic growth in the United States: approximately 15 percent per year. This expansion was reflected in stock market prices both in the United States and Europe, in stock trading volumes, and the volume of mergers and acquisitions, corporate restructurings, and related transactions.

By the end of the twentieth century, the proportion of all financial assets in the United States held by banks or insurance companies had declined to approximately 30 percent, from 45 percent in 1980, and the difference flowed into global financial markets that had developed to an extraordinary, completely unprecedented size—with market capitalization of stocks and bonds exceeding $72 trillion in 2000. These markets contained powerful forces that could quickly move funds in large quantities around the world to jump into (or out of) a suddenly discovered investment opportunity. These forces were energized by enormous turnover volumes—the value of consolidated world stock trading in 2000 was more than $47 trillion, one and a half times its market capitalization. About half of this trading occurred outside the United States, in stock markets in Europe, Asia, and Latin America.

In 2000, more than $4.4 trillion in new corporate debt and equity securities was issued, including some $2.3 trillion in investment-grade debt securities, $460 billion in asset-backed securities, $800 billion in medium-term notes, and $100 billion in high-yield debt securities, as compared to only $1.9 trillion in new syndicated bank loans and note issuance facilities. In 2000 as well, gross purchases and sales of U.S. securities (stocks, bonds, and government securities) by foreigners totaled $7 trillion, and gross purchases and sales of foreign securities by U.S. investors exceeded $3.6 trillion. Foreign investors, in the aggregate, owned about 10 percent of all U.S. stocks in 2000, the third-highest ownership after mutual and pension funds. Markets were well connected internationally and were linked by arbitrage opportunities and financial derivative instruments, such as interest rate and currency swaps, of which $66 trillion in notional amounts were outstanding in December 2000, and by a daily turnover in foreign exchange markets of more than $1.5 trillion, over 80 percent of which was attributed to financial transactions as opposed to trade.

The growth of financial markets, and the scale they achieved, was well beyond anything imaginable a generation earlier. In most of them, the volume attributed to transactions completed outside the United States was 30 to 50 percent of the world total, indicating that the rest of the world was quickly catching up with American financial market capacity. Overseas markets then provided virtually unregulated, fully competitive alternative marketplaces that could easily be used by U.S. corporations. The existence of such large, global financial markets, their trading power, and their changeable demands and whims, made them a challenge for all corporations seeking to locate new sources of low-cost capital, and to banks and others seeking to provide access to them.

Clinton Economics

Turmoil in the debt markets that followed the bursting of the late 1980s LBO boom, the Gulf War of 1991, and rising oil prices forced the economy into recession just as George H. W. Bush was running for reelection in 1992. Conservatives Reagan and Bush were criticized for having wrecked the country's financial position by over-borrowing and putting the burden for repaying the national debt on everyone's children and grandchildren. Ross Perot, billionaire EDS founder, was a third-party candidate in this election, during which he repeatedly stressed the importance of balancing the federal budget. Though unsuccessful, Perot secured almost 20 percent of the popular vote.

A lack of confidence in George H. W. Bush's ability to regain control of the economy during the campaign surfaced, and he was beaten by Bill Clinton who, predictably, promised—as John Kennedy did in 1960—to "get the economy moving again" and to undertake significant spending programs that were popular with the voters. Clinton was easily able to ride out the recession, which ended before he was inaugurated. But he had no convincing mandate, and two years after being elected, he lost control of the House of Representatives, enabling the Republicans to block his legislative agenda. He nevertheless made a significant contribution to the economy by focusing on interest rates, not the budget.

All Bill Clinton had to do was stay away from all the temptations that had beset Democrats from the days of Franklin Roosevelt. With reducing the deficit being seen as the necessary and patriotic thing to do (thanks to Perot), there was little pressure for new social programs or reforms, even if the Republican Congress would have allowed them. Clinton did narrowly pass a tax increase for further deficit reduction, and reappointed conservative Republican Alan Greenspan as chairman of the Federal Reserve, on whom he relied to keep interest rates down. But mainly he just waited for the deficit to reduce itself as economic growth, responding to the lower interest rates and other positive factors, began to resume. Economic values popped back into the system and helped to fuel a continuous period of growth in the economy that lasted even longer than the 106 consecutive months of the golden years of the 1960s. But unlike the earlier growth period, the Clinton expansion was not accompanied by a prolonged war or ambitious spending programs that would reignite inflation. The Clinton stock market (1993–2000), in which the Dow Jones tripled, was able to do so well because no such global uncertainties or big spending programs loomed ahead. To many, Clinton's economic policies seemed to be about what one would expect from a steady, mainstream Republican. The stock market felt it had nothing to fear from the Clinton administration and it continued to expand until the president's last days in office.

More Mergers

During the first years of the 1990s, the pace of merger-and-acquisition activities, reflecting market conditions, fell off sharply. The junk bond market collapsed, and banks became much more cautious about making highly leveraged loans, so financing for deals became scarce and the financial New Men who had been acquiring companies with borrowed money quit the scene. In any case, in light of stock prices at the end of the 1980s boom, there were no longer many low-priced, easy restructuring deals to be found. By 1994, however, the merger market was back in business, at an even faster pace than before. This time financial entrepreneurs played only a small role. The big deals were being done by companies seeking strategic partners, or repositioning themselves for the future in their changing industries. In the five-year period from 1996 through 2000, $3.1 trillion in U.S. domestic and cross-border M&A deals involving more than ten thousand companies took place, making this the most merger-intensive period of all times—in terms of five-year combined merger volume as a percentage of GDP. The activity in the 1996–2000 period eclipsed the much-acclaimed merger intensity of the 1898–1902 period, which had never been equaled even during the heyday of the

1980s.* The merger boom reached its peak in 2000, when nearly $1 trillion of domestic transactions were completed in the United States, the record year by far.

New Technologies

The bull market of the 1990s occurred during times of great change in technology, which greatly improved productivity in large sectors of the economy and also created entirely new industries and applications. Three new industry groupings, in particular, emerged as a result: the computer electronics and related fields (hardware, software and applications), the telecommunications field (embracing telephone, cellular, and wireless systems, and cable, satellite, and the Internet), and the reconfigured health care field (drugs, bio-tech, and health care delivery systems). Together, these groupings comprised about a quarter of the stock market capitalization of all of American industry at the end of 1998.

The computer industry was especially expansive, particularly in terms of new companies, products, and services being introduced to the market. A Goldman Sachs study of the industry in June of 1998 suggested that fifty-six companies in this industry group accounted for almost $1 trillion in market capitalization.[5] Of this, less than 22 percent comprised the eight companies that had been industry leaders in 1981 and were still independent. The rest of the group's market capitalization was attributable to new companies such as Cisco Systems, Compaq Computer, Dell, Microsoft, Oracle, and Sun Microsystems. Of the thirty largest computer/electronics companies by market capitalization in June 1998, only five were listed on the Fortune 500 list in 1981. IBM was the leading computer technology company in 1981, and its market capitalization at the end of 1998 was $170 billion. Microsoft's was $343 billion. Dell Computer's was $93 billion. The bubble saw technology valuations soar even further—at December 31, 1999, near their peaks, Microsoft was valued at $550 billion and Dell at $141 billion.

Similarly, in the high-tech sectors of the telecommunications industry

---

*The method used for determining merger intensity is to divide the value of completed domestic and U.S. cross-border transactions for the five-year period by the midyear nominal GDP of the United States. In 1898–1902, based on data compiled by Ralph Nelson, the volume of mergers was $6.3 billion, which, divided by the 1900 U.S. GDP of $18.7 billion, was 33.7 percent. The five-year total of mergers done in the United States in 1994–1998 was $2.64 trillion, based on data supplied by Securities Data Corp. This, divided by 1996 nominal GDP of $7.67 trillion, was 34.4 percent.

(leaving aside the traditional telephone businesses), thirty-one companies contributed $340 billion in market capitalization in 1989. This did not include another $133 billion in market capitalization of MCI WorldCom, which came together that year in an exchange of shares. Of the thirty-one companies, more than three quarters of the market capitalization was contributed by companies that were either nonexistent or insignificant in 1981, such as AOL, Comcast, Netscape, and Yahoo!

Similar high-tech communications companies were sold in an effort to pass their market capitalization on to larger, long-established companies. Examples include the purchase of McCaw Cellular Communications by AT&T in 1993 for $12.6 billion; Time-Warner's acquisition of Turner Broadcasting for $6.7 billion in 1995; and U.S. West's acquisition of Continental Cablevision for $5.3 billion in 1996. In 1999, Bell Atlantic merged with GTE in an $89 billion transaction, and Airtouch Communications, the West Coast cellular phone company, was merged into the British communications company Vodafone, in an exchange of shares valued at $58 billion. Olivetti, an Italian manufacturer that had converted itself into a telecommunications company, acquired control of the much larger Telecom Italia for $60 billion. Later in the year, Vodafone-Airtouch made a surprise hostile takeover attempt to acquire Mannesmann, a German cellular company, which finally agreed to a friendly merger for a price of $180 billion, still the world's largest deal. In January 2000, AOL organized a friendly merger with Time Warner in a transaction valued at $165 billion. AOL, one of the country's first Internet portal companies, had already acquired Netscape and CompuServe, two star performers of the Internet era.

All of these mergers, of course, were effected at high valuations, reflecting very high price-earnings ratios by ordinary standards. Accordingly, they released a great amount of new wealth to founders, key employees, and initial investors of the companies involved. They also provoked a substantial amount of post-merger restructuring, management changes, and asset sales. The merger wave of technology deals continued unabated into 2000.

The health care industry was another to explode in the 1990s. At the end of 1997, this industry, which was loosely defined as comprising pharmaceutical companies and health care service providers, represented more than $900 billion in market value. The eleven pharmaceutical companies among the Fortune 500 contributed most of this value, but in 1997 there were also thirteen health care service companies, such as hospital management companies and HMOs, among the Fortune 500, worth more than $60 billion in market capitalization. None of these companies was among the five hundred largest American companies in 1981. In 1999 and 2000, massive mergers occurred between the leading pharmaceutical companies, such as the $93 billion combination of Pfizer and Warner-Lambert, and the $75 billion merger of SmithKline-Beecham and Glaxo-Wellcome in January 2000.

Changed Market Dynamics

By the end of the 1990s, financial markets were vast, innovative, aggressive, and highly competitive. Institutional investors owned about 60 percent of all U.S. stocks, and accounted for about 90 percent of trading in the stock markets. Approximately two thirds of the institutional stock holdings were held by pension and mutual funds, whose managers had melded into about one hundred large investment management companies, which competed fiercely for assets to manage. They devised new funds aimed at exploiting the trends of the times, and paid handsomely to have them distributed by broker-dealers.

All of the mutual fund managers necessarily depended upon short-term results to continue to attract the assets from which they could draw fees. Investment results were published by numerous periodicals and by professional consulting companies with access to information about all investment managers' performance. Performance was the key, but it was hard for managers to beat the market under the weight of the steep management fees and expenses that the funds charged their clients. Some would try extra hard to catch trends before they happened, or otherwise to outsmart the market, but only a few managers could succeed at that. Most did what they could to enhance performance by fighting to receive IPO allocations (and selling immediately after the one-day gain, which in 1998 averaged 53.3 percent, and in 1999, an incredible 99.5 percent), and chasing hot tips where they could. Most, however, realized that to stay even with the S&P 500 (which was almost as good as beating it when the index was rising by 20 percent or more, which it did each year from 1995 to 2000), they had to own a representative proportion of technology stocks (even if they seemed to be overvalued) and to trade actively to track the index. Mutual funds averaged a portfolio turnover of more than 100 percent during these years (it was 17 percent in the 1950s), which meant that very few of these institutional investors were acting as long-term investors, looking after their clients' exposures to risks and being concerned about corporate governance or executive compensation.[6]

This focus on keeping up with the market's momentum caused institutional investors to become obsessed with quarterly performance to such an extent that any company (including Fortune 100 companies) missing performance expectations—i.e., failing to post the quarterly earnings result expected by the Street—might see its stock tumble instantly by as much as 25 percent.

For CEOs of companies benefiting from market attention, the 1990s were a perilous paradise. Market valuations and low interest rates combined to produce extremely low costs of capital for companies with access to the markets, and many individual CEOs were privately worth many hundreds of millions of dollars as a result of compensation arrangements tied to stock price performance that their boards had offered them. It was perilous, of course, because the market might be disappointed and the stock might drop into freefall, possibly resulting in the dismissal of the CEO. No matter how philosophical and long-range the thinking of individual CEOs, the market environment in which he or she worked was what it was. Great incentives were in place to motivate all CEOs to maximize their stock prices by pleasing market analysts, reporters, and an increasing number of financial broadcasters that the 1990s had produced, and to make sure these relationships, which were based on meeting quarterly expectations, did not turn sour.

Operating within the capital markets of the 1990s were also scores of vendors and service providers seeking to please their clients. Any corporation or investment manager could turn to a different vendor if the service wasn't up to par, and the way to gain more of a client's business was to be creative, responsive, optimistic, and willing to take risk and to offer packages of some important services bundled together that tied the client to the vendor. These vendors included banks, broker-dealers, and underwriters of course, but also accounting firms, law firms, consultants, and various other professional service providers. These last were captivated by a system in which consistent double-digit growth was expected from the best companies, to whom the rewards to investors and the managers could be enormous. But the ability to sustain double-digit growth indefinitely was well beyond the essential economics of most companies—only those with better ideas, more aggressive acquisitions, and special rapport with investors could be expected to survive this difficult challenge.

ANALYSIS OF A MARKET COLLAPSE

During the twentieth century four exceptional stock market booms took place in the United States that in retrospect have been called bubbles. Economist Richard Sylla describes these periods (1905, 1928, 1958, 1998) as times when the ten-year moving averages of real rates of return* on stocks reached peaks from which they rapidly descended, or crashed.[7] The crashes, of course, involved losses and other forms of collateral damage, although much of the losses were calculated using inflated market values registered at the market's peak.

What Professor Sylla identified as the bubble of 1998 became the crash of 2000–2002, a slower, more prolonged market correction than any since the 1930s. It began with a weakening, then a sharp fall in the high-technology sector, especially affecting Internet companies, but soon spreading to those more substantial companies on whom the Internet group relied for products and equipment. The collapsing prices in this sector acutely affected some other companies (such as Enron) that had invested heavily in them and lost control of their own financing as a result of these investments.

Enron was a reworked natural gas transmission company that had transformed itself into a "virtual" energy company, emphasizing trading and hedging rather than producing and distributing, and was a glamorous symbol of the New Economy. By 2000, weakening corporate results began to be reflected in a three-year run of increasing record levels of bankruptcies.

The terrorist attacks on September 11, 2001, pushed markets lower and instantly vaporized the confident, euphoric feeling of peace and prosperity that had characterized the optimistic markets of 1995–2000. In the December following September 11, the surprise bankruptcy of Enron occurred, and a few months later, the even larger failure of WorldCom, after a fraud designed to help prop up the stock price was discovered.

The 2000 crash involved more financial wreckage—however it is calculated—than earlier crashes, even than the crash of 1929, given the extraordinary levels that stock prices reached. Although the Dow Jones Index fell about 90 percent from its peak in 1929 to its low in 1933, the total amount of market capitalization lost was about $70 billion, or about

---

* The rate of return after inflation.

THE NEW ECONOMY BUBBLE · 291

59 percent of 1929 GDP. The loss of market capitalization in 1987, following the celebrated 22.6 percent Dow Jones one-day crash on October 19 of that year, was about $585 billion, or only 12.4 percent of 1987 GDP, and most of that was restored by a swift market recovery in the following months. However, even though the S&P 500 plunged by 48.9 percent from its high in September 2000 to its low in October 2002 (the Dow Jones, now a less used index containing few technology stocks, dropped by only 29.4 percent), the estimated loss in total U.S. market capitalization was over $8 trillion, or 80 percent of 2000 GDP. These figures represent only the loss in equity values, during a period when bond markets also shed about $100 billion in value and bank loan losses were estimated at more than $50 billion.*

The difference in loss experience between 1929 and subsequent crashes largely reflected the growth of securities markets as repositories for savings and investments of American financial institutions and individuals. In 1929, institutional investors were just developing and had not become powerful, important players in financial markets.

Another indicator of the magnitude of the effect of a bubble bursting is the amount of public attention and regulatory and legislative response that is generated. Lost market values, bankruptcies, and scandals lead to cries of outrage for punishment of the "guilty," and improved regulation to prevent future recurrences. In the 1930s, there was a massive effort to regulate the financial sector, resulting in the Banking Act of 1933 and the Securities Acts of 1933 and 1934. In the 1960s, there was no government response to that decade's bubble, other than the passage of a law to slow down the pace of hostile takeovers. In 1987, the federal government only formed a commission to look into the causes of the large one-day price collapse on October 19, after which some technical reforms were adopted by the New York Stock Exchange and by futures markets.

In 2002, however, the market crash and the scandals that soon followed were front-page stories for months. Public interest in the market collapse and its causes and consequences was intense—public ownership of stocks had reached an all-time high in 1998, when the Federal Reserve announced that 48 percent of all American households owned stocks, either directly or through mutual funds and pension funds. All of these

---

*The economic damage caused by the collapse of the real estate and mortgage bubble of 2007-2009 was about $10 trillion from the high-to-low change in stock prices plus about $1.5 trillion in estimated loan losses. This was also about 80 percent of the average GDP for 2007 and 2008, though the ensuing recession and government intervention was considerably greater.

investors were affected by the market's sharp and unexpected reversal, and their cause was picked up by politicians and the media. Various reforms were proposed and much discussed. The principal stated objective of these various efforts was to "restore investor confidence in the financial system," which many observers believed required the apprehension and punishment of those responsible and some far-reaching changes in how the system functions. These observers got what they asked for, but it wasn't at all pretty. Little did they know that within less than ten years the financial system would implode again.

Cleaning Up After Enron

Immediately after the Enron bankruptcy, committees of Congress began investigations and consideration of legislative action. These actions were accelerated with the collapse of WorldCom.

In March 2002, the Justice Department chose to indict the firm of Arthur Andersen, the auditor to both Enron and WorldCom, for obstructing justice. By this time a partner of Arthur Andersen had confessed to inappropriate document shredding, which was alleged to have been the consequence of a firm policy to destroy evidence that might be incriminating. Justice was also angered by Andersen's accommodating role in the Enron case, which it believed was in violation of a consent decree extracted earlier in a fraud case involving Waste Management Corporation. In June 2002, Andersen was convicted of the charges and, as a result, immediately went out of business. However, three years later, Andersen's conviction was overturned by the U.S. Supreme Court, because of faulty instructions to the jury by the judge, though the firm was no longer revivable.

In early July 2002, President Bush directed the Justice Department to establish a Corporate Fraud Task Force to include a variety of prosecutors, investigators, and technical experts. Within this group a separate Enron Task Force was also appointed. Henceforth, the Congress, the Justice Department, the SEC, and other enforcement agencies began an earnest and aggressive effort to close in on those thought to be offenders.

In late July 2002, a new federal omnibus accounting and corporate governance reform and improvement law, the Sarbanes-Oxley Act, was passed and signed by the president. This was the most comprehensive and extensive federal securities legislation since the 1930s, requiring the SEC to draft numerous new rules to provide for its implementation. The new rules, which would require auditors, among other things, to certify the adequacy of financial controls, would be expensive to implement and would apply to about ten thousand U.S. companies.

The Federal Sentencing Guidelines were amended by Congress in November 2004. These guidelines, established by Congress in 1991 to increase penalties for "white-collar" offenses (making prison terms for offenders much longer and less subject to parole), and to place significant burdens upon employers to cooperate with enforcement officials in order to avoid prosecution of their corporations, raised significantly the standards that corporations must meet to avoid indictment in criminal situations involving their employees. These new standards included the need to demonstrate preventive efforts to provide a "focus on ethics and organizational culture," and the ability to show that officers and directors understood and accepted greater responsibility for ensuring corporate compliance with these standards. However, the constitutionality of the sentencing guidelines was questioned in 2005 by the U.S. Supreme Court, which reduced them from "mandatory" to "advisory."

Prosecutions of some corporate officials began in 2002. By the end of 2005, officials of about thirty-five major public companies were charged with criminal activities. Several high-visibility executives were tried, convicted, and punished with lengthy prison sentences, including Bernard Ebbers (WorldCom), who received twenty-five years in prison; Jeffrey Skilling (Enron), twenty-four years*; John Rigas (Adelphia), twelve years, reduced from fifteen; Andrew Fastow (CFO of Enron), six years, reduced from ten for cooperation; Denis Kozlowski (Tyco), eight to twenty-five years; and Scott Sullivan (CFO of WorldCom), five years. These executives were also forced to turn over most of their remaining financial assets to the courts. The severity of these sentences was way beyond any handed out before for white-collar criminal offenses. Mainly they were the result of the tightening of the Federal Sentencing Guidelines by Congress to take into account to extent of damages caused, which in turn was a reflection of a growing public intolerance of financial abuses and fraud.

There was irony, however, in the fact that the system of checks and balances that governed corporate behavior during the bubble years, yet failed to restrain its greatest excesses, otherwise appeared to work fairly well. Certainly there was strong support among those invested in the

---

* Skilling's chairman and predecessor as Enron CEO, Ken Lay, was also convicted, but died before sentencing. Skilling's conviction was upheld on appeal but remanded for resentencing.

stock market (as half the American public was) for bold, aggressive actions by corporate CEOs, many of whom, including Ebbers, Skilling, and Ken Lay, were well known and admired corporate celebrities. No matter how well publicized their large compensation packages, the stockholding public did not seem to object. Further, hardly any objection was voiced about overly tame or inbred boards of directors that were meant to restrain their chief executives from taking excessive risks, but rarely did so. The corporate governance structure of the 1995–2000 period could be characterized as one in which the bias toward aggressive action to promote growth of shareholder value far outweighed any available quantity of sensible restraint in the interest of fiduciary responsibility. Despite such bias and temptation, only a small number (a tiny percentage of the 2,500 or so exchange-traded public companies) failed to govern themselves properly and fell into trouble. But those that did, including some spectacular examples of corporate misconduct and fraud, made headlines as never before.

During this period, the plaintiff's bar was especially active with class-action suits against banks, investment banks, and accountants, from which settlements aggregating more than $14 billion were agreed by midyear 2005. In the WorldCom and Enron cases, the principal plaintiff (a New York State pension fund) insisted on participation in the financial settlement by certain independent members of the boards of directors of the corporations, the participation to be personal, and not covered by insurance. This was an unprecedented outcome for litigation involving independent directors.

Friends of Frank

Wall Street and a few of its principal figures were also caught up in the effort to establish responsibility and accountability for the financial abuses of the Internet market years. In 2002, the SEC, guided by a tip apparently from a hedge fund, announced an unprecedented $100 million settlement with Credit Suisse First Boston for unspecified abuses related to technology IPOs. Frank Quattrone then headed CSFB's technology group, having been recruited to CSFB. This event attracted the attention of the Corporate Fraud Task Force, which indicted Quattrone in 2003 for obstructing a government probe into CSFB's IPO activities by forwarding an e-mail from the firm's legal group encouraging routine post-deal document destruction. The government had been looking into allegations that Quattrone maintained a list of "Friends of Frank," technology executives and others capable of directing business to CSFB, to whom significant allocations of hot IPOs would be made. This probe never bore fruit, but the investigators discovered the e-mail and used it, as in the Arthur Anderson case,* to provide a basis for prosecution. Quattrone's trial resulted in a hung jury, and a retrial. In the second trial he was found guilty, but the conviction was overturned on the grounds, as in the Anderson case, that the instructions to the jury were incorrect. The government subsequently dropped the charges, and Quattrone, who reportedly earned $160 million a year during his peak years at CSFB, has since founded a boutique investment bank called the Qatalyst Group.

The CSFB case also attracted the interest of New York State Attorney General Eliot Spitzer, who was elected in 1998. Spitzer is the son of a wealthy New York real estate developer who aced his way through Princeton and Harvard Law School, after which he worked for a prominent New York law firm, then went to the Manhattan District Attorney's Office where he learned to become a prosecutor. After this, he returned to private practice with another prominent firm, until his campaign for attorney general which he narrowly won. Despite the fact that licensed investment banks and the federal securities market are the regulatory province of the SEC, Spitzer decided that as the major securities firms are located in New York, he, too, should investigate them. New York State has a seldom-used statute on its books, the Martin Act (1921), which provides that criminal securities fraud cases can be brought without having to prove intent. In the hands of an intent prosecutor, which Spitzer certainly was, the Martin Act was a formidable weapon, far more powerful than anything the SEC (which can bring only civil cases on its own) had available to it.

Spitzer subpoenaed files and e-mails from all of the leading IPO underwriters, looking for evidence that Wall Street's research analysts were being used to solicit underwriting mandates (by offering more positive coverage than the companies deserved), or that IPO allocations were being made in such ways as to constitute commercial bribery. Were the now heralded Friends of Frank (or friends of other firms) being bribed for fu-

---

* A similar charge was brought against Martha Stewart, the domestic arts guru, in 2004, after failure to find evidence of insider trading. Stewart was found guilty and sentenced to five months in prison.

ture business by generous allocations of IPOs from the underwriters? Spitzer collared thousands of e-mails and assigned junior lawyers and law students to pore over them looking for evidence of misconduct. In 2002, Spitzer announced that he had evidence of corrupted research, IPO bribery, and conspiracy to commit fraud on the part of the leading IPO underwriters, and said he would prosecute under the Martin Act. E-mails were leaked that revealed Jack Grubman, Citigroup's star telecom analyst, and Henry Blodget, Merrill Lynch's Internet analyst, saying indiscreet and disparaging things about stocks they followed that were on their firm's recommended-for-purchase list. Spitzer also publicly charged a number of wealthy investors with commercial bribery for their acceptance of IPO allocations; these suits were settled out of court after promises of suitable charitable donations.

For several months the dozen Wall Street firms targeted by Spitzer negotiated with him for a settlement. The firms believed that Spitzer's charges were totally unsustainable, a few inappropriate e-mails notwithstanding. But they feared the Martin Act, under which a prosecutor only had to establish before a jury that things which might be construed as fraud had occurred in order to win a conviction. And a criminal conviction could have the same fatal consequences for the firms as the Arthur Andersen or the Drexel Burnham convictions had. Spitzer, on the other hand, did not really want to go to trial. He had very few, if any, individual offenders whom he could charge with criminal fraud; and without a clear case of fraud at the individual level, what sense did it make to indict a whole firm? Even then, the evidence against the individual firms, or the group of them as conspirators, was almost entirely circumstantial. He could lose, or be overturned on appeal, which would not make him look good. In April of 2003, Spitzer and the firms agreed to a compromise, to which the SEC had been invited to join.

The settlement involved a payment of an astounding $1.5 billion, contributed to in different proportions by ten firms, later expanded to twelve. Citigroup, burdened by Grubman and the legacy of WorldCom, had the biggest share ($400 million), followed by Merrill Lynch and CSFB ($200 million each). The firms admitted no guilt to the offenses charged, and the record of what actually happened was sealed. The firms would agree also to a complex set of rules regarding securities research (including agreeing for five years to provide free independent third-party research to any recipient of their own research) and internal restrictions on communications between security analysts and investment bankers. The firms would have to expend about $1 billion per year (for five years) to be sure they were in compliance with these agreed restrictions. Some portion of the settlement payment was to be used to reimburse victims of the hard-to-demonstrate offenses, and some was to be used for "investor education," though it appears that this has proven to be impractical to do. Wall Street leaders complained privately that the settlement was very unfair, but had to be accepted to get the matter out of the daily press, and to avoid the risk, however low the probability of it might be, of a terminal criminal conviction.

Crowned Heads Roll

There were no tears for the Wall Street firms involved in the settlement. Neither the press nor the public seemed to be sympathetic. Bad stuff had happened out there in the markets during the Internet era, they felt, whether technically illegal or not, and the firms had made a huge amount of money during the period—they could afford to give some of it back.

But the turmoil didn't end there. In October 2003, Sanford Weill, the powerful billionaire CEO of Citigroup, one of America's most admired and successful financial corporations, was forced to resign by Spitzer, who otherwise threatened to bring charges against him and the firm. Weill had been entangled with Jack Grubman in some unseemly ways, with Grubman allegedly swapping a favorable recommendation of AT&T stock for Weill's assistance in getting Grubman's two children admitted to the prestigious 92nd Street YMHA preschool. Weill, who was a member of the board of directors of AT&T, the chairman of which was a Citigroup board member, denied any quid pro quo. He said he had asked Grubman to take another look at his rating on AT&T (Grubman never liked the company's prospects) without pressuring him to do so. He also said he did no more for Grubman with the 92nd Street Y than he would have for any other senior employee of Citigroup who asked for his assistance. Weill's resignation was completely unexpected and considered by most people who knew him to be the last thing in the world he wanted to do.

In 2004, the former chief executive of the New York Stock Exchange, Richard Grasso, and Kenneth Langone, who had been chairman of the NYSE's compensation committee (and who had brought the EDS IPO to the market in 1968), were charged with fraud related to Grasso's allegedly excessive compensation, which had been approved by the Exchange's compensation committee and board of directors. Grasso's large and complex deferred compensation arrangements were revealed to the press, and a furor developed. Grasso was being paid as if he were a CEO of a hot Internet company, not a nonprofit public utility owned by the members of the Exchange. Grasso resigned under the weight of the public criticism, and then Spitzer decided to sue him and Langone under a New York law regulating not-for-profit organizations, for deceiving the other board members in relation to Grasso's pay. The two vehemently denied the charges and dug in to fight the issue in court. More than four years later, the case was decided when the New York Court of Appeals threw out the remaining charges against them. Langone announced that his and Grasso's legal bills for defending themselves against the charges approached $70 million, though this was covered by insurance.[8]

In 2005, Spitzer similarly secured a public relations victory in unhorsing yet another much-respected billionaire executive, Maurice Greenberg, the brilliant and long-serving CEO of insurance giant AIG, by threatening the company's board with a Martin Act lawsuit. The issue involved allegations of a criminal accounting fraud, which Greenberg hotly denied. Spitzer told the AIG board that he could not negotiate with Greenberg, so if they wanted to negotiate the issue with his office and avoid charges against the company, they would have to appoint someone else. The board caved in and asked Greenberg to resign. No further charges were made, and Greenberg, now over eighty, has continued to be in a state of open warfare with the AIG board and his successors.

The following year Eliot Spitzer ran for governor of New York, reminding the voters of all the Wall Street scandals he had discovered and brought to justice. These included discovering a number of instances of fraud in the mutual fund industry involving late trading and market timing, two schemes in which hedge funds or other traders are permitted, contrary to the rules of individual mutual funds (and the securities laws), to engage in trading with the funds' assets in such a way as to guaranty a small profit on each trade, and some similar actions in the insurance industry. Spitzer was elected in a landslide and sworn in January 2007, but he resigned fifteen months later after admitting to being a repeat client of an expensive New York call-girl ring.

Spitzer was seen as both a savior and a bully, like Rudy Giuliani in the 1980s, and used the publicity generated by the scandals and the settlements he championed to propel himself to higher office. His career ended sordidly, thus making it harder to evaluate in context. He did act in areas where the SEC was either too slow or unwilling to go, and he did call attention to many shoddy practices used by investment banks, mutual fund managers, and others in handling fiduciary relationships. In the scramble to make money in the bubble markets of the Internet era, Wall Street firms in general had repeatedly seemed to place their own interests ahead of those of their clients, counterparts, and the investing public in general, steering themselves to avoid only clear-cut illegalities rather than being guided by the basic principles of high standards and fair play. Spitzer may have addressed the problems he saw in research, share allocation, market manipulation, mutual fund management, insurance accounting, and executive compensation with an axe and a sledgehammer, but these problems, those of greedy and cocksure industries operating at full gallop, were certainly there, and perhaps getting worse, and he doubted that a customary slap on the wrist and a fine for a technical violation would slow things down or change anyone's behavior very much.

In many ways, Wall Street's experience with Eliot Spitzer demonstrated the power of the prosecutor to extract rough justice from those seen to have abused the public trust in financial markets. This power is enormous and disproportionate. Not even the mightiest corporations or CEOs can withstand it. Once it is set in motion, questions of legality or fairness may be swept aside, leaving those who have become the object of scorn highly exposed and vulnerable to a trial by media, which they will be unable to win. Indeed, the real lesson of the Spitzer episode is that firms must ensure, by internal scrutiny and enforcement, that their conduct in the marketplace, especially if known to the media, is seen as fair and reasonable. The firms cannot always know exactly what this entails, but the burden is on them to figure it out.

11

HEDGE FUNDS AND PRIVATE EQUITY

IN EARLY MAY 2008, JWM Partners LLC, a hedge fund management firm run by ex–Long-Term Capital Management chief John Meriwether, terminated nearly 20 percent of its employees and allowed investors to exit one of its funds. A number of JWM's strategies were hit hard with losses since the beginning of the year. Its $1 billion Relative Value Opportunity Fund, which made bets on currencies, stocks, and bonds, was down about 24 percent since January, and a $300 million global macro fund had lost about 14 percent for the year; both funds were well below published average hedge fund returns. Typically, hedge fund managers will lock up investors' money for long periods before allowing them to redeem, but Meriwether was giving his investors the opportunity to pull out early, an option he expected many would take.[1] JWM was among several high-visibility hedge funds that produced disappointing results during the market disruptions caused by the 2007–2008 mortgage crisis. *Hedge Fund Research* reported that the average hedge fund reported a loss of about 10 percent during the first half of 2008, with many firms, including some very well-known ones, doing much worse; 350 hedge funds closed up shop and returned what was left of their investors' money. All hedge funds braced themselves for redemptions by investors uncomfortable with the losses, or the volatility or both.[2]

John Meriwether is from Chicago, where he attended Catholic schools and worked as a caddy at a local golf course. An earnest young man, he won a caddy scholarship to Northwestern University and then attended business school at the University of Chicago (where one of his classmates was Jon Corzine), graduating in 1973. After business school, Meriwether made his way to Salomon Brothers, where he rose rapidly to become its very successful head of proprietary trading during the years when Salomon dominated the bond business in Wall Street. He was among several senior officers forced to leave the firm in 1991 when one of his traders, Paul Mozer, falsified bids in Treasury auctions. The Justice Department nearly sued the firm, Arthur Andersen style, for engaging in and for failing to prevent criminal fraud, but let Warren Buffett, Salomon's largest shareholder and ersatz chairman, talk them out of it.

After leaving, Meriwether recruited several of his trading colleagues and two future Nobel Prize–winning economists and formed Long-Term Capital Management in 1993, to engage in the same sort of proprietary trading strategies that he had perfected at Salomon. These were essentially bets that market aberrations would disappear over time and restore prices to normal. You could bet on them when they were out of line and, assuming you had the capital to wait out the inevitable market correction, make money when the corrections finally occurred. Despite the circumstances of his departure from Salomon, Meriwether had no trouble raising $1.25 billion from banks (mainly foreign banks), sovereign wealth funds, and sophisticated investors of various types. This was then the largest amount ever raised for a hedge fund, and Meriwether insisted on retaining 25 percent of profits (20 percent was normal) and 2 percent as an annual management fee. Until it failed in 1998, LTCM would have a glorious run, increasing investors' money fourfold without ever having a losing year. In 1997 it returned $1.82 for each dollar invested, while retaining the original dollar, but the following year it experienced what some of the LTCM people called a "hundred-year storm" in the markets following the unexpected moratorium declared by Russia on payments of its foreign bank obligations, which panicked financial markets and sent LTCM into a death spiral of margin calls from which it could not extricate itself. Meriwether and his partners made a great deal of money from the fees and profit sharing up until 1998, but most of this was reinvested in the fund and ultimately lost.[3]

The term "hedge fund" was first coined in 1949 by a legendary investor, A. W. Jones, who invested mainly in the stock market. Originally a method for protecting investors against unexpected market reversals by having a side bet on the downside of a position, hedge funds came to utilize a variety of skills, leverage, and investment strategies to make money, regardless of which way the market was going. Mainly, though, they were a way for really smart investors to raise a bunch of other people's money to invest, and for ordinary, but rich, people to hire star investors to manage their money for them. Hedge funds were able to avoid regulation because investments were restricted to a limited number of sophisticated investors, who waived their rights to protection under national securities laws. By the 1990s there were lots of hedge fund managers, and some of them were very well known in the private investment world: George Soros, Julian Robertson, Michael Steinhardt, Bruce Kovner, and John Meriwether, the only one of the all-stars to have migrated from a major investment bank. In 1998, when LTCM failed, there were 1,300 hedge fund management groups offering about 3,500 different investment vehicles with about $400 billion in capital under management. LTCM was one of the largest of these funds when it collapsed, with about $100 billion in fully leveraged assets on less than $4 billion in capital (which was lost), and its distress drew the attention of regulators fearing some sort of systemic failure or liquidity freeze-up that would affect markets everywhere. This didn't happen, mainly because a group of Wall Street firms took over LTCM's positions, but many observers considered the event a near miss and began to call for regulation of the industry.

The failure of LTCM was a second strike on Meriwether, but his reputation was still sufficient for him to pick himself up and start another fund. JWM Partners was founded in 1999 with LTCM alumni, almost immediately after the collapse of LTCM. This time, Meriwether's funds would involve less risk—leverage, for example, would not exceed fifteen times, as compared to thirty or more for LTCM—but the basic investment strategy would be the same. From 2000 through 2007, the larger Relative Value Opportunity Fund outperformed the Lehman Brothers aggregate bond index, but annual returns exceeded 10 percent in only two years. Capital peaked at $1.3 billion before 2008, when it dropped considerably after encountering a second hundred-year storm less than a decade after the last one.[4] The 2008 storm was brutal for the industry. JWM's Relative Value Opportunity Fund fell 43 percent, and net assets declined to $555 million. In a letter to its investors, Meriwether said four of its seven active partners would leave, and the staff would be cut from thirty-five to twenty-five. Many other leading hedge funds would experience similar results for the year.[5] In July 2009, Bloomberg reported that the Relative Value fund would close.

Such storms occur much more often than every hundred years, so there must be something else to explain why the supposedly low-risk hedge fund managers get caught off-balance as often as they do. Professor Steven Brown at New York University's Leonard Stern School of Business, an expert on hedge fund results, believes the failures have more to do with operational failings than market shocks, but market shocks such as those experienced in 2008 can also do a lot of damage.

The market for hedge funds in 2008, however, was very different from what it was a decade before. By then, as many as ten thousand hedge funds existed, and capital under management had increased nearly fivefold, to $1.9 trillion, according to a hedge fund market research group. Such a substantial shift in the flow of funds attracted Wall Street firms to find ways to participate in it. These hedge fund investments were concentrated in fewer than a hundred or so management groups, and many of these were large banks and investment banks, very few of which had been in the hedge fund business a decade before.

JPMorgan Chase claimed to be the world's largest hedge fund manager, but there were others: at Goldman Sachs, Citigroup, Merrill Lynch, Lehman Brothers, UBS, and Deutsche Bank. The Blackstone Group, formed by two Lehman refugees in 1985, managed $44 billion in hedge funds in 2007, and the industry was stuffed with former star traders or research analysts from major firms who decamped to start their own funds. Goldman Sachs has probably trained more hedge fund managers than any other financial organization, including top performers Leon Cooperman (Omega), Richard Perry (Perry Partners), Danny Och (Och-Ziff), Tom Steyer (Farallon), Dinakar Singh (TPG-Axon), Eric Mindich (Eton Park), and David Tepper (Appaloosa). Meriwether had started something, and others were watching. These funds, couched in the lingo of modern portfolio theory, would offer both to increase "alpha" (abnormal returns relative to a benchmark) and to lower "beta" (the variability of returns, or risk) relative to the markets. This would substantially increase their investors' risk-adjusted returns. How could they resist?

FLIGHT TO ALTERNATIVE ASSETS

The end of the high-tech market bubble in 2000 resulted in three consecutive years of negative returns in the stock market, something that had not occurred since the 1930s, and another three years during which the market slowly recovered to where it had been on December 31, 1999. Six years, in other words, of a totally flat return from investing in stocks. For some flexible and insightful investors who may have gotten out of the stock market in 2000 and back in again in 2003, the returns would have been much better, but for most pension funds (America's second-largest investors after mutual funds) that were not so flexible, or that stuck with their more conventional asset-allocation models, the six-year period was very rough. It was rough not only because stock market returns were nil but also because interest rates had declined, which increased the value of pension liabilities, suggesting that pension funds as a whole had experienced a six-year period in which assets did not grow but liabilities did, a time of serious capital shrinkage.

Pension funds are live, organic institutions, at least to their accountants and their sponsors. Employers have to provide part of the annual premium payments, and must top off the funds if the market value of their assets falls below the market value of their liabilities. If the reverse is the case, when pension assets exceed the liabilities, employers do not have to top off, and may be excused from their annual premium obligations or even permitted to make withdrawals. During periods in which liabilities are increasing faster than assets, sponsors face calls for cash from their pension funds. These deficits add to operating difficulties and existing budget deficits at some of America's largest companies (especially in the auto and airline industries, which were already losing money), and at many large state and municipal pension funds. The deficits threatened to turn into major crises for some of these industrial and municipal groups.

Most students of modern portfolio theory have learned that for pension funds with long-lived liabilities, the assets should be long-lived, too, and the best long-term returns have come from stocks, not bonds, so most pension funds now have most of their assets in portfolios of stocks. They have also learned that asset allocation among different, noncorrelated asset classes determines portfolio returns much more than picking the right stocks or bonds does. To diversify the risk of the stock market, they can look at other assets types that could provide equity-like returns but not (quite) equity risks. Asset types that are not highly correlated with equity market returns are called "alternative asset classes." These include hedge funds, private equity investments, and real estate. Indeed, in 1998 Goldman Sachs published a research study that demonstrated that from 1993 to 1997, four different types of hedge funds were less risky (as measured by the volatility of their returns) than the equity market as a whole, and had the same or better returns. Thus, the study concluded that hedge funds were more conservative than the stock market as a whole, and accordingly Goldman Sachs was urging its pension fund and wealthy family clients to consider increasing their investments in hedge funds, politely noting also that Goldman Sachs had a few of its own hedge funds to offer.

The pension funds may have been influenced by the Goldman Sachs report, but they were also aware of the outstanding investment performance of three Ivy League universities, Harvard, Yale, and Princeton, in managing their endowments. One of these, the Yale Endowment, which has a history of producing high investment returns over a long period, has long been committed to an asset-allocation model that rarely has had more than 15 percent of the endowment's funds in domestic common stocks, or more than 10 percent in fixed-income investments. On the contrary, for the five-year period 2002–2006, Yale maintained more than 25 percent of its assets in hedge funds, more than 20 percent in real estate, and approximately 15 percent in both private equity investments and foreign equities. Yale had returns of 41.0 percent in 2000, 9.2 percent in 2001, and 0.7 percent in 2002 during the three years of negative domestic stock market returns, and averaged over 20 percent from 2003 until 2007.

"Well," the average pension fund sponsor said, "if hedge funds and private equities are good enough for Yale and Goldman Sachs, maybe we ought to increase our allocation into these asset classes, too." So they did. During the five years or so before 2007, pension funds directed somewhere around $1 trillion into a variety of different hedge funds, and another $1 trillion into a variety of private equity funds. Much of the redirected investments came out of public equities and fixed-income holdings. Most of the pension funds just made modest increases in their allocations to provide more room for hedge funds and private equity, but the cumulative global effect—overseas pension funds were thinking the same thing—was very large. The new money flowed into hedge funds, and into private equity funds and real estate. All this new money being gathered into alternative investments constituted a bubble of its own only a few years after the last one had burst.

The Yale Endowment was not immune to the market difficulties of 2008; its value dropped 25 percent in the last six months of the year, and it reported its first negative return in the twenty years it had been managed by David Swensen and a professional staff of twenty-five. Swensen is much admired among professional asset managers and is the author of *Pioneering Portfolio Management*, for which a second edition was about to be released when he gave an interview to *The Wall Street Journal* in which he renewed his commitment to alternative assets and observed, "I don't think it makes sense for an institutional investor with as long an investment horizon as Yale's to structure a portfolio to perform well in a period of financial crisis. That would require moving away from equity-oriented investments that have served institutions with long time horizons well."[6]

HEDGE FUNDS

The investments flowing into hedge funds were deployed in various ways. Most of them, sometimes modestly leveraged, went into equity investments of different kinds: long-short positions or "event investing," in which a bet is placed that a particular transaction (such as an announced merger, recapitalization, or bankruptcy workout) would actually occur. Some of the money flowed into funds specializing in a variety of different fixed-income, foreign exchange, and commodity investments. These funds tend to be leveraged ten or fifteen times, or higher. Almost all hedge funds prefer to bet on arbitrages of various kinds rather than directional market movements, and accordingly promised "market-neutral," or "absolute," returns—meaning that they did not depend on how the market moved per se but on price adjustments within markets.

There are some outstandingly successful hedge fund managers, many with Wall Street origins. John Paulson, a former Bear Stearns managing director, founded Paulson and Co. in 1995; its assets more than doubled in 2007, to $28 billion, when the firm posted returns that were among the industry's highest by wagering against the subprime mortgage market. Paulson, with a personal net worth of $3 billion, was one of America's thirty-five or so billionaire hedge fund managers at the end of 2007.

The basic math of hedge funds can explain how such fortunes can be made. Assume a fund makes a relative value investment based on a perceived market anomaly aspiring to a simple 2 percent return on $10 billion in investment. If the investment, however, has been leveraged ten times (the original amount of capital committed being $1 billion), the 2 percent return will produce a gross return of 20 percent, which, less the management fee and 20 percent profit participation, will yield a net return of about 14 percent to the fund's limited partners (i.e., its nonmanagement investors). Such a result, however, would also yield about $60 million in fees to be distributed among the fund's general partners, of which the top two or three would divide most of the money. Keep that up for a few years, while increasing funds under management and launching new funds, and the managers will end up with some real money, far more than they could ever have made trading for Goldman Sachs or anyone else.

No wonder there was an exodus of trading talent from the big Wall Street firms in the years in which demand for hedge funds set all records. The talent could walk over to Merrill Lynch or one of the other firms that raised money for new hedge funds, point to a recent bull market track record, and walk away with a billion or so under management, some of which might be contributed by the old employer. After all, the employer was in the "prime brokerage" business, too, which coddled, nurtured, and helped along fledgling hedge funds with research, technical support, and other services in return for a goodly share of the actively traded hedge funds' sizeable commission and margin business.

Aggregate prime brokerage revenues grew to more than $25 billion a year for the industry by 2006, after five years of steadily increasing at 15 percent.[7] The prime brokerage business was dominated by three banks, Morgan Stanley, Goldman Sachs, and Bear Stearns, who shared about two thirds of the industry's revenues and developed bird's-eye views of what hedge funds were doing, and thus better understood market trends. But it was not long before the rest of the large banks began to horn in. Competition for prime brokerage became intense, and the brokers were forced to offer better deals and more credit to their clients in order to hang on to, or try to create, market share.[8]

Several large hedge fund managers, buoyed by their unusual ability to raise billions for their first funds, insisted on the right to set some of it aside, sometimes as much as 30 percent, for illiquid private equity investments. Some of this money found its way into leveraged buyouts and corporate takeovers, both of which surged to record levels in 2006 and 2007.

Eddie Lampert graduated from Yale University in 1984 (summa cum laude), where he was a member of Skull and Bones and Phi Beta Kappa. He became an associate at Goldman Sachs, and worked in the firm's Risk Arbitrage Department, directly with Robert Rubin, until he decided to go out on his own after only four years of trading experience. Rubin, quite naturally, warned him that this would be a bad career decision.

Lampert left Goldman to form ESL Investments (his initials), based in Greenwich, Connecticut, in April 1988. Richard Rainwater, another Goldman Sachs alumnus turned billionaire money manager, gave him $28 million in seed money and introduced him to some of his clients. That got him going. Lampert's investment style resembles that of Warren Buffett. He takes concentrated positions in a small number of stocks and holds the investments for years until they pay off. Unlike at most other hedge funds, however, Lampert uses his authority to invest in illiquid assets proactively. He acquired Kmart Stores and, in 2005, merged it with Sears Roebuck—two broken-down retailers with lots of real estate—to form the publicly traded Sears Holdings. Lampert's fund produced annual returns of 30 percent through 2007. His personal earnings in 2004 were estimated to be $1 billion, making him, then forty-four, the first Wall Street financial manager ever to exceed an income of $1 billion in a single year.[9]

Banks and Hedge Funds

Watching people such as Lampert perform encouraged some large banks to begin looking around to build or acquire successful hedge funds for themselves. The high returns from hedge funds were attractive, especially as most of their income was taxed at capital gains rates, as was the tie-in with prime brokerage and custody services, and all this could be had with relatively little capital—the funds could rely on client capital, or "other people's money," not its own. Of course the volatility of the funds could be a problem for them, and there could be some damage to the bank's reputation if things went wrong, but they tended to overlook the negatives when the fever was on. Many banks lacked the ability to start up high-performance hedge funds in-house, so the next best, and quickest, way to get into the business was to buy them. There was a risk that they would buy the wrong ones, or that the ones they bought would be too expensive, or the people who managed the funds would leave as soon as the ink was dry on the contract, but they were determined and went ahead anyway. Soon a market developed for existing hedge funds priced at somewhere between 10 and 30 percent of assets under management.

In 2004, JPMorgan Chase acquired a majority interest in Highbridge Capital, a fund manager with about $7 billion under management, for $1 billion, a price-to-assets ratio of close to 30 percent. When converted to a price-to-earnings ratio, the price paid would be very high, unless the hedge fund consistently produced returns of 30 percent or so, which for most funds was a very tall order. Highbridge ran several hedge funds and two statistical arbitrage mutual funds that were heavily marketed to wealthy JPMorgan clients, which helped attract more than $12 billion in new money, though after a couple of years of lackluster performance, clients withdrew about $8 billion.[10]

In 2007, Citigroup acquired Old Lane, a $3 billion fund managed by Vikram Pandit and some colleagues who had just left Morgan Stanley, for $800 million, also paying about 30 percent of assets, presumably justified by the fact that Citigroup would acquire the highly regarded Pandit as a potential future corporate manager. Pandit was paid $165 million for his stake, though he was required to invest $100 million in the fund. By the end of the year, Pandit was indeed named to replace Chuck Prince, after his unexpected retirement as Citigroup CEO, and he brought some of his Old Lane colleagues along to manage other Citigroup units. However, the redeployment of personnel triggered a clause in the Old Lane partnership agreement allowing investors to withdraw their money if as many as three of the original six managers left the fund. By March of 2008, after lackluster returns since the fund's acquisition, all of the investors elected to withdraw, and Citigroup was forced to take a $202 million write-off to close the fund.[11] Regardless of his abilities to manage the bank, Vikram Pandit had proven to be a very expensive new hire in terms of what it cost the bank to get him.

Downsides

But it was not all cakes and cream for the hedge fund people. There were other lessons out there waiting to be learned. There was a lot of competition among the thousands of hedge funds for the alpha, which proved elusive. Many of the traders had more or less the same ideas, which smoothed out the market aberrations and limited the profit potential. Managers had to look farther and wider to find the opportunities they needed, but often this meant that the search moved into areas and markets they knew little about. They invested in trendy things, riding the momentum of the dot.com or the mortgage securities booms until these died, hoping they would know when to get out. They pressured their bankers to give them large allocations of hot IPOs, and devised programs for "market- timing" trades with mutual funds to take advantage of small differences in daily price changes in underlying securities held that had not yet been reflected in the price of the fund's shares. (This led to a harsh investigation of the industry by Eliot Spitzer and severe penalties on some mutual fund management companies.) They were tempted to increase leverage, increase positions in less liquid markets, and, on the whole, increase their funds' risk in order to make up for the slimmer pickings. They knew that if they produced inadequate returns, their investors would likely withdraw money, tarnishing their reputation and prompting further withdrawals. Many such investors, especially conservative institutional investors, turned out to have a much lower tolerance for the high volatility of hedge funds than they thought.

They also learned that all these important investment banks that were eagerly soliciting their (prime brokerage) business when times were good could turn on them in a flash when the markets went against them. Peloton Partners, a $1 billion London-based fund launched in 2005 by two more former Goldman Sachs highflyers, Ron Beller and Geoff Grant, was one of the world's best-performing hedge funds until February 2008, when in a matter of days it lost $17 billion and closed. Peloton, in which Goldman Sachs had made an investment, was leveraged about ten to one, but the banks got nervous and pulled back their money, leaving the fund to liquidate positions in a very sour market. Beller and Grant were convinced that their positions were solid, though the markets were temporarily mispricing them—but the banks were not about to let loans backed by inadequate collateral remain outstanding, so they called them.[12] Not to be deterred, Grant formed another fund, Grand Capital, a few months later, with $100 million in backing from Société Générale, a French bank.

Hedge funds have been dangerous for banks to invest in, too. In 1998, the collapse of Long-Term Capital Management caused the dismissal of the CEO of UBS, the Swiss bank, which had a large investment in the fund. A decade later, in-house hedge fund losses triggered the resignation of another UBS CEO, and the failure of Bear Stearns. Such losses also were embarrassing to Goldman Sachs, which managed about $25 billion in hedge funds (and $25 billion more in funds of hedge funds) and had two of its best-known funds report declines in the area of 30 percent in 2007. The following year, a fixed-income hedge fund managed by Citigroup, Falcon Strategies, managed to lose 75 percent of its capital, causing great embarrassment to the bank. It paid out $250 million to allow retail investors to exit their positions without absorbing the fund's full losses. Three of its largest investors, banks that together acquired $1.6 billion in the fund for their employee life insurance programs, filed lawsuits looking for a settlement in which they would be made whole.[13] The suits were dismissed in 2008. Banks are natural deep-pocket targets in any kind of dispute in which a client experiences a big loss. These various experiences caused some banks to wonder whether investing in hedge funds was worth the downside exposure.

Bear Stearns must have thought it was taking a safe pathway to invest in the mortgage securities business when it set up two hedge funds to invest its own and client money in structured mortgage deals. These funds, which held at one time a total of $20 billion in predominantly subprime mortgage assets, were managed by Ralph Cioffi and Matthew Tannin, two experienced fund managers with their own money in the funds. The funds mainly would involve other people's money and would be off-balance-sheet, to insulate the firm from the trading risks involved.

The funds, however, suffered sizeable losses as the subprime market collapsed. Bear Stearns tried to rescue one of them with a large capital infusion, but by July 2007 the firm told investors they were unlikely to recover any money, and soon thereafter the funds filed for bankruptcy. The bankruptcy of these funds began Bear Stearns's struggle to remain independent as it faced an increasing loss of confidence by investors in its management and financial position. Keeping the funds at arm's length and off their balance sheet, and free of negative publicity for the firm, turned out to be impossible for Bear Stearns. In June 2008, Cioffi and Tannin were arrested, handcuffed, and hauled off to court, where they were charged with fraud based on subpoenaed e-mails showing that the two managers had a deep lack of confidence in the funds even while they were reassuring investors that they were comfortable with their holdings. As of September 2009, their cases had not yet gone to trial.

Along with the excitement of the buoyant markets came an influx of unsophisticated money into the hedge fund world. It was only natural that some of it would be taken advantage of by scam artists, such as Bernard Madoff, who was turned in to authorities by his two sons and business partners for having run an alleged $65 billion Ponzi scheme for many years that attracted thousands of hedge investors from all over the world.* Madoff, a former NASDAQ chairman and third-market operator well known in many Jewish philanthropic circles, had for years run a

---

* Based on reported account balances just before the fund collapsed.

hedge fund that he said specialized in low-risk convertible arbitrage. The returns reported by the fund seemed to be very steady from year to year, though some experts doubted that these returns could come from investing in convertible debentures and selling the underlying common stock short. Over the years, Madoff developed a cadre of loyal investors, who raved about him to others. In time Madoff took investments from funds of hedge fund investors and worked with brokers, who served as "feeder funds" for him. It was all a sham. For at least the last thirteen years, according to the court-appointed trustee in bankruptcy, no securities had been purchased: all of the incoming money had been used to fund payouts to the prior investors, a classic Ponzi structure. As of July 1, 2009, the trustee had been able to recover only $1.2 billion of the $13.2 billion of estimated losses suffered by investors since December 1995. In June 2009, while the roles others may have played in the fraud were still under investigation, Madoff was sentenced to 150 years in prison.

Hedge Fund Performance

It is estimated that more than a thousand new hedge funds were launched each year between 2002 and 2006, with more than two thousand being created in each of the last two of those years. The data on hedge funds, however, is very inexact. Many funds are created outside the United States, and therefore are not picked up by the reporting system. Many, perhaps a third, are funds of hedge funds, which double-count underlying invested assets. There is no accurate information as to the actual number of hedge funds around the world, nor of the value of assets managed, or allocation of assets by investment types or styles. There are some useful hedge fund databases, but these only aggregate un-standardized data that is submitted voluntarily, and contains survivor bias—i.e., they do not include the returns of funds that were closed, of which there were more than two thousand in 2005–2007 alone.

Nevertheless, the data sources collect information on several thousand funds and publish indices of performance. The published returns for the past few years showed that the average "investable" hedge fund* returns tracked the S&P 500 fairly closely, thus producing results that were probably well below what their investors expected. However, the indices

---

*This index excludes hedge funds that have been closed to new investment for several years, and includes only funds you could actually invest in.

show that there is a very large difference in returns between funds ranking in the upper and lower quartiles, and between different investment styles. A few funds lost sizeable amounts, such as Amaranth Advisers, which specialized in commodities and in 2006 very quickly lost $6 billion, or 65 percent of its capital, and a few made high, double-digit returns, but the average fund produced very little, if any, alpha. In an industry with a large variation between the returns of best and worst performers and a large amount of volatility in year-to-year returns of managers, the average return may not be very meaningful, nor certainly of much value in trying to forecast future returns.

Still, the indices are out there, and investors and the consultants who advise on the best funds to select do look at them. Individual funds are judged on the basis of how well they do relative to the market index most appropriate for them. In 2000–2003, when the S&P 500 index was down 40 percent, funds that were down only, say, 2 percent looked very good. Hedge funds may do better relative to their performance indices in bad markets rather than good ones, but they try to do better in good markets, too. Most individual funds have more volatility than the market, but diversified investments in different funds, or funds of funds, can reduce the volatility of the whole portfolio. All of this is taken into account when the performances of individual funds are evaluated, which occurs often.

The performance assessments at the end of 2008 were difficult to make. About $200 billion was withdrawn from hedge funds during the year. The average return for all hedge funds was down 21.7 percent, i.e., down much less than the S&P 500 index results for the year, but still well below expectations. Many funds had actually found it difficult to hedge their positions during the year after the Bush administration prohibited short-selling in 799 stocks in the midst of the market meltdown of the fourth quarter of 2008. Approximately 80 percent of the funds were "underwater" (i.e., they produced negative returns) and therefore received no performance fee, and because of "high-water marks," were not likely to return to paying performance fees for quite some time. Many funds decided to close; others, including many high-visibility funds, put restrictions in place on redemptions.

Funds that performed below expectations could expect a significant number of their investors to withdraw at the next opportunity rather than wait for the manager's luck to turn. After the credit crisis of 2007–2008, and market dislocations that turned sophisticated relative-value quantitative strategies to toast, the disappointments increased, and pension fund investors became much more cautious about putting their money into hedge funds.[14] By 2007 a number of hedge fund managers had begun to offer reduced fees on new hedge funds, to make up for losses on the funds that they had closed.[15] Some new funds also offered initial investors discounts on fees to induce them to invest.

Allowing for the use of borrowed money, McKinsey and Co., the management consultants, estimated the total of assets under management by the hedge fund industry was $6 trillion. A lot of this money was managed by groups that ran two or more multibillion-dollar funds. The people involved, usually trained at other large funds or on the proprietary trading desks of investment banks, tend to think alike. Often they made the same bets, both going in and getting out. It was starting to be clear that very large funds operated at a disadvantage to smaller, more flexible funds, and with so many competing for the magical alpha, was there really enough to go around? Many observers questioned whether there were enough high-performance investment opportunities to meet the need for investment returns promised by so many fund managers. If all this money was looking for the same sorts of market anomalies, wouldn't the anomalies begin to disappear? If they did, wouldn't that mean that the high fees paid to hedge fund managers might become increasingly hard to justify for ordinary market returns? A lower beta may not be much consolation if your fund can still collapse entirely at any time. Do some funds respond to the challenge of producing the desired returns by increasing risk, shifting investment styles, or lowering quality standards? If so, that would suggest that more nasty accidents are out there waiting to happen.[16]

PRIVATE EQUITY

In February 2007, the beautiful people of New York celebrated the sixtieth birthday of their newest idol, private equity* poster boy Steve Schwartzman, CEO of the Blackstone Group, who held a $3 million bash for hundreds of his closest friends at the Park Avenue Armory. The enormous place was turned into a replica of Schwartzman's $37 million, thirty-five-room triplex Manhattan apartment, once owned by John D. Rockefeller,

---

* "Private equity" is a category of investments made by qualified wealthy investors in unregistered private placements of securities with equity-like returns.

Jr., and was festooned with orchids, palm trees, and copies of the New Man's art collection. Comedian Martin Short was master of ceremonies for the party, which included performances from composer Marvin Hamlisch, soul singer Patti LaBelle, and the aging rock star Rod Stewart. *Fortune* put Schwartzman on the cover of its March 2007 issue, calling him "Wall Street's Man of the Moment." Schwartzman had finally edged out his crosstown rival, Henry Kravis of KKR, as the most visible private equity billionaire, a position Kravis had held unchallenged since the RJR Nabisco deal of 1988. Schwartzman had emerged as someone who lived large on many fronts. He owned lavish homes in Palm Beach, the Hamptons, St. Tropez, and Jamaica; he was also a generous philanthropist who had pledged $100 million to the New York Public Library and chaired the board at the Kennedy Center for the Performing Arts. The party, of course, ostentatious as it was, attracted all sorts of critical comment about the new Gilded Age, the return of the Robber Barons, and the extraordinary wealth and power they had accumulated. To his critics, Schwartzman was Wall Street's latest designated villain.

Schwartzman's performance, however, was not confined to his party. The main event was the initial public offering of Blackstone, a diversified investment manager with $88 billion in assets under management on which it had regularly produced high returns, which was announced in March and completed in June 2007. The offering, which included a non-voting $3 billion investment by the State Investment Company of China, was priced at $31 per share, and opened for trading at $36.45 per share, two days after two Bear Stearns hedge funds collapsed, ushering in the beginning of the 2007–2008 mortgage securities crisis. The offering valued Blackstone at about $38 billion, and revealed that Schwartzman would take out $677 million while retaining a 24 percent interest, valued at $10 billion. His co-founding partner, Pete Peterson, eighty, would withdraw $1.9 billion and retain a 4 percent interest valued at $1.6 billion; Tony James, Blackstone's president, would withdraw $189 million and retain a 4.9 percent stake. According to a friend of Schwartzman who worked at an investment bank, "You have no idea what an impression this made on Wall Street. You have all these guys who have spent their entire lives working just as hard to make twenty million. Sure, that's a lot of money, but then Schwartzman turns around and, seemingly overnight, has ten billion."[17]

Peterson and Schwartzman founded Blackstone in 1985, soon after Peterson was pushed out of Lehman Brothers, which he had headed since

1973, by an impatient Lew Glucksman, Peterson's co-CEO. Peterson, a former CEO of Bausch and Lomb, an industrial company, and secretary of commerce in the Nixon administration, was able to withdraw his capital as a result, and to negotiate an investment by Lehman in a new firm he planned to form with an initial investment of $400,000. He invited Schwartzman, then a thirty-eight-year-old merger specialist, to join him, and the two set out to see what they could do.

Peterson was very well liked by his many contacts among corporate CEOs, and he attracted boutique merger and other advisory business, which Schwartzman was good at executing. But they looked around after a while, especially at KKR, and decided to shift their focus from corporate advisory work to investing money on behalf of institutional clients in LBOs and real estate deals. In 1987 they began to raise their funds, which required a 2 percent management fee and a 20 percent share of profits. Their investors included university and other endowments and a few pension funds. In the twenty years since it was founded, until early 2007, Blackstone's funds had taken control of 112 companies with a combined value of $200 billion, and provided returns 10 to 20 percent higher than the S&P 500. At the time of Schwartzman's birthday party, it had completed the largest private equity buyout ever, the purchase of Equity Office Properties, for $39 billion, which topped the RJR Nabisco record. By the end of 2007, Blackstone managed over $100 billion in real estate, corporate private equity, and marketable alternative assets. Revenues for 2007 were $3.1 billion, and net income (after many adjustments to convert from a private partnership to a public limited partnership that distributes the bulk of its income directly to its investors) was $1.6 billion, down from a record income in 2006 of $2.3 billion. Peterson and Schwartzman, in modeling themselves after KKR, had recognized a good thing when they saw it.

We raise money to provide alternative asset opportunities for institutions that know us, they might have said. We charge hedge fund fees and use the money, plus a lot of leverage from banks and the junk bond market, to acquire companies we can improve and resell. We hire the industrial skills we need, use our connections to build a deal flow, and sit back and watch the money flow in, which is then taxed predominantly at capital gains rates. We keep the game going by selling new funds every couple of years, hopefully in large amounts. We avoid hostile deals, conflicts of interest, and regulation, and can stick to the high road because the nature of the business makes it relatively easy to do so. We only need a small staff for whom we provide a friendly, supportive environment, which earns the loyalty and dedication of our employees. We invest some of our money in our deals, but we don't need to retain a lot of capital otherwise, or borrow money or subject ourselves to trading risks. This has to be a lot better than cutthroat investment banking, competing for business with endlessly demanding clients against powerful competitors with huge balance sheets, or subjecting ourselves to a lot of market and other risks.

Blackstone's post-IPO share price valued the firm at about ten times book value, and 24 times earnings, as compared to an average of about 1.5 to 2.5 times book and 8 or 9 times earnings for the best of the investment banks. The IPO was a breakthrough for the secretive private equity industry that had prized its ability to avoid regulation and public scrutiny. Blackstone had proved that it could sell its shares to the public at a valuation of more than five times the price-to-book-value ratio of the leading investment banks. Other LBO operators would surely follow Blackstone's trailblazing example, and New York could expect more birthday parties for its celebrity financiers.

In fact, some other fund management companies had already gone public by the time the Blackstone deal came along. KKR had sold shares in a specialty finance company, KKR Financial Holdings, in London in June 2005, and followed up with an IPO of KKR Private Equity Investors on the Amsterdam market a year later. These funds were designed to allow small investors to invest in KKR's deals alongside the big guys, and were sold in Europe, where they didn't have to be registered with the SEC, which took a dim view of complex LBO funds luring unsophisticated investors into risky investments. Neither of these companies fared well in the markets, though, and KKR had to inject additional capital into Financial Holdings, which had been hurt by the mortgage crisis. There were also some hedge fund managers—Och-Ziff Capital Management, Fortress Investment Management, and GLG Partners—that had established public trading markets in their firms. In July 2007, just after the Blackstone IPO, KKR announced that it, too, was going to sell $1.25 billion in shares in an IPO scheduled for the fall, with all the money being retained in the firm and none of the firm's founders selling any of their shares. The initiative would signify a major shift in strategy for the firm, which saw itself branching out into a more comprehensive financial firm.

Blackstone's IPO coincided with the beginning of the market melt-down that began in the summer of 2007 and lasted for more than eigh-teen months. Blackstone had no exposure at all to the mortgage-backed securities business, and its exposure to real estate was limited to commer-cial real estate, which initially did not suffer so badly as the residential sector. Its principal exposure, of course, was to private equity investments, most of which were fully financed. Some deals in process were canceled or renegotiated without any harm to Blackstone. The problems lay in the virtual halting of all new deals (the banks, suffering as they were from major write-offs, did not want to make any new leveraged loans, which were also falling sharply in value), and the need to apply "Fair Value" ac-counting to the positions they did have following the introduction of new accounting rules in 2008. Soon after the IPO, the Blackstone share price began to drop, and continued to do so for most of the rest of the year, reaching a low of $3.35 per share in February 2009, a 90 percent decline from its high of $38. For 2008, Blackstone announced a net loss of $1.1 billion, as compared to a profit of $1.6 billion in 2007. The loss was at-tributable to restating the value of investment positions held at fair value and to a reduction in the amount of performance fees due on them. "We hold our assets for the long term," said Tony James, "and expect their value will rise as we come out of the cycle."

Building the Cycle

The cycle Tony James was referring to was the third one since LBOs be-came active in capital markets in the mid-1980s. The first one ended in 1990, when the junk bond market blew out. An active, but smaller-scale LBO business during the 1993–2000 period was halted by the collapse of the technology and telecommunications sectors and by the record levels of bankruptcies that ensued. In 2003, the third cycle began and peaked in mid-2007 when private equity fund-raising reached the $250 billion-per-year record level it had achieved in 2000, and then slightly exceeded it. During the four and a half years of the cycle, over $1 trillion was raised for private equity investments. During the first half of 2007, nearly one out of four U.S. acquisitions was in the form of an LBO, including a $45 billion transaction for the Texas public utility TXU, arranged by KKR and Texas Pacific Group, and a later record-smashing $52 billion deal for the Canadian phone giant BCE, led by Providence Equity Partners.

Most of the funds raised for private equity investments end up financing the equity component of leveraged buyout acquisitions, which are supplemented by substantial amounts of debt financing provided by banks or subordinated lenders. Private equity funds also exist to provide venture capital, mezzanine debt, financing for distressed company workouts or turnarounds, and to fund portfolios of private equity investments of various types acquired in the secondary market from original investors wanting to sell their positions before the termination of the funds they invested in. They also exist to finance real estate investments of various kinds. All of these different forms of private equity investments now operate globally—in Europe, Asia, and in the emerging market countries.

KKR is the biggest LBO firm; as of June 30, 2008, it had completed more than 166 transactions with an aggregate enterprise value of over $420 billion. KKR's equity investments were valued at over $68 billion on over $25 billion in invested capital. It controlled 46 companies with $185 billion in annual revenues and 825,000 employees worldwide.

Blackstone, TPG, and Goldman Sachs Capital Partners fill out the rest of the top ranks in the industry. The next six among the top ten private equity firms are Apollo Advisers, Carlyle Group, CVC Capital Partners and Permira (two European firms), Madison Dearborn Partners, and Warburg Pincus. In 2007 these ten firms shelled out $4.4 billion in merger and financing fees to investment banks, accounting for 18 percent of the industry's global revenues. Most of these fees were paid in the first half of the year, before the market closed down.[18] Goldman Sachs, the only investment bank with a private equity business big enough to appear on this list, paid a lot of those fees out to itself, providing it with another good reason to be in the business, as most of the major investment banks now are, though not on such as scale as Goldman.

During the most recent cycle, activity was accelerated by low interest rates and extremely easy borrowing conditions. Whereas the buyout firms have argued that their investment activity improves companies, creates growth and jobs, and meaningfully contributes to the economy, and academic studies support this claim, their critics say that the success of the LBO firms is all due to the use of leverage, and that because of the scale of the industry now, these firms subjected the economy to serious credit and liquidity risks.

In the period after 2003, LBOs of large, worn-out, difficult-to-improve companies (e.g., Burger King, Hertz, Kmart) occurred with little prospect for intrinsic value enhancement, but because of the ability to borrow lots of cheap money, and to borrow more later to pay special dividends, the

LBO operators could make a good and quick return. Leverage ratios of buyout companies increased after 2003, and credit quality standards deteriorated to what came to be known as "covenant light" loans, which required hardly any of the restrictive covenants agreed to by borrowers to keep them on the straight and narrow, because the loans were going to be repackaged into collateralized loan obligations (CLOs) and sold as asset-backed securities, in the same manner as mortgage-backed securities were being created and sold. Banks making these kinds of corporate loans were also eager to get themselves into the group of investment banks advising the private equity firms on their deals, so they could share in the fees and the credit to be reflected in league tables. These banks, especially Citigroup and JPMorgan Chase, became so competitive with their credit facilities that the investment banks were forced to meet them by offering credit facilities of their own. By the spring of 2007, with the market roaring along, the advantages in negotiating financing were all with the LBO fund managers.

They might call up three or four banks and say they were thinking of acquiring Smith Brothers and would need about $20 billion in credit facilities to back up $3.5 billion in equity. They would need $8 billion in senior debt, $10 or so in subordinated, and a few billion in "pay-in-kind" debt (in which interest could be paid by issuing additional debt of the same kind; sometimes with an option allowing the borrower to "toggle" when the PIK provisions would apply). They would go on to say, we want all of the financing good for five years, and for our banks to underwrite all of it now so we know it's in place. You can sell it or syndicate it after the deal is done.

However, such a deal with banks and investment banks to fund the LBO of First Data Corp. for $28 billion, negotiated in the summer of 2007 by KKR and scheduled to close in September, created all sorts of tensions. When the commitments for the debt were made to KKR, the lenders offered the loans at par, expecting to sell them at that price or a little better when they were permitted to do so. But in September, the market for the debt, already beginning to reflect the credit crisis, had declined to about 96 percent of par. At that price, the banks would be giving up all of their fee income on the deal, but some wanted to sell anyway, fearful of the deteriorating market and aware of their considerable inventories of such debt. The banks tried to negotiate improvements in the terms of the loan to make the sales easier, but KKR refused to do so. KKR, after all, had a lot of bargaining power; it controlled a lot of present and future investment banking fees. A modest portion of the debt was sold in the fall, but by February 2008, the market had fallen further, to about 88 percent of par, reflecting a write-down of the loan on the investment banks' books of 12 percent.[19] The same thing was happening to dozens of other unsold debt packages that were pending at midyear 2007, and cumulatively the losses mounted. By early 2008 there was still in excess of $150 billion of this debt overhanging the markets. There were lots of disputes, lawsuits, and catfights over terms and whether deals could be abandoned in order to cancel the need for the banks to make the loans. The collapse of the debt markets imperiled the investment banks in much the way that bridge loans did at the end of the first LBO cycle in 1989.

These conditions, however, did not deter KKR from its plans to go public. It recognized that an IPO would be nearly impossible in the turbulent markets that existed after it had filed its registration statement for a September offering, but it regrouped with another plan. In July 2008, a year after Blackstone's offering, which was then trading at a steep discount from its offering price, KKR announced that it would acquire its publicly owned Amsterdam affiliate in an exchange of shares that would create a public market for KKR, and that these newly issued KKR shares would be listed on the NYSE. The transaction was explained as offering investors an opportunity to acquire the Amsterdam traded shares at a large discount from what KKR believed to be their intrinsic value, even though the shares to be issued for them would also trade at a discount from the valuation levels KKR had earlier foreseen for itself. KKR was hoping that the New York listing would value the firm at $15 to $19 billion, but based on actual market prices then for the Amsterdam affiliate, the value might be more like $10 billion.[20] But the market continued to be difficult, and KKR's existing publicly held securities reflected the same declines as Blackstone's, and KKR was again forced to postpone the public offering of its shares indefinitely. In June of 2009, KKR came out with yet another plan: to merge all its operations into one company, the publicly traded Amsterdam affiliate, and then switch the listing to the NYSE so Henry Kravis and George Roberts, both sixty-five, could have a place to sell out their large stakes in the firm over time.

Banks in the Business

John Mack reversed Phil Purcell's decision in 2003 to have Morgan Stanley exit its private equity efforts by launching a $6 billion fund in early

2007, intending to put $2 billion of the firm's own capital into it. However, the huge write-offs that Morgan Stanley had to take to stem its position in the mortgage-backed securities business tied up its capital, and in the end required it to raise more of it. But the fund, focused on the middle market, got under way in late 2007 with a $310 million acquisition of a grocery chain, and in 2008 was seen trying to recruit private equity specialists from other firms. Most of the rest of the Wall Street banks have had similar on-again, off-again approaches to private equity, favoring the business while it's hot, but backing away when it's not.

By contrast is the aggressive approach to alternative assets that has been part of Goldman Sachs's core business strategy since the late 1990s. As of November 30, 2007, Goldman Sachs managed $151 billion in alternative asset funds (hedge funds, private equity, real estate, currencies, commodities, and asset allocation strategies), including $12 billion of its own capital invested in these assets. The firm's activities in this sector also include managing several large secondary-market funds that buy (and then hold) existing private equity portfolios from holders wishing to liquidate their positions at an approximate market valuation. In August 2008, Goldman Sachs's funds paid $1.5 billion for a portfolio of existing private equity investments involving thirty-two European companies and $450 million in capital as a part of the carve-up of ABN-Amro by Royal Bank of Scotland and others. In addition to these private equity investments, which totaled $9.7 billion, Goldman Sachs also held $10.9 billion in two especially large, strategic holdings in the Industrial and Commercial Bank of China and Sumitomo Mitsui Financial Group.

Goldman Sachs's Merchant Banking Division manages principal investments and private equity funds in LBOs, real estate, and mezzanine debt through various funds that have raised more than $50 billion, real estate funds that have raised more than $12 billion, and some additional funds aimed at urban and infrastructure development. The Merchant Banking Division employs around 250 people, who are led by a number of long-service Goldman Sachs managing directors.

Unlike most of the other private equity managers, Goldman Sachs has followed a policy of investing a substantial amount of its own money in the twenty or so private equity investment funds it has sold to outside investors, usually in the area of 20–25 percent of the amounts raised. This skin-in-the-game approach, it believes, provides it with superior investment opportunities and sets a threshold for expected returns that is attractive to investors and helps to align their interests with the firm's. It also gives Goldman Sachs an opportunity to set aside a portion of each fund for its employees to subscribe to if they wish. The returns on these funds have varied by type of investment, but have generally met the goals stated at the time the funds were raised.

Goldman Sachs believes that its involvement in alternative assets is important to its overall business in a number of ways. It uses its highly developed investment banking, trading, and real estate skills to create a variety of investment opportunities for its institutional and wealthy family clients. It makes use of the firm's global contacts with corporations and governments to create deal flow and special alliances in areas of the world where they are needed, to be able to invest with confidence. It provides the firm with the opportunity to leverage its own capital substantially to create funds of greater size, influence, and negotiating power, which widely distribute the risk. The fees and returns on its own investment in the funds provide a relatively high return on its shareholders' capital.

The principal investment platform is fully global—covering not only the developed world but emerging markets as well—and is available to assist the rest of the firm in building up contacts, relationships, and activities in promising parts of the world, such as Brazil, Russia, India, and China, where basic investment banking and investing activities have not yet developed to their full potential. At such times, principal investing can get the firm well plugged in, with something to do that can make money before capital markets develop enough to allow more normal investment banking opportunities to appear.

JPMorgan Chase has also followed an aggressive, though zigzagged path into alternative assets. As of the end of 2007 it had $121 billion in alternative assets under management, $76 billion in private equities, and $46 billion in hedge funds. JPMorgan came to this position by a strange route. Chase Manhattan Bank had an active venture capital and private equity group in the 1990s, which it merged with JPMorgan Partners, a private equity unit of JPMorgan, when Morgan was acquired by Chase. In the market downdraft that began in 2000, some of the bank's private equity positions began to reflect substantial losses, and as a result, the management of JPMorgan Chase decided to spin out JPMorgan Partners. The principals of that division formed CCMP Capital Advisors LLC, which focuses on buyouts in specialized areas, including energy, industrial production, health care, and media. Later JPMorgan Chase merged with Bank One, which owned One Equity Partners, a private equity arm. The merged bank decided to keep this unit, which in 2007 returned about two thirds of the bank's private equity gains, and having provided a rate of return of more than 50 percent from inception.

Merrill Lynch's 49.8 percent investment in BlackRock, like JPMorgan Chase's investments in One Equity Partners and Highbridge Capital, also represents a sort of outsourcing of investment management to smaller, more specialized units, which appear able to produce better returns than home-grown managers. BlackRock, however, with $1.4 trillion under management, is a much larger example. It was established in 1995 by Larry Fink and Bob Kapito, who gave up promising careers at First Boston—at twenty-nine, Fink was the youngest person ever to become a managing director of First Boston—where they had specialized in asset-backed securities in competition with Lew Ranieri at Salomon Brothers.

They left First Boston to join Blackstone in 1988, to create a money management arm just as the firm was getting started. They were nervous about giving up a sure thing to try something that might not work out—and didn't. In 1995, after a "rancorous split" Fink and Kapito left Blackstone to found their own firm, which would be almost anti–Wall Street in its attitudes. According to the *Financial Times*, "BlackRock was set up to manage money only for its clients, not for itself. It does not use its own balance sheet to compete with its clients by trading its own capital."[21]

BlackRock's success is attributed to Fink's decision to back the bull market in bonds for about twenty years, a timely switch to shares, and some successful acquisitions, which left it well positioned in equities, real estate, hedge funds, and commodities. In 2006, BlackRock acquired control of Merrill Lynch Asset Management in an exchange of shares that left Merrill Lynch with its slightly less than 50 percent interest in Black-Rock.

In March of 2008, the Federal Reserve hired BlackRock to manage $29 billion in distressed mortgage securities picked up from Bear Stearns, which followed a similar assignment from a State of Florida investment fund with respect to a $14 billion portfolio. In May of 2008, BlackRock acquired a $20 billion portfolio of mortgage-backed securities for $15 billion from UBS. Fink and his partners own 17 percent of BlackRock, which was valued at about $25 billion by the Merrill Lynch purchase. (PNC Financial also owns a 34 percent interest.) Fink has distributed ownership of the firm widely and owns only 1 percent himself, worth $250 million.

There are negatives, however, that come with a strategy of bank investments in alternative asset management. In 1990, Goldman Sachs formed an $800 million Water Street Corporate Recovery Fund, which aimed at investing in distressed or bankrupt companies, using workout and turnaround skills that the firm was developing, and being prepared to enter into the tough negotiations that always surround failing companies. This fund, however, immediately ran into conflicts with Goldman Sachs's institutional clients, who were investors in the debt of the companies being turned around. The investors objected to the way in which they were being treated by Goldman's recovery fund negotiators. After some soul-searching, Goldman Sachs decided to close the fund and withdraw from this business, which it has not reentered since. Fred Eckert, the Goldman Sachs partner in charge of the fund, resigned and set up his own business, which became the GSC Group, which has since raised several funds and been an active player in the distressed and turnaround area.

The same problem of conflicting interests potentially exists for Goldman Sachs's business with the large private equity fund managers, KKR, Blackstone, TPG, and the others, which in recent years have been Wall Street's biggest generators of investment banking fees. It's a delicate dance, but these fund managers have come to recognize that all of the banks they want to do business with have gone into private equity to one degree or another. They know they have to have the services of all of these firms available to them when they make acquisitions, or arrange IPOs spin-offs or financing for their deals, so they can't push too hard. But they can push some, and are not shy about it. Goldman Sachs, on the other hand, has proven to be a useful financing and co-investing partner for these large deal-makers, through either loans of its own capital or from its mezzanine debt fund. There are conflicts also among clients, who may want their investment bank to represent them when they are planning an acquisition, or a sale of their company, if the investment bank is also thinking about making a private equity investment in the company. Such conflicts occur regularly and have to be addressed with the best long-term interests of the firm in mind—which often involves giving precedence to clients when conflicts occur—even though it may necessarily require one part of the firm or another to give up an important piece of business.

Debt Markets and Other Casualties of the Meltdown

The 2007–2008 period of market turmoil brought most private equity activity to a standstill by June 2007, just in time for the Blackstone IPO. Many deals that were expected to close later in the year were either renegotiated or called off. LBO operators were reluctant to agree to changes in financing terms, but at the same time, they endeavored to get some deals canceled so they would not have to go through with them. One such dispute, involving Hexion, a company owned by the Apollo Group, which tried to walk away from an agreement to acquire Huntsman Corporation on the grounds that the combined company would be insolvent, was forced to proceed anyway and, when it couldn't, Apollo and its affiliates settled with Huntsman for $1 billion. Huntsman, greatly angered by what it regarded as bad business practices by both Apollo and its banks, also sued Credit Suisse and Deutsche Bank for failing to come through with the funds promised to support the acquisition. After a year of legal wrangling, the banks settled with Huntsman for $632 billion and an agreement to extent a $1.1 billion loan to it on favorable terms. The banks were worried that a Texas state-court jury—long feared by corporate defendants—might deliver a costly and unpredictable verdict.[22]

The entire industry felt the pain of the market meltdown. Their funds declined by 30 to 50 percent. They received no performance fees, and some were required to return fees earned in earlier periods. "High-water marks" (performance levels that have to be exceeded before fees can be paid) were so high relative to current levels that many feared they would never catch up. Besides, there were very few new deals on which fees might have been earned; nor were there any earlier deals ready to be refloated in the IPO market, which was virtually nonexistent in 2008. Further, many highly leveraged companies previously acquired through LBOs would find the global recession too difficult for them and be forced into bankruptcy. The private equity industry had never experienced such a storm of difficulty and hostile markets before. All private equity firms suffered large losses. Harvard University and other large investors announced plans to cut back allocations to private equity in the future, and several large investors threatened to seek to avoid future capital calls by assembling a majority of fund investors to vote to reduce the principal amount of the funds. New funding was extremely difficult, though Carlyle managed to raise some additional equity.

Without access to debt markets, and the high levels of leverage the

LBOs require, the industry was forced to look to other investment possibilities. Some, such as Goldman Sachs and BlackRock, took over portfolios held by others, especially ailing banks that were forced to undergo top-to-bottom restructuring as part of a merger arrangement or to fortify balance sheets. Others intended to use their capital like hedge funds to arbitrage the low prices of mortgage-backed securities or leveraged loans against their supposedly higher intrinsic value, or to make opportunistic investments in struggling banks. TPG organized a $7 billion investment in Washington Mutual, only to see the whole thing lost as the bank had to be taken over by its regulators a few months later.

Not all was entirely gloomy, however. Most private equity funds were of ten-year duration, with several years more to go before having to wind up. As markets recover, some of the write-downs may be reversed. Many private equity managers were also pointing out that they would be able to take advantage of the market declines by acquiring new investments at knock-down prices, often low enough to enable them to complete the deals with little if any leverage. As the recession entered its second year, a backlog of uncompleted restructurings in Europe, Asia, and America was overhanging the market. These deals were waiting to be done when they could be. And investors withdrawing their capital from private equity were not finding any other markets likely to provide solid equity returns. Many concluded, after efforts to reconsider portfolio rebalancing, that they might just as well stay where they were.

Over a longer term, private equity activity may prove to be less risky and worthy of higher price-to-book and price-earnings ratios than the traditional form of investment banking in which current income from fees and proprietary trading is entirely dependent on market conditions. But that might take some time; meanwhile, the memory of the sharp write-offs of values in their investment portfolios caused by the 2007–2008 market conditions lingers. This period also reminded investment banks that their hedge and private equity activities that had been parked off balance sheet, might not be so off balance sheet at all. Their names are on the funds, and investors expect them to meet whatever liabilities the funds have accumulated, even though such liabilities legally might not be the responsibility of the firms. Having to bail out such funds, as many firms did to one degree or another, could be very expensive and, as in the case of Bear Stearns, could suddenly force the firm to have to raise new capital under disadvantageous conditions. Investment banks in the hedge fund and private equity business also have to be careful of the negative public relations effects of being associated with aggressive actions that disrupt corporations and their supporters, especially in difficult economic times. These have been especially visible in Europe, where hedge fund and private equity funds have been referred to by government officials and the media as a "plague of locusts," and in Japan, where hostile deals, especially by foreigners, are viewed with great suspicion. They must also beware of the backlash effects of extravagant displays of wealth, as occurred, for example, with the press reports of the Schwartzman birthday party. A few days after the party was reported in the New York press, for example, hearings were proposed in Congress to eliminate the capital gains treatment of income from profit participation in hedge and private equity funds.

12

THE MORTGAGE CRISIS

IN MARCH 2006, in their annual letter to shareholders, UBS chairman Marcel Ospel and CEO Peter Wuffli proudly announced the completion of the Swiss bank's most successful year, in which it earned 14 billion Swiss francs ($8.5 billion), 75 percent more than the year before. Approximately three fourths of UBS's net income was attributed to its 140-year-old asset management businesses, which, with over $1 trillion in assets under management, was the world's largest wealth manager. The bank was also one of Europe's three principal universal banks, with total assets of its own of more than $1.2 trillion and a tier-one (Basel-based) risk-adjusted capital-to-assets ratio of more than 12 percent, one of the strongest in the industry. Highlights of the year included the naming of Peter Wuffli, forty-eight, as Europe's top banking CEO by *Institutional Investor* magazine. Wuffli had been CEO since 2003, when he replaced Ospel in the position, having previously served as CFO of the group and CEO of the asset management business.

During the year, UBS announced the integration of its two wealth management businesses (European and United States) under the name Global Wealth Management and Business Banking, and the creation of a new alternative investment management business, Dillon Read Capital Management, under the leadership of John P. Costas, former CEO of the

UBS group's investment bank, and a member of the ten-man group executive board. Costas, a forty-nine-year-old American—physically robust, handsome, and charismatic—was one of the bank's golden boys, having risen quickly since joining UBS in 1996 from Credit Suisse. He began at UBS as head of U.S. Fixed Income and Derivatives, then took over as Global Fixed Income chief in 1998, then chief operating officer of the Investment Banking unit in 1999 (in time to absorb the Paine Webber acquisition made in 2000), finally becoming deputy group chief executive in 2005. He had taken over the UBS investment bank in 2001 and spent $600 million expanding its trading floor (in Stamford, Connecticut) focusing on fixed income and proprietary trading. Costas, who would leave the bank's management team, was putting all this behind him to manage a group of hedge funds. UBS set up the funds in order to capitalize on the recent success of its proprietary trading operation, which had turned in exceptional results in the past few years. Costas convinced Ospel and Wuffli that the new hedge fund could add a valuable franchise to the UBS group, provide investment opportunities for its wealth management clients that might otherwise be provided by competitors, and give the bank the opportunity to leverage profits and diversify risk by bringing in outside capital. He also saw the opportunity to run the hedge fund as one from which to make a fortune for himself, and similarly as a means to retain key trading executives. The bank would transfer about $3.5 billion of its positions to the fund and offer participations in it to its wealth management clients. The new fund would be leveraged with $70 billion of the bank's credit and would charge both UBS and its new clients the unusually high fees of 3 percent annually and 35 percent of profits.[1]

Bringing in the outside investors proved to be more difficult than they had thought due to regulatory complications (and perhaps also to the fees), but the problems were overcome, and the fund, which had raised an additional $1.3 billion from outside investors, was launched in November 2006.

Six months later, in May of 2007, UBS announced that Dillon Read Capital Management would take a loss of $150 million for the first quarter of 2007, and close down. An internal audit revealed very large collateralized debt obligation positions in both the fund and the bank that needed to be marked down considerably. The bank needed to separate the outside investors so as to protect them from having to share in the losses from the legacy positions, and therefore the fund needed to be closed. The outside investors actually left with a return of about 16 percent, but losses from the fund and the bank's own positions would prove to be substantial. Closing the fund would cost approximately $300 million in severance and other payments. Costas would stay on during a transition period and then depart. The golden boy had turned into a goat.

When Costas left the bank to head up the fund, he was replaced as CEO of the Investment Banking Division by Huw Jenkins, an Englishman with no background in fixed income. Jenkins commissioned consultants to evaluate the division's competitive position and learned that the fixed-income business had fallen somewhat behind its principal rivals and had to be strengthened. The biggest gaps were in the credit, securitized products, and commodities businesses. The consultants recommended that emphasis be given to securitized products such as mortgage-backed securities. This advice was followed, and the investment banking division quickly set up a CDO origination and underwriting factory, which it pursued aggressively because of high structuring fees and the ability to sell the securities to an on-balance-sheet UBS "warehouse." The CDO desk would enter into an agreement with a collateral manager, for whom UBS would acquire residential mortgage-backed securities. These positions would be held for one to four months, until they could be securitized into a CDO and sold. According to a report on its write-downs by UBS's board in April of 2008:

> Generally while in the warehouse, these positions would be on UBS' books with exposure to market risk. Upon completion of the warehouse, the securities were transferred to a special-purpose vehicle, and structured into tranches. The CDO desk received structuring fees on the notional value of the deal, and focused on Mezzanine CDOs, which generated fees of approximately 125 to 150 basis points (high grade CDOs generated fees of 30-50 basis points). Key to the growth of the CDO structuring business was the development of the Credit Default Swap on asset-backed securities in June 2005.[2]

By far the majority of the securities in the warehouse were CDOs rated AAA.

By April 2007, UBS's risk managers no doubt had looked into the abyss and seen that altogether the bank owned many billions of dollars of mortgage-backed securities, enough if current market conditions continued, to force write-downs that would cause serious problems. Within a year, Switzerland's largest, most profitable, and proudest bank would be in shambles after having written off $49 billion in mortgage-backed securities and been forced to accept a $60 billion bailout from the Swiss government and to undergo extensive and humiliating management changes.

HOUSES, MORTGAGES, AND STRUCTURED FINANCE

Sometime before 2001, when the federal funds rate was 1 percent, a housing boom developed in the United States in which the value of home sales began to grow annually at between 10 and 20 percent. Mortgage loans were easy to get, and interest rates had been lowered by the Fed to counter the post-Enron recession. Indeed, mortgage rates were 27 percent lower than they had been in 2000, and by 2003 they were lower than at any time since 1972. As the stock market was in a slump until late in 2003, some investors must have thought, why not buy a house, or a condo, or an apartment building instead, finance it cheaply, and resell it in a few years? Real estate prices, at least, were still rising. Many did just that.

Mortgages could be created by brokers, sold to savings banks, sold again to larger banks seeking to package them into collateralized mortgage-backed securities, and sold a final time to market investors all over the world. The securities would join a vast pool of asset-backed securities already outstanding in the markets. This pool was valued at about $12 trillion in 2007 (having more than doubled since 2000), into which 39 percent of all bank mortgage loans had been sold. About $5.5 trillion of the securitized loans outstanding were backed by mortgages, and $6.4 trillion were backed by assets other than mortgages, such as credit card receivables, car loans, and student and home equity loans.[3] The securities were sold to pension and mutual funds, insurance companies, and a growing population of hedge funds. All of this securitization activity was thought to disperse risk from the banking system, lower costs to borrowers, and make markets safer and stronger. What more could you want?

This was the same business devised by Lewis Ranieri of Salomon Brothers in the 1970s, but it had developed a number of additional features since then. The market had essentially divided into collateralized debt obligations (CDOs) which repackaged real estate mortgages, and collateralized loan obligations (CLOs), which did the same for corporate loans, including leveraged loans used to finance LBOs. CDOs accommodated, in various proportions, prime loans (rated AAA when backed by federal loan guarantors or bond insurers), subprime (for loans of weaker credit quality), and something called Alt-A loans, which had credit ratings somewhere between prime and subprime. The value of subprime mortgages in the United States jumped from $190 billion in 2001 to $600 billion in 2006, and about 80 percent of these were securitized, up from 50 percent in 2001.[4]

CDOs included, in addition to fixed-rate mortgages, some that were adjustable-rate, with some of these subject to different inducements to attract the borrowers. The majority of these adjustable-rate mortgages were designed to be refinanced or to default within two to three years. By 2006, some special-purpose CDOs—"CDOs squared," which were collateralized not by mortgages but by other CDOs, and "constant-proportion debt obligations" (CPDOs, or forms of leveraged debt-investment derivatives)—were introduced to the market to add risk and other characteristics that might appeal to hedge funds and other institutional investors that asked for customized, risk-enhancing features to be designed for them. Working with all these different types of assets, credit qualities, and interest payment features, and taking into account the expectation that many of the loans would be prepaid before maturity, required special computer modeling capabilities, and significant commitments to sales and market making. In all, this particular brand of high-tech financial engineering was called "structured finance."

Investors could make money by capturing the spread between the yield on the highly rated CDOs and their funding costs, or by watching the price of the securities rise as interest rates dropped and/or other investors poured in, bidding up prices, and by leveraging the investments. Bankers could make money by collecting fees from packaging, underwriting, and distributing CDOs and by trading them for their own accounts or in hedge funds they managed.

The commitment to be made by bankers in this highly specialized business had to be considerable, and was beyond the means or interest of most banks. But for those relatively few large banks who made the commitment, the rewards could be very attractive, responsible for as much as 20–30 percent of the firms' total profits. Merrill Lynch, for example, earned $700 million in 2006 from CDO fees and other activities. Some firms, such as Merrill Lynch, Morgan Stanley, and Lehman Brothers, acquired or built their own mortgage brokers in order to be able to package mortgages more rapidly and profitably, and some, such as UBS and Bear Stearns, created hedge funds devoted to trading and holding CDOs that could be financed with margin loans or low-cost commercial paper. A Bear Stearns trader described how these hedge funds made money:

The managers were betting that the returns [on CDOs] were going to be stable. They were willing to buy up CDOs earning more interest than what they were able to borrow against . . . For example, a fund manager might buy up senior tranche CDOs—meaning those with the lowest risk factor and AAA credit rating—that earn LIBOR+ 100 basis points. In turn they borrow against the investor's cash and pay roughly LIBOR flat. The manager picks up 100 basis points per year, and if you lever that up 10 to 12 times, you end up with a return of 10 to 12 percent without subjecting yourself to a lot of financial risk. This is among the holiest of grails involved in running a fund. You find a double digit return with low volatility, and you've cracked the code.[5]

Finally, there were "structured investment vehicles" (SIVs), created by some banks to warehouse considerable holdings of CDOs off balance sheet, using techniques not very dissimilar from Enron in doing so.* The SIVs would allow banks to lock in large spreads between the rates paid on the CDOs and the commercial paper rates, which then were leveraged many times to produce a very attractive rate of return. Citigroup had seven offshore SIVs, supported by virtually none of its capital or reserve requirements, with investments totaling over $100 billion at their peak, earning sizeable profits for it as late as September 2007.

As the CDO market expansion accelerated after 2001, a competitive scramble for more supply and new ideas began. The mortgage pools began to get murky, and were made worse by a willingness of some mortgage lenders to lower appreciably the credit standards of borrowers, and of packagers to buy the shoddy mortgages and pass them on. The securities also became more complex and difficult to rate or classify, as they no longer fit the models developed by the rating agencies to evaluate them.

Still, this was all very good business for a few years, and several firms plunged into it in order either to catch up with competitors or to capture the lucrative profits to boost their results. No one wanted to stop because they were all making so much money. By this time a bubble had formed, which no one then was able to distinguish from what seemed to be a trend. Economist Robert Shiller described the chain of events that turned the bubble to a crisis:

---

* Enron was criticized for deceiving investors by transferring billions of dollars of liabilities into hundreds of off-balance-sheet subsidiaries, using accounting loopholes to do so.

Overly aggressive mortgage lenders, compliant appraisers, and complacent borrowers proliferated to feed the housing boom. Mortgage originators, who planned to sell off the mortgages to securitizers, stopped worrying about repayment risk. They typically made only perfunctory efforts to assess borrowers' ability to repay their loans—often failing to verify income with the IRS, even if they possessed signed authorization forms permitting them to do so. Sometimes these lenders enticed the naïve, with poor credit histories, to borrow in the ballooning sub-prime mortgage market. These mortgages were packaged, sold and resold in sophisticated but arcane ways to investors around the world, setting the stage for a crisis of truly global proportions. The housing bubble, combined with the incentive system implicit in the securitization process, amplified moral hazard, further emboldening some of the worst actors among mortgage lenders.[6]

Home prices began to fall in mid-2006. By late in the year there were clear signs that the market in CDOs was getting overheated and prices were getting out of line with their underlying values as expected default rates rose. In November, the ABS credit default swap index for BBB- securities* began to fall off, dropping from 100 to 94.

At this point, Goldman Sachs CEO Lloyd Blankfein, co-presidents Jon Winkelreid and Gary Cohn, and the firm's trading chiefs were gathered together by Goldman's CFO, David Viniar, and urged to reconsider the firm's exposure to the CDO business. The firm then decided to bring its overall exposure to nil, and later extended its cautious view to a negative one, and accordingly took on a very large short position in CDOs.

In mid-February 2007, the BBB-ABS credit default index dropped suddenly, to about 60. Also that month, an editorial by Jan Krahnen, professor at Goethe University in Frankfurt and director of the academic think tank Center for Financial Studies, noted that:

> The low quality of these loans was known for a long time. When interest rates in the United States began to rise, it was evident to analysts and investors that there will be losses. Since these losses did not come as a surprise, the sub-prime lending market is actually not the true driver of the credit crisis. Rather, the villain is the market for risk transfer, a market which analysts believed to merely distribute risk, thereby increasing the resiliency of the economy against shocks.
>   One practice not anticipated by analysts was the transfer of credit risk to special entities, called conduits [SIVs] rather than placing them

---

* A traded index for asset-backed securities rated BBB-.

outside the financial system. These entities were equipped with letters of comfort, or similar quasi-guarantees by the sponsoring banks.
These guarantees were substituting for equity which would otherwise
have been required to issue AAA rated Commercial Paper. The conduits contributed to the opaqueness of overall bank exposure, which
has triggered a near-shutdown of the Commercial Paper market, as
well as the Interbank market.[7]

Many banks and other investment groups with SIVs were devoted to
CDOs. Altogether these accounted for approximately $400 billion in out-
standing securities, but their principal funding source, the short-term
European commercial paper market, pulled back once it realized the extent to which the SIVs had been borrowing on the basis of no more than
a parent company "letter of comfort," or informal, nonbinding acknow-
ledgment that debt existed but would be entitled to no more than the
parent's best efforts to see that it was repaid. With commercial paper investors unwilling to roll over investments at maturity, the banks had to
find other sources of financing for their SIVs, the principal one being the
interbank market, which also began to show resistance to the sudden demand for borrowing on only a best-efforts basis. If the banks guaranteed
the SIV loans, they would have to take the SIVs back on to their balance
sheets, which they didn't want to do (but ultimately were forced to).

Once the interbank market began to reflect the pressure, everyone's
attention flew to their exposures. According to *The Economist*: "Keeping
track of the scale of exposures is even more difficult during a time of de-
leveraging, when the chains linking the different institutions suddenly
tighten: a margin call by one bank forces the closure of a hedge fund that
weakens a prime broker who has written a credit default swap on mortgaged backed securities" held in SIVs of large banks with whom you have
multiple exposures.[8] After the LTCM panic in 1998, market investors
began to look askance at hedge funds, needing to be reassured that they
knew what was in them. Now they were again beginning to doubt the
banks and one another. When this happens, as unlikely as any individual
default may be, no one wants to buy anything, and the market freezes
over, eliminating its liquidity.

The BBB-ABS credit default index recovered to 75 in May 2007 before plunging again to less than 40 in July. In June 2007, the higher-grade
AA ABS credit default swap index, which had been steady at around 100
since the beginning of the year, suddenly dropped to 85.

BANKS BEGIN TO STUMBLE

As prices fell, two high-grade structured credit funds (highly indebted, subprime-heavy hedge funds) managed by Bear Stearns began to post significant losses. Though the funds invested in the better-credit-quality part of securitized subprime mortgages, and had purchased credit default protection on them, the sudden loss of confidence in subprime paper caused the funds' lenders to require more collateral to offset the losses that the freefall had caused. The banks that had lent the funds the money against the mortgage-backed securities as collateral were marking the collateral down, steeply, and these marks (liquidation values, really) became virtually the only evidence of actual transaction values. The funds, of course, had to put up more capital or face having their investments sold out from under them at great losses. Bear Stearns advanced a $1.6 billion loan to the funds in an effort to save them from what was rapidly becoming an increasingly dangerous downward spiral. Despite the loan, additional bonds had to be sold to meet margin calls, causing further price pressure on the market. In a matter of a few weeks, the two hedge funds lost approximately $1.4 billion in capital and filed for bankruptcy in July. Bear Stearns's stock price fell by 40 percent.[9]

This news was accompanied by reports of a sharp increase in U.S. mortgage foreclosure rates, which concerned investors in CDOs, who couldn't tell how much of what they owned in the various packages of mortgages was subprime and might, therefore, be subject to foreclosure. By now the fat was in the fire, prices were plunging, and the fixed-income market was treating subprime anything as toxic waste, and dumping even high-grade mortgage-backed securities. The SIVs, unable to continue their commercial paper issuances, were stuck. They could neither buy nor sell (except at very steep discounts), nor fund their portfolios. For everyone else, these mortgage behemoths represented an overhang of sell orders that might soon be forced on the market.

In the summer of 2007, well after the closure of the Dillon Read fund, UBS began to warn of write-offs as its huge portfolio of mortgage-backed securities was priced to reflect actual market values (as panic-stricken as these may have been) as is required practice in the securities industry, known as "marking-to-market." UBS had accumulated its large mortgage exposure throughout the bank, thinking it was safe, despite its size, because of the AAA ratings the CDOs carried and the high level of liquidity the market for such securities had historically provided. But as the market for CDOs disappeared—because investors didn't know how much contaminated subprime paper was in each CDO, it also came to fear that the mono-line insurance companies* guarantying the ratings might fail. Thus investors no longer trusted the ratings assigned to the CDOs— indeed, all historical and statistical data were disregarded—and the market went into freefall. CDOs, regardless of their ratings, were marked down to fire-sale levels. So was just about every other kind of supposedly risky paper: other forms of asset-backed securities, junk bonds, and leveraged loans. As prices fell, all this paper had to be marked to market, causing more write-offs and more havoc.

The numerous hedge funds that had ventured into the mortgage sector were facing a continuous run of margin calls. Many of these funds had little or no more capital to put up. CDO prices fell further after taking account of all these technical factors. In August, BNP Paribas, a French bank, suspended withdrawals from three of its mutual funds that had invested in subprime mortgage securities because, it said, it couldn't assign a value to the assets in the funds because the market for them had disappeared.

These developments left banks, rating agencies, and investors in an awkward position with respect to the correct marking to market of securities held. Most had relied for risk management purposes on different sorts of sophisticated models to value CDOs, models that took into account changing interest rates, expected default rates, and repayment possibilities, and were considered accurate and reliable. But these models did not (nor could not) take into account a presumably temporary collapse in liquidity. When a market is panicked into a condition in which there are only sellers, prices drop to scrap level, where there is very little trading.

Fair Value Accounting

Auditors, having been severely held to task in the 2000–2002 corporate scandals and subjected to reregulation through Sarbanes-Oxley, were under great pressure to value the CDOs held by banks and hedge funds correctly. They had recently been made subject to Financial Accounting Standard 157 ("Fair Value Accounting," adopted for financial statements after November 2007), which requires a specific fair value framework

---

* Stand-alone bond insurance companies such as MBIA.

and places great emphasis on using actual market transactions, when they exist, as opposed to models. It was true, beginning in the summer of 2007, that some observers believed that market-driven fair value, and the early adoption of the rule by most financial firms, greatly exaggerated write-downs tied to the crisis. This, they believed, led to unnecessary chaos in the markets and forced banks to raise capital they actually didn't need. One such observer, William Isaac, a former chairman of the Federal Deposit Insurance Corp., criticized what he called the SEC's stubborn refusal so far "to abandon its very destructive approach of forcing banks to take excessive and unjustified write-downs on their assets." The destructive approach he had in mind was requiring banks to apply FAS 157. When they did, however, the banks did not have to mark everything to market as the investment banks did. The banks could designate certain assets as ones that would be held to maturity, and thus could still be valued at cost less a reserve for expected losses. The only assets that would have to be marked to market were those held in trading accounts that the bank did not expect to retain.

These assets would be marked to market if a market existed—but if there was no market, they could be valued using a discounted cash flow model—and by the end of the crisis period, the banks had been able to value some of their tradable assets this way (which produced a result similar to valuing at cost less reserve for losses, a much more favorable valuation method than accepting the so-called "fire-sale" valuations in the market). In essence, they were able to declare the market for their asset-backed paper to be so severely impaired as to negate the idea of a market altogether. The SEC and the bank regulators allowed the banks generous leeway on this issue, and in April 2009, the Financial Accounting Standards Board (the author of FAS 157), under great pressure from Congress to do so, modified the terms of the rule to allow the more favorable interpretation of it. So the banks (not the Wall Street firms) never did mark everything to market, and they were allowed an increasing amount of wiggle room to minimize the amount of assets that were marked down to market levels. Their write-downs, in other words, could have been a lot worse.

Nevertheless, because the banks still held a large amount of these assets in trading positions, by the end of September 2007, they did indeed begin reporting large amounts of losses from mortgage-backed securities. Several reported that they had tried to hedge their exposure by selling some of the weaker mortgage credits short and buying stronger ones, but those hedges didn't work very well—they had a hard time selling the weak ones, and the good ones they bought went way down in price, too.

The Government Intervenes

The financial crisis had spread through all the markets, causing a rush to safety—assets such as U.S. Treasury bills and gold bars soared in price. The Federal Reserve was doing all it could to manage its way through the mess by cutting interest rates and pumping huge amounts of liquidity into the markets. Some of this liquidity was used to shore up the banks and investment banks that had come under pressure, but otherwise the enhanced liquidity was not finding its way into the well-spooked mortgage securities market, or the market for home loans. Absent new mortgages, home prices continued to fall across the country, and forecasts of recession could be heard from many of the economic talking heads who were frequent guests on the nearly incessant TV programs of the financial media.

In October 2007, Secretary of the Treasury Hank Paulson announced a plan to create a new entity to acquire a large quantity of the mortgage securities that were overhanging the market, in order to return liquidity conditions to normal. The effort, he insisted, was not a case of a government "bailout" of the CDO industry, but a free market initiative to be inaugurated by the private sector with the full support of the Treasury, which had been working earnestly for months to broker such a deal. The new entity would be known as a Master Liquidity Enhancement Vehicle, or MLEC, and it would be organized and advised by the three largest U.S. wholesale banks, Citigroup, JPMorgan Chase, and Bank of America, all of which had considerable exposure to the CDO market. Having set the thing in motion, the government, it said, would have no further role.

The MLEC soon became known as a "super-conduit," an SIV for the SIVs. It would somehow organize funding from the market for the new super-conduit to purchase assets from the old conduits. The banks would endeavor to syndicate a sufficient credit line of several hundred billion dollars to fund the MLEC, though many of the banks invited into the syndicate might be reluctant to contribute to rescuing their competitors, and to do so by taking on a load of mortgage-backed securities in the middle of a liquidity crisis. The key question would be at what price would the purchases of CDOs occur? Would they be valued at margin-call liquidation prices or at much higher cash-flow-modeled intrinsic value prices?

If at liquidation, why would the bank-owned SIVs want to sell? If at modeled prices, why would the funding banks want to buy? It was a dilemma that was never resolved. By December 2007, after six months of a liquidity shutdown that had spread widely within financial markets, and had already resulted in hundreds of billions of write-offs, the MLEC project was dropped.

Write-offs Peak

By the end of December 2007, the write-offs had mounted to extraordinary levels, and would continue to rise for several more quarters. Though there would be some further write-offs in the second quarter, by the end of April 2008, Bloomberg News reported that approximately $250 billion in loan losses for both CDOs and CLOs had been taken by banks in the United States and around the world, with the former, the mortgage-related loans, being about three fourths of the total. Leading the list of reported loan losses in 2007 were: Citigroup, $41 billion; UBS, $38 billion; Merrill Lynch, $32 billion; Bank of America, $15 billion; and Morgan Stanley, $12.6 billion. JPMorgan Chase, which disposed of an SIV before the crisis began, reported losses of only $9.7 billion. Deutsche Bank and Credit Suisse were in at $7.4 billion and $6.3 billion, respectively. About thirty other foreign banks had more than $75 billion in write-offs. Outside the banking system there was another $100 billion or so of losses being absorbed mainly by insurance companies, hedge funds, and other institutional investors. By midyear 2008, the estimated industry write-offs would rise to $500 billion, and rise still further through the third quarter.

The Bank of England in its May 2008 Financial Stability Report, suggested that the write-offs taken by the banks, under pressure from their auditors, may have been excessive. Using mainstream, fairly pessimistic assumptions on defaults and loss rates, the bank determined from its model that about $900 billion (at par value) of mortgage-backed securities then had a fundamental worth of 81 percent of par, yet market prices, as determined by credit default swap indices, were then valuing the securities at 58 percent of par. Thus, the bank said, the write-offs may have overshot the paper's true value by more than $200 billion, leaving room for some stouthearted investors to profit from the market's inevitable repricing of the risk.[10]

There were, however, other estimates of the total value of losses produced by the credit crisis that were larger than the Bloomberg and Bank of England numbers, including an especially gloomy one from the International Monetary Fund that estimated the total global damages at around $1 trillion. This was an effort to include even the kitchen sink in order to capture all of the economic effects of the mortgage crisis. The IMF's estimate put the 2007 crisis as being larger, in terms of dollar value of losses incurred, than either the Japanese banking crisis of the 1990s or the U.S. S&L crisis of 1986–1995. The IMF also measured the impact of the crisis at about 7 percent of U.S. GDP, which was only about half the economic impact of the Japanese crisis, but somewhat more than the impact of the S&L crisis. The impact of the 2007 crisis was delivered over a period of only a year, as compared to a much longer time for both the Japanese and S&L crises. However, the collapse of the new economy bubble (2000–2002), with total market value losses between its high and low points of more than $8 trillion, was, at this point, considerably greater in terms both of losses and of economic impact. But the 2007 crisis predominantly affected large financial institutions in the United States and Europe, and these were the first to feel the shock and the damage. As the crisis spread to the global real economy, its impact worsened and invoked large and unprecedented intervention efforts by government that had not occurred in earlier crises.

HEADS ROLL

The consequences of the mortgage crisis would have a lasting effect on the banking industry as all the banks pulled in their horns and cut back on their lending businesses. Several were forced to change the leadership of their firms and reconsider their basic business strategies. Most also raised new capital to replace that consumed by the mortgage business, significantly diluting their previous shareholders' interests, and there were acquisitions made under conditions of distress.

UBS

In July 2007, Peter Wuffli, UBS's CEO, was forced to resign, and was replaced by another Swiss executive, Marcel Rohner, the bank's chief risk officer. In October, UBS announced that it would likely report an overall pretax loss for the quarter; that Huw Jenkins would step down and be replaced by Rohner as head of Investment Banking; and that Clive Standish, group CFO, would retire.

In December UBS announced additional write-offs of $10 billion, with the expectation that it would report a loss for the year, and that it quietly had raised $11 billion in new capital from sovereign wealth funds in Singapore and the Middle East. In January 2008 more losses were announced, with the total attributed to the U.S. residential mortgage market being $18.7 billion.[11] In February, Jerker Johansson, former head of institutional equities at Morgan Stanley, was appointed CEO of the Investment Banking Division, the fourth person to hold the job in three years. Losses from other credit sectors, including leveraged loans, brought the total write-offs to an astonishing $38 billion. At the UBS annual meeting, the bank's hitherto "Teflon" chairman, Marcel Ospel, announced that he would not stand for reelection, and would be replaced by an outside director, Swiss lawyer Peter Kurer. Ospel, fifty-eight, had been the key figure at UBS since 1997, the year before the merger of Union Bank of Switzerland and Swiss Bank Corporation that created UBS. He and the rest of UBS's shareholders were forced to watch the UBS stock price drop 66 percent from its all-time high in June 2007, from which lofty heights it had looked down condescendingly on its two chief European rivals, Credit Suisse and Deutsche Bank. These events were considered essentially unbelievable by UBS's core Swiss shareholders: that the proud and mighty UBS could be brought to its knees by a bunch of U.S. residential mortgages was inconceivable. To us "this was like a nuclear bomb," said Konrad Hummler, a managing partner of Wegelin and Co., a Swiss private bank and substantial UBS shareholder. In May 2008, UBS was forced to raise another $15 billion in equity through a rights offering to shareholders at a steep discount from an otherwise very low share price.

Merrill Lynch

In late October 2007, Merrill Lynch fired Stanley O'Neal, fifty-six, its chairman and CEO, after announcing a large incremental write-off of mortgage-backed securities. O'Neal, the first African American ever to head a major Wall Street firm, is a totally self-made man. The son of a small-town Alabama farmer and the grandson of a slave, O'Neal took a job on a General Motors assembly line in Atlanta when his family moved there so his father could work in an auto plant. GM spotted him as a bright, hardworking kid and invited him to attend its General Motors Institute, an in-house university for stand-out employees. He excelled there and, after graduating, was accepted at Harvard Business School. From there he returned to General Motors as a junior executive, before moving on to Merrill Lynch in 1986, at the invitation of a former GM colleague who had been transplanted there. At Merrill, he rose rapidly through the managerial ranks and became a favorite of some of its top officers. He was appointed CFO in 1998 and CEO in 2002, replacing the popular David Komansky, who, though a previous O'Neal supporter, soon turned on him for his "attempted destruction of the value system and culture that existed at Merrill Lynch." This was a maternalistic culture known within the firm as "Mother Merrill." Messing with Mother Merrill, Komansky said, may have been more important in explaining O'Neal's forced exit than the mortgage losses, but the mortgage losses certainly put him on the spot.

Merrill's stock price had performed well enough within the industry during the time when O'Neal was CEO. It had been behind Goldman Sachs, one of its two rivals, but ahead of the other, Morgan Stanley. Under O'Neal, Merrill's profits and margins had improved significantly, though he had achieved this through supposedly un-Merrill-like layoffs, expense cuts, and the replacement, according to one observer, of "more than half of the firm's top managers, often with younger executives from Asia or Europe, rather than from Queens and Long Island."[12]

O'Neal faced other criticisms among his colleagues at Merrill, Wall Street's most authentic Irish American institution, in which all the previous top guys looked like beat cops in tough neighborhoods. O'Neal, once in power, proved to be a loner—cold, aloof, and occasionally unpleasant to his subordinates. He was no schmoozer in a firm full of them. Instead, he was seen to be a numbers man without a soul and an insecure leader who got rid of anyone who he thought was, or might be, a threat to him or his position. The mortgage crisis certainly hit Merrill hard, but it affected others in the industry, too. Merrill's losses were certainly high, but they were still less than the losses at Citigroup and UBS. Certainly the losses reflected a much increased exposure to trading risk during O'Neal's tenure, but the board had been well advised of it as it developed, and should not have been surprised by the exposures.

Indeed, the board knew that shortly after he became CEO, O'Neal authorized an expansion of the mortgage securities department. He recruited a thirty-four-year-old expert in CDOs from Credit Suisse, and within two years the firm jumped from fifteenth place in the mortgage securities league tables to first. In 2006, Merrill paid $1.3 billion for First Franklin, a California mortgage loan broker that had issued $29 billion in home loans the year before, and by the end of the year would boost this figure to $44 billion.

These volumes of loan originations included an increasing proportion of "non-traditional loans," that is, those involving virtually no credit standards at all. But the volume of loans coming through the chutes into the sausage factory that turned them into securities helped Merrill dominate the highly profitable CDO origination process. The trouble was, Merrill was creating more mortgage paper than it could sell, and the paper was building up on its balance sheet, a balance sheet that was already leveraged more than twenty to one. This is a perilous position to be in, even if the firm had not been in the midst of a bubble, which certainly it was by the end of 2006, though apparently no one at Merrill seemed to notice. In February 2007, HSBC, a large British bank, announced that it was taking a $10 billion reserve to cover mortgage loans. In April 2007, New Century, a large mortgage originator, declared a large loss for the previous quarter and filed for bankruptcy. But despite these and other warnings, Merrill kept the mortgage securitization factory going at full speed. By June of 2007 it had taken $32 billion in unsold CDOs on its books, and they were still being accumulated. But by then it was all over. The market was collapsing, and there was no way out of the mess Merrill was in. The write-off for the third quarter of 2007 was $8.4 billion ($7.9 billion from mortgage-backed securities), leaving the firm with a loss for the quarter of $2.3 billion.

Certainly in retrospect it is obvious that no one was watching Merrill's trillion-dollar balance sheet and worrying about the increasing mortgage exposures that were occurring while the market was softening. Maybe the watchers were distracted by O'Neal's aggressive 2006 share repurchase program, which involved further increasing leverage by borrowing $9 billion to buy back stock in the market in order to improve Merrill's return-on-investment ratio.

In any event, after the disastrous 2007 third-quarter results were posted, O'Neal knew that Merrill Lynch would have to raise additional capital, and quickly. So in October he approached Ken Thompson, CEO of Wachovia Bank, about a possible merger with Merrill Lynch, but did so without informing anyone on his board of directors. The board heard about it a few days later, and many members were upset, not only at the terrible results for the quarter, which had put the firm in the position it was in, but that O'Neal had not kept them informed or received their authorization to speak with another company about a merger. It was too much, and several board members turned on O'Neal and wanted him fired. At that point, even Mother Merrill could not have saved O'Neal from being axed, and his forced retirement was announced at the end of October. This didn't end the problems, of course. For the fourth quarter of 2007, Merrill would write off an additional $11.5 billion, including write-offs of leveraged loans used to finance leveraged buyouts, and even then the firm would reveal that it still owned $30 billion in CDOs.

A search committee of the board was formed to find a successor to O'Neal, and it quickly located and retained fifty-two-year-old John Thain, CEO of the New York Stock Exchange and a former president of Goldman Sachs, who was named Merrill Lynch CEO on December 1, 2007, the first ever appointed from outside the firm. Thain, a risk-managing technician who had been CFO of Goldman Sachs for several years, moved quickly to stop the bleeding. More write-offs would follow, but by April 2008, Thain had raised $16 billion in new equity capital, including a combined $6.6 billion from Temasek Holdings of Singapore, the Kuwait Investment Authority, the Korea Investment Corporation, and Mizuho Bank. Even so, Thain was unable to prevent additional write-offs of the remaining CDOs on Merrill's books, and the firm's stock price continued to fall. In late July 2008, Thain decided that he had to purge Merrill Lynch of these toxic holdings and did so by selling $30 billion in CDOs to Lone Star Funds, for twenty-two cents on the dollar, a price that involved a further write-off of another $6 billion (bringing Merrill's total write-offs to $47 billion). Thain also announced that Merrill would raise another $8.5 billion in new capital.[13] After the Merrill sale, other banks felt pressure to clear out their CDO holdings, even at distress prices (which the stock market had already discounted), and several large hedge funds had raised funds to buy up these positions.

Stan O'Neal was not the only Wall Street banker to lose his head after announcing third-quarter results in 2007. In late November, Morgan Stanley announced a major management change in which the firm's two co-presidents, Zoe Cruz and Robert Scully, would step down after the firm announced major CDO losses that would total about $9 billion by the end of the quarter. Cruz, a twenty-five-year Morgan Stanley fixed-income veteran, was Wall Street's highest-ranking and highest-paid woman executive, a friend and protégée of the popular John Mack, who had returned to the firm as CEO after the resignation of Phil Purcell in 2005 under pressure from a group of former Morgan Stanley partners. The losses revealed a number of weaknesses in the risk management function that Cruz supervised, and Mack apparently lost confidence in her. She retired, but Scully agreed to be repotted into a new "Office of the Chairman," where he would help look after clients. Two new co-presidents would be appointed, Walid Chammah, a Lebanese who headed Morgan Stanley International and who had a background in structured finance, and James Gorman, an Australian who headed the Global Wealth Management Group. Mack, a hands-on fixed income veteran, was lucky to have kept his job after losses of that magnitude from a strategy that he had to have backed fully. The board had only just hired him, however, and didn't think it could do any better replacing him, so it accepted the jobs of the two co-presidents instead.

Citigroup

A week following the resignation of Stan O'Neal, Charles O. ("Chuck") Prince III, chairman and CEO of Citigroup, also resigned unexpectedly. Prince had replaced Sandy Weill in 2003 after Weill's surprise resignation. Prince's announcement followed third-quarter write-offs that would later climb to $24 billion. Many of these losses were on previously off-balance-sheet assets held by various Citigroup SIVs and asset-backed commercial paper conduits. Citigroup had been tagged as the bank with the biggest exposure to mortgage-backed securities and the most aggressive in using "variable-interest entities" to park its exposure to them off balance sheet. These were controlled affiliates of Citigroup that met certain accounting conventions that permitted them not to be consolidated on the balance sheet of the parent. Altogether, such off-balance-sheet assets on September 30, 2007, consisting of SIVs and a lot of other structured finance vehicles, would amount to $343 billion, an amount that had increased by $38 billion since the beginning of 2007.[14] As large as it was, it was still only 15 percent of Citigroup's total assets at the time, but it was certainly a large amount relative to the size of the trading market in mortgage-backed securities, Virtually all of these off-balance-sheet assets were financed in the markets without the use of any Citigroup capital under the auspices of a "letter of comfort."[15]

For many Citigroup investors, this episode of losses was the last straw. The four years since Prince had taken over from Sandy Weill had been nothing but trouble: reams of expensive litigation related to Citigroup's aggressive mandate-grabbing corporate lending practices; a scandal in Japan resulting in the loss of its private banking license; another embarrassing headline in Europe, where Citigroup bond traders tried to corner the market in government bonds with a sudden $13 billion destabilizing short-selling raid; censure from the Federal Reserve, which threatened to oppose any future Citigroup acquisitions unless it got its ethical act together; a year spent trying to do this by reeducating its 350,000-strong global workforce; continuous management reshuffles at the top; and now a deluge of further losses in mortgage-backed securities. The stock price had never risen more than 1 percent during the four years that Prince had been in charge, and now, having announced the mortgage losses, it was down about 30 percent on the year, dropping well below all of its principal universal banking and investment banking competitors. Prince had earlier said in a press conference that the time for excuses had passed, and that he would have to be accountable for returning Citigroup to the growth and profitability levels that it had enjoyed during the first years after the merger.

A corporate lawyer with virtually no line operating experience, Chuck Prince was an awkward and improbable choice to become CEO of the world's largest and most complex banking organization. He had joined Consumer Credit Corporation in Baltimore as a corporate lawyer, and met Sandy Weill and the Travelers team when they took over his company in 1986. He proved to be an effective, loyal, and dutiful staff guy and hit it off with Weill, who moved him up to executive vice-president of Travelers ten years later and then, appreciative of his troubleshooting work on the Citicorp merger and the various episodes of litigation and regulatory trouble after 2000, to chief administrative officer in 1998, to chief operating officer in 2001, and to chief executive of the Investment Banking Division in 2002. A year later he was selected to become chief executive on Weill's departure, which was announced in July of 2003, with the turnover to occur on October 1. Weill would stay on as chairman until 2006, just to keep his hand in. He did, but in light of all the other problems that cropped up, and the setbacks that Citigroup faced, he kept a low profile as chairman.

As it was, Weill picked his closest confidant of the time and asked the board to approve his choice, even though Prince, lacking operational experience, must have been seen as being only barely qualified for the job. Of course he was a loyal Weill friend and supporter, but Weill had had many of these throughout his career with whom relations had turned sour soon after a transfer of significant responsibilities occurred. The board well remembered the case of Weill's previous protégé, Jamie Dimon, whom Weill had made president of the bank, but fell out with afterward, causing Dimon to leave Citigroup in 1998. In 2000, Dimon became CEO of Bank One; in 2000 Bank One was acquired by JPMorgan Chase, and Dimon became president of JPMorgan, and soon succeeded Bill Harrison as CEO. In any event, there was no search committee appointed by the Citigroup board, no looking around outside the bank for a suitable candidate (possibly including Dimon). The board simply rubber-stamped Sandy Weill's choice.

Prince did the best he could to build up revenues and improve the stock price so as to catch up with his competitors. It was a difficult struggle to do so, not only because of the distractions that were occurring and the fires that needed to be put out, but also because the top managers of the group, on whom he depended for operational execution, were constantly being reshuffled. Robert Willumstad, Citi's chief of consumer services until 2002, when he was appointed president and chief operating officer, left the bank in 2005 after being passed over for the top job, to become chairman of the board of AIG, the insurance group. Sallie Krawcheck, a thirty-seven-year-old CEO of a research boutique, Sanford Bernstein, had been recruited by Weill to become head of the Smith Barney unit, but then suddenly was made chief financial offer, a position she had never held before and one that in a few years she would turn over to Gary Crittenden, an experienced CFO with industrial companies but not any in financial organizations. When Prince was elevated to CEO, he appointed Robert Druskin, a longtime operations expert and cost-cutter for Weill, to replace him as head of the investment bank; Druskin had never been an actual investment banker dealing with clients, deals, or trading. A few years later, Druskin would be appointed chief operating officer, and also head Global Wealth Management, the third such chief in five years. Prince had to rely on key executives who were often inexperienced in their jobs to carry out the bank's many different strategic plans and manage its risks. This created a serious disconnect between top managers and what was really going on several layers below them.

Prince himself appeared to be happy with the bank's aggressive lending stance in July of 2007, when he said that his bank hadn't pulled back from making leveraged loans for private equity deals, despite a skittish credit market and concerns that the recent run of big buyout deals could be losing steam. As he told the *Financial Times*, "As long as the music is playing, you've got to get up and dance. We're still dancing."

Wall Street CEOs might be sympathetic with Prince for continuing to dance to music played by their important corporate and financial clients, such as the LBO firms certainly were at the time, but there is little reason to extend the sympathy to the mortgage business, where few such clients were involved and where only the uncertain prospect of more profits kept the music going.

Certainly internal pressure was generated to increase profits, and the message was not lost on lower-level employees. To these mid-level managers responsible for large parts of Citigroup's enormous balance sheets, it usually meant "increase profits or expect to be replaced"—and profits really could be increased in many businesses only by taking on more and more complicated forms of risk. As at Merrill Lynch, it was difficult for mid-level risk managers to argue that the money-making machine that had been put in place should be slowed down because of concerns about risk. After all, the top guys in the bank were saying that "We're still dancing." Still, somebody senior had to know that Citigroup had embarked on a major commitment to structured finance and CDOs at a time when the market fundamentals were weakening and the bank's exposures were very large. Somebody must have signed off on the idea that the risks were manageable, and were being managed.

Under these circumstances it is difficult to see how Prince might have survived, though the board had expressed support for him right up until his resignation was announced. Within a month of the announcement, the board further announced that, though it had formed a search committee this time and had gone through the motions of looking outside the bank (apparently at John Thain, who for a time was being considered by both Merrill and Citigroup), it decided to name Vikram Pandit, an ex–Morgan Stanley division head who had joined the bank only a few months before when Citigroup acquired his hedge fund, Old Lane LP, and put him in charge of Alternative Assets. An Indian national with a Ph.D. in finance from Columbia University, Pandit had worked at Morgan Stanley since 1986, mainly in equities. He rose there to become head of the Institutional Securities Division (which included securities trading and sales and corporate finance), only to be forced out in 2005 by Phil Purcell, who was struggling to save its own position. Pandit and five others formed Old Lane immediately thereafter and had raised $4.5 billion for the fund by the time it attracted the attention of Citigroup. Bob Rubin, in particular, was eager to acquire the fund to get Pandit, who he thought had future managerial potential.

Bob Rubin, actually, might have been a natural choice to have succeeded Weill or Prince, but Rubin was adamant that he did not want any more managerial responsibility at this time of his life (he was sixty-nine in 2007), and he wanted to be free to involve himself in presidential politics in the campaign of 2008 (he was a prominent supporter of and advisor to Hillary Clinton) and to keep up with his other interests. When Prince resigned, the board thought that it would be best to appoint a non-executive chairman of the board, to keep that job separate from the CEO's until the new man had proven himself to some extent. Rubin was again urged to become chairman, but refused. Instead, the board asked another of its members, Sir Winfried Bischoff, former chairman and CEO of Schroder and Co., a British merchant bank acquired by Citigroup in 2000, to take the job, which he did.

The board also decided, beginning in the fall of 2007, to raise additional capital to shore up its balance sheet and to protect itself against any kind of downgrading of its debt ratings. The common dividend was cut by 40 percent, and private sales of preferred and common stock raised approximately $40 billion, including an issue of $7.5 billion to the government of Abu Dhabi, by the end of April 2008. These stock issues were especially expensive to long-standing shareholders, as they were made at unusually low prices, reflecting the fact that Citigroup's share price fell further during this period, to a point lower than where the stock price had been at the time of the 1998 Travelers-Citicorp merger. Pandit moved quickly to set up his own management team, making several important changes to the group put together by Prince, and to review all of the group's different businesses. He promised to tighten up Citicorp's balance sheet and to rid it of about $400 billion in nonessential assets, which sounded like a lot but was less than 20 percent of the bank's total assets.

Citigroup was by no means the only large bank to see its stock price hammered as a result of loan losses. Bank of America suffered a drop in its share price to a price-to-book value ratio of 0.79 by the end of the second quarter of 2008. (Citigroup's ratio was 0.77; JPMorgan Chase's was 1.00.) Bank of America had suffered fewer write-offs, but in August of 2007 it moved opportunistically to acquire a $2 billion stake in Countrywide Financial, the country's leading mortgage broker, which was in serious trouble. In January 2008, it offered $4 billion in stock to buy the rest of Countrywide, which Ken Lewis, Bank of America's CEO, called a "steal" at the time (at one-sixth of Countrywide's market value before the crisis), and later renegotiated the price to $2.5 billion. It would replace all the top managers and provide the capital to pull Countrywide through the crisis, but the market wasn't sure the move was such a good idea and took out its feelings on the Bank of America stock price. Meanwhile, Bank of America's crosstown rival, Wachovia, was struggling under the weight of a 2006 $25 billion acquisition of Golden West Financial Corp., a large mortgage-originating savings bank, which was suffering its share of problems. Wachovia's stock had dropped to 0.46 percent of book value by July 2008, and the bank's board replaced its prominent CEO, Ken Thompson, after a search that produced Robert Steel, undersecretary of the treasury and a former senior executive of Goldman Sachs, as his replacement.

RESCUING BEAR STEARNS

Both Citigroup and Merrill Lynch moved quickly to raise additional equity capital once their CDO and CLO exposures became clear. So did fourteen other banks and investment banks tracked by Bloomberg, which in aggregate raised approximately $250 billion in new capital to replace about that amount lost in the mortgage market during 2007 and first half of 2008. The new capital raised substantially stabilized the risk to the world economy of broad financial collapse, and reassured creditors of the firms that they would be acceptable counterparts for future trading activity, and reassured clients whose assets were held at the firms that they would be safe. The issuance of this large amount of new capital confined the damages from the crisis mainly to the shareholders of the firms involved, which is the way you want such things to work out. But each loss was a hit to capital, and the losses continued as the marking to market valuation of CDOs and leveraged loans continued to decline. After July of 2008, the losses began to exceed by significant amounts the amount of new capital raised, and the stock prices of the banks, reflecting all this and the dilution of the stock by the new capital raised, continued to slump, making further capital raising more difficult and more expensive.

One firm, however, took a different approach. Bear Stearns, the fifth-largest U.S. investment bank with significant mortgage market exposure, did not raise capital to shore itself up during this period, though it had several opportunities to do so. Its management decided (despite significant internal opposition) that the capital being offered was at too low a price and the firm, an opportunistic, street-smart trading organization that almost always made money, could tough it out. But it couldn't. Most Wall Street veterans would have named Bear Stearns as one of the least likely of the increasingly large and hard-to-manage firms on Wall Street to lose control of its balance sheet and end up in a forced merger that was only a little bit better than outright liquidation. But that's what happened to the firm in mid-March of 2008, when, at the urging of and with considerable assistance from the Federal Reserve Bank of New York, it accepted an offer to be acquired by JPMorgan Chase for the derisive price of $2 per share for stock that had traded at $170 per share a year before.

Bear's problems began in June 2007, when two subprime mortgage securities hedge funds that it managed reported substantial losses in the downward-spiraling price freefall that occurred then. Markdowns triggered margin calls, which precipitated even lower markdowns, and so on, until the capital in the funds was depleted. These funds went bankrupt on July 31, 2008. As a result, Bear Stearns's CEO, seventy-four-year-old James Cayne, fired the firm's well-liked and -respected co-president and head of securities trading (and Cayne's bridge-playing rival), Warren Spector.*

Despite the setback, Cayne still thought the firm had enough capital to get through continued market turbulence, and wasn't crazy about raising more at the $100-per-share price to which the stock had fallen over the summer. So the firm did not attempt to raise capital then or later. As market conditions deteriorated, Cayne would be criticized in the press for spending too much time playing golf or tournament bridge (he had been a champion player for more than thirty years) and too little minding the store. For the third quarter of 2007, Bear Stearns reported its first quarterly loss in its history, after a $1.9 billion write-off of mortgage-backed securities that the firm owned itself—in addition to those held by its hedge funds. The quarterly loss was certainly a sizeable one in relation to the firm's total capital, then of only $12 billion. In December, Cayne was assisted in deciding to stand down as CEO in favor of Alan Schwartz, the other co-president, while remaining as chairman. In January 2008, the firm looked at an offer from an Asian bank to acquire 30 percent of the firm for the then-current market price—about $100 per share—and

---

* Spector was able to cash in his stock and options as a result of being dismissed for a $23 million gain.

turned it down, despite urgent appeals from some of its senior traders to accept the offer and unload its remaining mortgage-backed securities, even at a loss.[16] In all, Bear Stearns backed away from at least six different efforts to raise billions in new capital, including one involving the sale of a stake to KKR.[17]

For Bear Stearns the worst of the storm was felt during the first quarter of 2008. Stock prices in general were dropping fast out of concern that the liquidity crisis, then more than six months old—the longest-lasting liquidity squeeze in anyone's memory—had spread to all other fixed-income markets and, it was assumed, driven the economy into a recession. Financial firms were under the gun, and rumors spread wildly about firms that were unable to meet trading obligations or were facing large client withdrawals. Rating agencies were looking at investment banks with raised eyebrows, wondering whether to pull ratings that kept the firms viable. This was a bad time to be undercapitalized.

On Friday, March 14, 2007, after a week of customer withdrawals, counterparty concerns, and rumors of collapsing credit sources, Bear Stearns's stock fell 47 percent, to a nine-year low of $30 (its book value), on rumors (which proved to be true by the end of the day) that its ratings were to be downgraded. A lowering of a credit rating can require a firm to post additional capital against some of its obligations, and it can make trading counterparties reluctant to trade with it and investors unwilling to roll over maturing debt. In normal market conditions, such things can be adjusted by paying higher interest rates or by raising additional capital. In panicky markets, everyone runs for the door at the same time. Suddenly Bear's regular trading counterparties would no longer trade with it and were trying to unwind large outstanding repurchase, derivative, and other positions. Rumors spread that the firm was struggling to stay afloat, and denials were disregarded.

The Federal Reserve, which had been monitoring Bear Stearns's deteriorating position closely for months, dispatched a team to its offices to look at its books. There, in something of a surprise, the team discovered that Bear Stearns was much more involved with securities counterparties than they had thought. Bear was a major clearing firm for smaller brokerages, hedge funds and asset managers, which would be greatly inconvenienced if they lost access to their funds while Bear Stearns sorted out the niceties of bankruptcy. Worse, the firm was also counterparty to institutions on more than five thousand credit default and other swaps agreements with a "notional" (or face) value of $11 trillion.

All of the major firms, as market makers in derivatives, maintained similar portfolios of swaps. The portfolios included positions in which the firm was owed money, and offsetting ones in which it owed the money. The two sets of positions were balanced, and marked to market, with daily settle-up payments being made between counterparties. Under normal conditions, the derivative positions would not have constituted a significant net risk to the firm, and indeed another firm could take over the entire portfolio at little cost or trouble. But if the firm should suddenly be forced into bankruptcy, the whole situation would change. The assets and liabilities would be treated separately in bankruptcy, under the supervision of a judge trying to sort out the various claims of those to whom the firm owed money. This process would destroy the daily valuation symmetry of the portfolios, meaning that the net risk of the positions (now valued at fire-sale prices as individual assets or liabilities) would increase as the firm lost control over them. This could create a big mess in the derivatives market—especially in view of the size of the Bear Stearns portfolio—affecting prices and liquidity of derivatives owned by others, and bringing more panic to the already troubled market. Further, there were billions of dollars of outstanding credit derivatives swaps outstanding that insured the credit of Bear Stearns itself, and these would all come due in bankruptcy, forcing their holders (other banks and financial institutions) to face potentially very large losses.

Finally, Bear was also a major participant in the repurchase, or repo, market, in which owners of government securities can raise cash by selling them overnight with a contract to repurchase them later. This market turns over approximately $2.5 trillion every night. Bear used the market to borrow heavily from money market mutual funds. According to one senior official at the Fed,

> If Bear had failed all these money-market mutual funds, instead of getting their money back on Monday morning, would have found themselves with all kinds of illiquid collateral, including CDOs and God knows what else. It would have cause a run on that entire market. That in turn would have made it impossible for other investment banks to fund themselves.[18]

At 2:00 a.m., on Friday, March 14, Timothy Geithner, president of the New York Fed, who had been overseeing the investigation into Bear Stearns's financial position, reported to a colleague at the Fed that he doubted that the fallout from the failure of Bear Stearns could be contained, because the firm's trading positions were so numerous, large, and inter-connected. By 4:00 a.m., Geithner spoke to Ben Bernanke at the Fed, who had not previously thought it would be likely that Bear Stearns would be rescued by its intervention, and the two agreed that firm had to be as-sisted. They would make a twenty-eight-day loan to JPMorgan, which would on-lend it to Bear Stearns. In enabling the loan to a nonbank, the Fed would rely on Section 13(3) of the Federal Reserve Act of 1932, which permitted them to extend credit outside the immediate banking system in "unusual and exigent circumstances."[19]

Bear Stearns had concluded on its own that after the preceding week's run on its credit facilities, customer withdrawals, and trading counter-party defections, unless it could secure government assistance, it would not be able to open for business on Monday morning, March 17. Accord-ingly, it and Lazard Frères, whom it had hired to assist it, had been search-ing the market for buyers of all or part of Bear Stearns, and Alan Schwartz had called Jamie Dimon of JPMorgan Chase to propose a sale to it. The weekend was hugely intense, with Treasury Secretary Paulson telling Schwartz that he "had to have a deal by Sunday night."[20]

JPMorgan Chase, which was a major creditor of Bear Stearns and counterparty to a great many of its positions, also had a strong interest in seeing the firm avoid bankruptcy, but it couldn't help, Dimon said, with-out government assistance. It was all just too big and too rushed. JPMor-gan offered to take over Bear Stearns's assets and liabilities, with substantial support from the Fed, if a price low enough to cushion its risks could be agreed upon. On Saturday, March 15, Morgan told Lazard that its cur-rent thinking was that it could acquire Bear Stearns at a price of $8–12 per share, depending on a number of matters to be resolved. Bear Stearns replied that it would not be able to agree to any material conditions on an offer from Morgan, or commit to customary representations and warran-ties in closing the deal, as the market would be unhappy with a deal with any risk of not being closed promptly. Later, Morgan lowered its price expectations to $4 per share.

At this point both Bear Stearns and JPMorgan realized that bank-ruptcy for Bear Stearns might be a reality. If it were to happen, because of its billions of dollars of exposure, the event could be very damaging to JPMorgan, as well as to the whole financial system. Bear Stearns, un-happy with the lowball offers being thrown its way, might reject them all and announce that it would file for bankruptcy. This option, which they called the "nuclear card," if played, might result in a higher offer. Jimmy

Cayne was the strongest advocate for playing this hand: "I knew that there was a strong probability that if Bear Stearns went down, there might be systemic failure. I knew I had a nuclear card. Of course you can't play such a card . . . but if anybody on earth would have played it, it would have been me."[21]

But Jamie Dimon knew it, too. If he held back, on the grounds that the deal was too risky for JPMorgan, then at the last minute the Fed might offer up the guaranty that he had been fishing for all along, without, so far, getting any bites on the line.

In the end, the Treasury and the Fed yielded, afraid of the consequences of a Bear Stearns bankruptcy, but in doing so, insisted that the price of the acquisition not be so high as to appear to be a bailout of the stockholders, and lowered it further, to $2 per share. The Federal Reserve Bank of New York would commit to lending up to $30 billion against Bear's less-liquid assets, and JPMorgan Chase would guaranty all of the firm's outstanding and future liabilities.[22]

At $2 per share and the government guarantying all the uncertain assets, Dimon figured he had a great deal with more than enough cushion under it for him to be able to cope with unexpected discoveries, difficulties, and legal claims. He was interested in Bear's top-performing prime brokerage business, its large and usually profitable clearing business, its valuable new office building, and some of the firm's top banking and trading performers. These businesses and professionals alone would well be worth the price, even if the rest were worth nothing. Bear Stearns objected to the price, of course, which was not much more than liquidation value, but was in no position to bargain if it wanted the Fed's assistance. Without such assistance, the firm would be toast on Monday, so it very reluctantly agreed to the terms, creating a howl of protest from stockholders and employees loud enough to be heard across the Atlantic.

That howl was heard by British billionaire Joseph Lewis, living in the Bahamas. On September 10, 2007, he had paid $860 million in an all-cash purchase of a 7 percent stake in Bear Stearns, which by December he had raised to a total of eleven million shares or 9.4 percent, for which, according to Bloomberg News, he paid an average price of $107 a share. Lewis lost over $1 billion on the forced merger. Approximately a third of Bear Stearns's stock was owned by its employees, including 5.6 million shares owned by James Cayne and over 1 million owned by Alan Schwartz. At its high, Cayne's stake had been worth more than $1 billion.

The market opened on Monday with Bear Stearns's stock at $5.29 per share, a substantial premium over the agreed $2. The market believed that the story was not yet over, and that another shoe would soon drop. But amid such uncertainty, the customer and counterparty withdrawals continued to strip the firm of any remaining liquidity, which would have to be made up by Morgan. With the price where it was, there was room for another bidder to challenge Morgan's rock-bottom valuation. There was also the need to have the deal voted on by the Bear Stearns stockholders, many of whom were angry and disinclined to do so, which could threaten the Morgan deal, but leave it having already guaranteed many of Bear Stearns's liabilities. If someone else were to offer to pay more to rescue the deal, the Fed would be hard pressed then to say no, even though the cosmetics of its guaranty that made the bailout possible would worsen considerably. On Monday the stock closed at a very optimistic $11.25. Dimon then stepped in and raised JPMorgan's bid to $10 per share, which ended the uncertainty. JPMorgan would immediately purchase new shares equivalent to 35 percent of the recapitalized company to infuse new money right away, and it would guarantee Bear Stearns's trading and other obligations, including Bear Stearns's borrowings from the Federal Reserve. The New York Federal Reserve Bank would also provide a $30 billion special financing, collateralized by mortgage-backed securities, with the first billion in any losses being absorbed by JPMorgan. The Fed would also retain BlackRock, to advise it on the value of the mortgage-backed securities in the portfolio.

This may have been the only deal in history that experienced a fivefold increase in valuation over a weekend, but in any case it was not much of a victory for Bear Stearns's employees and other shareholders, though certainly $10 per share was better than $2. From the point of view of JPMorgan Chase and the Federal Reserve, increasing the offer was a little sloppy and embarrassing, but sometimes messy deals occur in the "fog of war" that can present itself when things are moving fast, the stakes are large, and information for decision-making is changing and never all that clear. In the aftermath, most observers, including serious critics of bailouts of any kind, were satisfied that both the bank and the Fed did what was best for the system, and indeed the event seemed, at the time, to signal the turning point in the long, painful liquidity meltdown in the mortgage markets.

Within weeks of the Bear Stearns deal, so-called vulture investors had appeared in the market, buying up mortgage securities at distressed prices, and returning some of the liquidity to the market. In May, Black-

Rock announced its $15 billion purchase of UBS's mortgage portfolio at a value of about 75 percent of par value and for which UBS would provide $11.25 billion in financing, and other groups were putting together private equity funds to acquire other distressed mortgage portfolios. For them, the apparent improvement in market conditions would prove to be a false recovery.

Two months after the second Bear Stearns deal was agreed, Alan ("Ace") Greenberg, eighty, was in his spacious office at the firm, quietly trading away for his own account, when he was interviewed by a reporter from the *New York Times*. During the turmoil surrounding the merger, it was revealed that Greenberg, who had preceded Cayne as CEO (and was forced to turn over the reins to him in 1993), had sold all of his several million shares of stock in the firm over the past few years. Greenberg and Cayne had had a bitter and tumultuous relationship since Cayne took over, and when asked whether his counsel had been sought during the mortgage crisis, Greenberg replied that "Jimmy was not interested in my point of view. He was a one-man show—he didn't listen to anybody. That is [why] the real break [between us] took place." Told that Cayne had lost much of his entire net worth and was suffering personally, Greenberg responded by saying, "Oh, really. Goodness, that's a shame."[23]

There were also grumblings among former Bear Stearns senior executives that the Treasury's action to force the sale to JPMorgan was really a form of "payback" for Cayne's blunt refusal to participate in the bank group that bought out the assets of LTCM in 1998; others also claimed that Bear Stearns had been the target of a bear raid by short sellers bemoaning the fact that the SEC had issued short-term restrictions on short-selling of certain banking stocks a few months after Bear was taken down. However, no evidence to support either charge was ever produced.

Within two months of the acquisition, Jamie Dimon, recently hailed as the new King of Wall Street by an adoring press, announced that the bank may have underestimated the cushion it would need for legal, financing, and acquisition costs, and therefore it may have overpaid in its generous upping of the purchase price to $10 per share. After better understanding Bear Stearns's balance sheet, Dimon and his colleagues added $3 billion to the $6 billion reserve they had established to effect the acquisition, which meant that it had in effect paid book value for the firm, not a substantial discount.[24] Time will tell; Dimon is skilled at integrating merged businesses and is known for his practice of underpromising and overperforming, but the announcement of the added reserves moved the market away from thinking that JPMorgan Chase, by acting quickly, had scored a lot of points by buying Bear Stearns on the cheap.

MORTGAGES IN PERSPECTIVE

All financial crises are unique, but they also have a number of things in common. What was unique about this one is that the bulk of the debt involved in the write-offs was low-risk, secured debt rated AAA. This was the type of debt that people bought in a crisis, not the kind they sold. And the debt was supposed to be safe—secured by mortgages on valuable real estate—so a lot of it could be borrowed. So the banks confidently loaded up on it, hoping to sell it to investors chasing yield during a liquidity glut, or to hang on to it to capture the yield for themselves. In the end the banks had to learn that too much of anything, even super-senior secured debt, can still be too much.

One of the things the crisis had in common with other financial crises is that banks made it worse for themselves by turbocharging the asset-backed securities market with a continuous supply of increasingly leveraged, risk-enhancing packages and ever-more-complex low-grade products that undermined the quality of the paper they were producing. The dynamic of winner-take-all marketplaces can be very powerful, dragging everyone into the action, as happened in this case. When the prices of houses peaked and then began to decline (for the first time in recent memory), mortgage defaults became inevitable. Then they accelerated into an avalanche of foreclosures. By the end of the second quarter of 2008, more than four out of every one hundred mortgages were in foreclosure or were 90 days past due, the highest level reported in twenty-nine years by the Mortgage Bankers Association.[25] This could only cause the market to reverse itself, which it did.

Once the defaults began to increase, the markets seized up. It was not that all mortgages were thought to be bad, but no one really could tell which CMOs contained the weakest subprime mortgages; not knowing, and fearing the worst, the yield-chasing investors dumped it all: CMOs, whole loans, and anything else connected to real estate. The folks left holding the bags of unsellable mortgages were banks, thrift institutions, and hedge funds. These are, in essence, opaque institutions, something that no amount of required transparency seems to be able to alter. One investor in UBS and other bank stocks, Henry Herrmann, CEO of Waddell and

Reed Financial, a major U.S. mutual fund management company, noted, "We were shocked when all this came to light. UBS was the one [bank] we perceived in a better light than the others. But, like the others, it didn't fully appreciate the magnitude of the debt buildup."[26] Herrmann might have added that his well-paid analysts at Waddell Reed didn't see the buildup, either. Trillion-dollar balance sheets can hide a lot of mistakes and a lot of mischief, and investment advisors don't always see what they should.

Once the banks were seen to be in trouble, just about everything they owned was suspect. If mortgages could suddenly go wrong, couldn't all those leveraged loans and credit card receivables do the same? And if the banks were caught up short, wouldn't they begin to unload their positions in the market, driving prices further down as they did? It is just such thoughts as these on the part of investors suddenly discovering the downside of things that turn expected financial market adjustments into crises.

And it seems also that each time a crisis develops, it reveals yet another failure of the industry's risk management systems. In 1987, firms learned not to trust their portfolio hedging mechanisms that depended on derivative markets. In 1994, they learned about "value at risk," and the problems of long-tailed exposures in which the probability of disasters can be very low, but still disastrous. In 1998, the markets discovered again that all expectations about correlation or noncorrelation of investment exposures go out the window in the midst of a real mess. This time the lesson was that long-held assumptions about liquidity could be useless during crises, and even AAA ratings (which many thousands of CMOs were rated, even though only a handful of industrial companies were) could not protect you. Risk managers tend to be a little like generals reconsidering how to fight the last war when the next one is always different. There is always something that can go wrong that hasn't before. Common sense tells us that risk needs to be limited to a size that can't blow up the firm. John Thain, a former risk manager at Goldman Sachs, observed after he became Merrill Lynch's CEO that "Risk should be sized to the return and earnings profile of the division. It is not acceptable for a division to have a position that wipes out its own earnings, let alone those of the entire firm."[27] Or, as Ace Greenberg, former CEO of Bear Stearns, put it, "we don't have limits on traders buying things they *don't* like."[28]

The problems were with what they *did* like. The only way so much risk could be built up to the levels it did in the banks was because the top managers were willing to waive the limits (or other rules) or ignore what they saw because they wanted to keep harvesting the profits from the CDOs for as long as they could. They needed the profits to keep their stock prices up, and there weren't too many other places to get them from, so they hung in there, convincing themselves that they were in the midst of a long-term trend rather than a bubble about to burst.

A NEW ROLE FOR GOVERNMENTS

In the 1980s, a consortium of central banks orchestrated by the Bank for International Settlements, the Bank of England, and the Federal Reserve introduced the concept of "systemic risk" to the world financial system after a decade of excesses in lending practices by commercial banks that culminated in serious banking failures in the United States, then in Europe, and finally in Japan. Concerns about risks that could bring down the global financial system led to the Basel Accord for risk-adjusted, minimum capital adequacy for banks in 1988, and its implementation by the central banks of all of the leading industrial countries in 1992. There have been other economic crises since then, and the central banks, together with their treasury ministries and the World Bank and IMF, have combined in various ways to sort them out. Each of these crises has involved some amount of moral hazard resulting in bailouts, which were always tolerated to prevent something worse from happening. The U.S. government has also intervened in various other ways to support such nonbanking institutions as TVA, federal mortgage lending institutions, Penn Central Railroad, Chrysler, Lockheed, and New York City. Though the ghost of Adam Smith shudders at the thought, the U.S. government, over the last fifty years, has become an intervener in situations of economic distress sufficiently often so as to encourage the populace to expect it in almost all such situations when they arise.

The Federal Reserve's unprecedented intervention in the Bear Stearns case was just another example. The Fed changed its rules by assisting a nonbank, which it was technically allowed to do only in special situations, but had not done for many years, and never done for an investment bank. Despite the fact that the investment banks had become huge institutions engaging in many of the same activities as banks, and engaging with them as counterparties, the Fed regarded investment banks as outside its job description. Under Alan Greenspan, the Fed's predisposition was to allow markets to sort out their problems and not to intervene beyond flooding the markets with liquidity when they needed it, though Greenspan was around for the Mexican and Asian currency crises and the Long-Term Capital Management incident in 1998.

But the Fed, now under a new man, Princeton professor and Depression scholar Benjamin Bernanke, and facing a potentially huge crisis, had to act more boldly. The standard Greenspan approach would not have been enough. Together with Wall Street veteran Hank Paulson, Bernanke saw Bear Stearns's plunge to the earth as potentially catastrophic for the financial system. A bankruptcy of the large, highly interconnected Bear Stearns, they feared, could be the financial equivalent of a small nuclear weapon detonating in Wall Street.

So they decided to act by extending to Bear Stearns a twenty-eight-day line of credit from the Fed—its lender-of-last-resort window—while it tried to find a buyer for the firm. But once it concluded that Bear was facing a run, it dropped all pretenses. The Fed undoubtedly pushed Bear Stearns into the arms of JPMorgan Chase at $2 per share, but the deal would not have happened without the Fed's willingness to guaranty nearly $30 billion of Bear Stearns's assets.

The event was the first in which the possible collapse of an investment bank was seen to have been important enough to endanger the system to the same extent that a large commercial bank's failing might have. So the market read the action as a signal that any firm larger than Bear Stearns (such as Lehman Brothers) would also be rescued, and its creditors bailed out, if it should get in to trouble. Thus the creditors of large investment banks thought they were being offered a free ride—they would be guaranteed if the firms got into trouble—the same as depositors were guaranteed by the FDIC, but without any size limit. After Bear Stearns, with no information to the contrary from the government, the guaranty was out there in the market, presumably guarantying the liabilities of any too-big-to-fail investment bank. And the guaranty was free, because, so far, the government had made no effort to apply insurance costs or to assert more stringent regulation of the investment banks, though this was thought to be a temporary condition that the government would get around to adjusting when it could.

As the summer after Bear Stearns's demise unfolded, the market quieted down. There was a lot of comment suggesting that the government had overreacted and extended its guaranty of Bear Stearns's assets too quickly, but for the most part the decision was accepted as necessary and appropriate. In July, Paulson and Bernanke approached Congress for powers to intervene in the case of Fannie Mae and Freddie Mac, if needed, though such an intervention was not thought to be urgent or imminent. This action also involved moral hazard—the bailing out of Fannie and Freddie's creditors—which appears to have offended Paulson, in particular, who badly wanted to set down a marker that would limit the expectation of future bailouts.

As we saw in chapter 1, Paulson pulled the trigger on Fannie and Freddie in the first week of September, but refused to help Lehman Brothers, while nonetheless committing to an enormous intervention in the case of AIG. The Lehman bankruptcy, whatever the effect of its message on moral hazard, set off the Armageddon in global financial markets that kept them writhing in pain and confusion for the next four months, and panicked the real economy into its sharpest drop in nearly a century. This in turn drove financial markets down further. Wall Street staggered under the weight of these events, which several firms would not survive, but would profoundly change the industry for those that did.

13

AN UNCERTAIN FUTURE

REVIEWING THE FINANCIAL SERVICES industry at the end of
2008 was similar, some may have thought, to looking over Pearl Harbor
at the end of 1941. There was wreckage everywhere then—everywhere
the remnant hulks of proud ships once thought to be unsinkable. Similarly, in a short period of time, the banking and financial services industry
had been torn apart by bankruptcies, forced mergers, and extraordinary
efforts to endure and resist market runs on credit sources and stock prices.
Of the top five investment banks, only two were still afloat under their
own power; the others had either sunk or were under tow. The two top
mortgage financing providers and the world's once most valuable and
admired insurance company had been nationalized. The largest retail brokerage firm, the largest commercial mortgage provider, one of the largest
savings banks, the fourth-largest commercial bank, and the fifth-largest
investment bank had been sufficiently damaged that they had to be merged
into other, stronger firms. And beyond this level of destruction, another
twenty-three American banks or savings-and-loan organizations had
been seized by their regulators during the year.

The devastation from the collapse of the global financial system was
not confined to the United States. The largest bank in Britain, the architect
the year before of a $100 billion hostile takeover of the largest bank in
Holland, had collapsed, and the government was required to step in and

acquire a 70 percent voting interest in the firm; the UK government was also forced to acquire a controlling interest in the country's largest mortgage lender. The largest Swiss bank sold $60 billion in bad assets to its government, and the second-largest German bank had to be assisted with a loan package that left the government owning a 25 percent interest. A variety of other government rescue efforts to keep the banking industry afloat took place in Europe. These collectively involved several trillions of government funds by the end of 2008, and the expectation was that more money would be needed before all the damage had been contained.

It was clear that the damage to the financial services industry from the events of 2007 and 2008 had been cataclysmic. By the beginning of January 2009, Bloomberg estimated that more than $1 trillion in write-downs had been taken by the world's largest banks and brokerage firms since the beginning of 2007, forcing them to raise a total of about $950 billion in new capital from various sources. During this time markets, many markets, froze up and resisted all efforts to thaw them out. Capital markets were effectively inoperative for almost a year, a longer period of illiquidity than anyone alive could remember. This extraordinary market failure caused enormous damage to banks and other intermediaries, much of which would take years to repair.

How could all this have happened in a highly regulated industry that is principally owned by sophisticated institutional investors? What was going on that allowed such a terrible systemic collapse to happen? There are several answers to these questions; many different things led to the collapse, but altogether it may have been a case of an industry, after decades of unchecked pedal-to-the-metal expansion, finally just blew itself apart.

REGULATORY FAILURES

Certainly the regulatory environment for financial services was benign throughout the Greenspan years, when the chairman's authority was unquestioned. Glass-Steagall was repealed, permitting banks to engage in the fast-moving securities industry that few understood, and large bank mergers were continuously allowed with hardly any hesitation over what effect such deals might have on systemic risk. Banking regulators overlooked a variety of bad practices associated with the extension of mortgage loans, their securitization and off-balance-sheet parking of assets, and rarely asked questions about the adequacy of internal control and risk management systems, especially those of the largest banks which were thought to be capable of looking after themselves..

Further, the federally chartered government-backed mortgage financing entities, Fannie Mae and Freddie Mac, were allowed for years to engage in accounting chicaneries and to operate without adequate capital; the derivatives markets were allowed to escape regulation, even the relatively mild oversight associated with moving the over-the-counter market for credit default swaps onto a traded exchange, where it would involve less systemic risk. The SEC allowed investment banks to increase operating leverage to dangerous levels, scam artists such as Bernie Madoff to escape scrutiny, and rating agencies to issue over sixty thousand AAA ratings for asset-backed securities without wondering how come. In the two most important regulatory actions of the decade, the $1.4 billion settlement forced on Wall Street underwriters by New York Attorney General Eliot Spitzer (for alleged abuses in technology investment research and underwriting practices) and the passage of the Sarbanes-Oxley Act to improve corporate governance and accounting, the SEC played only a comparatively passive, go-along role. Despite several scandals in the midst of two bubble markets within a decade, the regulators seemed content that they had the dangers of systemic financial failure under control.

Systemic risk, after all, they thought, was something that had already been dealt with through the Basel Accord which had worked fine since the early 1990s. But despite fifteen years of having the system in place, and several years spent trying to improve it, it had all came to naught—the very crisis the Basel Accord was designed to prevent happened anyway.

There were three principal flaws in the system that everyone was relying on.

First, the Basel Accord was among central banks, and these only regulated banks, not investment banks, broker-dealers, insurance companies, hedge funds, or other elements of the so-called "shadow banking system." These nonregulated entities that owned and traded financial assets had grown to operate on about the same scale as the large banks, but they were outside the Basel regulatory system and not required to adhere to it.

Second, technical deficiencies in the methods for determining risk-adjusted capital enabled the system to be gamed by the banks. One such deficiency was that secured debt (such as mortgages or mortgage-backed securities) was considered to be very low risk, because the collateral was thought always to be sufficient, and liquidity never a question. Neither collateral nor liquidity, however, were things the system attempted to

value, measure, or regulate. As financial instruments became more sophisticated and complex, the Basel rules were changed to allow responsible banks to use their own high-tech risk management models, which
often used bond ratings supplied by rating agencies to determine capital
requirements. During 2007 and 2008, these risk models did not provide
for enough capital to support the positions carried, and the correlation of
ratings and market values went terribly awry. When the models did require capital, some banks found ways around the rules by putting assets
into an off-balance-sheet special investment vehicle. By playing the game
so as to minimize the amount of capital needed to support the assets
held—through the risk-adjusting mechanisms—banks could end up with
unusually high total assets-to-equity ratios. Further, the banks were able
to manipulate the ratios so as to be able to substantially increase their
total amounts of leverage. Deutsche Bank, for example, survived the
mortgage crisis to which it was not heavily exposed. Nevertheless it had
$1.5 billion in proprietary trading losses in the last quarter of 2008.
These losses derived from a balance sheet with a leverage ratio of 38 on
June 30, 2008, substantially higher, according to one analyst, than the
leverage ratios of Goldman Sachs or other investment banks.[1]

Third, the regulators themselves relied too much on the Basel ratios
and did not exercise independent judgment as to the capital needed by
the banks under their control. Regulators allowed banks to operate from
large, complex multi-platform structures with inadequate enterprise risk
controls; they allowed the banks to grow assets at exceptional rates without sufficient attention to quality or diversification; and they allowed
several large banks to undertake serial acquisitions at such a pace as to
make integration and control of operations very hard to achieve. As long
as the banks could point to their good standing under Basel, however, all
else would be forgiven. To some degree this regulatory forbearance was
the result of a commitment to free market principles under the long reign
of Alan Greenspan at the Federal Reserve, and to some extent the result
of effective lobbying by the large banks and investment banks to protect
their freedoms and privileges. There was an effort in the Clinton administration to try to bring the shadow banking system under the same
regulatory umbrella as the banks, but it never advanced very far.
Greenspan, in testimony to Congress in 2008, explained that a mistake
he made during his time in office was to rely on the banks to govern
themselves carefully so as to avoid bankruptcy—in their self-interest—
and thus not to overextend themselves. But as he pointed out, that as-

sumption proved to be wrong. Something was driving the banks into such a competitive frenzy as to relax their concerns about the risks they were taking that could endanger their own safety.

STRATEGIC ERRORS

On January 9, 2009, Bloomberg News announced that Citigroup was negotiating the sale of 51 percent of its Smith Barney retail brokerage business to Morgan Stanley. The report was denied as a rumor, thought to be the result of pressure from the Federal Reserve which had asked Citigroup to simplify its organization and to raise as much capital as it could by selling off assets not essential to the basic banking business. Indeed, as recently as November 21, 2008, Vikram Pandit had said, "I have no desire to sell Smith Barney. I love that business." About that time, Citigroup presented a "Town Hall Meeting" for securities analysts and proclaimed yet again that it was fully committed to its universal banking strategy. Smith Barney was the core of the business that Sandy Weill assembled after leaving American Express, a business that preceded the acquisition of Travelers, Salomon Brothers, and Citicorp.

Nevertheless, a few days later Citigroup announced the joint venture with Morgan Stanley, in which both companies would contribute their retail brokerage businesses to a new firm, with a sales force of twenty-two thousand, to be 51 percent owned by Morgan Stanley. The new company, which the two firms valued at $21 billion, would be far larger than Merrill Lynch. Citigroup would be paid $2.7 billion to cede control to Morgan Stanley and would record a capital gain on the transaction of about $10 billion. A few days later, Citigroup announced a further disappointing quarterly loss, about twice what was expected by analysts. The stock dropped again, and Pandit announced that Citigroup would split into two parts, Citicorp (the bank under a new, old name) and Citi Holdings, which would include its nonbanking businesses and the troubled assets guaranteed by TARP.

The sale of Smith Barney was seen as a major (if unwilling) step in breaking up the multi-platform, universal banking business model that had been aggressively assembled by Weill. At the time, this was thought to be the inevitable business model for the industry, most analysts then believed, one that would enable it to displace the so-called stand-alone investment banks. The Smith Barney sale, of course, was necessary because

Weill's business model hadn't worked. It had either been ill conceived or poorly executed (perhaps both), though it took several years for this to become evident.

On the same day that the Smith Barney sale was reported, Bob Rubin announced that he was retiring as Citigroup's senior counselor and would not stand for reelection to its board. This news was reported in the *Financial Times* with a large photograph of an unsmiling Rubin, looking all of his seventy years, standing behind a Citibank lectern with his hands spread apart with their palms up (as if to say, "hey, what can you do") before a backdrop with "Legacies of Leadership" written in large letters. The *FT*'s headline for the piece was "Scapegoat for the Woes That Nearly Sank Citigroup."

Some months after leaving the Treasury, and a year or so after the Citigroup merger had been completed, Weill invited Rubin to join the board and become chairman of its executive committee, a non-executive job. It was clear that Rubin would have considerable influence with the other members of the Citigroup board, of which few members were financial people. Rubin did not want to be tied down with day-to-day managerial responsibilities, and made this plain, but Weill knew that Rubin had enormous door-opening powers and could be a valued "consigliere" (a term Rubin liked), so he arranged for him to be paid enough to keep him interested and loyal. That amounted to an annual compensation (not including the use of the airplanes and other perks) that totaled $125 million in cash and stock over a bit less than ten years. By the time he left the bank in 2009, he had accumulated 5.3 million shares of common stock and options, which at that time had depreciated in value to a mere $15 million, after a 90 percent drop in value over the previous year. Rubin always claimed that he earned at Citigroup only what he would easily have been able to get at a hedge fund or as the CEO of another banking group. This certainly is true, though he might have had to take on a little more responsibility at the other places to earn what he did at Citigroup. Someone with Rubin's celebrity, reputation, and Rolodex undoubtedly could have landed an equally lucrative position somewhere else.

Clearly Rubin was a valuable addition to the board at the time. But his role was unclear from the start. He was paid as if he were a full-time executive, but he described his role as purely non-executive. The role and purpose of the executive committee that he chaired was never clear. But what was clear, was that at critical moments he supported Sandy Weill and sustained his legacy as, for example, when John Reed proposed that both he and Sandy Weill resign together and be replaced by an independent, nonaligned CEO from the outside; or when Sandy exceeded the normal retirement age and wanted to continue as CEO; or when Chuck Prince was appointed CEO on Weill's recommendation without a search committee being formed. Rubin was also reported to be strongly in favor of the bank's acquiring the Old Lane hedge fund for $800 million in order to secure the services of Vikram Pandit, who was soon elevated to CEO without ever having held a similar position anywhere else. In retrospect, all of those decisions taken by the board seem questionable, as does its agreeing, after Weill's departure and apparently based on Rubin's urging, to increase the bank's trading exposures without commensurately beefing up its risk management capabilities. Some Citigroup shareholders might also have thought that Rubin seemed insufficiently committed to the corporation during its more difficult moments to have been paid quite so well—he refused to serve as chairman after Weill left, and again after Prince left, forcing the board to select London-based Winfried Bischoff to serve instead, despite Bischoff's seeming to be out of touch with the crucial operating issues of the bank at the time. There were times when Rubin seemed out of touch as well.

But it wasn't Rubin who sank the ship, though he may have done little to save it. All the way until its second bailout, which effectively nationalized the bank, the board had been mesmerized by the legacy of Sandy Weill (whom a senior Citigroup executive, several years after Weill had left the CEO position, described to my students as a "living icon at Citigroup"). Sandy's colossal, multi-platform, cross-selling, pay-for-performance, double-digit-growth machine had an inertia all its own,* even long after he left and it had become apparent that the business model wasn't working. Citigroup had been more or less continuously entangled in loan and trading losses, hugely expensive legal disputes, and serious regulatory infractions and penalties since 2000, while still engaging in an ongoing acquisition program. Its risk management and control systems were nowhere near what they needed to be for it to handle 350,000 employees from a variety of dissimilar corporate cultures engaged in hundreds of different product lines, all operating globally under unrelenting pressure to produce results or else. Considering the weakening state of the bank's financial health, and the desperate condition of Wachovia in September 2008, it is very hard to see how that acquisition could have appeared to make sense to the

---

* Citigroup's balance sheet assets more than tripled over ten years.

Citigroup board, but the board was in denial about the bank's shortcomings and saw the opportunity only as a sound and necessary strategic move. Between them, Citigroup and Wachovia would report combined loan losses and write-downs in 2007–2008 of $180 billion. Nonetheless, Citigroup was both devastated and embarrassed when Wells Fargo stepped in to top its bid. In fact, losing out to Wells Fargo may have enabled Citigroup to dodge a very large and dangerous bullet aimed right at its heart.

Citigroup's strategic thrust was undone by the high cost of supporting it: cross-selling generally involved subsidies given to customers that diminished revenues or increased risks, some of which (as in Citigroup's multiple exposures to Enron and WorldCom) were the result of risks-for-mandates exchanges that the bank regularly made. The strategy was designed to enable the increasingly enormous corporation to grow profits at around 15 percent indefinitely, but its quest for growth led it into making more acquisitions of dissimilar cultures and businesses than it could manage, and to incentivizing its traders and bankers beyond its ability to control the risks they created. On top of that, add frequent high-level management changes, regulatory and brand-image problems, and a stock market that became unconvinced by the continuous sales pitches delivered by top executives, and you get a sense of where Citigroup's multi-platform, high-growth strategy delivered it. In January 2009, it announced an $8.3 billion loss for the fourth quarter of 2008 (based on loan write-downs of $12.1 billion), and an $18.7 billion loss for the year. This was the fifth consecutive quarterly loss, which together aggregated $28 billion. It also announced that Richard Parsons, a long-standing director and former chairman of Time-Warner, would replace Sir Win as chairman of the board. Later, Citigroup announced that its 2008 loss had been increased by $9 billion to $27.7 billion, among the largest in U.S. corporate history.

In February 2009, the Treasury Department announced that it would increase its ownership of Citigroup to 36 percent. Pandit would remain, but Citigroup would shake up its board so that it would contain a majority of truly independent directors, a move that federal regulators had already been pursuing. Under the deal, the Treasury Department agreed to convert up to $25 billion of its preferred stock investment in Citigroup into common stock, giving the company relief from the heavy burden of the preferred dividends. Taxpayers would have more risk but also more potential for profit if the company recovered. The Treasury would convert its stake to the extent that Citigroup could persuade private investors, including several foreign government investment funds, to go along, though the terms of the exchange effectively forced conversion. The Treasury would match the private investors' conversions dollar for dollar, and do so at the most favorable price and terms offered to any other private investor.

By then Citigroup had become something of a zombie, unable to get itself back into a profitable mode, staggered by the weight of troubled assets that it had been unable or unwilling to sell, and stuffed to the gills with government capital that it is supposed to repay within a few years out of profits, or the proceeds from the sale of common stock, neither of which looked very likely. The government had forced Citigroup to eliminate its dividend and recruit new independent directors, and nudged it to sell Smith Barney and to give up its long-held resistance to allowing judges to modify terms of mortgages to keep them out of default, a position strongly opposed by its principal competitors in the mortgage industry. The government's role, originally described as passive, was proving to be anything but.

Citigroup's business strategy, however, had set the model for other large universal banks, which had to keep up with it in terms of balance sheet size, push for market share in investment banking, and reliance on proprietary trading profits. It had the greatest influence on JPMorgan Chase, which was the consolidation of Chemical Bank, Manufacturer's Hanover, Chase Manhattan, JPMorgan, and Bank One over a fifteen-year period, to which were added some smaller-scale investment banking firms, before then acquiring Bear Stearns and Washington Mutual. But it also affected the strategic thinking of Bank of America, and of a number of European universals such as Deutsche Bank, UBS, HSBC, and Credit Suisse.

What made the universal banking strategy work, while it appeared to, was the credibility it had with institutional investors and other financial professionals. Investors believed that Sandy Weill was a money maker and they bought into whatever he was doing, and made money doing so, over a long period of time. In his prime, Sandy was the freshest thing in bank investing since Walter Wriston, and he attracted a following among money managers and analysts that pushed the stock price to a price-earnings ratio of 25. After the acquisition of Citicorp, the stock fell off initially, but then began an extended recovery that pushed it to $50 in mid-2000, when the technology bubble deflated and other problems, including Eliot Spitzer's attack on Weill that caused him to resign, came to be revealed. These problems drove the stock price down to $30, but it recovered and climbed back up to $55 in late 2006, but by then Sandy had left and the price-to-earnings ratio had been halved as investors became more skeptical, though Citigroup's stock performance from 2002 to 2007 was still better than that of its two principal rivals, JPMorgan and Bank of America. After 2007, however, even the most loyal institutional investors must have had doubts about the business model, which appeared to have collapsed entirely, after Citigroup's injurious involvement in the mortgage and leveraged loans markets became evident. Indeed Citigroup came under a lot of pressure to change the business model, but Pandit, Rubin, and the board brushed it off, despite a stock price that traded as low as one dollar per share in early 2009. Just prior to receiving its second, unexpected but necessary, round of financing from TARP in late November, Pandit defended the company's strategic approach: "This is a fantastic business model," he said.[2] But events have proven otherwise and the business model will have to change. Indeed, it has already done so in the announcement of the sale of Smith Barney and the creation of Citi Holdings. The only question remaining at Citigroup is whether or not the government-backed management team can restore the Citicorp banking business, having disposed of the rest. If not, presumably it would be dismantled further and sold off to repay the taxpayers.

EXCESSIVE LEVERAGE

The principal difference between the speculative bubble that burst in 2000 and the one that burst seven years later was that the latter was much more highly leveraged, and when things go wrong, leverage hurts those who use it. Certainly in 2007, when the mortgage market imploded, suddenly and deeply dropping prices of CMOs and CDOs, those who were most leveraged suffered the most: hedge funds, proprietary traders, private equity firms, and those banks and prime brokers that supplied the leverage.

Banks, even those in compliance with the Basel rules, suffered enormous losses. So did investment banks and hedge funds not regulated by Basel. For all their arguments that banks were more regulated and less leveraged than investment banks, their gross leverage ratios were about the same: in the 25-to-30 range. Large investment banks actually were regulated by the Consolidated Supervised Entity rules of the SEC, which required them to report Basel capital adequacy ratios. But investment banks, having only limited access to deposits, had to depend on the market for their own credit facilities, and the market had credit standards of its own and was prepared to sell out collateral when prices dropped. To obtain the financing, investment banks had to mark their positions to market daily, whether the securities were to be held until maturity or not. These market value rules put limits on how much leverage investment banks could bring to bear to finance their positions.

Banks had more freedom to determine how assets were valued, and their discretion was increased as fair value accounting rules were relaxed. Banks had more flexibility in deciding what types of assets to own in order to maximize leverage under the Basel rules, and had access to the Federal Reserve's lending window when desperate. Some also created off-balance-sheet vehicles in which to stash assets without having to provide capital for them. Banks also had a substantial source of low-cost demand and time deposits, though for large banks these rarely amounted to more than 40 percent of total assets, suggesting that they were using the same money markets to finance trading positions that the investment banks were. On balance it is hard to say whether Bear Stearns, Lehman Brothers, or Merrill Lynch was actually more leveraged than Citigroup, UBS, and Deutsche Bank, despite the complaints registered by many banks that they were. Still, it is possible to say that both types of banks were more leveraged that they should have been when the market break finally came.

COMPENSATION AND MORAL HAZARD

The capital markets industry operates in a very sophisticated and competitive environment, one that responds best to strong performance incentives that are locked into it as part of its DNA. These set up internal competition among skilled, highly motivated individuals. People who flourish in this environment are those who want to be paid and advanced based on their individual and their team's performance, and who are willing to take the risk that they might be displaced by someone better or that mistakes or downturns may cause them to be laid off or their firms to fail. Those who have survived the changing fortunes of the industry have done very well, so well in fact that they appear to have become symbolic of greedy and reckless behavior during another "Gilded Age" on Wall Street.

In January 2009, New York State Comptroller Thomas DiNapoli released an estimate that the "securities industry" paid its New York City employees bonuses of $18 billion in 2008, 44 percent less than the year before. This would signify that perhaps as much as half of the bonus pool was not tied directly to the profits of the firms. The point was underscored by the news that Merrill Lynch, after reporting $15 billion in losses, had rushed to pay $3.6 billion in bonuses on the eve of its merger with Bank of America.

In normal times, the erosion of the integrity of the bonus system might not have been noticed outside of Wall Street, but because Merrill Lynch and Bank of America were receiving substantial government funds to keep them afloat, the subject had become part of the public business, and the idea that the banks had paid out taxpayers' TARP funds in undeserved bonuses to employees, together with a leaked report of John Thain's spending $1 million to redecorate his office a year earlier, understandably provoked a blast of public outrage against Wall Street. The issue was so hot that President Obama interrupted his duties to call the bonuses "shameful," and the "height of irresponsibility," and announced a new set of rules for those seeking "exceptional" assistance from TARP that would limit cash compensation to $500,000 and restrict severance pay, frills, perks, and boondoggles. "In order to restore our financial system," Mr. Obama said, "we have to restore trust and to restore trust, we've got to make certain that taxpayer funds are not subsidizing excessive compensation packages on Wall Street."

Many Americans at the time were convinced that any bonuses at all for top executives of Wall Street firms would constitute "excess compensation." But none actually got any: no Wall Street CEO taking TARP money received a bonus in 2008, and the same was true for most of their senior colleagues. Not only did those responsible receive no bonuses, but the value of the stock in their companies paid to them as part of prior-year bonuses dropped by 70 percent or more, leaving them, collectively, with billions of dollars of unrealized losses. That's pay for performance, isn't it?

The Wall Street compensation system has evolved from the 1970s, when most of the firms were private partnerships, owned by partners who paid out a designated share of the firm's profits to non-partner employees while dividing up the rest for themselves. The non-partners had to earn their keep every year, but the partners' percentage ownership in the firms were also reset every year or two. On the whole, everyone's performance was continuously evaluated, and rewarded or penalized. The system provided great incentives to create profits, but also, because the partners' own money was involved, to avoid great risk.

In time there was some significant erosion of the simple principles of the partnership days. Compensation for top managers followed the trend into excess set by other public companies. Competition for talent made recruitment and retention more difficult and thus tilted negotiating power further in favor of stars. Henry Paulson, when he was CEO of Goldman Sachs, once remarked that Wall Street was like other businesses, where 80 percent of the profits were provided by 20 percent of the people, but the 20 percent changed a lot from year to year and market to market. You had to pay everyone well because you never knew what next year would bring, and because there was always someone out there trying to poach your best-trained people, whom you didn't want to lose even if they were not superstars. Consequently, bonuses in general became more automatic and less tied to superior performance, more like entitlements, as compensation became the industry's largest expense, accounting for about 50 percent of net revenues. Warren Buffett, when he was an investor in Salomon Brothers in the late 1980s, once noted that he wasn't sure why anyone wanted to be an investor in a business where management took out half the revenues before the shareholders got anything. But, of course, he recently invested $5 billion in Goldman Sachs, so he must have gotten over the problem.

As firms became part of large, conglomerate financial institutions, the sense of being a part of a tight cohort of similarly acculturated colleagues was lost, and the performance of shares and options in giant multi-line holding companies rarely correlated with an individual's idea of his own performance over time. Nevertheless, the system as a whole worked reasonably well for years in providing rewards for success and penalties for failures, and still works even in difficult markets.

At most firms, much or most of the bonus is paid in the firm's stock, which vests over several years, to reward long-term performance. But the market for talent is competitive, and many firms have been compelled to offer guaranteed or minimum bonuses to recruit the people they wanted, and some star traders have been able to negotiate specific profit-sharing arrangements regardless of what happens to firm-wide earnings. Indeed, most of the Wall Street bonuses paid in 2008 were largely directed to those with contracts providing for guaranteed minimums, to those whose efforts during the year contributed to making things better rather than worse, and to middle- and junior-level employees whom the firms wanted to retain during difficult times. Soon after the DiNapoli bonuses estimate, Bloomberg reported that UBS hired more than two hundred experienced brokers in the United States by offering "super-size" bonuses, so even in tough markets, poaching of valuable employees still occurred.

At the senior-most level in Wall Street, where executives are major shareholders of their firms, all have suffered with the financial crisis. Several present and former CEOs lost hundreds of millions of dollars as their firms disintegrated. The share prices of once-mighty firms Fannie Mae, AIG, Lehman Brothers, Citigroup, and Bank of America all fell to less than the cost of a cup of coffee. Many top Wall Street executives, including seven CEOs in the United States and several more in Europe, were sacked. Not many other industries have such a harsh, up-or-down compensation system that is so closely tied to performance.

The virtues of the Wall Street bonuses notwithstanding, it must be recognized that the system contains some serious flaws. The most important of these is the amount of moral hazard it creates. Great rewards to executives are paid for successful risk taking, but the penalties for unsuccessful risk taking end up being borne mainly by shareholders or taxpayers. One remedy for this is to ensure that top managers be held more closely accountable for the trading results of their subordinates. Another is to apply the full cost of risk to traders' profit-and-loss tabulations, which would correctly reduce the profits of the riskier trades and thus the bonuses paid on them.

The short-term orientation of the compensation system is another flaw. This needs to be fixed by increasing the proportion of bonuses that reflect performance over a longer term, such as a whole market cycle, and to provide for "clawbacks" of bonuses accrued when positions or transactions go awry at a later time. Many firms have already done this.

Those who are still unconvinced that the industry will reform itself, however, may have less to worry about compensation excesses in the future. A recent study by Thomas Philippon (New York University's Leonard Stern School of Business) and Ariell Reshef (University of Virginia) of compensation in the U.S. financial services sector since 1909 demonstrates that financial jobs were relatively skill-intensive, complex, and highly paid until 1930, and became so again only after 1980. Wall Street compensation relative to other industries peaked in 1930, and again between 1995 and 2006. The authors link the high compensation periods to deregulation and high demand for corporate financial services and to increased exposure to credit risk—in short, to periods of high value-added innovation, leverage, bullish markets, and extensive trading and risk-taking. Assuming that these causative factors will be less important now, and the industry is entering a cautious, post-bubble recovery period, Wall Streeters may have to wait for quite a while for relative compensation conditions to get back to the way they were in the good old days of 1930 or 2006.

Wall Street, often associated with financial excesses and flamboyant behavior, periodically needs reminding that a system of free market capitalism operating inside a vibrant, popular democracy can succeed only if the people accept its benefits and are not offended by what they may perceive (rightly or not) as greedy, abusive, or in-your-face conduct on the part of the capitalists. In 2010, we are still less than ten years away from the last time there was public rage against Wall Street, and to the extent that excessive compensation is the problem, the solution is for the industry simply to curtail it. Otherwise, our free-market financial system becomes subject to the risk of being dismantled by voters annoyed by a system they think is unreasonable and offensive.

REBUILDING THE INDUSTRY

On January 1, 2009, Bank of America's acquisition of Merrill Lynch was completed by the issuance of common stock worth $19.4 billion (though valued at $46 billion when the deal was struck), to the great relief of the shareholders of Merrill Lynch and to Ben Bernanke and Hank Paulson. It was, however, a close-run thing. Merrill Lynch was continuing to hemorrhage losses—its fourth-quarter results would show a net loss of $15.3 billion, far above Ken Lewis's worst-case expectations in September 2008, when the deal was agreed upon. At the time, Lewis had said, "We actually thought Merrill Lynch's capital structure was very good and had a lot more of a base of common equity than some others we had seen, so it looked good."[3]

Subsequently, markets worsened considerably, lowering the value of Merrill's legacy positions further still. In October, TARP invested $15 billion in Bank of America and $10 billion in Merrill. November saw the market's low for the year. Nevertheless, Bank of America's shareholders voted approval of the deal on December 5, 2008, and a major push was on to close the deal by the end of the year. Three days later, on December 8, Merrill's board approved the year-end bonuses for employees (based on a nonpublic attachment to the merger agreement that outlined the maximum Merrill could pay), after consulting with Bank of America and, at its request, increasing the percentage paid out in cash to 70 percent (from 60 percent), with the rest to be paid in Bank of America stock after the deal had closed.[4] The bonus package was only 6 percent less than the previous year, despite the firm's poor results, but this was partly because of previous bonus guarantees and other contractual arrangements. Merrill's bonus package was bound to be distasteful to Bank of America employees, whose average compensation in 2008 was less than a third of the average Merrill Lynch employee's.

The following week, Merrill's accountant began to tally up the preliminary fourth-quarter results. According to Thain, the results were reported to Bank of America as soon as they were produced. They showed considerable additional write-downs, particularly of the legacy positions that Merrill had been carrying for at least a year. Bank of America had every incentive at the time to write down everything it could before consolidating Merrill's results and financial position with its own after January 1. Further, since the tax rule change at the time of the Wells Fargo–Wachovia deal, Bank of America may have been able to deduct some of these losses, which would give it a tax incentive for maximizing the write-downs. Bank of America had considerable experience in acquiring troubled businesses, such as Countrywide Financial, which it closed in July 2008, and was very familiar with all the pre-closing accounting and tax issues involved.

Lewis, however, was concerned that the unexpectedly large Merrill losses (which would include $8 billion in proprietary trading losses and $7.3 billion of other items, such as "goodwill impairment" of $2.3 billion and "credit valuation adjustments related to monoline financial guarantor exposures" of $3.2 billion) might backfire on him with shareholders and the government. On December 17, Lewis approached the Treasury and said that he was considering dropping the Merrill deal because of its "monstrous losses." Bernanke and Paulson were horrified: You can't do that, they said. Merrill would become another Lehman and send the markets back into another terrible downward spiral. Paulson was telling Lewis that regardless of his duties to his shareholders, he had a public duty to go through with the Merrill acquisition. Tensions increased, and the Treasury got tougher. The matter was finally resolved when the Treasury offered to extend additional TARP funds and guarantees after the Merrill deal closed. Lewis, perhaps grinning a bit like Br'er Rabbit, must have thought he had struck a good deal; the Treasury funds were cheap capital for Bank of America at the time, and the capital infusion was necessary to offset the Merrill losses. Later that month, Lewis was honored by *American Banker* as "banker of the year."

Ken Lewis was born in Meridian, Mississippi, the son of an army sergeant; his parents divorced when he was twelve. He worked his way through high school and Georgia State University as a business major, and joined North Carolina National Bank upon graduation in 1969. He later picked up an MBA from Stanford and became a protégé of the bank's legendary CEO Hugh McCall, who built NCNB into a national banking franchise through a series of high-profile mergers that included the acquisition of the original Bank of America in 1998 and adopting its more prestigious name. Not long afterward, David Coulter, Bank of America's former CEO and McCall's designated successor, was forced out after a loss associated with the failed hedge fund Long-Term Capital Management. Lewis rose to head various operating divisions and succeeded McCall in 2001. He has continued McCall's strategy of making highly opportunistic (if sometimes overpriced) mergers and integrating them roughly but efficiently into the main body of the bank. Like his mentor, Lewis has carried a chip on his shoulder for years, as if to challenge the notion that you have to be a smooth Easterner with a well-born Ivy League background to rise to the top in American finance.

To colleagues and associates, Lewis was determined, tough—and dangerous if you were in his way. A former banking industry analyst who now runs a hedge fund and a finance blog, Thomas Brown, said that in 2004, after an exodus of top talent, the Bank of America board asked how deep the bank's managerial bench was, and a table was put together showing the names of eighty-five promising executives. Four years later sixty-five of those executives had departed.[5]

On January 1, 2009, the enlarged Bank of America, with approximately $2.5 trillion in assets, became the largest commercial banking business in the United States and the largest wealth management business in the world with approximately twenty thousand financial advisors and more than $2 trillion in client assets.

On January 16, the Treasury announced its promised $20 billion TARP financing to Bank of America, together with a guaranty of up to $118 billion in troubled assets, mostly Merrill Lynch's, for which Bank of America would issue some additional preferred stock to the government. Bank of America also agreed, as Citigroup had done after its second tranche of TARP money, to restrict its common dividend to $0.01 per share per quarter; to comply with "enhanced restrictions on management compensation"; and to "implement a mortgage loan modification program." On the same day, Bank of America reported a fourth-quarter loss of $1.8 billion (not including Merrill Lynch's results), in a year in which its earnings fell to $4 billion from $15 billion.

The Merrill Lynch deal, however, was putting Lewis into an increasingly tight spot. The write-downs, the further government investment, dividend cuts, and other restrictions were not popular with the common stockholders. Bank of America's stock price began to sink in mid-December from $15 per share (it had been $30 in September, when the Merrill deal was announced) to just below $4 per share six weeks later. The bank also announced it was cutting thirty-five thousand jobs and was selling a $2.8 billion stake in China Construction Bank. Many stockholders thought Lewis had been overly aggressive in an extremely adverse market (in addition to Merrill and Countrywide, Bank of America had also acquired LaSalle National Bank from ABN-Amro in October 2007 for $21 billion) and was in well over his head. But Lewis stood firm, defending the Merrill Lynch acquisition: "We just thought it was in the best interests of our company and our stockholders and the country to move forward with the original terms and timing. Renegotiating the deal would have cost more than it would have saved," he said.[6]

On January 22, the *Financial Times* reported the story of Merrill's year-end bonuses and how they had been accelerated to December 28 from early January to enable Merrill to pay out the cash portion itself (while it still was an independent company, just in case Bank of America should decide not to), and the image that spread around was that Merrill was using its last days to pay out excessive bonuses to undeserving employees before Bank of America could do anything about it. After this story appeared, New York State's attorney general, Andrew Cuomo, announced an investigation into the payment of the Merrill Lynch bonuses.

To make it all worse, a second story appeared on CNBC that contained all the details of the $1.2 million cost paid by Merrill Lynch to redecorate John Thain's four-room office suite a year before, making Thain appear to be as thoughtless and greedy as most Americans had come to think that all Wall Street bankers were. Both stories had the appearance of having been leaked.

Also, on January 22, Ken Lewis flew to New York closely tracked by the media for a fifteen-minute meeting with Thain, after which Thain, apparently the last to see it coming, was fired. The next day, Bank of America issued a statement to the *Financial Times* laying full responsibility for the December bonus flap on Thain.[7] Whether this was true or not, Thain ended up as the fall guy for the Merrill Lynch acquisition, and he fell where he stood, in his expensively decorated New York office suite, with a knife in his back. All this did great damage to his thirty-year reputation as a super-competent, super-clean Wall Street Boy Scout. An editorial in the *Financial Times* on January 26 seemed to sum up the instant disapproval that had been dumped on him since the bonus story appeared: "What is it that bankers don't get? Unable to own up to a collective failure, some still display a sense of entitlement that bears no relation to their current status as wards of the state supported by the taxpayer. Step forward John Thain."

Finding someone to blame didn't end Lewis's problems, however, which now included class-action lawsuits that accused him of withholding important information from shareholders before their vote to approve the transaction. The lawsuits claimed that Merrill's losses occurred during November, when the fixed income markets plummeted, not during the week after the shareholders' meetings, as Lewis claimed, when the markets were calm.[8] The lawsuits were accompanied by cries for Lewis to resign, though the Bank of America board was reported as still being very supportive. Many Wall Street veterans, however, familiar with the blood-in-the-water aspects of Lewis's situation, were ready to write him off as dead meat.

At its February 2009 low point of $3.14 per share, Bank of America's stock was well below where it had been when Lewis became CEO eight years before, and there were many questions among investors about how the bank would, or whether it could, recover the considerable lost ground under the current management team. Even assuming the markets recovered, and the bank began to report increasing quarterly earnings, there were doubts about how it would be able to integrate the highly dissimilar businesses of Merrill Lynch and Countrywide Financial into the Southern, conservative, countrified culture of the Charlotte-based bank. In 2002, Lewis had told a group of students at Wharton Business School that the particular culture of Bank of America "would be preserved," even after large and dissimilar acquisitions: "Our culture can't change. It has to [represent] our values. We wouldn't tolerate a taint on our culture, or [any] subculture [of it]."[9]

In March, things started to turn around for Bank of America, as its stock price recovered to the area of $10 per share. Its first-quarter 2009 earnings of $4.25 billion (up from $1.21 billion in 2008) far exceeded analysts' estimates. The results included a $1.9 billion gain from the sale of China Construction Bank, and $20.34 billion of additions to loan loss reserves and charge-offs. According to Lewis, Merrill Lynch and Countrywide were the two "stars" driving profits during the quarter. Nevertheless, at the bank's annual meeting, shareholders voted to split the roles of chairman and chief executive, and Walter E. Massey, a serving director and president emeritus of Morehouse College, was named chairman, with Ken Lewis remaining as president and CEO.

The bank, however, continued to owe more than $45 billion to the Treasury, and therefore in April of 2009 was still sitting in a pretty big hole. That's a lot of money, including dividends on the preferred stock, to repay to the government from future profits or sales of common stock. Then, in May, the government announced the results of its long-awaited "stress tests" applied over the preceding months to the country's largest banks, noting that of the $65 billion of new capital needed by all of the banks combined, Bank of America would be required to raise $34 billion. (Wells Fargo would need $15 billion, Citigroup $5 billion.) This certainly added to Lewis's problems, but he and his team wasted no time in attempting to address the issue. The bank said it would immediately commence to sell certain less important businesses, consider joint ventures, make an offer to preferred stockholders to exchange their shares for common, and sell new common shares to the public. By the end of May, these efforts had raised $26 billion of new common equity, and were expected to raise $10 billion more from asset sales, aiming to meet the $34 billion requirement within just a few months rather than having to request additional TARP funds from the government. A third round of TARP financing would almost certainly force the government to take more drastic action than it had so far, forcing further board and management changes (as was done at AIG), or even taking the bank over altogether, with the idea of salvaging what it could from the various units acquired over the past years. Lewis remained optimistic that he could turn things around and repay the government its TARP money in due course, but until he did, the bank would be a virtual hostage to the markets and the economy.

Citigroup meanwhile had squeaked out a $1.6 billion profit for the first quarter from trading gains and accounting benefits, and it was endeavoring to sell its Japanese businesses and other assets. The bank had also made some board changes but its stock price lingered in the range of

$2 to $3 per share, and at the end of the first quarter it had a market capitalization of only $14.8 billion.

In contrast to its two traditional rivals, JPMorgan Chase was in a much better position. It had exceeded analysts' estimates in the first quarter, earning $2.1 billion, after $5 billion of loan write-offs and additions to reserves. It survived the stress test with flying colors (needing no new capital) and was in a position to repay TARP as soon as the government permitted it to do so. Its investment banking business was doing well and increasing its market share. It had already benefitted from Bear Stearns's prime brokerage and clearing businesses, which absorbed large amounts of incoming asset transfers after the Lehman bankruptcy, and Bear's surviving trading businesses had been tamped down so as to lower or insulate market risk exposures. Jamie Dimon, widely held in high esteem during the difficult markets of 2008, was announcing how active the bank's ongoing lending business was (though net new loans were still down) and how diligently the bank was pursuing mortgage modification and assistance programs to keep mortgage holders from defaulting. It would still have to consolidate WaMu, and was feeling the weight of its own credit card and other consumer financing businesses as these experienced harsh recessionary periods before it could claim to be on safe ground again, but JPMorgan was clearly looking like the market leader among the large bank holding companies. It was not under pressure to change its business model or to break itself up to stay afloat. The WaMu acquisition, and the Bank One acquisition in 2004, were two clear signals that the bank saw its future as being tied mainly to the retail and consumer sectors, as opposed to the wholesale, investment banking sectors, despite its opportunistic acquisition of Bear Stearns.

Meanwhile, Wells Fargo, now America's fourth-largest bank holding company, was busy integrating Wachovia, which closed on December 31, 2008, onto its platform. This involved a further $11.2 billion fourth-quarter loss for Wachovia (which also included a lot of pre-merger write-downs), $37.2 billion in credit write-downs on $93.9 billion in high-risk loans segregated in Wachovia's loan portfolio, and a variety of "de-risking" actions. Wells Fargo also recognized a $10.9 billion tax benefit from the combination, which left it with $1.3 trillion in assets even after absorbing Wachovia's mortgage and loan loss write-offs, which were greater than those of any other bank in the world. Though Wachovia had a sizeable securities brokerage and asset management business, it was not an important player in investment banking—nor by choice had Wells

Fargo been, but in the spring of 2009 John Stumpf, the bank's CEO, began talking about beefing up the securities arm of Wachovia into a contender for market share in the investment banking area.

The world's top ten investment banks, ranked by their midyear 2009 market capitalizations, were led by JPMorgan Chase ($130 billion), Wells Fargo ($110 billion), Bank of America ($101 billion), Goldman Sachs ($73 billion), BNP-Paribas ($68 billion), Credit Suisse ($52 billion), Deutsche Bank ($37 billion), Morgan Stanley ($36 billion), UBS ($35 billion) and Citigroup ($15 billion). The stock prices of all of these banks had recovered significantly from their levels of the beginning of the year, as positive net earnings were reported and the market's fear of a systemic collapse and nationalization by the government faded.

For the new bank holding companies, Goldman Sachs and Morgan Stanley, the future had been especially uncertain at the beginning of January 2009. They suffered from brutal trading conditions in the fourth quarter, a drying-up of their principal fee-based revenue sources, and from a prospect for industry reregulation that could make their long-standing business strategies obsolete. Many analysts predicted that they would be forced to operate with far less leverage, and that would substantially reduce their growth rates and returns, even when their revenue sources returned to normal. Would their investors and/or their regulators now expect them to diversify their businesses and their funding sources by acquiring retail deposit-taking branches? Could they keep the same quality of talent and motivation that had separated them from the other banks with a less risky and less abundant profit stream?

Morgan Stanley and Goldman Sachs both finished 2008 in the black, though with profits well below those of the year before. Both had raised $10 billion in new capital plus $10 billion in TARP funds. At November 30, 2008 (then the fiscal year end for both firms), they had both shown considerable flexibility under stress by rapidly reducing assets and risk exposures. Morgan Stanley posted year-end assets of $658 billion, down from $1.05 trillion in 2007; and Goldman Sachs, $884 billion, down from $1.12 trillion. Morgan Stanley announced a tier-one capital ratio of 17.9 percent, and Goldman, 15.6 percent, both significantly higher than the average for large wholesale banks, which had been increased to approximately 10 during the fourth quarter of 2008 (due to TARP funds) from a previous average of about 8.5.

The two firms had been tooth-and-claw competitors for forty years, with each firm regarding the other as its principal rival. Both firms were devoted to serving all institutional users and suppliers of capital, wherever in the world they should be located. Over the years their businesses became different, however, when the original Morgan Stanley was sold to Dean Witter and joined a large retail brokerage franchise, and when Goldman Sachs developed its proprietary trading and alternative asset management businesses, which became the firm's principal sources of income.

After John Mack's return to Morgan Stanley in 2005, he began to tug at the reins to steer Morgan Stanley into greater proprietary risk exposures, though this proved to be an untimely move in light of the financial crisis that followed. After being reborn as a bank holding company, Morgan Stanley, already possessing a substantial retail base, suggested that it might acquire a bank with a solid deposit-gathering base and expand its business along retail lines, without, of course, diminishing its interest in maintaining a leadership position in wholesale banking.

The January 2009 announcement that Morgan Stanley would contribute its retail brokerage business to a joint venture with Smith Barney seemed to clarify Morgan's strategic direction. The deal, which was accelerated to close in June 2009, seemed to be a promising and timely one for Morgan Stanley, which may have benefitted from the government or the Citigroup board pushing management to downsize the company. For a cash payment of $2.7 billion, Morgan effectively purchased the right to control the new venture, of which the Smith Barney portion was considered the more valuable. The venture would create the world's largest brokerage organization with a sales force a third larger than Merrill Lynch's.

Meanwhile, Merrill Lynch was entering a painful process of being absorbed into a troubled and tightfisted Bank of America, where presumably it would be expected to operate synergistically with the bank's vast retail branch network and conform to its culture, leadership style, and pay scale. Such efforts to integrate retail financial services businesses had a long history—Ross Perot and DuPont Glore Forgan, American Express and Lehman, Sears Roebuck and Dean Witter, Prudential Insurance and Bache, the Equitable and DLJ, among others—with very little evidence of success. An obvious question was whether Bank of America (already occupied with a complex effort to integrate Countrywide Financial) could pull off a successful integration where others had failed to do so. By midyear 2009, John Thain and several other senior Merrill Lynch officers had left, including eighteen important veteran investment bankers out of about three hundred who had come over to Bank of America, leaving an impression that neither high-flying Wall Street deal doers nor the old-time

Mother Merrill crowd felt comfortable or appreciated inside the culture of a distressed Southern retail banking organization with a chip on its shoulder.[10] On the other hand, many Merrill crossovers had no better offers and became resigned to finding a place for themselves in the soon-to-be transformed firm. The expectation, however, was that Bank of America was not in a position to back expansion into the more competitive and risky parts of investment banking and would focus instead on absorbing the safer and steadier retail branches.

If, however, Bank of America's own fortunes do not improve further, it may be forced to conclude that in different hands and in better markets, Merrill Lynch might be worth more to Bank of America shareholders and the government if it were resold or spun off. It is too early to assume that the disappearance of Merrill Lynch as an independent player is a sure thing, but for the time being, it is locked into the Bank of America business, where no doubt it will struggle for a year or more before being tamed or let go. No matter what happens to Merrill in the long run, it is now in for a period of management distraction in which internal battles will equal or outshine external, competitive ones, and rival companies will use the opportunity to chip away at Merrill's market share, which had already begun to decline in 2009.

Morgan Stanley's acquisition of the Smith Barney retail brokerage business was also a considerable threat to Merrill and Bank of America, as it was to UBS, which was still reeling from its experience of the mortgage crisis, a $780 million settlement with the U.S. Department of Justice concerning tax evasions by U.S. clients of the bank, and the surprise appointments in April of Oswald Grübel as CEO and former Swiss finance minister Kaspar Villiger as chairman. Grübel, a no-nonsense former CEO of Credit Suisse, immediately began layoffs of another 7,500 positions and a review of all of the bank's "high-risk" businesses and locations. Later Grübel announced that he had considered selling UBS's Paine Webber business in the United States, but had decided to shake up management instead and perhaps wait for a better time to sell. In general, UBS, which had lost its position as the world's largest private bank to the Bank of America–Merrill Lynch merger and to a continuing outflow of client assets, was struggling hard to remain viable. It would not be an aggressive competitor in any sector of investment banking for the foreseeable future.

Despite its Smith Barney move, Morgan Stanley's position in basic investment banking, i.e., underwriting and corporate finance services—Morgan's legacy business in which it had maintained a leadership position since the firm's beginning in 1933—was still a powerful threat to its competitors. Even in 2008, a miserable year for investment banking, with most of its markets drying up, Morgan Stanley had been lead manager for $938 billion in transactions, ranking fifth in the global industry, just behind Citigroup (which was down from first). Though Morgan Stanley reported a small loss for the first quarter of 2009 and adjusted to the shortfall in revenues by reducing staff, it only did so to the extent of approximately 10 percent, in order to have execution capability on hand when the markets recovered and corporations and others would be able to complete transactions that had been barred by market conditions for nearly two years. With Citigroup and UBS disabled, Merrill distracted, and Lehman and Bear Stearns gone, Morgan Stanley looked forward to picking up market share in investment banking.

So did Goldman Sachs. It finished 2008 with net record revenues in Equities, Asset Management (despite the market's decline, which reduced the value of assets under management), and Securities Services. Investment banking revenues were down by 30 percent for the year, but trading revenues, a principal profit engine for the firm, were down by 70 percent. The trading results included losses of $3.6 billion from markdowns of principal investments. For the first quarter of 2009, however, Goldman Sachs reported a profit of $1.8 billion, double analysts' forecasts, and soon thereafter raised $5 billion of additional capital from a sale of stock. The firm had about $20 billion in bank deposits, which it was considering expanding through an online banking unit that would sell certificates of deposit and other products, but it rejected suggestions that it needed to acquire a retail banking business to lessen its dependence on money markets for funding its activities. David Viniar, CFO, said in early 2009 that the firm was "very cautious" about considering acquisitions because of the long record of unsuccessful deals in the financial sector: "I would not pick up *The Wall Street Journal* every morning looking for the big Goldman Sachs acquisition because I think you will be disappointed. We don't really like or know the retail business and I don't expect that to change too much."[11]

Though there were questions about its future strategy, in early 2009 Goldman Sachs was the acknowledged market leader in investment banking, according to almost any metric. It had come through the financial crisis in reasonably good condition, with two new shareholders, Warren Buffett and TARP, and in early June it, along with JPMorgan and Morgan Stanley and some other banks, was allowed to redeem its preferred shares from TARP.

Lloyd Blankfein, previously Goldman Sachs's president, replaced Hank Paulson as CEO when Paulson went to Washington in May of 2006. He is the son of a postal clerk who grew up in New York City public housing and attended Thomas Jefferson High School, where he was valedictorian of the class of 1971. He went to Harvard College on a scholarship and graduated from Harvard Law School in 1978. Lloyd worked as a corporate tax lawyer for a prominent New York firm, but preferring business to the law, he joined Goldman's commodities trading arm, J. Aron, as a gold bar and coin salesman. He soon found his niche as a trader, and his skills at managing other traders and trading risk led him to the top. In his mid-fifties, he is short, balding, and jovial. He has impressed the Goldman Sachs's old guard as being a deep thinker, an adaptable strategist, and an effective and tireless leader. He also has a good sense of balance. After a series of hectic meetings—weekend after weekend—in September of 2008, he and a colleague were heading for yet another session at the New York Fed when his companion complained of being exhausted from all the work and tension. Blankfein replied that he should keep things in perspective: "Hey, you're about to arrive at the Fed in a Mercedes—you're not getting out of a Higgins boat on Omaha Beach."[12]

In December 2008, at an annual gathering of former partners of the firm, Lloyd reassured the group that though he did not know what lay ahead, he was pretty confident that the firm, with adequate capital and good people, would find a way to adapt to whatever it had to and still perform as a market leader. "We'll think it through, and do what we have to do." Some of us in the audience had heard the same sentiment from Lloyd's predecessors on one or more of the several occasions during the past thirty or forty years when the firm also had to adapt to survive: after the back-office crisis in the late 1960s; after the Penn Central bankruptcy in 1970; the oil shock; when fixed commission rates were abolished in 1975; when the markets were internationalized in the early 1980s; when stock markets crashed in 1987, and again in 1994 and 1998; the repeal of Glass-Steagall; and after the technology bubble burst, the Spitzer lawsuit and Sarbanes-Oxley. Adaptation and change was an ordinary and necessary thing in the business, and those who would be successful had to reinvent themselves periodically. Those who didn't either failed or were taken up into mergers. Goldman Sachs had managed all these adaptations and reinventions well, and in 2009 it was the only major firm existing in the 1960s that was operating today under its own name, never having given up control to others.

After 2008, the firm had to be prepared to face more challenges to the industry. In an op-ed article in the *Financial Times*, Blankfein said that "self-regulation has its limits," and problems in the industry, after the crisis, were such that the banking industry required more effective, global, and coordinated regulation than it had been receiving, and that all financial institutions—banks or otherwise, that were big enough to be "a burden on the system in a crisis" (e.g. investment banks, insurance companies, and hedge funds)—should be subject to some degree of regulation." He offered several specific best-practice ideas for risk management, accounting practices, and executive compensation that Goldman Sachs had already adopted. He may have intended to influence the coming debate on regulatory reform that he expected to occur in the coming months, concluding his article with a plea for governments not to increase regulation to the extent that it "takes risk completely out of the system, which [would] be at the cost of economic growth."

A NEW GOVERNMENT ASSERTS ITSELF

During 2008, as the banks were falling apart, a lot was done to keep them solvent. Some banks raised additional capital on their own, but hundreds turned to TARP for funds until most of its initial funding authority of $350 billion was committed. The problem, as the financial crisis entered its third year, however, was that the recession it had precipitated was threatening to require the banks to write off as much as another $1 trillion or so of assets, according to an IMF projection, and there were other estimates of even greater amounts of losses to come. Several economists were saying that the U.S. banking system was already insolvent, as the falling market prices of their assets had wiped out the banks' remaining capital.

This was the same problem that beset American banks in the 1980s, when the declining market value of Latin American and other loans, less the banks' liabilities, left them without capital. The banking regulators (then led by Paul Volcker, chairman of the Federal Reserve, now returned to government as an advisor to the Obama administration) took over Continental Illinois, the country's seventh-largest bank by assets, because it was unable to roll over maturing certificates of deposit and other liabilities. But there were many other banks, bigger and smaller, that were effectively kept on life support by their regulators until they could absorb the write-offs that had to be taken. The life support provided, however, enabled the banks to write off their bad loans gradually, over about ten years, during which time the regulators kept the banks in a penalty box, allowing very little growth and forcing assets sales and other moves to recover whatever capital they could. Though there was a serious recession in the early 1980s, and another a decade later, national economic growth moved ahead in the 1980s, fueled by financial resources delivered by expanding capital markets that rose to the occasion by inventing new products, such as securitization, junk bonds, and derivatives, to inject capital into the system where it was needed.

In early 2009, significant parts of the banking system again seemed to be hanging by a thread, hoping for economic recovery that would reverse the decline in asset-backed securities and other loans to give some much-sought relief to their capital positions. But many economists believed that the economy would not be able to turn around unless the banking system were there to help it do so, at least while the volume of new financing in capital markets was so far below the levels of previous years. The banking system needed both short- and long-term fixing, and that task fell to the newly inaugurated Obama administration.

The task was surely difficult. It involved trade-offs between public and private interests, between efficiency and expediency, between what was seen to be fair and what was not, and between positions that were theoretically valid but untried, and those that were experimental or simply hoping for the best.

If the banks were insolvent, some said, they should be nationalized, separated into good and bad banks, and refloated as soon as possible.

Nationalization, others said, could involve a fair number of banks, some of which were huge. Such a program would require a massive bailout of risk-taking bank investors with taxpayer money, a terrible and unfair idea that might cost trillions.

Letting them go bankrupt would avoid the bailout problem, but would subject the markets to another round of mayhem far worse than what was experienced after Lehman's failure, causing even more damage to people's savings, investments, and economic expectations.

Nursing the banks along with doses of "regulatory forbearance" (a kind of benign neglect of the rules for banks) would only preserve the banks as zombies while putting off the resolution of the problems until a later day.

Anything done to fix the banks would have to be done in plain sight of everyone involved, under modern accounting rules and with full reporting to shareholders. But whatever was done would be subject to harsh criticism from one side or another. The public at large had shown little support for bailouts of any kind, and anything that favored bank executives (such as paying them bonuses) seemed sure to trigger more outrage and anger.

What most people did agree on (conservatives and liberals alike) after the fourth-quarter GDP was reported to have declined by a stunning 6.3 percent (the steepest decline in twenty-six years), was that the economy appeared to be in freefall, and government would have to step in some way to save the day. And that would mean stepping in big time, as the government had done in the 1930s, but not since. The people also seemed to agree with the new Obama administration that the government would have to provide—all at once—an enormous economic stimulus and recovery plan, mortgage assistance plan, a banking system rescue plan, an industrial policy (for dealing with the failing U.S. automobile industry, another problem that the Bush administration passed along), and major reforms to the global financial services regulatory system. All of these were complex, big-ticket items with huge down-the-road consequences for the American economy, many of which could not then be foreseen.

An $800 billion stimulus package began to be debated soon after the inauguration. The Democrats had a strong majority in the House, and the stimulus bill began there, as it is required to do. The House passed a version a few weeks later without any Republican support. The Republicans were unhappy with the balance between tax cuts and spending programs, favoring more tax cuts, and many also disliked the something-for-everyone spending provisions inserted by the House's democratic leadership. The Senate passed a smaller bill, with less spending, and after working out the differences between the two, a $789 billion compromise bill was passed by Congress on February 13, and quickly signed into law, still with only a handful of Republican votes. The bill passed after a late-night insertion by Senator Christopher Dodd, chairman of the Senate Banking Committee, which greatly restricted the total compensation (including compensation in the form of restricted stock) of the twenty highest-paid persons in any bank receiving capital from the government.

A bank rescue plan came out of the box next. On February 9, 2009, a revised plan for using the remaining (previously approved but still unfunded) $350 billion in TARP funds was announced by Treasury Secretary Timothy Geithner at a press conference at the Treasury. The event had been subject to a major buildup: elements of the new bank plan were leaked, but the plan itself was kept secret. The press conference was delayed a day or two to allow Geithner and other members of the economic team to get the stimulus bill behind them, and then to have everyone focus on the banks.

THE FINANCIAL RECOVERY PLAN

The Geithner financial recovery plan had to pick up where the Paulson plan left off after the first $350 billion in TARP funds had been distributed. In addition to stabilizing the banks, the Paulson plan was to have the benefit of enabling banks to increase lending as an offset to the recession, but this never happened. Net lending of banks decreases when they are deleveraging (which virtually all of them were after being overleveraged), and in recessions (when good creditors don't need to borrow, but weaker ones, of which banks are wary, do). The preferred stock arrangements may have been symbolically important in demonstrating their solvency, but most of the banks utilized various explicit Federal Reserve guarantees of their deposits and other liabilities or used direct access to the discount window to renew their maturing obligations, so the preferred stock infusions (with a few exceptions) may not have been of great importance in ensuring the stability of the banks as a whole.

Several of the banks that had accepted TARP funds, however, saw their stock prices fall sharply, partly because several were continuing to report losses from write-offs, but also because the investment was seen as a signal that the next step might be a harsher form of nationalization (such as at AIG or Fannie Mae) that would kill off any remaining common shareholder value. But even without this fear, common stockholders had to wonder how the banks were going to pay down or refinance such large amounts of preferred stock when losses were still being reported and equity markets were closed to them. For the common stockholder of Citigroup and Bank of America, each with approximately $50 billion in preferred stock owned by TARP, paying preferred dividends averaging about 7 percent that would rise to 9 percent within three years—but no common dividends—the outlook was more than a little bit gloomy.

One problem with the first round of TARP money was that if Treasury priced the preferred stock where the market said it should be priced, then no one would take the money—the cost of capital would be too high to do much good, particularly with attractive debt-subsidization programs available from the Fed.* Paulson initially wanted to get a convoy of large banks and investment banks going with the TARP money—to validate the program with other banks and to show that there was no stigma attached to taking the money—so it had to offer the capital at bargain rates. So the floodgates were opened to smaller banks, which saw the preferred stock as cheap capital and moved to get what they could. As a result, the TARP funds were being distributed across many banks that didn't actually need the money, reducing the availability of funds for those that did and for any effort to support the market for MBSs, the continuing panic which was forcing banks to take even more write-offs. The initial round of TARP funds was also distributed without any strings attached through which the government could exercise control of the banks. Members of Congress, however, seeing the so-called Paulson plan as a bailout, never really liked it and soon began to assert themselves into various aspects of bank governance, especially the compensation and business expenses of banks receiving TARP funds, which became ex-post-facto constraints on bank activities which the banks, of course, disliked and considered intrusive and inappropriate. Then the government changed with the inauguration of Barack Obama, and he appointed Timothy Geithner, a chairman of the Federal Reserve Bank of New York, as Paulson's successor.

Geithner, forty-eight, was a fast-rising career Treasury civil servant before being named as president of the New York Fed in 2003. He had worked for Henry Kissinger for a few years after graduating from Dartmouth, and had served in a number of international positions at the Treasury, including a tour at the IMF. Though a protégé of Bob Rubin and Larry Summers (who was appointed as Obama's chief economic adviser), he probably owed his appointment as Treasury chief to the fact that he had worked on the crisis since its beginning, with Paulson and Bernanke, who also had confidence in him. He knew what had happened before, why things were done they way they were, what worked and what did not, and what the obstacles were in getting things through Congress. Though he had some hard-to-explain personal tax problems that surfaced during his Senate confirmation, his appointment was approved because he was

---

* On February 6, 2009, the Congressional Oversight Panel issued a report claiming that the Treasury "overpaid" for investments in bank-preferred stock and warrants to the extent of $78 billion.

seen to be a necessary and useful player in trying to sort out the mess. When he took over from Paulson, he had too much of the TARP money in mispriced bank preferred stock, where it wasn't doing much good, and not enough left over either to shore up banks that really needed it or to make a difference in the markets for the troubled assets, the original intention of the TARP.

On February 10, 2009, Geithner made his debut as treasury secretary at a press conference, standing before five or six American flags in the Treasury's elegant nineteenth-century "Cash Room." There he announced the new administration's four-part Financial Stability Plan. The first component was to be the beefing up of the largest banks, those that carried systemic risk, after applying a "stress test" to be sure the banks were adequately capitalized to withstand a worsening economy. The government would decide whether they were, and if not, how much additional capital they would need. If necessary, such banks could raise additional capital from the TARP, but only under conditions that would be much tougher than before: the new securities would be acquired at market prices, with tight restrictions on dividend payments, acquisitions, lobbying, "luxury" spending, and executive compensation. These conditions would also, no doubt, necessarily subject the banks to greater operational control by regulators, including possibly the requirement to sell or spin off troubled assets or assets not essential to a "good bank" business. The idea was to force the banks to recognize the stressed value of their assets and to adjust their capital accordingly (even if it meant having the government acquire a controlling interest in some banks) as quickly as possible. Until this was done, the banks could not be returned to normal, good bank status.

The second component was the formation of a "Financial Stability Trust" to acquire, together with the private sector, troubled assets at a discount either directly from banks or from the market. The Treasury would invest $50 billion in seed money for the trust and solicit private capital to invest up to another trillion. Geithner hoped, he said, that such a trust would help to put a floor on the price of asset-backed securities and other assets for which there was then not a ready or liquid market.

The third component was to be an expansion to $1 trillion from $200 billion in funds available to the Term Asset-backed Loan Facility (TALF), which was organized by the Fed in November to acquire commercial mortgage-backed securities and other loans secured by credit card or automobile receivables and student loans.

Finally there was to be a Comprehensive Housing Program, in which the Treasury would invest $50 billion to stem mortgage foreclosures by offering modifications to existing mortgage loans, and would require other banks receiving TARP loans to participate in the plan.

The market was very disappointed with the plan. The Dow Jones index dropped 380 points on the news. *The Wall Street Journal* pronounced it a plan to have a plan; *The Economist*, an opportunity squandered. Few commentators disagreed. The plan lacked details, some said, and would be unworkable. It was naïve to think that private equity money would be attracted to the co-investment proposition unless the assets were priced at significant discounts from market values, prices at which banks would not wish to sell them.

A more positive interpretation of the plan was possible, however, after a careful reading of it. The stress test would be mandatory for those nineteen banks with more than $100 billion in assets. The test was to be "forward looking, accurate and realistic" and be "coordinated among all relevant financial regulators." This statement stopped short of announcing that the test would involve marking all assets to market, but it implied that the regulators would be very tough-minded as to asset prices, and be consistent as to asset prices among banks (including Goldman Sachs and Morgan Stanley, which continued to mark to market religiously after becoming bank holding companies). The stress test would reveal to regulators (and become transparent to the markets) the capital positions of the banks, and those thought to be undercapitalized would be required, no doubt in whatever way most appropriate for individual banks, to obtain additional capital to top up, perhaps by spinning off or selling divisions or other business lines.

If such efforts were not sufficient, the banks could acquire additional capital from TARP II (now called the Capital Assistance Program, or CAP), but this time at prices that would reflect realistic market values. The new preferred stock would be fully convertible into common stock (not accompanied by warrants to acquire stock worth only 15 percent of the value of the preferred shares), and the conversion price would be set at "a modest discount from the prevailing level of the institution's stock price as of February 9, 2009." For example, if Citigroup needed another $20 billion, it would have to issue new preferred stock convertible at, say, $3.75 per share (the closing price on February 9 was $3.95) into 5.3 billion shares, or 49.5 percent of all outstanding shares, which would rise to exceed 80 percent when the warrants associated with the previously issued preferred shares were exercised into common stock. For all practical purposes this would mean the de facto nationalization of the bank even if an amount somewhat less than $20 billion in new equity capital was injected. Conceivably there could be several banks needing to be so nationalized after their stress tests. Conceivably, too, if banks were so nationalized, they also would be subjected to board or management changes to align them with the public interest more closely. In the meantime, the large banks would be kept on a short leash by regulators. They would be kept alive by the Fed's guarantees of their maturing liabilities, but otherwise they would be expected to do whatever the regulators told them to. In order to cool things down, the Treasury would go about its stress tests carefully (and slowly) while it figured out what else might be done to have the troubled banks raise capital on their own.

In order to assist banks in "cleansing" their balance sheets of "legacy" assets, the Financial Stability Plan provided for an imaginative approach to attract private equity investors to "co-invest" with the government through a "Public-Private Investment Fund" that would involve seed capital from TARP "side-by-side, using public financing to leverage private capital on an initial scale up to $500 billion, with the potential to expand up to $1 trillion." Further, the plan "allows private sector buyers to determine the price for current troubled and previously illiquid assets" by bidding for them at auction.

Was this too good to be true? Private investors get to set the price, and the government will provide leverage for them? That could be great for the investors (and would protect the Treasury from criticism for having priced the paper it was buying too generously, always a sticky issue), but, critics asked, why would a distressed bank sell assets at prices low enough as to make private equity investors happy? Wouldn't that just create more losses?

Under the plan, two things made this situation different from what preceded it. First, the government having forced marking to market (or something close to it, to be accurate and realistic) for the stress test, and rebasing capital needs on these prices, the banks should be indifferent as to whether to sell at the prices at which the assets were then carried on their books. And, second, if the banks had taken TARP money, the government is likely to have both the will and the ability to force them to make the sales, in order to clean out the balance sheet.

The government, for example, could simply announce that Citigroup was going to auction off its legacy assets and that those who wanted to buy them through the leveraged Public-Private Investment Fund should submit their bids. Not only could such a program move the bad assets off Citigroup's balance sheet (where it was a part of Citi Holdings), it would also set prices for the assets that could be translated into the secondary markets in general. With up to a trillion dollars of purchasing going on, the markets would firm up around the new prices being set, creating a floor, thereby attracting others seeking to buy these assets at distressed levels in the hope that they would rise to their default-adjusted expected values if held to maturity. The market would then be doing the government's work for it, and rising prices would take pressure off the extremely low asset valuations. There was considerable doubt that it would actually work like this, however, and there were concerns on the part of investors that the government would apply its compensation and other restrictions to them (if they used Treasury funding for the asset purchases) and there were arguments over the terms of the purchase contracts the Treasury was circulating for investors to accept. By early July (six months after it was announced) very little had happened and this initiative appeared to have gone cold, though the Treasury was still assembling its group of lead investors and promised activity when it was complete.

Geithner's plan to extend the TALF initiative to a trillion dollars also seemed a step in the right direction, but it too was very slow going, for the same reasons. Between the two trillion-dollar programs, the Treasury prospectively would add a great deal of support to the asset-backed securities markets that had been completely dysfunctional since the collapse of the two Bear Stearns subprime hedge funds in 2007. By early 2009, capital markets otherwise were beginning to return to normal, with nonfinancial new issues of bonds, commercial paper, and other instruments recovering both the volume and rate levels of mid-2008. If the Treasury's program for troubled assets started to work, then with their securitization functions restored, the capital markets could return to their normal functions, infusing funds into the economy as needed, helping to end the recession. The banks, on the other hand, clearly would take longer to return to normal lending activity.

But the clumsy introduction of the Financial Stability Plan, its need to be decoded and read between the lines, and the slow speed of its adoption meant that the market did not have confidence that the plan would amount to much in the near term. If it was so urgent, many wondered, why such a long delay before things started to happen? Most assumed the answer was because the details of the plans had not been worked out yet, and until they were, no one could take them seriously.

It would take some time for all this to clear up, and Geithner learned that he should not have assumed at the time when his plan was announced that the market would give him the benefit of the doubt. Indeed, the market had learned the hard way that Treasury plans were often not what they were presented to be. About a month later, Geithner made a second, amplifying announcement, filling in much of the details of how private investment companies could borrow low-cost funds from the government to purchase troubled assets, and the Dow Jones rose 489 points as a result. This time there were some who thought it just might work.

Meanwhile, the stress tests were to be conducted over the next several months. This part of the Financial Stability Plan worked well. No banks experienced the sorts of runs that bedeviled them in the fourth quarter, most returned to profitability (partly as a result of using the government guaranty of their debt to obtain very low-cost funding), and thanks to rising bank stock prices several were able to raise new capital in the markets. When the results of the stress tests were announced in early May, most of the banks were deemed to need no new (or only a little) additional capital, with only Bank of America, Wells Fargo, General Motors Acceptance Corp. (another new bank holding company), and Citigroup required to raise $65 billion among them. The following month, ten of the original TARP banks were allowed to redeem their preferred stock from the TARP for approximately $60 billion.

A SYSTEMIC REGULATOR

In late March of 2008, when the deficiencies of the financial regulatory system had become apparent, Treasury Secretary Paulson stepped into the breach to propose an entirely new structure. The old system, he said, was broken, and had to be adjusted to meet different needs. He proposed a new system (he called it a "blueprint") to replace the present one, in which there are several different, poorly coordinated regulators, each addressing different parts of the financial marketplace, as if it were a silo unto itself, with none having oversight or authority over all. The new plan would create three new regulators instead: a "market stability regulator," who would extend some of the powers of the Federal Reserve to examine and guide any institution (bank or nonbank) that might pose a risk to stability in financial markets; a "prudential financial regulator," who would consolidate regulation of all types of deposit gathering institutions (to make sure they were safe and sound and behaved prudently); and a "business conduct regulator," to provide for consumer protection across a wide range of financial products, thereby extending the role of the SEC and perhaps combining it with other agencies.

Paulson accompanied his recommendations with an appeal to Congress, which would have to approve his plan, to avoid creating layers of new or redundant regulation, but instead to focus on redistributing the regulation we already have in a more efficient way. He also wanted to minimize taxpayer liabilities in future rescues, and suggested in a later speech that there was a need for a new mechanism for the orderly disposal of any seized assets. In any event, he added somewhat despondently, Congress was not likely to take up this issue during the last year of President Bush's term, so he was throwing it out only for long-term consideration. Thus the proposal, like the president himself, became a "lame duck" soon after it was put forth.

A year later, Secretary Geithner announced his plans for systemic risk regulation. There were four intertwined issues: (1) The regulation had to apply to any financial enterprise (including nonbanks) capable of imposing systemic risk (e.g., GE Capital, a captive finance subsidiary of an industrial corporation); (2) this designation had to capture not only the very large, complex institutions at the center of the markets, but also those thought to be risk transmitters through their "interconnectedness" with important market players; (3) these systemic risk institutions would have to be subjected to tighter regulatory restrictions and controls than those not carrying systemic risk; and (4) the new regulatory regime would have to apply globally, not just nationally.

Like Geithner's other announcements, this one, which also covered a lot of ground, was nonetheless vague as to certain details. Presumably, he was leaving some options open, and would have to negotiate his ideas further with Congress and representatives and lobbyists of the financial services community. But he did insist on a single, independent regulator (he had the Fed in mind) to have responsibility for "systematically important firms and the critical payment and settlement systems," and for higher capital and risk management standards for these firms. He also asked for the registration of moderate-size hedge funds, comprehensive oversight for the OTC derivatives market, and for improvements in the regulation of money market mutual funds.

These March 2009 proposals resulted in a quiet sort of approval—a lot of heads nodding because the expected, obvious issues had been addressed—but most observers knew the devil would be in the details and wanted to see what these would be. In June, Geithner released further details of his regulatory plan, reflecting a great deal of input from other parts of government and interested parties since the first announcement. These included the creation of a new committee of regulators to retain oversight of the financial regulatory system (that would dilute the concentration of power into the hands of the Fed), provision for "robust, accountable regulation" for systemic risk institutions (now called "Tier 1 Financial Holding Companies"), higher standards for all financial firms (involving capital requirements, management, compensation, and accounting), increased transparency and consumer protection, and structural changes in who regulates what (seven agencies or other entities would replace six existing bodies, with two being combined into others). There was a lot in the plan, and a lot about it that was predicted to generate heated debate and compromise. President Obama said he hoped the plan would be ready for congressional debate by the end of 2009.

In the fall of 2008, two banking scholar colleagues and I wrote a paper for a volume of NYU Stern policy recommendations aimed at the new administration called *Restoring Financial Stability*. Titled "Enhanced Regulation for Large, Complex Financial Institutions," it addressed the systemic issues that later surfaced in Geithner's proposals.[13] We wrote then that a new system should single out systemic risk carriers (the large, complex financial institutions) and subject them to enhanced regulation by a stand-alone, specialized regulator with adequate powers to control the powerful, politically active institutions in question, together with a mandate to expand the existing Basel Accord global framework so as to absorb these new regulatory elements. The systemic regulator, using information collected in this role, would be better able to price accurately the government guarantee that inevitably underpins the systemic risk carriers. This can enable setting a fair baseline insurance cost (similar to deposit insurance premia now paid by banks) linked to the asset size and institution-specific risk attributes of individual large firms.

Most important, however, is that the new regulator have the statutory power and the duty to ensure that those carrying systemic risk consistently operated with priority attention to the institution's safety and soundness, even if this could be achieved only at the cost of reduced growth and profitability. The large, systemic banks, in other words, would have to be turned back into, and maintained as, responsible public utilities (that which Walter Wriston fought so hard against), or they would maneuver around or over the restrictions, or the regulator, and return the systemic risk situation to what it was before the mortgage bubble. It must be tough, as the Fed was in the Volcker days, and stay tough, or it would represent little, if any, improvement over the present system.

THE UNCERTAIN FUTURE

Wall Street has certainly traveled a long distance in the forty-four years since Sidney Weinberg offered me a job at Goldman Sachs. Very little of this journey could have been foreseen at its beginning. Driven uncontrollably by forces of institutionalization, technology, deregulation, and ultimately globalization, Wall Street has little resemblance to the small, fragmented community of broker-dealers clustered in downtown Manhattan that it was for the first 150 years of its existence. It has evolved instead into a vast, high-pressure global financial marketplace, dominated by a handful of very competitive large, complex financial institutions, only two of which, Goldman Sachs and Morgan Stanley, are independent survivors of the transition from the old Wall Street.

Throughout this period many paper fortunes have been made and lost. Many firms, too, have come and gone. Mergers have been made and dissolved, people have moved from firm to firm, cross-pollinating. Some very large firms with trillion-dollar balance sheets have emerged even while some of the best and brightest individuals in the industry have moved to smaller, "boutique" operations where they have been able to offer "old-fashioned client service," or to run hedge funds or private equity investing shops. The global capital markets industry that has evolved from such simple beginnings—even now involving more than $125 trillion of market value of securities around the world—has never been more fluid and changeable.

One lesson learned over the past forty-four years is that to endure, Wall Street has to continuously change.

And it is about to do so again.

The largest, most complex financial institutions are now under threat from two directions. Regulators want to curtail their risk taking, to keep them from again damaging the world's delicate economic and financial system, and are proposing tighter restrictions on them that could degrade their profitability and competitiveness. The government may or may not fully succeed in getting what it wants in the legislative arena, but even if it doesn't, it still possesses substantial regulatory powers that it could use to force banks and bank holding companies to limit the risks they take. At least as long as the memory of the current crisis lingers, the regulators will still be able to control the whip hand, and the industry will have to adapt to more restrictions on its activities.

The institutions also have to reestablish themselves with their investors, the long-term patient capital that all large, established firms require to be well represented in their shareholder bases. A large part of the institutional capital supporting large banking firms had left by early 2009, after the incredible price volatility and trading volumes of the fall of 2008, turning their positions over to hedge funds and other speculative traders with very short-term investment horizons. Until this situation is reversed, it is difficult to see how the large banks will be able to see their stock prices return to the two-to-three-times–book-value level some of them enjoyed a few years ago. For such levels to be sustained there has to be less likelihood of sudden, large trading losses or similar surprises. By reducing the risk of the business, and the extreme competitiveness in the industry that risk taking can permit, banks can revert to enjoying large market shares and reasonable margins and efficiencies without exposing their investors to being ruined by a sudden market reversal or mishap. There is value in being a little more boring and predictable.

After a decade of experience, many investors have now understood that the large, multi-platform, trading-and-banking entity, such as Citigroup, has been proved to be unworkable, too prone to loss of management control or recklessness. Regulators want to tame these beasts to have them revert to being the kind of banks they used to be, more stable, solid, and prudent, but of course they also run the risk of their becoming too stolid, unimaginative, risk-averse, and expensive. For the moment, anyway, the regulators seemed to be prepared to take this risk, and the recovery of most bank share prices in 2009 suggests that investors agree with the regulators.

This being the case, banks ought to recognize the change and go with the flow: simplify their businesses and, as in the 1990s, get back to the basics. This will be the case especially for those banks that have taken more TARP funds than they can easily redeem within a few years. These banks need to free themselves from TARP, and that, of course, means shedding some of their other businesses and assets so as to be able to raise capital and recover good bank status as soon as possible. But even then, those remaining as large, systemic risk carriers, even after having escaped TARP, will have to face the fact that their regulatory burden is going to be heavier and their actions more constrained than those of their market competitors that are not systemically important. Even if they could keep their proprietary trading, hedge funds, or private equity businesses after TARP, they may not want to. Those businesses may not thrive under heavy-handed systemic risk regulation, and therefore the banks might be better off selling them or spinning them off to their shareholders.

Indeed, the industry may be driven into an era of downsizing, the first in its history. Generally, downsizing is not seen as a viable pathway for growth and prosperity, but there may be good reasons to consider it strategic repositioning instead.

Most large, complex financial institutions will benefit from a period of de-conglomerating, and their shareholders' will, too. Conglomerates trade at a premium over their breakup value only while investors are admiring their power and prowess, usually only a relatively brief period early in their history. Mostly, they trade at discounts, sometimes ones large enough to invite breakups orchestrated by their own boards of directors or by outsiders. Many of the largest American and European banks have traded at discounts from their breakup values for several years.

Commercial banks have never found it easy to be successful in investment banking, so, under pressure and with a clear-eyed look at reality, some of them might decide to sell or spin off their investment banking units. This could mean that whole investment banking businesses could be returned to the market as new forms of Salomon Brothers, Merrill Lynch, Paine Webber, or Prudential Securities (perhaps even a Lehman Brothers in a third incarnation). These reborn investment banks would have an incentive to keep themselves small enough so as not to be classified as systemic risk institutions, and thus escape enhanced regulatory constraints. The commercial banks could devote themselves instead to serving the vast nationwide marketplace for consumer financial services and for services to those midsize businesses lacking their own access to capital markets. Wells Fargo, never tempted by investment banking until recent events, developed its retail banking franchise to make it far more valuable for every dollar of income than Citigroup, JPMorgan Chase, or Bank of America. Wouldn't their shareholders rather own a stock that traded at twelve to fifteen times earnings (typical of some successful regional banks) instead of one that aspired to leadership in investment banking but, even then, traded at only eight to ten times earnings?

For Goldman Sachs and Morgan Stanley, changes to be made may be less obvious, but as systemically important bank holding companies they both may need to move some activities outside the confines of the regulator's tent. Goldman's large proprietary trading business may thrive better outside the enhanced regulatory structure; so might its hedge fund and private equity activities, which altogether are the size of a Blackstone Group. In its heyday, Blackstone traded at ten times book value, as compared to Goldman Sachs's three to four times in its best years. Goldman Sachs's shareholders might be better off with those businesses, and some of its riskier proprietary trading activities, being owned separately from the investment bank. The remainder, Goldman Sachs's fine wholesale and institutional business could be reoffered to investors as a much more predictable, less risky, global, market-dominating banking house with great power, influence, and reach, similar to what the original J. Pierpont Morgan was in the late nineteenth century. Such a business ought to command a higher price-earnings ratio than 8 or 9, especially if accompanied by a healthy dividend.

Morgan Stanley has committed itself to becoming a large Merrill Lynch remake. But it, too, has a very strong wholesale and institutional business, like Goldman Sachs's, which may seem to it to be better off separated from a giant retail brokerage business, especially if in doing so, the two parts could each be declassified as large, complex financial institutions, thereby escaping the enhanced regulation altogether.

It will take time, of course, for all this to sort itself out. But wouldn't it be ironic if the Wall Street of the future evolved into a small group of powerful, but restrained, money-center banks surrounded by a whole host of smaller, risk-seeking specialized financial firms stuffed with New Men who were constantly pushing, innovating, and challenging each other for market share and profits?

If so, Wall Street will have reinvented itself back into what it was fifty years ago.

EPILOGUE

BY THE END OF THE SUMMER OF 2009, nearly a year after the bankruptcy of Lehman Brothers, one of the greatest financial hurricanes in modern history had passed, leaving a lot of damage to Wall Street in its wake. There had been recriminations and efforts to embarrass not only all the bankers involved but also the officials who had to deal with the mess as it cascaded down on them. Tim Geithner, Ben Bernanke, and even the once revered Alan Greenspan, were subjected to rude and rough treatment by members of Congress. Hank Paulson, who had retired to Johns Hopkins School of Advanced International Studies, was summoned to testify before the House Committee on Oversight and Government Reform in mid-July and boldly and vigorously defended the high level of government intervention that he had initiated on the grounds that it all would have been very much worse if he and the others in government at the time had not acted as they did.[1]

But meanwhile, the economy, which had been plunged into a steep recession as a result of the financial crisis, was starting to come around, and financial markets, though still suffering in some ways, had more or less returned to normal. Large banks, buoyed by the many government market interventions and guarantees, reported substantially increased profits for the second quarter, and several had redeemed their preferred shares from the TARP, though the FDIC had had to take over more than eighty smaller banks since the first of the year, far more than during the year before. Mortgage foreclosures were still taking place, unemployment was nearing 10 percent, and bank credit continued to be very tight, but there were signs that the worst was over and the economy was recovering. Prices of high-grade CMOs had increased about 50 percent from their lows (lower-grade CMOs, however, were only up about 10 percent) as markets acted on their own to close the valuation gaps that had opened over the past year. The government's PPIP and TALF investment programs to support MBSs—after considerable delays and some downsizing—had still not yet kicked in, so the market was acting on its own. Stock prices had risen about 50 percent from their March lows and the VIX volatility index was back down to around 25. The stock prices of most major banks had more than doubled with some rising three to fourfold.

The stocks of Goldman Sachs, JPMorgan, and Morgan Stanley were trading again above book value (Goldman, after reporting record second-quarter results, was trading at 1.5 times book in early August, higher than the others), but Bank of America and Citigroup, which had not repaid TARP and were still subject to extensive micro-management by their regulators, were trading well below book value. Citi had completed its previously announced, crammed-down preferred-for-common-exchange offer that increased its tangible book value per common share, but it resulted in the government exchanging some of its preferred for a 34 percent interest in the company's common stock. Both Citi and Bank of America had made several new board appointments and management changes at the government's request. In early August, Bank of America agreed to a $33 million settlement with the SEC over its alleged failure to properly disclose its Merrill Lynch bonus arrangements, and announced a succession plan to select a new leader to replace Ken Lewis, sixty-two, over the next few years, and the appointment of Citigroup's former asset management chief, Sallie Krawcheck, to head its Global Wealth Management division.

These two banks, and some other Wall Street firms, had been greatly weakened by the events of the past year, and this soon triggered a global battle within the industry to pry market share loose from them. Some of the competition was from the market leaders, but also joining the fray were smaller investment banks and boutique firms and some of the private equity shops and hedge funds that had survived the past year. Vigorous efforts were made to recruit the best producers and to steal what clients they could. Wall Street believed that a wave of new business was around the corner, when long-postponed debt, equity, and merger deals started up again. Headhunters were having a field day. Bonuses were offered, positioning risks were increased, and intra-industry competition revved up again. By late June there were some shifts in aggregate market shares for the origination of corporate finance transactions (the combination of syndicated bank loans, global debt and equity issues, and merger and acquisition advisory assignments): moving up significantly were Morgan Stanley, Barclays, and HSBC; moving down significantly were Bank of America and UBS, with JPMorgan (which moved into first place in 2008), Citigroup (which dropped from first to fourth in 2008), Goldman Sachs, Deutsche Bank, and Credit Suisse staying about where they were. However, for 2009, the combined market share of the top five firms increased to 56 percent from 50 percent, and for the top ten to 87 percent, as the crisis shifted business to those more likely to survive.

More shifts in market share can be expected, especially if some of the leaders are prevented from returning to fully competitive engagement in the markets because of their considerable government ownership. Bank of America's Merrill Lynch affiliate is likely to be hobbled by the normal problems of integrating a complex merger, but also by the government's aversion to risk. UBS, too, was operating more cautiously, though the government had sold its 9 percent interest in the bank in August, as management, wanting no unpleasant surprises from its investment banking unit, focused on shoring up its ailing asset management business. Indeed, the prospect of moving up in the league tables to replace those departed from them or otherwise in trouble was attractive to many players outside the top ten. Barclays, after buying the North American businesses of Lehman, announced a major further commitment to the capital markets business. Nomura Securities of Japan, by buying Lehman's European and Asian businesses, did the same. Wells Fargo, having acquired the large broker-dealer business that is part of Wachovia, told the press that it saw great opportunities in investment banking. The effect of all this scrambling about for market share was to put pressure on both attackers and defenders to pay their people well enough to keep them, and to be aggressive enough in searching for mandates to take on at least some of the clients' risks. This meant, of course, that even before the recession was over and its bank-related problems put to rest, the industry had started ginning up again for the next round of competition. Most believed they had little choice in the matter, and that they could not afford to fall behind at a time like this.

But, after all the taxpayer financed intervention to save the financial system, the government (which now included any part of the government with an interest in banks) and the media (with its many, many bloggers and commentators), expected the banks to be contrite, apologetic, and subdued. They were surprised and much annoyed to discover that the banks were not, and turned nasty.[2] They were upset that the banks appeared to resist the government's efforts to increase bank lending (to weaker credits in a recession), were slow to cooperate in modifying (i.e., forgiving) home-owners' mortgages, and continued to expose themselves to substantial trading risks and to paying large bonuses to traders, regardless of the banks' poor results during the prior year. The banks (and other outfits like AIG and FNMA) claimed that they were only trying to avoid further write-downs on loan losses and to preserve the value of their trading inventories and businesses franchises, and to do that you had to take market risks and pay market rates. Besides, they noted, they had fiduciary duties to their investors not to lose money deliberately to support someone else's idea of the public interest.

The banks' case was not helped by the publication of a report by New York Attorney General Andrew Cuomo in July that revealed that nine of the largest banks receiving TARP funds in 2008, which together lost $81 billion during the year, nonetheless had paid out more than $32 billion in bonuses to 4,800 employees. JPMorgan, according to the report, paid bonuses of over a million dollars to more than 1,100 people; even Citigroup, which had lost the most money and was now in the arms of the government, had a total bonus pool of $5.3 billion in 2008, with million-dollar payments going to 738 employees.

It wasn't clear why Mr. Cuomo was investigating these bonuses (did he think they were criminal?), but his report created quite a stir. A day or two later the House of Representatives passed a bill introduced by Barney Frank, chairman of the House Financial Services Committee, that would require regulators of all financial service companies with assets of more than $1 billion (not just those with TARP money or those thought to be potentially too big to fail) to write rules that would prohibit compensation systems that provided "perverse incentives" for taking "imprudent" risks. The House had passed a bill earlier in the year that placed severe restrictions on compensation for employees of firms receiving government assistance, but it was not taken up by the Senate. In June, the Treasury suspended the TARP's compensation restrictions in favor of a new effort that empowered Kenneth Feinberg, who had served as special master for the compensation claims of 9/11 victims, to serve in a similar role to assure that compensation programs for employees of banks in which the TARP was invested were fair and appropriate. But this wasn't enough for Chairman Frank, who said of the bill passed in July, "this is the first step towards comprehensive financial regulatory reform." Frank, a smart and cagey politician with no sympathy for the point of view of the banks, would be a key player in all the other steps that the Congress would take to achieve the comprehensive reforms he referred to.

There was little dispute that the compensation incentives contributed to banks taking on excessive risk during the mortgage crisis—indeed Paul Volcker and the Group of Thirty had said so earlier—but few thought it was the principal cause of the risk-taking. Nevertheless, the size of the bonuses seemed way out of place to most Americans, especially in view of the fact that taxpayers had to bail out the banks to prevent the entire global economic system from going under, even while executives were being paid millions. Barney Frank said "their mistakes got us into trouble— for them to be paying themselves this kind of money amounts to a moral deficiency." Larry Summers told *The New York Times* that "those in the financial system must consider carefully their obligations to their fellow citizens," something banks, like other capitalists, had never been much in the habit of doing. In August, French President Nicolas Sarkozy proposed that his government would no longer do business with banks that did not subscribe to a set of compensation guidelines it would prepare, and urged other EU countries to follow suit, which the leaders of Germany and the UK said they would do. The bonus rage was still on and was likely to affect the rest of the regulatory reform efforts that were slowly making their way through the legislative process.

The Geithner reform package seemed to have been accepted as a workable template for the bill that many different groups had an interest in. The key provision was the effort to control systemic risk, though other parts of the package were seen to be important, they were not as important as this part. Ben Bernanke, making an unprecedented appearance at a town meeting TV show in July, announced that too big to fail had to be done away with. This was to be accomplished in three ways: by indentifying those large banks and nonbanks that were or could be carriers of systemic risk, to find ways to closely monitor and restrict this risk from becoming excessive, and to empower regulators to seize (as bank regulators already have the power to do) any such nonbank risk carrier (e.g., a Lehman Brothers or AIG) if necessary to prevent it spreading risk throughout the system. In late August, just prior to a G20 meeting, Tim Geithner wrote an op-ed piece for *The Financial Times* in which he said he and his colleagues were considering imposing higher capital cushions for all banks, and higher ones yet for Tier-1 banks, together with new standards to limit leverage and maintain liquidity, which he hoped the other countries would adopt.

In general there was plenty of agreement that these or similar steps were the right ones. But there was a lot of disagreement over how to put them into effect. The disagreement began with who was to do all this: the administration wanted the Fed to be the systemic risk regulator in chief. This was because the Fed already understood the issues better than any other regulator, it had the staff and know-how to handle the program, and in any event it would be bound by the oversight of a committee of high-level government officials to be sure it acted properly. In Geithner's mind, the integrity of the whole reform effort depended on this point: the Fed must be in charge, not some new group cobbled together from all over the place or a committee of some kind. Those who objected to the Fed having such powers, including an Investors Working Group chaired by former SEC chairmen Arthur Levitt and Bill Donaldson, did so on the grounds that the Fed had failed to act to prevent the mortgage bubble from forming, even well after others had seen it happening, and that it had an inherent conflict of interest between managing monetary policy and banking risks, in which stimulating the former tended to stimulate the latter. There were others, especially congressmen from the Middle American states, who deeply mistrusted the Fed,[3] thinking it favored money center banks, and feared giving so much power to an organization that was independent of both the Congress and the administration. These people feared the Fed was an elite, nonpolitical (therefore not responsive to public opinion) institution, and wanted to control it. Accordingly, there were battles to be expected over who the systemic regulator would be, and if not the Fed, then who? And would this body be competent and free of the profound political interference that invests most government agencies (including the federal national mortgage finance entities that stumbled into ruin without their regulators being able to do much about it)?

It will come down to whether the new systemic risk regulator proves to be up to the hands-on oversight of the banks' risks, risk management capability, and corporate governance standards that the legislation assumes. Will the regulator have the courage and the ability to threaten to shut a major bank like Citigroup (with lots of political friends and lobbyists) in the prime of an economic boom because its risk management practices are thought to be shoddy, out of date, or overridden by orders from the CEO to "keep dancing while the music is playing"? Is it an illusion to think all this can happen no matter who the systemic regulator is? It may be. The Sarbanes-Oxley Act of 2002 was featured as the most important corporate regulatory event since the 1930s; it was to end the accounting and boardroom lapses that enabled Enron and other scandals. Within just five years, however, it seems that Sarbanes-Oxley did nothing to prevent the next round of corporate excesses. Where were the boards of directors of Citigroup, Merrill Lynch, Bear Stearns, or Lehman Brothers when their risk management and control systems were disintegrating? Where were they when the excessive compensation plans were approved? Where was the Accounting Oversight Board when some of the banks resorted to Enron-like off-balance-sheet reporting of their Special Investment Vehicles? Where were they when the Fair Value Accounting rules were being resisted, then modified after adoption under heavy pressure from the banks and their allies?

The dilemma for policy-makers today is the same as it was in the 1930s: they must face the essential trade-off between economic growth and stability, between keeping the cost of capital low and allowing too much risk into the system. This is a difficult balance to strike—and maybe it is one that is beyond the capabilities of politically influenced regulators to maintain. In the 1930s, the solution was to use a meat axe to separate banking and investment banking, and although some have proposed that Glass-Steagall be reinstated as a crude but effective remedy to the current problems of systemic risk, the world of finance has changed too much since the 1930s to make that a practicable alternative.

For the past thirty years the United States has favored economic policies that have embraced open markets, deregulation, and globalization. These policies have widely been judged to have been effective in increasing competition, innovation, and risk-taking, all of which were thought to be uniquely American approaches for encouraging national economic growth. The policies—as policies—have been successful and have encouraged most of the rest of the world to adopt them, in one form or another, which has led to a world that is now more economically integrated than at any other time in its history. These policies have encouraged economic growth in other parts of the world, have allowed for free financial flows that reward effective economic organizations and regimes, and have assisted in the formation of an emerging global consensus on the rights of private property and its regulation. Altogether, these represent enormous steps in global economics that have smoothed the way for the emergence of democracies and unprecedented political cooperation. All this is wonderful, but these policies have also contributed to a loss of control over the enormous, market-based, integrated global financial environment that replaced the gold-backed system of protected national finance that ended with the collapse of the Bretton Woods Agreement in 1971. Markets overreact periodically, and cause problems, but as the size and mobility of the global pool of financial resources has increased, it may have evolved into a mechanism that can periodically present real dangers to the world economy. After all, it has enabled and then ignited two world-shaking, hundred-year bubbles in the last ten years. There is now wide international agreement that something has to be changed to prevent such a large danger from continuing to threaten us. Two generations of liberal economic policies applied across the globe has produced a wolf among the sheep, and it must be tamed.

But reinstating Glass-Steagall is not the way to do it. Banks today would find it very difficult to separate lending from underwriting: the markets have fused these two functions, which in themselves do not necessarily create much in the way of systemic risk. American banks would find themselves to be at a great disadvantage in global marketplaces if they were forced to return to the Glass-Steagall restrictions while banks in Europe and Asia were not: if they were, a great and valuable leadership role in finance now enjoyed by American banks would probably be lost.

It may be instead that separating banking from proprietary trading and investing (where the most of leveraged risks at Citigroup, Merrill Lynch, UBS, and Lehman Brothers were located) would be a better answer. Banks could remain as large, regulated, oligopolistic service providers, lenders and managers of other peoples' assets, but not as large proprietary risk takers. The proprietary businesses could be spun off into units that would face serious disincentives in becoming too big to fail. And surely it would be easier for our poor, underpaid, underfunded, and overworked regulators to control what cannot be done than to attempt to regulate all the high-pressured nuances of what can be.

But one thing we do know, no matter what regulatory changes are forced upon it, the global capital markets industry—that we now know as Wall Street—will adapt and continue. It may not end up in the form that we now know it, but the demand for the functions and services of the global capital markets industry will certainly continue, and you can be sure that the smart folks of Wall Street will figure out a way to apply their skills and risk-taking talents to it.

NOTES

1: Armageddon

1. Henny Sender, Francesco Guerrara, Peter Larsen, and Gary Silverman, "Brinksmanship Was Not Enough to Save Lehman," *Financial Times*, Dec. 16, 2008.

2. Yalman Onaran and John Helyar, "Fuld Sought Buffett Offer He Refused as Lehman Sank," Bloomberg.com, Nov. 10, 2008.

3. Susanne Craig, Jeffrey McCracken, Aaron Lucchetti, and Kate Kelly, "The Weekend That Wall Street Died," *Wall Street Journal*, Dec. 29, 2008.

4. Onaran and Helyar, "Fuld Sought Buffett."

5. Susanne Craig, "Lehman Struggles to Shore Up Confidence," *Wall Street Journal*, Sept. 11, 2008.

6. Carrick Mollenkamp, Susanne Craig, Jeffrey McCracken, and Jon Hilsenrath, "The Two Faces of Lehman's Fall," *Wall Street Journal*, Oct. 6, 2008.

7. Ibid.

8. Craig, McCracken, Lucchetti, and Kelly, "Weekend That Wall Street Died."

9. Ibid.

10. Onaran and Helyar, "Fuld Sought Buffett."

11. Ibid.

12. John Cassidy, "Anatomy of a Meltdown," *The New Yorker*, Dec. 1, 2008.

13. U.S. Treasury press release, Sept. 7, 2009.

14. Aline van Duyn, Deborah Brewster, and Gillian Tett, "The Lehman Legacy" (quoting Neil McLeish of Morgan Stanley), *Financial Times*, Oct. 13, 2008.

15. Ibid.

16. Jeffrey McCracken, "Lehman's Chaotic Bankruptcy Filing Destroyed Billions in Value," *Wall Street Journal*, Dec. 29, 2008.

17. Jeff Poor, "Knock Out: CNBC Confirms Lehman CEO Punched at Gym," *Business and Media Institute*, Oct. 6, 2008.

18. Lorraine Woellert and Yalman Onaran, "Fuld Blames Lehman's Fall on Rumors, 'Storm of Fear,'" Bloomberg.com, Oct. 6, 2008.

19. Matthew Karnitschnig, Deborah Solomon, and Liam Pleven, "US to Take Over AIG in $85 Billion Bailout," *Wall Street Journal*, Sept. 17, 2008.

20. Michael Lewis, "The Man Who Crashed the World," *Vanity Fair*, August 2009.

21. Craig Torres and Hugh Son, "AIG Gets Up to $85 Billion Fed Loan," Bloomberg .com, Sept. 16, 2008.

22. "The End of Wall Street," *Wall Street Journal*, Sept. 23, 2008.

23. Robin Sidel, et al., "WaMu Is Seized, Sold Off to J.P. Morgan," *Wall Street Journal*, Sept. 26, 2008.

24. Jesse Drucker, "Obscure Tax Breaks Increase Cost of Financial Rescue," *Wall Street Journal*, Oct. 18, 2008.

25. John Gapper, "Hank Paulson's Strong-arm Tactics with Wall Street," http://blogs.ft .com/gapperblog/, May 18, 2009.

26. Mark Pittman and Bob Ivry, "US Pledges $7.7 Trillion to Ease Frozen Credit," Bloomberg.com, Nov. 24, 2008.

27. Cassidy, "Anatomy of a Meltdown."

28. "The TARP Trap," *The Economist*, Nov. 22, 2008.

2: The "New Men" of Finance

1. Opinion of Harold R. Medina, in *US v. Henry S. Morgan, et al.*, Feb. 4, 1954, p. 171.

2. Robert Sobel, *Panic on Wall Street* (New York: Truman Talley Books/E. P. Dutton, 1988), p. 400.

3. Roy C. Smith, *The Money Wars* (New York: E. P. Dutton, 1990), pp. 2–4.

4. Walter Bagehot, *Lombard Street* (London: Henry S. King and Co., 1987), pp 1–20.

5. Lisa Endlich, *Goldman Sachs: The Culture of Success* (New York: Alfred A. Knopf, 1999), pp. 44–48.

6. Ibid.

7. Ibid.

8. Ibid.

9. Robert E. Bedingfield, "Mr. Wall Street to Mark his 60th Year at Goldman Sachs," *New York Times*, Nov. 16, 1967.

3: The Go-Go Years

1. Roy C. Smith, *The Money Wars* (New York: E. P. Dutton, 1990), p. 80.

2. John Brooks, *The Go-Go Years* (New York: E. P. Dutton, 1973), pp. 136–47.

3. Author conversation with Langone, 2001.

4. Brooks, *Go-Go Years*, pp. 1–25.

5. Eric J. Weiner, *What Goes Up* (New York: Little, Brown, 2005), p. 188.

6. Smith, *Money Wars*, pp. 87–88.

7. Cary Reich, *Financier* (New York: William Morrow, 1983), pp. 71–73.

8. Ken Auletta, *Greed and Glory on Wall Street* (New York: Random House, 1986), pp. 30–35.

9. Reich, *Financier*, pp. 14–50.

10. Auletta, *Greed and Glory*, p. 31.

11. Reich, *Financier*, pp. 14–50.

12. William D. Cohen, *The Last Tycoons* (New York: Doubleday, 2006), pp. 3–49.

13. Weiner, *What Goes Up*, p. 118.

14. Brooks, *Go-Go Years*, p. 187.

15. Ibid.

16. Terry Robards, "F.I. DuPont Rescue Seems to End Wall St. Crisis," *New York Times*, Dec. 17, 1970.

17. Weiner, *What Goes Up*, p. 122.

18. John Steele Gordon, *The Great Game* (New York: Scribner, 1999), pp. 277–79.

19. Weiner, *What Goes Up*, pp. 11–25.

20. Ibid., p. 165.

4: The Industry Reinvented

1. Eric J. Weiner, *What Goes Up* (New York: Little, Brown, 2005), p. 29.
2. Patricia Beard, *Blue Blood and Mutiny* (New York: William Morrow, 2007), p. 42–47.
3. Weiner, *What Goes Up*, p. 151.
4. Ibid., p. 178.
5. Ibid., p. 180.
6. Ibid., p. 183.
7. Martin Meyer, "Merrill Lynch Quacks Like a Bank," *Fortune*, Oct. 20, 1980.
8. Roy C. Smith, *The Money Wars* (New York: E. P. Dutton, 1990), p. 89.
9. Cary Reich, "Profile of John Whitehead," *Institutional Investor*, June 1987, pp. 22–29.
10. Leonard Stone, "Gustave Levy, Investment Banker Who Led Goldman Sachs, Is Dead," *New York Times*, Nov. 4, 1976.
11. Reich, "Profile of John Whitehead," p. 28.
12. Roy C. Smith, *Comeback: The Restoration of American Banking Power in the New World Economy* (Cambridge, Mass.: Harvard Business School Press, 1993), pp. 207–11.
13. Kurt Eichenwald, *Serpent on the Rock* (New York: HarperCollins, 1995), pp. 430–47.
14. Steve Lohr, "Phibro's New Commodity: Money," *New York Times*, Aug. 9, 1981.
15. Beard, *Blue Blood and Mutiny*, pp. 70–72.
16. Robert J. Cole, "Sears Will Purchase Dean Witter in Plan to Offer Financial Services," *New York Times*, Oct. 9, 1981.
17. Ken Auletta, *Greed and Glory on Wall Street* (New York: Random House, 1986), p. 190.
18. Monica Langley, *Tearing Down the Walls* (New York: Simon and Schuster, 2003), p. 21.
19. Auletta, *Greed and Glory*, pp. 196–210
20. Roy C. Smith and Ingo Walter, *Street Smarts* (Cambridge, Mass.: Harvard Business School Press, 1997), p. 189.
21. Michael Blumstein, "Equitable Life Will Purchase Securities Firm," *New York Times*, Nov. 6, 1984.

5: The Banks

1. Phillip L. Zweig, *Wriston* (New York: Crown Publishers, 1996), p. 1.
2. Roy C. Smith, *Comeback: The Restoration of American Banking Power in the New World Economy* (Cambridge, Mass.: Harvard Business School Press, 1993), pp. 51–78.
3. Ibid., p. 56.
4. Roy C. Smith and Ingo Walter, *Street Smarts* (Cambridge, Mass.: Harvard Business School Press, 1997), p. 15.

6: Internationalizing

1. Charles Ashman, *Connally: The Adventures of Big Bad John* (New York: William Morrow, 1974), p. 62.
2. Ibid.
3. Ray Vicker and Richard Janssen, "Pressure Increases for Formal Devaluation: IMF Head Calls It Aid to Monetary Stability," *Wall Street Journal*, Aug. 24, 1971.
4. William Greider, *Secrets of the Temple* (New York: Simon and Schuster, 1987), p. 146.
5. Roy C. Smith, *The Global Bankers* (New York: E. P. Dutton, 1989), pp. 223–43.
6. Roy C. Smith, *Comeback: The Restoration of American Banking Power in the New World Economy* (Cambridge, Mass.: Harvard Business School Press, 1993), p. 246.
7. Roy C. Smith and Ingo Walter, "Risks and Rewards in Emerging Market Investments," *Journal of Applied Corporate Finance* 10, no. 3 (Fall 1997): 8–17.

8. Roy C. Smith, "Enterprise Capital in Emerging Markets." *The Independent Review* 12, no. 1 (Summer 2007).

7: The Innovation Decades

1. John Brooks, *The Takeover Game* (New York: E. P. Dutton, 1987), p. 15.
2. Roy C. Smith, *Comeback: The Restoration of American Banking Power in the New World Economy* (Cambridge, Mass.: Harvard Business School Press, 1993), p. 52.
3. Michael Lewis, *Liar's Poker* (New York: W.W. Norton, 1989), p. 107.
4. Robert Sobel, *Salomon Brothers* (New York: Salomon Brothers, 1986), p. 183.
5. Smith, *Comeback*, p. 90.
6. Roy C. Smith, *The Wealth Creators* (New York: St. Martin's Press, 2001), pp. 185–87.
7. Richard Ferri, *All About Index Funds* (New York: McGraw-Hill, 2006), pp. 12–22.
8. John Bogle, "*The First Index Mutual Fund: A History of Vanguard Index Trust and the Vanguard Index Strategy*," report published by the *Bogle Financial Center*, 2002.zzz
9. Eric J. Weiner, *What Goes Up* (New York: Little, Brown, 2005), p. 279.
10. Ibid., p. 289.
11. Anise C. Wallace, "The Brady Report: Looking for Flaws; Study Cites Portfolio Insurer's Role as a Key to the Market Meltdown," *New York Times*, Jan. 11, 1988.
12. Smith, *Comeback*, p. 302.
13. Roy C. Smith and Ingo Walter, *Street Smarts* (Cambridge, Mass.: Harvard Business School Press, 1997), pp. 17–18.
14. *Ibid.*
15. *Ibid.*

8: Restructuring

1. This chapter draws heavily on chapter 4 of Roy C. Smith, *The Money Wars* (New York: E. P. Dutton, 1990).
2. Smith, *Money Wars*, p. xx.
3. "Greed in America," *Time*, Dec. 5, 1988.
4. Bryan Burroughs and John Helyar, *Barbarians at the Gate* (New York: Harper and Row, 1990), pp. 497–98.
5. Carl C. Icahn, "The Case for Takeovers," *New York Times Magazine*, Jan. 29, 1989, p. 34.
6. *Smith v. Van Gorkem*, 488 A.2d 858 (Delaware 1985).
7. Merrill Brown and Caroline E. Meyer, "US Ends Antitrust Suits Against AT&T, IBM," *Washington Post*, Jan. 9, 1982.
8. Christopher Byron, *New York Times Magazine*, Sept. 1989.
9. Roy C. Smith and Ingo Walter, *Street Smarts* (Cambridge, Mass.: Harvard Business School Press, 1997), pp. 156–60.
10. Eric J. Weiner, *What Goes Up* (New York: Little, Brown, 2005), pp. 327–28.
11. Wayne Barrett, *Rudy!: An Investigative Biography of Rudy Giuliani* (New York: Basic Books, 2000), p. 204.

9: Power Shifts

1. "The Big Squeeze," *Wall Street Journal*, Aug. 12, 1991.
2. Roy C. Smith, *Comeback: The Restoration of American Banking Power in the New World Economy* (Cambridge, Mass.: Harvard Business School Press, 1993), pp. 91–93.
3. Roy C. Smith and Ingo Walter, *Street Smarts* (Cambridge, Mass.: Harvard Business School Press, 1997), pp. 123–28.
4. Michael Siconolfi and Laurie Cohen, "How Salomon's Hubris and US Trap Led to Leaders' Downfall," *Wall Street Journal*, Aug. 19, 1991.
5. Smith and Walter, *Street Smarts*, pp. 11–13.

6. History of American Express, from its Web site, http://home3.americanexpress.com/corp/os/history.asp, accessed in 2009.

7. Joshua Milla, "Parent Sets a Spinoff of Lehman," *New York Times*, Jan. 25, 1994.

8. Patricia Beard, *Blue Blood and Mutiny* (New York: William Morrow, 2007), pp. 47–49.

9. Ibid., p. 49.

10. John Authers and John Waters, "US Firms in $24 bn Alliance," *Financial Times* (U.S. edition), Feb. 6, 1997.

11. Ibid.

12. Beard, *Blue Blood and Mutiny*, pp. 300–20.

13. Monica Lange, *Tearing Down the Walls* (New York: Simon and Schuster, 2003), pp. 205–25.

10: The New Economy Bubble

1. Significant portions of this chapter are extracted from chapter 1 in *Governing the Modern Corporation*, by Roy C. Smith and Ingo Walter (New York: Oxford University Press, 2006).

2. Eric J. Weiner, *What Goes Up* (New York: Little, Brown, 2005), p. 347.

3. Ibid., p. 348.

4. Karen Lowry Miller, "Too Much Money," *Newsweek*, Aug. 18, 2003, quoting Robert Hormats of Goldman Sachs and Co.

5. Abraham Bleiberg, "Tech M&A, Size Does Matter," Goldman Sachs Investment Research, June 1998.

6. Smith and Walter, *Governing the Modern Corporation*, pp. 13, 128–32.

7. Richard Sylla, "The New Media Boom in Historical Perspective," *Prometheus* 19, no. 1 (2001).

8. Jenny Anderson, "Stock Exchange's Former Chief Wins Court Battle to Keep Pay," *New York Times*, Jul. 2, 2008.

11: Hedge Funds and Private Equity

1. Mark Ginocchio, "JWM Losses Result in Job Cuts," *McClatchy-Tribune Business News*, May 3, 2008.

2. Louise Story, "Hedge Funds Are Bracing for Investors to Cash Out," *New York Times*, Sept. 29, 2008.

3. Roger Lowenstein, *When Genius Failed* (New York: Random House, 2000), pp. 1–120.

4. Jenny Strasburg, "A Decade Later, John Meriwether Must Scramble Again," *Wall Street Journal*, March 27, 2008.

5. Adam Bradbery, "Meriwether Hedge Fund to Cut Staff," *Wall Street Journal*, Dec. 23, 2008.

6. Craig Karman, "Yale's Investor Keeps Playbook," *Wall Street Journal*, Jan. 13, 2009.

7. Richard Beales and Joanna Chung, "Banks Take a Supporting Role as Hedge Funds Flourish," *Financial Times*, Aug. 8, 2006.

8. Ibid.

9. Robert Berner, "The Next Warren Buffett?" BusinessWeek.com, Nov. 22, 2004.

10. Gregory Zuckerman and Jenny Strasburg, "Banks Fumble at Operating Hedge Funds," *Wall Street Journal*, May 31, 2008.

11. "Heard on the Street," *Wall Street Journal*, Feb. 12, 2009.

12. Cassell Bryan-Low, Carrick Mollenkamp, and Gregory Zuckerman, "Peloton Flew High, Fell Fast," *Wall Street Journal*, May 12, 2008.

13. David Enrich, "Citigroup Hedge Fund Loss Weighs on 3 Banks," *Wall Street Journal*, May 20, 2008.

14. Craig Karmin, "Pension Managers Rethink Their Love of Hedge Funds," *Wall Street Journal*, Aug. 27, 2007.

15. James Mackintosh, "Managers Cut Fees to Help Make Up for Old Fund Losses," *Financial Times*, May 2, 2008.

16. "Money for Old Hope," *The Economist*, March 1, 2008.

17. James B. Stewart, "The Birthday Party," *The New Yorker*, Feb. 11, 2008.

18. Dana Cimilluca, "Buyout Firms Take Knocks," *Wall Street Journal*, Jan. 4, 2008.

19. Liz Rappaport and Peter Lattman, "Anyone for Some Used Corporate Debt?" *Wall Street Journal*, Feb. 6, 2008.

20. Henry Sender, "KKR to Go Public Via Fund Merger," *Financial Times*, July 28, 2008.

21. Henry Sender, "The Rock of Wall Street," *Financial Times*, May 11, 2008.

22. Peter Lattman, "Huntsman, Banks Settle for $1.7 Billion," *Wall Street Journal*, June 24, 2009

12: The Mortgage Crisis

1. Stephanie Baker-Said and Elena Logutenkova, "UBS $100 Billion Wager Prompted $24 Billion Loss in Nine Months," Bloomberg News, May 19, 2008.

2. "Shareholder Report on UBS' Write Downs," Apr. 18, 2008.

3. Financial Economists Roundtable, *Statement on the Role of SROs in Securitization,* Oct. 18, 2008. Data based on a variety of sources, including four investment banks, Markit .com, and IMF staff estimates.

4. "Paradise Lost," *The Economist*, May 17, 2008, p. 7.

5. Bill Bamber and Andrew Spencer, *Bear Trap: The Fall of Bear Stearns and the Panic of 2008* (New York: Brick Tower Press, 2008), p. 32.

6. Robert J. Shiller, *The Subprime Solution* (Princeton, N.J.: Princeton University Press, 2008), p. 6.

7. Jan P. Krahnen, "Securitization Crisis: How the Credit Market Teaches Us a Lesson," Center for Financial Studies, Frankfurt, Feb. 2007.

8. "Paradise Lost," p. 12.

9. Bamber and Spencer, *Bear Trap*, pp. 37–39.

10. "The Old Lady Sings," *Financial Times* (Lex column), May 2, 2008.

11. "Shareholder Report on UBS' Write Downs."

12. John Cassidy, "Subprime Suspect," *The New Yorker*, March 31, 2008.

13. Susanne Craig and Randall Smith, "Merrill Aims to Raise Billions More," *Wall Street Journal*, July 29, 2008.

14. Citigroup, 10Q filing with the SEC for the third quarter of 2007, footnote 13, page 72.

15. Paul J. Davis, "10Q Clue to Anatomy of Citigroup's Losses," *Financial Times*, Nov. 8, 2007.

16. William Cohan, "The Capital Blunders That Led to Bear's Demise," *Financial Times*, April 9, 2008.

17. Kate Kelly, "Lost Opportunities Haunt Final Days of Bear Stearns," *Wall Street Journal*, May 27, 2008.

18. John Cassidy, "Anatomy of a Meltdown," *The New Yorker*, Dec. 1, 2008.

19. Ibid.

20. Kelly, "Lost Opportunities."

21. William D. Cohan, *House of Cards: A Tale of Hubris and Wretched Excess on Wall Street* (New York: Doubleday, 2009), p. 91.

22. JPMorgan Chase and Co., Form S-4 filing with the SEC, April 11, 2008.

23. Landon Thomas, "Bear's Family Feud," *New York Times*, May 7, 2008.

24. Richard Beales and Lauren Silva, "Bear Market for Bailouts" (Breakingviews.com), *Wall Street Journal*, May 15, 2008.

25. Government Accountability Office, "Troubled Asset Relief Program," Dec. 2, 2008 (GAO-09-161).

26. "Paradise Lost," p. 6.

27. "Paradise Lost," p. 12.

28. Cohan, *House of Cards*, p. 105.

13: An Uncertain Future

1. Aaron Kirchfield and Jacqueline Simmons, "Deutsche Bank Trading Losses Reveal Industry Setback," Bloomberg.com, Jan. 12, 2009.

2. David Enrich, "Pandit's Puzzle: How to Fix Citigroup," *Wall Street Journal*, Jan. 16, 2009.

3. Dan Fitzpatrick, Deborah Solomon, and Susanne Craig, "BofA's Latest Hit," *Wall Street Journal*, Jan. 16, 2009.

4. Susanne Craig and Dan Fitzpatrick, "BofA's Lews Is Subpoenaed Over Merrill; Thain Talks," *Wall Street Journal*, Feb. 20, 2009.

5. Greg Farrell, "The Red-blooded Banker," *Financial Times*, Feb. 1, 2009.

6. David Mildenberg and Linda Shen, "Bank of America Posts Quarterly Loss After Bailout," Bloomberg.com, Jan. 16, 2009.

7. Gregg Farrell, "Lynched at Merrill," *Financial Times*, Jan. 26, 2009.

8. Gregg Farrell, "Shareholder Lawsuits Put Pressure on Lewis to Go," *Financial Times*, Jan. 26, 2009.

9. Ibid.

10. Matthew Karnitschnig and Susanne Craig, "Old Merrill Quickly Disappears Inside BofA," *Wall Street Journal*, Jul. 8, 2009.

11. Christine Harper, "Goldman Sachs Would Like to Pay Back TARP Money," Bloomberg.com, Feb. 4, 2009.

12. Susanne Craig, Jeffrey McCracken, Aaron Lucchetti, and Kate Kelly, "The Weekend That Wall Street Died," *Wall Street Journal*, Dec. 29, 2008.

13. Anthony Saunders, Roy C. Smith, and Ingo Walter, "Enhanced Regulation for Large, Complex Financial Institutions," in Viral Acharya and Matthew Richardson (eds.), *Restoring Financial Stability* (New York: J. Wiley and Sons, 2009).

Epilogue

1. Paulson has written a book on his time in office to be published in the fall of 2009.

2. *Rolling Stone*, an unusual commentator on financial matters, published an article in July 2009 that claimed that Goldman Sachs engaged in a conspiracy to use its influence in government to exploit opportunities for profit, and described the firm as "a great vampire squid wrapped around the face of humanity."

3. As they had, for the same reasons, since Andrew Jackson's time when the charter of the Second Bank of the United States, a rough equivalent of a central bank, was not renewed and the U.S. was without a central bank of any kind until 1913.

INDEX